DETERRENCE

STUDIES IN CRIME AND JUSTICE

DETERRENCE
*The Legal Threat
in Crime Control*

(

Franklin E. Zimring
Gordon J. Hawkins

With a Foreword by
James Vorenberg

THE UNIVERSITY OF CHICAGO PRESS
CHICAGO AND LONDON

The University of Chicago Press, Chicago 60637
The University of Chicago Press, Ltd., London

International Standard Book Number: 0-226-98352-8
Library of Congress Catalog Card Number: 72-89584

To Norval Morris

Grammaticus rhetor geometres pictor aliptes
Augur schoenobates medicus magus, omnia novit.

Juvenal

Contents

Foreword

Deterring future misconduct is probably the principal aim of criminal sanctions. Yet decisions are made by legislators, sentencing judges, and parole boards with virtually no knowledge and little analysis about the future effects which their actions will have. The authors have taken an important step in beginning to fill this gap. Their book is an authoritative and stimulating analysis of deterrence in criminal law.

The first book in Studies in Crime and Justice, *Delinquency in a Birth Cohort*, by Wolfgang, Figlio, and Sellin, was a report of a major research study. The aim and approach of Zimring and Hawkins are different. Taking one of the most difficult and crucial issues in criminal administration, they sift and analyze such research and theoretical work as has been done in an unusually intelligent and straightforward way. They make a number of interesting and penetrating forays into theory on specific issues, but it is as an organizer of thought rather than as a developer of new theory that the book is particularly valuable. The result is a book which not only deepens knowledge and insights about crime and the criminal justice system but should challenge others in the field to go further.

It is consistent with the approach of the authors that they avoid becoming embroiled in the sterile, overgeneralized debate on whether the threat of punishment deters, but instead focus attention on the differential effects on compliance resulting from changes in particular sanctions. Consequently, the reader is rewarded not only with a clear picture of what the major issues are but also with an understanding of how varying resolutions of these issues, on the basis of research which the authors propose, would affect policy judgments about penal sanctions and criminal administration. For example, at a time when most jurisdictions are experimenting with the early diversion of offenders from the criminal justice system, and a few are closing down reformatories and prisons, clear thinking about the effects of deterrence is crucial.

One of the great strengths of the book is the chapter "The Strategy of Research," in which the authors analyze research methods that they believe would begin to shed further light on issues raised throughout the book. This chapter not only elucidates the issues relating to deterrence; it also provides an important model which should be followed in the growing literature in this field. It substitutes for the typical combination of pontification and hunch that characterizes much criminological writing an honest and thoughtful recognition of what we do not know and a careful plan to begin to acquire the data we need. Much of its strength is that it carefully explains the value and limitations of various research approaches. And the point that the lack of any one perfect method should not lead us either to total reliance on imperfection or to despair is important and well presented. Thus, like its predecessor in the present series, this book makes an important contribution to research methodology.

In sum, anyone working in the criminal field—including administrators, legislators, law revisers, and academics—should read and ponder this book. If we take seriously its warnings and advice it can help move criminal administration out of the dark.

JAMES VORENBERG

Acknowledgments

In preparing this book we have freely availed ourselves of what Thomas Carlyle called "the indisputablest" of all the rights of man: the right of the ignorant to be guided by the wiser. In particular, we are deeply indebted to Johannes Andenaes, Dean of the Faculty of Law and Director of the Institute of Criminology and Criminal Law at the University of Oslo, who has been largely responsible for the current renewal of serious interest in the subject of deterrence.

Some part of that indebtedness will be immediately apparent to the reader. The frequency of reference to his writings, and the fact that in many places our discussion of topics is directly responsive to his treatment of them, make it sufficiently plain. In addition, we have had the benefit of lengthy discussions and correspondence with him, in the course of which he has subjected our ideas to searching criticism and refinement. He has been both our harshest and our most generous critic. In making our final revision of the manuscript, we were greatly helped by his detailed critique of it. His influence has been, in short, pervasive.

Among others to whom we are indebted, the foremost are Norval Morris and Hans W. Mattick, Codirectors of the Center for Studies in Criminal Justice at the University of Chicago. Without the stimulus they provided, this book would not have been conceived; without their support, it would never have been completed.

We are grateful also to Saleem Shah and George Weber of the National Institute of Mental Health's Center for Studies of Crime and Delinquency. At a critical stage, they provided both encouragement and financial aid. Two colleagues in the University of Chicago Law School, Hans Zeisel and Owen M. Fiss, also assisted us by reading parts of the book in manuscript. They are responsible for substantial changes made in response to forceful and cogent criticism. James Vorenberg, Professor of Law at Harvard University, provided valuable criticism of the manuscript.

Richard Bowler, Reference Librarian in the Law School Library, provided assistance in our search for available literature. Among the many persons who were at times subjected to physical and psychological strain by our importunate demands for typing and retyping, we would especially like to thank Sylvia Karjala, Karla Moras, and Evelyn Clarke.

Finally, we owe a particular debt to Maurice Zimring of Hilo, Hawaii, for editing an early draft of chapters 2 through 4.

FRANKLIN E. ZIMRING
GORDON J. HAWKINS

1   The Task

Belief in the deterrent efficacy of penal sanctions is as old as the criminal law itself. It has informed and does inform political, administrative, and judicial policy to so great a degree that deterrence has been described as a "primary and essential postulate"[1] of almost all criminal law systems.

The nature of that postulate as traditionally conceived is succinctly stated in earlier editions of C. S. Kenny's classic *Outlines of Criminal Law*. Kenny, who cites as authorities "the most generally accepted writers—as for instance Beccaria, Blackstone, Romilly, Paley, Feuerbach—"[2] defines "deterrence by punishment" as a "method of retrospective interference; by holding out threats that, whenever a wrong has been actually committed, the wrongdoer shall incur punishment."[3] The object is "to check an offence by thus associating with the idea of it a deterrent sense of terror. . . . The restraint of terror . . . is supplied by the criminal law very efficiently."[4]

1. Morris, "Impediments to Penal Reform" (1966) 33 *U. Chi. L. Rev.* 631.
2. Kenny, *Outlines of Criminal Law* (13th ed., 1929) 30.
3. *Ibid.* 29.
4. *Ibid.* 29–30.

Kenny's belief that the criminal law provided a very effective "restraint of terror" was, unlike that of many of his contemporaries, not entirely unsupported by evidence. In a footnote he said: "That the fear of punishment *can* deter is shown . . . vividly by its efficacy in the training of animals and even of fishes; a pike can be taught to swim amongst tench innocuously, or a flea to abstain from jumping."[5] Today, however, in the face of widespread skepticism about the whole institution of punishment, a pacific pike and a frightened flea can hardly hope to sustain so heavy an inferential burden.

Until quite recently, discussion of punishment in general and deterrence in particular has been in the main quite unscientific in character. The bulk of the literature consists of deductive argument. The level of dialectic subtlety is often high; the factual content is minimal. Matters of fact are passed over with candid confessions of ignorance, occasionally supplemented by random speculation. Discussion of what we are justified in doing not only takes precedence over, but even precludes consideration of, what in practice we can do.

Indeed, the theory of punishment as traditionally conceived is largely made up of recommendations or prescriptions; of rhetorical statements rather than propositions which could be evaluated on the basis of fact. As Professor H. L. A. Hart says:

. . . Theories of punishment are not theories in any normal sense. They are not, as scientific theories are, assertions or contentions as to what is or what is not the case; the atomic theory or the kinetic theory of gases is a theory of this sort. On the contrary, those major positions concerning punishment which are called deterrent or retributive or reformative "theories" of punishment are moral *claims* as to what justifies the practice of punishment—claims as to why, morally, it *should* or *may* be used.[6]

And clearly, insofar as this is true, such theories cannot be subjected to empirical investigation.

It is true that in recent years the need for empirical research has been emphasized even in philosophical literature. And deterrence has received an increasing amount of attention from

5. *Ibid.* 31 n. 1.
6. Hart, "Murder and the Principles of Punishment: England and the United States" (1957) 52 *Northwestern U. L. Rev.* 446–47.

scholars in a variety of fields. The volume of empirical studies of crime control policies has increased. Research relevant to deterrence in social psychology and other fields has grown impressively since World War II.

Nevertheless, the net effect of increasing attention and study is something less than a knowledge explosion. There are doubts about both the reliability and the relevance of much of the psychological experimentation that has been done. Lack of methodological rigor combined with extrapolative extravagance have in many studies produced counterfeit conclusions. There have been modest increments in understanding; but most results have been suggestive rather than definitive. Many questions remain unanswered, among them inevitably those as yet unformulated.

The Dialectics of Deterrence

There are many reasons for this unsatisfactory state of affairs. We shall not attempt to list them here. One, however, needs to be mentioned at this stage. It relates to the nature of the evidence which is available for study in this area, and some conclusions which have been drawn from it. For while it is true that much of it is ambiguous and susceptible of various interpretations, there are also bodies of evidence which move observers to two clearly antithetical conclusions.

On the one hand, there is the potent, ubiquitous, seemingly irrefutable thesis that attaching unpleasant consequences to behavior will reduce the tendency of people to engage in that behavior. This proposition is so basic that it can rightfully claim to be the ancestor of such unimpeachable formulations as the first law of demand in economics and the principle of conditioning in psychology. Moreover, despite fashionable skepticism about the efficacy of legal controls there is in some areas impressive evidence of the effectiveness of criminal law enforcement as a means of social defense.

We will refer here to only one simple but striking example. It has been shown in a great many studies carried out in various countries that the imposition of speed limits has, in general, the effect of reducing speeds and accidents.[7] A dramatic

7. Great Britain, Department of Scientific and Industrial Research, Road Research Laboratory, *Research on Road Safety* (1963) 155–63.

instance of this may be found in an experiment conducted in Great Britain by the Ministry of Transport's Road Research Laboratory. The experiment dealt with increased police enforcement of a 30 m.p.h. speed limit on six roads in different parts of the country over the period of one year. It demonstrated clearly that the enforcement of speed limits on roads can substantially reduce speeding and consequent accidents and casualties. It was found not only that speeds were reduced on the experimental roads but also that injury accidents were reduced by 25 percent, and driver and passenger casualties were cut in half.[8]

On the other hand, there are areas in which attempts to control or suppress behavior by means of the threat of punishment seem, to many observers, to be hopeless failures. The American experience with the prohibition of the sale, manufacture, and transportation of alcoholic liquors during the fourteen years from 1920 to 1933 is not infrequently cited as evidence that "goodness cannot be legislated into men."[9] More recently the application of criminal enforcement and penal sanctions in the field of drug control is often said to have met with similar lack of success. Thus, the President's Crime Commission Task Force on Narcotics and Drug Abuse reported that despite the application of increasingly severe sanctions to marijuana "the use and traffic in that drug appear to be increasing."[10]

The existence of these two contrary types of evidence has meant that discussion of the deterrence issue has often taken a dialectic form. On one hand, evidence of the effectiveness of legal controls is adduced in support of an irrefutable theory of universal deterrence. It is irrefutable because any failure to achieve a deterrent effect is interpreted as an indication of the need for more severe and certain punishments.

On the other hand, there is an equally incontrovertible but antithetical theory of nondeterrence. As Enrico Ferri put it

8. Munden, *An Experiment in Enforcing the 30 mile/h Speed Limit* (Road Research Laboratory Report no. 24, 1966) 1.

9. Byse, "Alcoholic Beverage Control Before Repeal" (1940) 7 *Law and Contemp. Prob.* 569.

10. U.S. President's Commission on Law Enforcement and Administration of Justice Task Force Report, *Narcotics and Drug Abuse* (1967) 11.

nearly a century ago, "The daily bankruptcy of penal justice as a defense of society against crime" demonstrates that "criminal phenomena are independent of penal laws."[11] More recently our experience with Prohibition has been said to confirm that social problems "cannot be solved by a statute."[12] Deterrence is "belied by both history and logic."[13] At best the criminal law is merely epiphenomenal, a dependent variable shaped by current mores and prevailing norms. At worst the threat of punishment is likely to provoke more of the behavior it is intended to control or suppress.

With some aspects of this ideological polarity we shall deal further later in the text. But the truth is that, like so many dialectical arguments, the antithesis upon which this one rests is false. It is a matter of common observation that men seek to avoid unpleasant consequences and that the threat of unpleasantness tends to be deterrent. It is equally indisputable that not all criminal prohibitions are completely effective. But these propositions are not contradictory or mutually exclusive.

It is always possible to argue that some imaginable threat might have been more effective, just as it is always possible to find examples of deterrence failure. But neither assertion speaks directly to the real issues which are involved in the operation of the machinery of threat and punishment, because the important issues are far removed from that level of generality.

Thus, in the case of Prohibition the crucial question is not whether it could conceivably have been made absolutely effective, or whether or not a single potential alcoholic was prevented by it from becoming an alcoholic. The significant question is whether that particular policy created benefits worth its cost, and why that particular policy might have had different results than other threats in other areas.

Such questions are in principle answerable, and it is to questions of that kind that we address ourselves rather than to the construction of general theories. We do not take sides in the deterrence debate, which seems to us, if not meaningless, at

11. Ferri, *Criminal Sociology* (1884; trans. Kelly and Lisle, 1917) xli and 218.
12. Byse, supra note 9.
13. Barnes and Teeters, *New Horizons in Criminology* (2d ed. 1951) 338.

least largely irrelevant to any material concern. Instead, we attempt a classification of the great variety of factors which condition the differential effectiveness of legal threats.

Dimensions of the Study

We begin our detailed treatment of the subject of deterrence in chapter 2 by considering what we have called the rationale of deterrence and in particular its function as a motive of official action.

We distinguish four aspects or four elements of official crime control ideology which are of crucial importance. In the first place, we examine those beliefs regarding the operation of deterrence which provide motivation for general crime control strategy. We attempt to analyze the foundations of the official beliefs upon which action is based.

The second aspect of official ideology with which we are concerned relates to a series of important ethical considerations regarding the use of criminal sanctions for deterrent purposes. Next, we deal very briefly with the economic implications of official policy. We offer a very simple model for dealing with the problem of costs and determining the investment of resources in crime prevention. Finally, we discuss a political aspect of the use of deterrents in crime control policies.

Having cleared the ground a little in chapter 2, we adopt in chapter 3 a more synoptic approach to the subject. It is a truism, but no less important for that reason, that the kind of answers we get will be largely determined by the questions we ask. It is of crucial importance to define our field of inquiry because the concept of deterrence is a complex and difficult one.

The point at issue has been well put by Leslie Wilkins:

Many concepts in criminology, and the concept of deterrence in particular, are not developed beyond the impressionistic stage. Impressionistic concepts cannot be used in scientific analysis. Nor are they really effective for communication, because they have a tendency to change meaning with context and with the personality of the user. Such concepts are fertile ground for argument but not for research progress.[14]

14. Wilkins, "Criminology: An Operational Research Approach," in Welford (ed.) *Society: Problems and Methods of Study* (1962) 326.

By way of illustration, consider the gulf between those who like Jeremy Bentham construed deterrence as being the prevention of crime simply by "intimidation or terror of the law,"[15] and later writers like Paul Tappan, who included within his definition of the term what he called "the educative moralizing function,"[16] of punishment.

Of course, it does not necessarily follow from the fact that a concept is "impressionistic" that it is meaningless or that it is not susceptible to analysis. The concept of deterrence after all *has* been widely used for communication. It might seem obvious that what is required is merely observation of the way in which it has been and is used. Then ideally the concept can be broken down into its elements. Rigorous, operational definitions can be derived. And the application of scientific methods of investigations can proceed.

The essential point, however, is simply that both in technical and in less formal discussion of punishment the word *deterrence* is currently used with a variety of meanings and diverse connotations. It is therefore important for purposes of discourse and exposition that we provide some definition of key terms. Accordingly, in chapter 3 we offer some definitions basic to the discussion of issues in deterrence.

In chapter 4, the longest in this work, we attempt to define and survey the principal issues involved in the use of threats as a means of inducing compliance to law. Deterrence, as we make clear in our essay in definition in chapter 3, is principally a matter of the declaration of some harm, loss, or pain that will follow noncompliance; in short, the central concept is that of threat. Having already considered in chapter 2 the view of legal threats subscribed to by threatening agencies, we now move to the responses of the threatened audiences.

This is the crux of the whole problem of deterrence: what we have called the deterrent effect. Discussion of this subject frequently used to begin, and in some quarters still does begin, with the traditional question, Does punishment deter crime? This question, though not entirely meaningless, is unanswerable in categorical terms, for we confront a complex of issues about human behavior in a great variety of situations; and

15. Bentham, "Principles of Penal Law," in 1 *Works* (1843) 396.
16. Tappan, *Crime, Justice, and Correction* (1960) 247.

there are significant differences in situation which condition the existence, extent, and nature of deterrence. The critical issue is the differential effectiveness of threats.

This shift from the general to the specific is, of course, no more than an elementary step in logic. It helps to define our inquiry as the search for those variations in circumstance that account for differences in the results of threats.

The conceptual organization we have imposed on the data should be viewed as tentative. In the light of the distinction between etiology and taxonomy drawn by Michael and Adler in their celebrated examination of the state of knowledge and research in criminology forty years ago, our approach may perhaps best be defined as taxonomic. Taxonomy they saw as representing some kind of intermediate stage between "descriptive knowledge" and "perfect empirical science."[17]

We have attempted to draw together some of the more significant empirical and analytical material. We have indicated what seem to us to be the principal issues. But we have provided not so much a map of the area as a preliminary sketch in which, within a provisional projectional system, many of the contours are conjectural.

In chapter 5 we move from the analytical to the empirical level. Having stated what we consider to be the principal issues in deterrence, we attempt to outline some methods by which these issues may be investigated. There is no point in discussing methodological points here, for they are dealt with in some detail in the text. There is, however, one point which may properly be made in this introduction. It is this: We do not claim that the methods of research we discuss are the best of all conceivable procedures for assessing crime control policies. Most of them, as we are at some pains to point out, are imperfect. Nevertheless, we do maintain that a combination of these imperfect methods of assessment is, at the present time, the most effective and least hazardous of the practical means by which knowledge about the effects of threat and punishment will be obtained.

Having dealt in chapter 5 with the strategy of research, in the sixth and final chapter of this study we come to the tactical

17. Michael and Adler, *Crime, Law, and Social Science* (1933) 23–25.

level. We have considered modes of operation in general terms, and the ends we may hope to achieve. The next step is to consider those areas which should be given priority in the disposition of available resources for research.

It is our view, as we shall presently make quite clear, that the practical social needs of the moment are more important than such ends as the acquisition of knowledge for its own sake, the achievement of theoretical insights, or the disinterested pursuit of truth. Any program for research should therefore be designed with that practical aim. We begin chapter 6 by stating the criteria which we believe should govern the selection of the problems in deterrence for intensive study. Since priorities will inevitably be dictated by the exigencies of particular situations, we do not offer a definitive program. Rather, we indicate some specific areas which conform to our criteria for determining priorities and merit immediate study.

Limits of the Study

We have looked at the use of threat almost exclusively in a criminal law context. A moment's consideration of the pervasion of the basic deterrence hypothesis throughout human thought and experience will demonstrate how small a part of the area available for study we sought to penetrate and explore.

Deterrence as a motive is immanent throughout the civil as well as the criminal law in most countries. It informs in part the concept of damages, both punitive and compensatory; and it even emerges in discussions of doctrines as arcane as the old Louisiana rules on wrongful death actions brought by illegitimate children after the death of a parent.[18] Moreover, beyond the field of law—whether the subject be international politics, child rearing, or economic theory—the reaction of groups or individuals to the prospect of possible unpleasantness is a significant and recurrent theme.

Obviously, in a work of this kind it is necessary to find some

18. "Plaintiff-Appellant, on behalf of the children contends that the denial of this right to illegitimate children solely because of their status is, as to them, a denial of due process and equal protection. . . . Denying illegitimate children the right to recover in such a case is actually based on morals and general welfare because it discourages bringing children into the world out of wedlock." Levy v. Louisiana, 192 So. 2d 193 (1966) at 194–95. But see also Levy v. Louisiana, 391 U.S. 68 (1968).

stopping point short of the totality of human response to threatened loss. It has been wisely observed that "exhaustive treatments are exhausting."[19] To treat deterrence issues in the whole of law would, theoretically, make it possible to distinguish and analyze the similarities and differences in various areas and perhaps arrive at some tenable synthesis which would both comprehend and illuminate the whole. But while we recognize the existence of many similarities between areas of law, the differences have impressed us as being too great for such an enterprise to succeed.

Consider only the unique character of the criminal sanction with its special stigmatic component; the specific types of audience that must be reached to deter serious crime (very different, we suppose, from the characteristic groups involved in the prevention of traffic accidents or the use of disincentives to corporate mergers); and the enormity of the losses threatened in the higher reaches of criminal sanctions. Given these differences, the singular importance of social defense against crime, and the need for some detailed study of deterrence, we have opted for the narrower range of criminal law.

Still, the distinction between absolute and marginal deterrence, the stress on the importance of communications, and the distinction between the subjective credibility of threats and the objective probability of apprehension all have a bearing on the operation of deterrence outside the field of criminal law. Indeed, they have all, to a greater or less degree, been noted by others engaged in related studies.

Some of what we have to say will be of limited significance because much of our discussion is confined to the American experience. The limitation imposed by this feature of our study is twofold.

In the first place, a particular culture may condition the way in which an audience will react to legal threats. Thus, Andenaes, in discussing the effectiveness of the British Road Safety Act of 1967, rightly says, "It cannot be assumed that similar legislation, even when enforced in the same manner as in Great Britain, will have the same effects in a country whose citizens view obedience to the law differently."[20]

19. Lucas, *Freedom of the Will* (1970) 2.
20. Andenaes, "Deterrence and Specific Offenses" (1971) 38 *U. Chi. L. Rev.* 552.

In the second place, cultural values also impose certain limits on punitive measures. So the fact that we have been especially concerned with punishment ranges that are political possibilities may well lend a further degree of insularity to some of our conclusions. If our discussion were placed in a different political context, some of our conclusions would probably be different.

Were we living in Peking earlier in this century when the authorities once exhibited the heads of drivers executed for exceeding the speed limit alongside the signs indicating that limit (15 m.p.h.),[21] no doubt some of our scruples would seem weakly sentimental. It is conceivable that if we lived under an absolutist political regime, capital punishment for tax evasion might not only be regarded as a feasible and salutary preventive of governmental losses but even be accepted as just. However, we do not. And the major part of our discussion of marginal deterrence is limited to that which is politically possible and morally acceptable in the Western context. Such limitations are inevitable in studies of this nature, and in the circumstances are not entirely disagreeable.

It is necessary to make one other point. Despite our emphasis on political possibilities the structure of our book makes it necessary to omit some aspects of the deterrence issue which are of crucial interest to political scientists and sociologists. For their purposes, a more systematic perspective involving the interrelationships between punishment policy, social norms, and societal reactions would be preferable.[22]

Thus, instead of considering deterrence as a motive for official action separately from consideration of the deterrent effect, we might have merged the two and asked how penalty increases affect the administration of justice in various different situations. Or we might have attempted to distinguish in greater detail the social and political factors that correlate with successful attempts to use the threat of sanctions as a mechanism for reorienting public attitudes to particular kinds of activity, in contrast with the dismal failure of the law to change some cus-

21. Griffiths, "The Limits of Criminal Law Scholarship" (1970) 79 *Yale L. J.* 1455–56.
22. For discussion of some of these matters, see Zimring and Hawkins, "The Legal Threat as an Instrument of Social Change" (1971) 27 *J. of Social Issues* 33–48.

tomary behavior. Our study stops short of attempting any such synthesis, although in the final section of chapter 2 we deal briefly with one aspect of the politics of punishment.

Theory and Practice

We have already referred briefly to our preference for research which is oriented toward practical ends. Since this is one of our basic themes, it may be as well to declare explicitly here our position on the tension between practical and theoretical perspectives in deterrence studies.

The crux of the matter may be simply stated as follows. In any consideration of the methods by which knowledge about deterrence can be obtained, it is proper to note that the type of knowledge obtained may be of differential significance to the social scientist and to the individual who is responsible for making decisions about crime control.

The social scientist will often have more interest in *whether* particular effects exist than in the *extent* of such effects. The role of the policy planner, on the other hand, is to make determinations about whether a particular policy, which by necessity is a mixture of a number of different threat variables, will produce results worth its cost.

At times, the tension between ideal agenda for scientific inquiry and the kind of program necessary for intelligent policy planning has led observers to despair of any fruitful collaboration between the two perspectives.

If we practice self-deception, we shall fail to appreciate how ignorant we are and to realize that efforts to develop a science of criminology are of greater practical importance than immediate efforts at crime control. Preoccupation with urgent practical problems too often leads the practical man into impracticality. As a result, he unwisely shuts his eyes to the importance of research or insists that research shall be undertaken with his practical problems immediately in view. It is a result of such insistence that a great part of criminological research has been promoted and undertaken. The insignificance of the knowledge which such research has yielded and its inutility in practice indicate that scientific research cannot be fruitfully directed toward the solution of immediate practical problems except in those fields in which there exist highly developed empirical sciences.[23]

23. Michael and Adler, supra note 17, at 231.

Yet it is by no means clear that insights of importance to the practical realities of crime control policy are necessarily of no interest to the theoretical scholar. Rather than assume a zero-sum relationship between practical and theoretical knowledge, we suggest that any really useful insights into the practical significance of particular crime control policies cannot help but advance theoretical knowledge of the deterrent influence of legal sanctions. At the same time, significant progress in the scientific assessment of deterrence effectiveness will even in the short run be of great importance to the practical decision maker. It is almost inconceivable that the two perspectives should operate at cross-purposes, and far more likely that each type of finding will possess a great potential for enriching the substance of the other.[24]

Moreover, if forced to choose between theoretical and policy findings, we would opt for the latter. We do not conduct this inquiry in a vacuum; we write in a city whose streets are far from safe at night. In an area of clear social importance, the fundamental significance of knowledge is its use.[25]

A Recurrent Theme

In conclusion, it is appropriate to draw attention to a distinction which is fundamental and recurs as a basic theme throughout the book. That is, the distinction between the issues of absolute and of marginal deterrence, which are often confused in the discussion of deterrence.[26]

24. Cf Radzinowicz, "Criminological and Penological Research," Address to Second U.N. Congress on Prevention of Crime and Treatment of Offenders, London, August 1970. "We should not allow ourselves to be intimidated by those who contrast with a supercilious air, so-called pure research with applied research. The latter, if well conducted, will not only increase the social utility of criminology but will bring with it a refinement in method and a more exact perception of the things which matter."

25. On the broad issue of the relationship between the theoretical and practical aspects of criminology we are inclined to agree that "practical needs are particularly strong in the study of crime and punishment." Mannheim, 1 *Comparative Criminology* (1965) 20; and that "to rob it of [its] practical function is to divorce criminology from reality and render it sterile." Radzinowicz, *In Search of Criminology* (1961) 168.

26. Although Nigel Walker draws a distinction between the absolute and the comparative efficacy of a deterrent which reflects the difference

The problem of absolute deterrence relates to the question, Does this particular criminal sanction deter? The problem of marginal deterrence relates to such questions as, Would a more severe penalty attached to this criminal prohibition more effectively deter? In the capital punishment debate the issue is not that of absolute deterrence—whether the death penalty is a deterrent. It is that of marginal deterrence—whether it is a more effective deterrent than the alternative sanction of long imprisonment.

We are rarely in a position to study absolute deterrence, that is, "to compare a situation in which there is *no* deterrent with a situation in which there is *only that* deterrent."[27] This is not to say that the results of the criminalization or decriminalization of behavior should not be studied. But the research we recommend in chapter 6 will reveal more about marginal deterrence than about absolute deterrence. We shall be putting this knowledge to use long before basic issues about the effects of threat and punishment approach a resolution.

In the foreseeable future most research opportunities are likely to be provided by modest changes in threat composition, and are likely to be spread over a wide range of issues. Irregular opportunities make systematic research difficult and make for uneven progress in our understanding of deterrence. Nevertheless, as more becomes known, experimental variations in the conditions of threat and punishment can be increased if advances in knowledge make public and official attitudes about crime control more flexible.

Unfortunately, the relationship between increased knowledge and changes in official attitudes is by no means either simple or direct. A communication gap already exists between the level of available information about the effects of legal threats and the level of official beliefs. Progress in penal policy will depend as much on closing this gap as on our willingness and ability to increase knowledge. In the following pages we shall examine closely some of the factors which determine official attitudes and beliefs in this area.

---

we have in mind. See Walker, *Sentencing in a Rational Society* (1969) 56.
    27. *Ibid.*

2   The Rationale of Deterrence

The term *rationale* is an ambiguous one. For this reason it serves our purpose admirably because the topics we deal with under this heading, although related, are diverse. Our primary concern is with the ideology of deterrence as it is reflected in crime control policy. We seek to analyze some aspects of the theoretical basis upon which that policy rests. At the same time, we supplement our critical examination with some positive suggestions.

The aspects of the theory and practice of deterrence which we have selected for examination are fourfold. After a brief introductory note in section 1, in section 2 we attempt to elucidate and evaluate the theoretical foundations of official beliefs. In section 3 we consider ethical aspects of the problem and draw attention to certain ethical principles which should govern the use of deterrent punishment as a means of social control. In section 4 we examine the economic implications of this crime control method and offer a model for the rational assessment of costs in relation to crime prevention strategies. In section 5 we comment briefly on an aspect of the politics of punishment.

SECTION 1 INTRODUCTORY NOTE

There is a celebrated passage in Immanuel Kant's *Philosophy of Law* which runs:

Even if a Civil Society resolved to dissolve itself with the consent of all its members—as might be supposed in the case of a People inhabiting an island resolving to separate and scatter themselves through the whole world—the last Murderer lying in the prison ought to be executed before the resolution was carried out.[1]

There is an equally celebrated passage in Jeremy Bentham's *An Introduction to the Principles of Morals and Legislation* which runs:

But all punishment is mischief: all punishment in itself is evil.[2]

The passage from Kant has been qualified by numerous exegetists, and Bentham supplied his own qualification in terms of the prevention of crime. But the juxtaposition of these passages reflects an antithesis which is present in popular thought on the subject of punishment.

For there are those who believe simply that criminals deserve punishment and that the institution needs no further justification. Moreover, even among those who feel the need for further justification in terms of social benefit, the necessity for some positive evidence of advantage gained is often given little weight if it is not disregarded altogether.

There is little doubt that the argument advanced by Professor Van den Haag in a recent article "On Deterrence and the Death Penalty" reflects a widely held popular view. Van den Haag argues that "though we have no proof of the positive deterrence of the penalty, we also have no proof of zero, or negative effectiveness." He goes on to say that therefore "our moral obligation is to risk the possible ineffectiveness of executions."[3] On a most charitable interpretation this is a highly attenuated form of utilitarian justification.

1. Kant, *Philosophy of Law* (trans. Hastie, 1887) 198.
2. Bentham, "An Introduction to the Principles of Morals and Legislation," 1 *Works* (1843) 83.
3. Van den Haag, "On Deterrence and the Death Penalty" (1969) 60 *J. Crim. Law, Crim., and Police Science* 147.

At the opposite extreme there are those who believe that punishment is "futile" and that if we were "honest" about it we would admit that the idea of deterrence "is simply a derived rationalization of revenge."[4] On this view the institution of punishment provides for "the popular masses" a vehicle for "a disguised living out of their own aggressive hostile impulses."[5]

Because such views are held and strongly held, and because attitudes to punishment are among the most deep-rooted of all our beliefs or convictions, it might seem that the approach developed in the pages which follow is unrealistic. Our discussion of such matters as the ethics of deterrence or of the evaluation of penal measures could be said to bear little relation to the way in which people actually think, talk, act, and make political decisions in this sphere. It might be argued that we display a naïveté and a simple-minded rationalism characteristic of the academic when he ventures into the world of realpolitik.

We must therefore point out that our model was conceived and can be interpreted on two different levels. First, it may be regarded as a political paradigm, that is, as an example or pattern of the sort of approach which *should* be adopted in dealing with the problems considered. And insofar as it represents an ideal, to object that it does not correspond to reality, although semantically correct, can scarcely be regarded as a very serious criticism.

On the second level our model reflects an approach to crime control which in its implementation may create its own constituency. The absence of information can itself both give rise to and ensure the continued dominance of irrational modes of thought and action. For the vacuum created by the absence of data is rapidly filled by the inrush of prejudice, surmise, random speculation, and unsupported assumption. And since the only rational policy is that which is selected as the best on the basis of the observed evidence, the lack of the necessary evidence means that irrationality can often be preemptive. But people's attitudes to punishment are neither always nor wholly

4. Barnes and Teeters, *New Horizons in Criminology* (2d ed. 1951) 337–38.

5. Alexander and Staub, *The Criminal, the Judge, and the Public* (2d ed. 1956) 221.

irrational. For many, it is likely that information about the effectiveness of crime prevention programs would itself be a decisive factor in determining attitudes.

SECTION 2 THE FOUNDATIONS OF OFFICIAL BELIEFS

A Official Ideologies

"English judges," says Professor R. M. Jackson in *Enforcing the Law,* "have a great belief in the general deterrent effect of sentences."[6] This belief is not confined to English judges. As Norval Morris has pointed out: "Every criminal law system in the world, except one, has deterrence as its primary and essential postulate. It figures most prominently throughout our punishing and sentencing decisions legislative, judicial and administrative."[7]

And although it would be foolish to regard all those with legislative, judicial, and administrative power in our society as being unquestioning adherents of an established faith in deterrence, it is undeniable that some community of attitude exists. Different groups of officials do appear to share attitudes about deterrence to the extent that generalization does not seem unfair. This is not to say that there is an official dogma which has been formally stated or authoritatively proclaimed. Yet there is an official ideology of deterrence which, though not a system of integrated assertions or an organized body of concepts, does have sufficient definable content to make analytical discussion possible.

When confronted with a crime problem, legislators often agree that the best hope of control lies in "getting tough" with criminals by increasing penalties.[8] Police subscribe to the no-

6. Jackson, *Enforcing the Law* (1967) 207.

7. Morris, "Impediments to Penal Reform" (1966) 33 *U. Chi. L. Rev.* 631. In a footnote it is indicated that the exception referred to is the Greenland Criminal Code of 1962.

8. *Crime and Penalties in California* (1968), a publication of the California Assembly Office of Research, discusses two episodes of increased-penalty response to rising rates of marijuana use and assaults on police during the 1961 term of the California legislature (at pp. 10–13). Other frequent candidates for "get tough" legislation in the United States include dangerous drug use and sale, gun robbery, and organized criminal activity.

tion of "getting tough," but are apt to put more emphasis on what is termed "strict law enforcement,"[9] a concept that accords the major role to policing. Even correctional officers who are publicly committed to a rehabilitative ideal will sometimes privately confess allegiance to a more punitive approach with deterrent purposes in mind.[10] There are of course significant exceptions to these patterns. Many legislators, but far from a majority, now doubt the efficacy of the death penalty as a marginal deterrent when compared with the threat of protracted imprisonment. Many police express less than total faith in the ability of "strict law enforcement" alone to make a very positive contribution in such areas as the control of prostitution and illegal gaming.

But the exceptions are relatively few, and people more often seem to think in a straight line about the deterrent effect of sanctions:[11] If penalties have a deterrent effect in one situation, they will have a deterrent effect in all; if some people are deterred by threats, then all will be deterred; if doubling a penalty produces an extra measure of deterrence, then trebling the penalty will do still better. Carried to what may be an unfair extreme, this style of thinking imagines a world in which armed robbery is in the same category as illegal parking, burglars think like district attorneys, and the threat of punishment will result in an orderly process of elimination in which the

9. The difference in emphasis between "getting tough" and stricter law enforcement appears to be that the former emphasizes the severity of sanctions while the latter emphasizes the risk of apprehension.

10. In this connection see also Morris and Zimring, "Deterrence and Corrections" (1969) 381 *Annals of AAPSS* at 143: "... when the correctional officer faces a disciplinary problem within a prison: then special and general deterrent purposes can be heard resoundingly to dominate decisions."

11. A remarkable example of thinking in a straight line about deterrence can be found in James Fitzjames Stephen's article "Capital Punishment" (June 1864) 16 *Frazer's Magazine* at 753–54. Stephen was convinced that "the punishment of death when vigorously inflicted has tremendous deterring force." He goes on to say that if it were shown that capital punishment did not deter "it would prove too much. It would prove that legal punishments do not deter at all." He concludes: "The truth is that if it is denied that the punishment of death deters from crime, the deterrent theory of punishment ought to be altogether given up, and we ought to resort to the doctrine ... that crime ought to be treated exclusively as a disease."

crime rate will diminish as the penalty scale increases by degrees from small fines to capital punishment, with each step upward as effective as its predecessor. Other officials, however—frequently those engaged in correctional work, the discouraging end of deterrence—will sometimes take a different but equally unitary view: Since human behavior is unpredictable and crime is determined by a variety of causes, deterrence is a myth.[12]

Commonly, both those who assert the necessary and universal effectiveness of punishment threats and those who deny their relevance to human behavior do not provide more than alternative slogans or catchwords. So it is impossible to determine what evidential bases their views rest on. The truth is (and it is a cheap point) that deterrence is far too complicated a matter to be contained within either of these procrustean views.[13] Such beliefs have no truth value. Nevertheless, it is of considerable importance to examine the bases upon which they rest. The discussion which follows represents an attempt to provide the necessary analysis.

12. This approach is exemplified in Barnes and Teeters, *supra* note 4, at 337–38. They talk of the "futile contention that punishment deters from crime. In this concept of deterrence there is a childlike faith in punishment. . . . The claim for deterrence is belied by both history and logic." See also Ellingston, *Protecting Our Children from Criminal Careers* (1948) 43: "The belief that punishment protects society from crime by deterring would-be law breakers will not stand up before our new understanding of human behavior."

13. Norval Morris, *supra* note 7, at 631 says: "The deterrence argument is more frequently implicit than expressed: the debate more frequently polarized than the subject of balanced discussion. . . . There is rarely any meeting of minds on the issue central to the discourse." And it is true that the dialogue frequently exemplifies the mathematician Frank Ramsey's point: "I think we realize too little how often our arguments are of the form:—

    A: I went to Grantchester this afternoon.

    B: No, I didn't."

Ramsey, *The Foundations of Mathematics* (1931) 289. As a corrective to this kind of polarization one might refer to Wittgenstein's reply to the question, Why do we punish criminals? "There is" he said "the institution of punishing criminals. Different people support this for different reasons, and for different reasons in different cases and at different times. Some people support it out of a desire for revenge, some perhaps out of a desire for justice, some out of a wish to prevent a repetition of the crime, and so on. And so punishments are carried out." Wittgenstein, *Lectures and Conversations on Aesthetics, Psychology, and Religious Belief* (ed. C. Barrett, 1966) 50.

When crime rates rise, law enforcement officials are frequently held—and many hold themselves—in some degree responsible. Some of them, it is true, may feel either that the problem is insoluble or that the solution lies beyond their sphere of influence. But, for the most part, law enforcement officials and society at large find themselves in agreement that fluctuations in the crime rate are subject to political control and responsive to crime-control policy.[14]

The law enforcement official, however, soon finds that he has a limited range of crime control options. He is not in a position—nor will he always feel the need—to introduce millennial measures to end poverty or eradicate social and economic inequity. He can make crime physically more difficult in only a limited number of situations—by urging citizens to lock their cars; fostering the use of automatic locks on bank vaults; raising the height of fire alarm boxes to secure them from the whims of five-year-old children; doubling and trebling the number of police on the street to hamper the mugger, the purse thief, and the random attacker.

Many prevention strategies are expensive, and the administrator is the first to feel the brunt of this type of expense. To double the police force, we must more than double our budget for police. If citizens are required to take expensive precautions, they will object. If precautions are not made mandatory, many will not heed warnings. Beyond this, many of the most serious of crimes—homicide, aggravated assault, rape, indoor robbery, larceny, and crimes against trust—are committed where police cannot prevent them.

Thus, a belief in the efficacy of deterrent measures is attrac-

14. There is, to be sure, some official ambivalence about the relationship between law enforcement efforts and crime rates. In discussing the nature of homicide, police authorities are quick to point out that there is little by way of direct intervention that police can do to reduce the rate of violent killings. "Criminal homicide is, to a major extent, a social problem beyond police prevention." *Uniform Crime Reports — 1967* at 8. At the same time, police and many other officials have asserted a direct relationship between rising crime rates and constitutional restraints on police procedures imposed by the United States Supreme Court in recent years. And four of the eleven factors listed by the FBI as "conditions which will affect the amount and type of crime that occurs from place to place" concern police, prosecution and court policies. See *Uniform Crime Reports 1967* at vi.

tive, because it offers crime control measures where alternatives appear to be unavailable and does so without great apparent cost. It is not surprising that deterrence through threat and punishment is among the most valued official weapons in the war against crime. Nor is this merely a matter of political expedience. For it is difficult to deny that, as Professor Packer puts it, "People who commit crimes appear to share the prevalent impression that punishment is an unpleasantness that is best avoided."[15] To threaten with punishment is therefore a very promising strategy for influencing behavior. And deterrence is a strategy that shows promise of working in areas of behavior where the official has no other technique for crime reduction at hand.

Yet it is one thing to believe that deterrent measures may be a promising strategy in some situations and quite another to espouse a monolithic theory of deterrent efficacy. And it is not immediately apparent why so many people do hold monolithic attitudes about deterrence—whether affirming or denying the effectiveness of legal threats. It seems that they allow themselves to hold only one idea about the nature of deterrence. Once the complex of issues about deterrence is transformed into a yes-or-no question, the results are of course predictable. If the only question at issue is whether deterrence is possible or not, those who believe that it is possible will achieve a substantial majority as a matter of common sense. But when a complex series of different issues is bent into the form of a yes-or-no question, the margin of error obtained from answering that question either way approaches 50 percent.

The tendency to have only one idea about deterrence is not peculiar to officials, nor is it confined to those who deal with the subject of deterrence. The "single idea" phenomenon is a characteristic of prescientific speculation in most areas of human knowledge.[16] One factor is no less basic than human nature; we all would prefer to have simple rather than complicated explanations for the questions that perplex us. Com-

---

15. Packer, *The Limits of the Criminal Sanction* (1968) 149.
16. The basic fallacy in this context, as in many others (e.g. the causation of crime) was identified over a century ago by that neglected American genius Alexander Bryan Johnson (1786–1867). "The search after the unit is the delusion," he said. Johnson, *A Treatise on Language* (ed. D. Rynin, 1947) 77.

plicated explanations evolve from the pressure that experience exerts on our simple initial constructs by a process of trial and error. Since so little evaluative research has yet been done in the area of deterrence, there is little pressure toward rethinking unitary positions. Thus, there are few inconsistent results to sensitize officials to the differences in situation which may, in turn, condition differences in threat effectiveness. Moreover, the limited amount of data available can be comfortably fitted into the official's initial opinion—it can be either accepted at face value or rejected as inconclusive. The absence of reliable research in deterrence does not mean that officials are without any basis for their opinions. In most cases they will have personal and administrative experience in the light of which to test their views of deterrent effectiveness.

The official's personal experience is in most cases likely to lend support to his belief in deterrence. Having worked hard to achieve the regard of his fellows, he is more sensitive than most to the threat of social stigma. He likes to regard himself as a rational man, and will be anxious to give himself credit for responding in the only rational manner to threats. The official is also a law-abiding man and attributes some of his obedience to the threat of sanctions. He remembers slowing down when seeing a police car on the highway, remembers considering the possibility of audit when filling out his income tax return. He is less likely to recall deviations.

It is probable that another source of information is the official's own experience with crime control policies. In his official capacity the legislator "tries out" deterrent threats; the results of these trials are integrated into his attitudes about deterrence. In the absence of controlled research, the apparent results of ongoing crime control policy are the most important data available about deterrence, and these results will inevitably have a profound effect on official attitudes. Unhappily, as we shall see, the unquestioning acceptance of the unanalyzed results of experience with crime control policy is not a satisfactory substitute for careful evaluative research.

B The Lessons of Experience

We cannot demonstrate the truth of our assertion that an important source of those shared beliefs about deterrence which influence penal policy is to be found in the experience of our lawmakers and law enforcers. Nor can we show conclusively that their beliefs are derived from their experience in the manner which we suggest. We can only adduce argument in support of our view, mainly by showing that officials rationalize their beliefs by pointing to that experience. Moreover the study of such rationalization is itself important.

We do not claim to be, in T. S. Eliot's phrase, "expert beyond experience."[17] But experience as a teacher has defects other than the commonly observed characteristic that it seems to inspire reminiscential garrulity. The truth is that there are different types of experience from which knowledge may be derived, and it is necessary to distinguish from one another at least two meanings of the word *experience*.

First, by experience we may mean the experiences which men accumulate as a result of direct participation in events and being engaged in a particular activity without making any special effort to explore, investigate, or test hypotheses. Second, we may refer to the special data of experience which men collect by undertaking methodical research and making systematic observations.

Our contention is that the experience of lawmakers and law enforcement officials is usually of the first kind and that it is subject to serious limitations as a source of knowledge. It is particularly defective when used as a basis for generalization or inductive inference. In order to emphasize some of the common pitfalls that officials encounter in trying to read the significance of the results of crime control policies, we may start with three examples of common errors made in inferring more from statistics than the statistics will support.

i Aunt Jane's Cold Remedy

One common inferential error, or failure to satisfy the conditions of valid or correct inference, can be illustrated by an example drawn from the field of folk medicine. Aunt Jane's Cold Remedy is a mixture of whiskey, sugar, and hot water. It is widely recommended as a treatment for the common cold which can be guaranteed to be effective as a cure within ten

17. Eliot, "Whispers of Immortality," in *Poems 1909–1925* (1925) 57.

days. In a great many cases, moreover, it does appear to be effective. The great majority of those who take the remedy are likely to be quite satisfied with it because every time they take it their cold disappears within the nominated period.

However, apart from some possible temporary, symptomatic relief, Aunt Jane's Remedy has no known effect on the common cold. The cold goes away within ten days because most colds run a course of from three to ten days whether treated or not—that is the nature of the malady. Yet if the adherents of Aunt Jane's Remedy are faithful, they will have no way of knowing that the remedy did not effect a cure. And if, as is quite possible, they have some kind of emotional investment in believing in the cure,[18] they may staunchly resist the suggestion that the remedy is useless, even when their colds go away without being treated with it. Such untreated colds, when recovered from, can be explained away as milder infections.

Legislators and law enforcement officials treat crime, not colds, but they are prone to adopt similar modes of inference. When life is proceeding normally, no great pressure is put on the legislator to increase penalties or on the police official to double or triple patrols. Pressure for strong new countermeasures comes when the crime rate suddenly spurts. Often the scenario then follows this course: (1) spurt in crime rate, (2) countermeasure, (3) return of crime rate to more normal historical level.

Did the countermeasure reduce crime? If so by how much? The headlines read, *Police dogs reduce ghetto crime by 65%*, or *Computer reduces false alarms by 35%*, and enforcement officials are reluctant to avoid credit for the change. But if we remember that an unusual spurt in the crime rate was responsible for the countermeasure, another possible explanation of the reduction exists: The crime rate simply returned to its usual level, which would have been the case whether or not the computer or police dogs or new patrols had been introduced.

18. It is characteristic of such folk remedies that they are handed down from parents to children, or within intimate family groups, and thus attract a loyalty which is based on extrinsic factors irrelevant to the nature of the remedy but no less potent for that reason.

At a later stage we shall be considering documented examples of law enforcement techniques being credited with achieving reductions in crime that were partly the result of other factors. In some cases we find that, after account has been taken of regression to normal levels of crime, the preventive effects attributed to a particular program probably had nothing to do with it. In other cases there may be genuine preventive effects which cannot be explained in terms of regression.

It is sometimes impossible to tell what the crime rate would have been if a particular program had not been introduced. So it is not always possible to determine how much of the reduction can be attributed to natural causes and how much can be credited to the program. But in most cases, knowledge that the program was introduced in a peak period should at least make observers sensitive to the possibility that a good part of the decrease might have been unrelated to the new program. Detailed study of historical trends in the crime rate, or comparisons with untreated areas, could show that the decrease was not solely attributable to Aunt Jane.

Still, if officials desire to maintain a unitary faith in deterrent countermeasures, they can easily do so. Because new programs are normally tried during periods when the rate of the particular crime is high, the official can take credit for any decreases in rate that follow the introduction of the new measures. If the crime rate stays high, who can say that it would not have climbed higher were it not for the new program? Indeed, the rise in crime shows conclusively that we need more of the new countermeasures.[19]

Subjecting our crime prevention strategies to evaluative research will prove less comforting but, in the long run, more valuable. In some situations, close analysis will show that the crime rate could have been expected to decrease even if no new treatment had been administered; in others, a steady rise in crime over a long period of time that can be attributed to

19. According to the California Assembly Office of Research study, *supra* note 8, "In the City of Los Angeles, the rate of attacks on police went from 2.5 per 100 in 1952 to 8.4 in 1961, to 15.8 in 1966. . . . In 1961 the first special penalties for attacks on the police were enacted by the Legislature and such penalties were further increased in . . . 1963 and 1965."

factors such as an increase in the population at risk will indicate that, in the absence of a new treatment, the crime rate would probably have continued to increase.[20] Evaluative research may be able to provide rough estimates of how much the rate would have increased or decreased in the absence of treatment and thus give us a baseline for testing the value of new treatments.

Providing a baseline, so that reliable determinations can be made about the degree of crime reduction attributable to particular countermeasures, is an absolute necessity in any but the most wasteful of crime control policies. Without such a baseline, it may be assumed that some strategies reduce crime when in fact they do not. The preventive effects of other programs may be underestimated because we fail to account for expected increases in crime. When countermeasures do have some effect on crime, overestimating that effect by neglecting the possibility of natural decrease may provoke the use of programs that are not worth their cost—and, worse still, postpone the development of new and more effective strategies.

ii Tiger Prevention

Alexander King prefaces his *May This House Be Safe from Tigers*—the second volume of his memoirs—with an anecdote about a Buddhist prayer which provides him with his title and will provide us with an illustration.[21]

There are many versions of the story King tells, but that which we favor seems more closely analogous to the way in which what we call the tiger prevention fallacy may both vitiate official thinking and set up a formidable barrier to the

20. Thus, it is not possible to conclude, as was done in *Crime and Penalties in California, supra* note 8, at 11, that increased penalties for assaults on a police officer were of no deterrent effectiveness merely because the rate of such crimes continued to increase after penalties for that offense increased.

21. King claims to have a Zen Buddhist friend who, when leaving after a visit, invariably stops in the doorway, presses his hands together Hindu fashion, and says: "May this house be safe from tigers." One day King asked him the meaning of the prayer, and the following dialogue ensued: "What's wrong with my prayer?" he said. "How long have I been saying it to you?" "Oh, about three years, on and off." "Three years," he said. "Well—been bothered by any tigers lately?" King, *May This House Be Safe From Tigers* (1959) v.

revision of crime control strategies. In our version a man is
running about the streets of mid Manhattan, snapping his
fingers and moaning loudly, when he is intercepted by a police
officer. Their conversation follows:

> P. O.: What are you doing?
>
> Gtlm.: Keeping tigers away.
>
> P. O.: Why, that's crazy. There isn't a wild tiger within
> five thousand miles of New York City!
>
> Gtlm.: Well then, I must have a pretty effective technique!

Other factors than the Buddhist's benediction are responsible for Alexander King's immunity from tigers, just as other
factors account for the absence of tigers in New York City.
But as long as those who practice such preventive methods continue to do so they will not find that out.

In crime control, the tiger prevention problem is subtle and
difficult to resolve. Officials who administer very high penalties
acquire the firm conviction that only those penalties stand
between them and huge increases in the crime rate. Having
assumed that the penalty is the only reason for the absence of
a crime wave, the official has "proved" that high penalties
deter crime more effectively than less severe penalties.

One of the most celebrated examples of the tiger prevention
approach to crime control is British Chief Justice Lord Ellenborough's now classic response to a nineteenth-century proposal that, while the death penalty for shoplifting should remain,
the value of the goods stolen which incurred that penalty be
raised from five to ten shillings. Speaking in the House of
Lords, Ellenborough said:

> I trust your lordships will pause before you assent to an
> experiment pregnant with danger to the security of property. . . .
> Such will be the consequence of the repeal of this statute that
> I am certain depredations to an unlimited extent would
> immediately be committed. . . . Repeal this law and . . . no
> man can trust himself for an hour out of doors without the
> most alarming apprehension that on his return, every vestige
> of his property will be swept off by the hardened robber.[22]

22. Parliamentary Debates: House of Lords, 30 May 1810. Cited in
Calvert, *Capital Punishment in the Twentieth Century* (1927) 7–8, and
subsequently by others too numerous to mention. Another example may
be found in the celebrated passage in "The Saint Petersburg Dialogues"
in which Joseph de Maistre writes of the public executioner: "And yet

The proof is the same as that offered by the tiger preventers except in one respect: because penalties may well influence crime rates, it cannot be assumed, as in the tiger examples, that the countermeasure bears no relation to the rate of crime. Being unable to assume that there is no relation between penalty level and crime rate, we can only determine whether and how much the two are related by varying the penalty. But since that would involve risk taking, the status quo and the "proof" of deterrence built into it persist. The tiger prevention argument is not refutable when posed as a barrier to experimental decreases in punishment; it is, however, patently absurd to present high penalties combined with low crime rates as proof of deterrence.

Studies of different areas with different penalties, and studies focusing on the same jurisdiction before and after a change in punishment level takes place, show rather clearly that level of punishment is not the major reason why crime rates vary.[23] In regard to particular penalties, such as capital punishment as a marginal deterrent to homicide, the studies go further and suggest no discernible relationship between the presence of the death penalty and homicide rates.[24] Although imperfect, these studies certainly utilize the best methods available of testing whether more severe sanctions have extra deterrent force in particular situations.

But even in comparative and retrospective studies, the tiger prevention fallacy may crop up in a more sophisticated form. Consider a study that shows homicide to be both the most severely punished and the least often committed crime in a particular jurisdiction.[25] Proof of deterrence? Or tiger prevention? It is quite possible that the rate of homicide would remain

---

all grandeur, all power, all subordination rests on the executioner: he is the horror and the bond of human association. Remove this incomprehensible agent from the world, and at that very moment order gives way to chaos, thrones topple, and society disappears." *The Works of Joseph de Maistre* (ed. J. Lively, 1965) 192.

23. See Rusche and Kirchheimer, *Punishment and Social Structure* (1939) 193–205.

24. See the studies collected in Bedau, *The Death Penalty in America* (1964); also U. N. Dept. of Economic and Social Affairs, *Capital Punishment Developments, 1961–65* (1967).

25. Tittle, "Crime Rates and Legal Sanctions" (1969) 16 *Social Problems* 409.

low even if the penalty for homicide were less severe, because of the strong social feelings against homicide. Indeed, one reason why the penalty for homicide is so high may be that citizens view this crime as so terrible. Both the low rate and the high penalty may be effects of the same cause: strong social feelings against homicide. Thus, showing that crimes which are punished more severely are committed less often may only be one way of showing how accurately a penalty scale reflects general feeling about the seriousness of crimes.

This problem can also arise in connection with some forms of comparative research. Assume we find out that homicide is punished more severely in one state than in another, and that the homicide rate is much lower in the severe penalty state. Does the higher penalty cause the lower rate? It may be that the higher penalty shows that people in that state have stronger social feelings about homicide; and these feelings, rather than the extra penalty, may explain the difference in homicide rate. In order to test the effect of penalties alone, areas that are similar to each other in all respects except penalties should be sought out and compared. This would be a strategy far more cumbersome than assuming that harsh criminal sanctions are keeping the tigers away but, again, far more reliable and rewarding.

iii The Warden's Survey

A third type of faulty inference is found most frequently among those who work at what we have called "the discouraging end of deterrence." Once again the argument is based on experience, but this time the conclusion drawn is diametrically opposite to that exemplified above.

The earliest example we have come across of the type of argument we have in mind occurs in a 1931 article by Warden George W. Kirchwey of Sing Sing.[26] Writing as one *"that has known the convict"* (our italics), Kirchwey maintains that "it argues a curious ignorance of human psychology to attach much importance to the doctrine of deterrence." He goes on to say that belief in "the deterrent effect of exemplary punishments

---

26. Kirchwey, "The Prison's Place in the Penal System" (1931) 156 *Annals of AAPSS.*

or in their moralizing effect on the community at large is "a blind faith."[27]

The same sort of inference is drawn much more explicitly in a book by another celebrated Warden of Sing Sing, Lewis E. Lawes, published in 1940.[28] In his *Meet the Murderer* Lawes states that "the threat of capital punishment lacks the deterrent force most people believe it posseses." On the basis of "*many years' acquaintance with all types of murderers*" (our italics again) he avers that "a person who commits murder gives no thought to the chair."[29]

Lastly, more recently (1962), and even more explicitly we find Warden Clinton T. Duffy of San Quentin giving his views on the effectiveness of the death penalty as a deterrent in his *88 Men and 2 Women*.[30] "But the prison man knows this threat is no deterrent," says Duffy, "*for convicts have told him so again and again*" (our italics).[31]

The warden's survey is unpersuasive for two reasons. First, in none of the instances cited is it at all clear that the prisoners would have told the warden even if they *had* been deterred by penalties at some time in their lives. It could hardly be in their interests to do so. But more significantly, in each case the warden's sample of people to ask about deterrence and base his inference upon is hopelessly biased. For he has based his conclusion on experience with groups of men who have evidently *not* been deterred or they would not be in prison.

At a later stage we will be considering more rigorous studies in deterrence and will demonstrate that the warden's survey fallacy is one which recurs even on quite sophisticated levels of inquiry, including a study conducted for the President's Commission on Law Enforcement and the Administration of Justice.[32] In studies which involve this particular fallacy attention is concentrated on groups of deterrence failures; and *general*

---

27. *Id.* at 17–18.
28. Lawes, *Meet the Murderer* (1940).
29. *Id.* at 177.
30. Duffy, *88 Men and 2 Women* (1962).
31. *Id.* at 22.
32. Goodman, Miller, and DeForrest, "A Study of the Deterrence Value of Crime Prevention Measures as Perceived by Criminal Offenders (1966). Unpublished paper submitted by the Bureau of Social Science Research, Inc., to the Institute for Defense Analysis.

conclusions are drawn on the basis of evidence relating to *particular* groups, which are unrepresentative precisely because they have not responded to the threat of punishment for crime. All of the law's successes, if there were any, would be found outside these groups.

Our tiger preventers and our wardens make contradictory assumptions about the relation between those criminals in jail and the potential crime problem. The tiger prevention advocate assumes that large numbers of law-abiding citizens are held in check by the threat of penalties; indeed, that only severe penalties can perform this job. The warden seems to assume that, when he interviews prisoners, he is talking to the totality of the potential crime problem, or at least to a representative sample. Consequently, because these assumptions are unsupported, both the "proof" and "disproof" of deterrence must fail.

But the fact that these patterns of thinking fail to prove or disprove deterrence does not mean they are unimportant and can be ignored. Officials will continue to act on sincere convictions, whether or not these convictions are well founded. Thus, a significant step toward more rigorous research in deterrence, and ultimately toward a more rational crime control policy, would be to make officials more sensitive to new insights and more understanding of the complexities that undermine monolithic attitudes about deterrence. For this reason, the careful study of "cold remedy," "tiger prevention," and "warden's survey" patterns of inference are an important part of a program for progress in crime control.

SECTION 3 THE ETHICAL ASPECT

In order to make the threat of punishment believable, the criminal law must follow through by punishing those offenders it apprehends. As Justice Holmes put it, "The law threatens certain pains if you do certain things. . . . If you persist in doing them, it has to inflict the pains in order that its threats may continue to be believed."[33] Punishing people in order to deter them (or others) from committing future offenses raises some questions about the *justice* of pain inflicted for deterrent purposes, which should be distinguished from the *efficacy* of deterrent strategies.

33. Holmes, *The Common Law* (1881) 46.

When concerned with the efficacy of punishment-for-deter-rence, we ask the question, Will it work?; when concerned with the justice of punishment-for-deterrence, we ask, Is it morally acceptable to punish for this reason? These two issues are not identical. It is easy to imagine punishments that would be effective but unjust; for an extreme example of this, we need only consider the random execution of every tenth parking violator.

A The Philosophy of Punishment

This is not the place to attempt any very significant or sub-stantial contribution to the philosophy of punishment, but we cannot ignore the subject altogether. A recent collection of papers written since 1939, *The Philosophy of Punishment*, edited by Professor H. B. Acton, is useful and illuminating in this connection.[34] It is not least valuable for the way in which it reveals the complexity and difficulty of problems involved. Yet as one of the contributors makes clear, some of that com-plexity and difficulty is not intrinsic to the subject but rather generated by the way many writers in this field have conducted the discussion. K. G. Armstrong in "The Retributivist Hits Back"[35] successfully demonstrates that a great deal of unre-warding debate on the theory of punishment has been the result of the confusion of three different problems: the definition of punishment, the moral justification of the practice, and the problem of penalty fixing.

We shall therefore begin by declaring our position regarding these problems, without, however, entering into detailed argu-ment about them.

With regard to the definition of punishment we agree with Armstrong that "some sort of retributive theory now seems to be fairly generally accepted";[36] in short, that punishment is pain or deprivation inflicted on an offender for his offense. This is not to say that for certain purposes a more rigorous definition such as that offered by John Rawls in his "Two Concepts of Rules" might not be preferred.[37] But our definition serves

34. Acton (ed.), *The Philosophy of Punishment* (1969).
35. Armstrong, "The Retributivist Hits Back," in Acton, *supra* note 34, at 138–58.
36. *Id.* at 156.
37. Rawls, "Two Concepts of Rules," in Acton, *supra* note 34, at 111–12: "I begin by defining the institution of punishment as follows:

our purpose here: to distinguish punishment from other methods of social control which are employed to prevent antisocial behavior.

As for the moral justification of the practice or institution of punishment, two observations are called for. In the first place we can see no way of avoiding or eliminating what Professor Acton refers to as "the general difficulty of justifying a practice or institution, the difficulty that we must make a dogmatic stop somewhere or else go on *ad infinitum*."[38] In the second place we are inclined to agree with Professor Flew that philosophers have been mistaken in seeking "to find a single unitary and comprehensive justification for all justified punishments."[39] Indeed, relatively few philosophers today seek to justify punishment exclusively in terms of a single principle. Most utilitarians recognize that punishment is retributory at least in the sense that, for a pain or deprivation to constitute a legitimate punishment, it must be inflicted on someone who has committed an offense. And as Professor H. L. A. Hart points out in the "postscript" to his *Punishment and Responsibility*, "Most contemporary forms of retributive theory recognize that any theory of punishment purporting to be relevant to a modern system of criminal law must allot an important place to the utilitarian conception that the institution of criminal punishment is to be justified as a method of preventing harmful crime, even if the mechanism of prevention is fear rather than the reinforcement of moral inhibition."[40]

Similarly, the problem of penalty fixing is one which is rarely dealt with in either purely retributivist or purely utilitarian terms. To determine the amount or severity of punishment *solely* in terms of the gravity of the offense involves all the

---

a person is said to suffer punishment whenever he is legally deprived of some of the normal rights of a citizen on the ground that he has violated a rule of law, the violation having been established by trial according to the due process of law, provided that the deprivation is carried out by the recognized legal authorities of the State, that the rule of law clearly specifies both the offence and the attached penalty, that the courts construe statutes strictly and that the statute was on the books prior to the time of the offence."

38. Acton, "Introduction," *supra* note 34, at 27.

39. Flew, "The Justification of Punishment," in Acton, *supra* note 34, at 101.

40. H. L. A. Hart, *Punishment and Responsibility* (1968) 235–36.

notorious difficulties and multiple ambiguities of the "severity/ gravity" equation. At the same time it ignores the fact that punishment has a social and political function which cannot be fully defined in terms of the requirements of morality.

On the other hand, purely reformatory or deterrent theories lack what are essential safeguards against inhumanity and the infringement of human rights. In this connection we favor the compromise solution which employs the retributive notion of appropriateness as fixing an upper limit to the range within which penalties may be selected on utilitarian grounds.[41] The discussion which follows is in the main a development of this compromise view as applied to the general problem of the use of punishment for deterrent purposes and to specific instances of ethical issues which arise in relation to penalty fixing.

B The Morality of Deterrence

Having said this, we turn to the special problems that arise in connection with punishment for deterrent purposes. One of the principal problems is that such punishment appears to have so little to do with the particular offender. It is not determined by the degree of reprehensibility of his conduct, as retribution is, and it cannot be justified as being designated to benefit the offender, a familiar justification of rehabilitative measures.[42] Indeed, because it stems from other considerations, such deterrent punishments may generate conflict with rehabilitative and retributive precepts.

i The Kantian Principle

One of the most familiar and influential statements of objec-

41. See Longford, *The Idea of Punishment* (1961). For discussion of the "principle of the punitive ceiling" in relation to correctional practices, see Morris and Howard, *Studies in Criminal Law* (1964) chap. 5, and Morris, *supra* note 7, at 627–56.

42. "[Deterrence] is peculiar in that it ignores the personal quality of the offender." Temple, "The Ethics of Penal Action," first Clarke Hall Lecture, 1934. See also G. B. Shaw, *The Crime of Imprisonment* (1946) 32–33: "[Deterrence] necessarily leaves the interest of the victim wholly out of account. It injures and degrades him, destroys the reputation without which he cannot get employment; and when the punishment is imprisonment under our system, atrophies his powers of fending for himself in the world. . . . He is, at the expiration of his sentence, flung out of the prison into the streets . . . [with] no compunction as to society, and why should he have any?"

tion is contained in a passage from Immanuel Kant's *Philosophy of Law.* "Punishment," says Kant, "can never be administered merely as a means for promoting another good. . . . For one man ought never be dealt with merely as a means subservient to the purpose of another."[43] Now Professor Andenaes in a recent article on "The Morality of Deterrence,,[44] deals with this objection, and what we have to say on this point can conveniently be stated by reference to his treatment of it.

Andenaes states Kant's principle as being "that man should always be treated as an end in himself, not only as a means for some other end."[45] He goes on to say that "realistically, societies often treat people in ways designed to promote the good of society at the expense of the individual concerned." By way of example he cites military conscription, quarantine regulations, the confinement of dangerous mentally ill patients and the detention of enemy citizens in wartime. And he concludes that "the Kantian principle, in practical application, is of doubtful value."[46]

Nevertheless, Professor Andenaes admits that the Kantian principle "lends itself to different interpretations."[47] And it seems to us that a different interpretation both preserves what is valuable in the Kantian position and at the same time does not constitute an irrebuttable objection to deterrence. The point is a very simple one. It is that Kant did not say we must never treat men as means. He said that men should never be treated *merely as a means* or, as Andenaes puts it, *only as a means.* This interpretation is favored by Professor H. L. A. Hart in his discussion of Chief Justice Holmes's theory of objective liability.[48]

Kant, Hart maintains, insisted that we should never treat men *only* as means "but in every case as ends also." Hart goes on to say that this means "we are justified in requiring sacrifices from some men for the good of others only in a social system which also recognizes their rights and their interests.

43. Kant, *supra* note 1, at 195.
44. Andenaes, "The Morality of Deterrence" (1970) *U. Chi. L. Rev.* 649–64.
45. *Id.* at 649.
46. *Ibid.*
47. *Ibid.*
48. Hart, *supra* note 40, at 38 and 242–44.

In the case of punishment, the right in question is the right of men to be left free and not punished for the good of others, unless they have broken the law where they had the capacity and a fair opportunity to conform to its requirements."[49] Insofar as this interpretation is valid, the Kantian principle does not necessarily imply the rejection of punishment based on deterrence; but it manifestly implies some limitations upon its use.

It may be noted at this point that all of the ethical problems we shall be considering relate to the imposition of suffering in nonpunishment as well as punishment contexts. But where the innocent or nonblameworthy are involved, the imposition of suffering is more easily recognized as morally objectionable. In the case of the guilty the position is rather different in that the infliction of pain or deprivation is widely felt to be appropriate and deserved, which is one reason for the popularity of the institution of punishment. And this popularity makes it much easier to overlook ethical considerations, which might be readily perceptible in a nonpenal context. To further explore these issues we need to refer more specifically to the context in which ethical problems in deterrence arise.

ii The Retributive Limit to Deterrence

Punishment for deterrence seldom involves administering harsh penalties solely for deterrent motives to people who would otherwise go unpunished. Except for regulatory offenses, deterrent motives condition the degree of punishment far more often than they represent the single justification for punishing crime.

In most cases of serious crime we have no difficulty classifying those who commit them as blameworthy. A street robbery is objectively dangerous behavior, and the offender's intentions are seldom in doubt. When we catch him, the quality of his conduct makes it clear that he is eligible for punishment. But having decided that punishment is justified, we still face the question, How much punishment is just?

Beyond deciding that the robber's punishment is appropriate, legislators have prescribed a range of from one to ten years in

49. *Id.* at 244.

prison, a judge has sentenced our offender to five years, and the parole board has refused to let him out after serving three. The particular penalty for robbery in this situation exists for many purposes: to physically isolate robbers and thereby prevent some crime, to assist in the rehabilitation of the robber, to express society's retributive feelings toward robbers, and to add potency to the threat of the law, in order to promote the deterrence of apprehended robbers and others who might become robbers.

If we assume that robbery would be punished by a two-year rather than a five-year prison sentence, were it not for deterrent motives, we encounter in a real world context a complex of issues about the justice of punishing for deterrent purposes. Our robber will argue that he is, in fact, being punished twice: two years of prison for the offense of robbery, three years of prison for the service of mankind. The legislators may reply that once it is determined that an individual is blameworthy, the term of punishment is just, so long as it is set as a result of proper balancing of legitimate punishment objectives; and deterrence is certainly one legitimate objective of punishment.[50]

The prisoner may then argue that, while deterrence is a laudable goal of public policy, the second sentence he is serving, if it is designed to deter him from future robbery, seems unjust because it is not at all clear that he would commit robbery again in any event.[51] On the other hand, if his extra sentence is motivated by the desire to prevent others from entering the path of crime, he feels unfairly put upon. Why should his grief pay for their moral education?[52]

---

50. "When a man has been proven to have committed a crime, it is expedient that society should make use of that man for the diminution of crime: he belongs to them for that purpose." The Rev. Sydney Smith as quoted by Radzinowicz and Turner, in "A Study on Punishment: Introductory Essay" (1943) *Can. Bar Rev.* 92.

51. A similar complaint could be registered by those confined in preconviction preventive detention and those held in restraint by civil processes because of "dangerousness to others." The relationship between ethical problems associated with the rationale of constraint and the need for evaluative research appears to be similar in these areas.

52. Not unexpectedly, prisoners place little value on the deterrent potential of increased sanctions. See Goodman et al., *supra* note 32.

Such a dialogue is only possible because it has been assumed that an extra measure of punishment was assessed for deterrent purposes only. It is not deterrence as an objective that is cause for concern but the escalation of sanctions for deterrent purposes. Thus, the moral problems raised by punishment for deterrent purposes arise only when we impose a punishment for deterrent purposes that is more severe than would otherwise be imposed. Yet increases in penalty for exclusively deterrent purposes are far from rare if the reasons given for legislative and judicial change in policy are taken at face value.

The robber's complaint can be understood most forcibly in those cases where the punishment is harsh and the disparity between the punishment that would be set in the absence of deterrent motives and the one that is actually set is most extreme. Sending offenders to prison for parking violations, much as it might reduce overtime parking, would excite our sense of injustice because the penalty seems so grossly disproportionate to the wrongfulness of the conduct. The same sense of disproportion has overcome many critics of drastically escalated penalties for the possession of marijuana.

These disparities are likely to be most clearly perceived in connection with behavior that is not considered a serious threat to the community. In these cases, the community's sense of "just deserts" or retributive justice creates a limit beyond which punishment seems unfair. The notion that the severity of the punishment should fit the crime, and not grossly exceed it, is one natural limit on the imposition of sanctions for deterrent purposes.[53]

It might be suggested that a retributive principle can hardly be applied to offenses which are not generally regarded as morally blameworthy. Thus Professor H. L. A. Hart writes of "a vast area of the criminal law where what is forbidden or enjoined by the law is so remote from the familiar requirements of morality that the very word 'crime' seems too emphatic a description of law breaking." In this area, he says, "many modern retributivists would concede that punishment

53. See for example Commonwealth v. Koczwara 379 Pa. 575,155. 2d 825.

was to be justified and measured mainly by Utilitarian considerations."[54]

But even if utilitarian considerations may be regarded as paramount in such cases, it does not follow that their application should be unrestricted. For it would be ridiculous if the protection afforded by the notion of retribution as setting a maximum for punishment were to be confined to crimes which are regarded as immoral, and the principle of reasonable proportion between crime and punishment were to be abandoned in the case of offenses not so regarded. The fact that there is no lower limit to the punishment called for by retributive principles does not mean that there is no upper limit to what would constitute "just deserts." Rather, the absence of a minimum punishment necessary for retribution means that the maximum punishment allowable for deterrent and other reasons is confined by a relatively low upper limit to the community's sense of just punishment.

Where criminal conduct has been more serious, the community is less likely to have any sympathy for the offender, and the gap between deterrent increases and punishment levels which might be set in the absence of a desire for marginal deterrence will be smaller if only because the base penalty is larger. It nevertheless remains true that we are taxing the offender in order to influence the behavior of others. Our preliminary statement regarding this problem is simply the rather weak one that if this is the only way in which we can reduce the crime rate, the practice seems inevitable, and can be more easily justified than if alternative methods of crime control were available.[55]

Professor Packer in his *The Limits of the Criminal Sanction* speaks of "the inevitability . . . of punishment." He says, "In our present state of comparative ignorance about the sources

54. Hart, *supra* note 40, at 236.
55. Cf. Andenaes, "Some Further Reflections on General Prevention," working paper, Center for Studies in Criminal Justice, Chicago University Law School, at 60: "But in the ordinary run of things, where general preventive considerations are taken into account in determining the general level of penalties, the question seems to me to be primarily not one of principle, but one of degree. How much human suffering are we willing to accept as the price of a reasonable protection of life, property and other interests."

and control of human conduct there is no escape from the use of punishment (whether criminal or not) as a device for reducing the incidence of behavior that we consider antisocial."[56] Packer is clearly right, but the history of crime control and penal methods should warn us that complacent conclusions about inevitability and the assumption that no alternatives exist have in the past all too often been taken to justify barbarity and inhumanity.

It may well be that in some instances more effective police work, possibly involving the expansion of police forces, could provide the same or even better protection for the public than an increase in penalties. Where alternative methods of crime reduction do exist and are not employed, we are in the even less enviable position of explaining to the offender that his extra punishment is our method of saving other scarce resources.

That the search for alternative methods of control may be regarded as morally imperative can be supported by another consideration. We have referred above to offenses not regarded as morally blameworthy. A problem arises here because there is no necessary correlation between the accepted moral evaluation of a particular type of conduct on the one hand, and the social undesirability of that conduct and the consequent need for deterrence on the other. Drunk driving may be cited as the sort of behavior in regard to which this discordance obtains in some societies. Moreover, it may often appear that precisely because a particular type of conduct is not subject to strong moral condemnation, therefore heavy penalties will be necessary to suppress it.[57]

It could be argued that in some instances punishment can serve a moralizing or educative function and that this should be welcomed. But there is apt to be tension between the use of punishment as an instrument for the reorientation of the community's moral views and the limiting principle of retribution or just deserts. This may mean in practice that while a strong case can be made for increasing the punishment for

56. Packer, *supra* note 15, at 249.
57. Deterrence may work better in such cases. The fewer the moral barriers to behavior other than legal threat, the more likely the legal threat will have significant influence on behavior. See chap. 4, Sec. 1(c), *infra*.

some crimes beyond the community's normal expectation, such increases should not *grossly* exceed those expectations. It may also mean that particular types of punishment, either permanent in effect or especially severe, may be objectionable as initiating instruments in a campaign of moral reform. Here more than anywhere else the existence of effective alternatives other than increased offender suffering places a moral obligation on enforcement officials to employ alternative means.

The possibility that alternatives to heavier penalties as a means of control exist should always be explored. In the example cited—drunk driving—increasing the likelihood of apprehension and conviction by the use of the breathalyzer might serve. It should never be taken as axiomatic that greater severity will provide a more effective deterrent. Finally, however, the idea of retribution or just deserts as setting an upper limit to the range in which penalties are to be chosen should always be borne in mind.

iii Two Further Principles

Two further principles emerge. First, the harm suffered by offenders as a result of the extra measure of punishment administered for deterrent motives must be recognized as a cost, not insubstantial, to the community as a whole. If the community should gain satisfaction from punishment as an expression of retributive feeling, no joy should come from punishment in excess of that required to express collective feelings of outrage. Our own reading of the Kantian principle is that the offender is a citizen, and the community's decisional process exists to protect his welfare as well as that of others.[58]

Incidentally, Bentham, who has often been accused of crude utilitarianism, was quite explicit on this point. "It ought not to be forgotten" he wrote, "although it has been too frequently forgotten, that the delinquent is a member of the community, as well as any other individual . . . and that there is just as much reason for consulting his interest as that of any other. His welfare is proportionately the welfare of the community— his suffering the suffering of the community."[59]

58. See Temple, *supra* note 42.
59. Bentham, "Principles of Penal Law," in 1 *Works* (1843) 398.

If the offender's suffering is not taken into account as a cost, the usual resolution of the choice between extra offender suffering and alternative crime reduction methods will be to opt for the extra suffering. The situation is reminiscent of the story of the man who was advised that the best method of increasing his horse's efficiency was violently to castrate the animal with two bricks. When he asked, "Doesn't that hurt?" his mentor responded, "Not if you don't get your thumbs in the way."

Of course, the important question is, "Whom does one count when determining if the action hurts?" When the community asserts its right to punish offenders at higher levels for exclusively deterrent purposes, it must protect them against unjustified punishment by fully considering the offenders' interest in freedom from excessive punishment.[60]

A second principle to be drawn from an otherwise unresolved dialogue is that administrators have a moral duty to the punished offenders to do research on the deterrent effect their policies pursue. When the law enforcement official imposes extra punishment for deterrent purposes, he holds the lives of the least lovable segment of our society in trust. To base extra punishment on a *belief* in deterrence is morally acceptable only as long as it is necessary. When facilities exist for the evaluation of sanction policies, failure to test policies while continuing to penalize offenders in the name of deterrent beliefs becomes morally obnoxious.

It has been rightly said that "anyone who purports to set out a justification for the institution of punishment has got to come to terms with the problem of action in a state of ignorance."[61] In relation to deterrence this means that an obligation exists both to test the effectiveness of the policies pursued in the light of available information and also to search for further information.

---

60. There is a further point, in addition to the calculus of social benefit and individual suffering, to be considered in this connection. This is that some methods of punishment (e.g., imprisonment) may themselves be criminogenic. Insofar as this is the case the preventive effect of punishment on other potential offenders has to be weighed against the possible criminogenic effect on the offender.

61. Griffiths, review of Packer's *The Limits of the Criminal Sanction* (1968), in (1970) 79 *Yale L. J.* 1428.

It has also been suggested that empirical ignorance imposes an obligation to "act on reasonable assumptions related to a plausible and testable theory."[62] And, although there can be no obligation to perform the impossible, it seems reasonable to assert that whenever possible the implementation of deterrent policies should be pursued in such a way as to provide opportunities for evaluative research.

But if administrators have an obligation to test their methods, it is an easy obligation to ignore. Offenders are the least powerful of pressure groups, and officials are subject to very real temptations to avoid research. In addition to the cost of evaluation, any honest effort to test a program is a threat to its continued existence and a potential shadow on the prior judgment of its administration. Criminal law administration thus represents an almost ideal mixture for evaluative inaction: powerless subjects, economic excuses for resistance to research, and an administrative incentive to avoid the testing of long-held beliefs.

When the genuine obstacles to effective research are added to this already potent brew, the absence of research is as easy to explain as it is difficult to justify.

C The Exemplary Sentence: A Special Case

The "exemplary sentence" is one designed to meet the needs of deterrence felt in a particular case or group of cases. This topic has been recently discussed both by Nigel Walker in *Sentencing in a Rational Society*[63] and Professor Andenaes in his article "The Morality of Deterrence."[64] Such sentences are usually imposed to deal with specific offenses which have suddenly become, or appeared to become, more frequent or more frightening. In such cases, as Walker puts it, judges "will sometimes impose sentences which are markedly more severe than the norm for the express purpose of increasing their deterrent

---

62. *Id.*
63. Walker, *Sentencing in a Rational Society* (1969) 68–70.
64. Andenaes, *supra* note 44. This topic is also discussed by Professor W. T. H. Sprott, who talks of it as "specific deterrence." Sprott, "Sentencing Policy," in Halmos (ed.) *Sociological Studies in the British Penal Services* (1965), 35–38.

effect."[65] A number of ethical problems beyond those previously discussed arise in connection with this practice.

i Fair Notice

We must first consider to what extent it is fair to raise the penalty for a particular offender who made his commitment to a given criminal outlet without notice of the penalty increase.

It is, of course, true that there is some doubt as to how effectively the multiple threats of punishment embodied in the criminal law are communicated to the public. Leslie Wilkins, for instance, regards communication as "perhaps the most unsatisfactory point in the doctrine of deterrence." Indeed, he goes so far as to suggest that it is "probable that in most serious offences the offender is not aware of the true possibilities of being caught, nor is he aware of the likely penalty should he be caught."[66]

Professor Wilkins is concerned with the empirical rather than the ethical aspect of "the doctrine of deterrence," and we shall be considering this at length later on. We have already dealt with the moral duty to do research on the effectiveness of deterrence, and such research must necessarily include attention to the problem of communication. It is interesting to note, here and elsewhere, how empirical questions, and thus inevitably empirical methods, interact with ethical issues in deterrence.[67]

The fair notice issue, however, specifically concerns the justice of increased penalties which are "markedly more severe than the norm." One view might be that as long as there is notice that a particular behavior is forbidden, escalation in

65. Walker, *supra* note 63, at 69.

66. Wilkins, "Criminology: An Operational Research Approach," in Welford (ed.) *Society: Problems and Methods of Study* (1962) 324. See also Wootton, *Crime and the Criminal Law* (1963) 97–98; Ball, "The Deterrence Concept in Criminology and Law" (1955) 46 *J. Crim. L., Crim., and Police Science* 351; Hawkins, "Deterrence: The Problematic Postulate" (1969) 2 *Aust., N.Z. J. Crim.* 136–38.

67. What we have in mind may be illustrated by the following dialogue:

    A: It is proper to do X.
    B: It is only proper to do X if Y is a fact.
    A: I know that Y is a fact.
    B: How do you know?
And there we are.

penalty raises no substantial issue of fair notice, since the duty to obey the law is absolute and violators do so at their own risk. On the other hand, if we believe that escalation in sanctions may persuade offenders to abstain from a particular criminal act—and this is the rationale for exemplary sentences—it seems incongruous to impose extra punishment on persons who have never had the benefit of the extra deterrent force of the escalated threat. But, in our view, if the increased penalty is within the legislatively prescribed range, then the fair notice issue is blunted and it becomes a question of inequality of treatment as beween the offender and his predecessors—or violation of the principle of equality before the law—which we discuss below. If, on the other hand, the sentence exceeds the maximum penalty applicable at the time the crime was committed, then of course exemplary punishment raises separate and substantial ethical problems.[68]

ii Particular Efficacy

A basic requisite of exemplary sentencing is that there be reason to suppose that the punishment imposed for a deterrent purpose will achieve its intended goal. Walker devotes his entire discussion to this problem and demonstrates by means of examples "how difficult it is to draw confident and definite conclusions from the available evidence."[69] It is evident that if the exemplary sentence in a particular case is aimed at the community at large rather than at the offender before the court, the audience had better be listening.

iii Problems of Equality

The exemplary sentence, because it is designed to attract public attention, generates tension between the tactual benefits of "singling out" an individual or group for more serious punishment than other offenders and the ethical notion that equally culpable offenders should be treated equally. The proponent

68. While the ex post facto law and ex post facto penalty are distinguishable in that in the latter case there is notice of the forbidden nature of the behavior, at least part of the reason why the former is objectionable can be found in the imposition of the latter. See in this connection Bentham in "Principles of Morals and Legislation" on "cases unmeet for punishment" I *Works* (1843) 84.

69. Walker, *supra* note 63, at 70.

of exemplary sentences might argue that more deterrence can be achieved with less total suffering if one publicized offender receives harsh punishment while others are treated more leniently. But the singled-out offender will find small comfort in the fact that he may be saving fellow offenders some suffering. If deterrent motives compel that extra punishment be imposed on offenders, then why not impose it equally upon all?

This argument could be read in support of punishing all at the higher level required for the exemplary sentence, but that policy would involve extra offender suffering without any necessary extra deterrent returns. Or it could be seen as a plea for leniency to the singled-out offender, which sacrifices the presumed marginal deterrent impact of the exemplary sentence.

There are a variety of ways an exemplary sentencing strategy may attempt to accommodate the claim that equally culpable offenders should be treated equally. First, even assuming that only a small number of the equally culpable are to be singled out, it can be argued that the random selection of that few from the many is equality of treatment, because each member of the class has the same initial exposure of risk. Yet the unequal punishment remains troublesome: imagine, for example, the unseemly impression that a formal lottery to assign punishments would create.

It would thus seem more promising if some principled basis for assigning exemplary punishments could be found. One such standard, and this we believe to be implicitly accepted by many courts, is to administer exemplary punishments in cases most likely to capture public attention—such as those involving public figures or newsworthy circumstances. The utilitarian justification is that these are the cases where the exemplary sentence is apt to achieve the greatest amount of attention and therefore presumably the greatest deterrent impact. But since this distinction is not necessary related to differences in culpability, it is not an adequate rejoinder to the objection to unequal treatment. It is only when an exemplary sentence can be justified on other than deterrent grounds that the general problem of inequality can be avoided.

Two other questions of equality concern the timing of exemplary sentences but are distinguishable from the fair notice issue referred to above. The first, raised by Professor Andenaes, is whether an increase in the crime rate can ever justify an increase in sentence level in the case of a defendant who may have had no part in the crime rate increase. One view is that, subject to the limitation of just deserts referred to above, the offender is fair game for maximum punishment designed to serve any of society's legitimate punishment aims.

Professor Andenaes, however, draws a distinction here. On the one hand, he apparently concurs in the Norwegian Supreme Court's rejection of leniency, in the appeal of a youth sentenced for bag-snatching, on the ground that "recently there has been a great increase in bag-snatching."[70] In regard to this case Andenaes says that "it is ethically defensible to increase the penalty because of changes in the crime rate."[71] Yet he seems unwilling to extend this principle to a situation in which a rise in the crime rate takes place "after the commission of the act of the defendant."[72] For he says "subsequent developments should be excluded as an aggravating factor in sentencing."[73] We find it difficult to distinguish the two cases, unless one is prepared to assume the defendant in the first case guilty of crimes other than that for which he was convicted; and even if that were the case, general deterrence would not be the ground for increasing his sentence.

The second temporal problem arises when the special demands of crime control call for the singling out for harsh treatment at a particular time of a group of offenders who are in no sense especially blameworthy, while other equally guilty offenders before and after that time are treated more leniently. By way of example, the reputed treatment of drunk drivers in Chicago during the Christmas period may be cited.[74] It is important to note that in Chicago there is a time lag of a month or more before such offenders are brought to trial. Christmas is supposed to be a peak period for drunk driving offenses, and exemplary sentences are therefore likely to be awarded. Yet because of the time lag, those likely to be awarded the exemplary sentences, if such sentencing is confined to the peak

70. Andenaes, *supra* note 44, at 659.
71. *Id.* at 660.
72. *Id.* at 661.
73. *Ibid.*
74. Now extended because of the success of the experiment.

period, are those whose offenses were committed earlier. More-over, those at whom the deterrent is aimed may benefit from regression to a more normal crime rate and sentencing pattern. In regard to this problem, we would observe that from the viewpoint of justice, once again subject to the just deserts limi-tation, such a pattern although anomalous cannot be dismissed categorically as unacceptable. Nevertheless, if it were—as it might be—equally effective to impose the exemplary penalties on the peak period apprehendees, then clearly such a course would be preferable, at least when they have been exposed to special appeals that were not aimed at the earlier group.

It may not have escaped attention that we have invoked the principle of equality before the law without defining it. In this we are not alone. Thus Professor Andenaes, who says, "It may, to be sure, often be difficult to determine what equality means,"[75] does not essay that task himself. Professor H. M. Hart says, "The very ideal of justice is offended by seriously unequal penalties for substantially similar crimes,"[76] but does not elaborate. Professor H. L. A. Hart says no more than that one of the ways in which "Principles of Justice" are widely taken to bear on the amount of punishment "is the somewhat hazy requirement that like cases be treated alike."[77]

We shall not attempt to lend precision to a notion which is in fact vague, or to draw sharp lines where none exist. It is sufficient to say that the cases we have discussed exemplify significant aspects of what is commonly understood by the principle. Our general conclusion on the topic is that exem-plary sentences do clearly violate the principle, but that this may not always be objectionable. As Professor H. L. A. Hart says, "Some sacrifice of justice to the safety of society is in-volved though it is often acceptable to many as the lesser of two evils."[78]

In regard to exemplary sentences we have distinguished three fundamental issues: that of fair notice, the question of the efficacy of such sentences and finally the principle of equality

75. *Id.* at 656.
76. H. M. Hart, "The Aims of the Criminal Law" (1958) 22 *Law and Contemp. Prob.* 439.
77. H. L. A. Hart, *supra* note 40, at 24.
78. *Id.* at 24–25.

before the law. We see no reason to disagree with Andenaes's conclusion that while it cannot be said "that it is unjust under all circumstances to attach weight in sentencing to the deterrent effects of the particular sentence . . . at least we are in an area which demands extreme caution."[79]

D Conclusion

Professor H. L. A. Hart in his celebrated "Prolegomenon of the Principles of Punishment" speaks of a need to develop a "sense of the complexity of punishment" and the necessity for "realization that different principles . . . are relevant at different points in any morally acceptable account of punishment."[80] He is writing there of such general principles as deterrence, retribution, and reform. But it is no less true when we consider a particular principle as we have done here that multiple issues and a number of values are involved.

It seems to us that the principles which need to be observed if deterrence is to be morally tolerable can be seen as a hierarchy. Three are of paramount importance: the retributive limit or the principle of just deserts, the principle that the offender's suffering should be regarded as a cost, and the principle that action in ignorance imposes a moral obligation to do research. Also of major importance, although infrequently at issue, is the fair notice principle in relation to offenders punished beyond the maximum authorized at the time they committeed their offenses. Still important, but at a lower level, are the principle of equality and the principle of fair notice when unusual but authorized sentences are imposed. It is scarcely necessary to add that in current practice these principles are not generally observed, nor in some cases are they even recognized.

SECTION 4 THE ECONOMIC ASPECT

A Introductory

The question of cost is rarely raised in discussions of deterrence, but has not been totally ignored. Bentham, in his *Panopticon: or The Inspection House* (1791) and again in

---

79. Andenaes, *supra* note 44, at 656.
80. H. L. A. Hart, *supra* note 40, at 3.

Panopticon versus New South Wales (1802), gave the subject of "pecuniary economy"[81] a good deal of attention. Indeed, he regarded as one of the principal advantages of his scheme, upon which he dilates at some length, the fact that it would be substantially cheaper than the transportation system."[82]

Bentham did not stop at the discussion of particular costs but made a serious attempt to deal with the more general problem of the proper place of economic considerations in this context. Very briefly his view was that "Economy" ought to be included—along with Example ("beyond comparison the most important"), Reformation, Incapacitation, and Compensation or Satisfaction—as one of the "several objects or ends of penal justice."[83] He added, however, that whereas the other four were *direct* ends, Economy should be regarded as "an *indirect* or *collateral* end" which "ought not to be departed from to any greater distance, than the pursuit of the other direct ends shall be found to render unavoidable."[84]

Apart from Bentham, the question of cost effectiveness has not only been neglected but even on occasion deliberately rejected as a matter of concern. To give an example, the history of "hard labor" as a penal method represents a repudiation of economic principles. It was an attempt to achieve a deterrent effect by "the punishment of hard, dull, useless, uninteresting monotonous labour."[85] And as Sir Lionel Fox has noted, "the derivation here was entirely from penal theory divorced from social or economic principles, since its essence was that the labour should be unproductive—it aimed at punishment of the body and spirit by monotony and fatigue and nothing more."[86]

This type of decision making seems to imply that cost is irrelevant to punishment policy. To the official, however, cost is an important matter. To talk of the effects that particular programs might have, without addressing the issue of cost,

81. Bentham, "Panopticon: or The Inspection House," in 4 *Works* (1843) 47.

82. Bentham, "Panopticon versus New South Wales," in 4 *Works* (1843) 201–11.

83. Bentham, *supra* note 81, at 174.

84. *Ibid.*

85. DuCane, *The Punishment and Prevention of Crime* (1885) 175.

86. Fox, *The English Prison and Borstal Systems* (1952) 177.

tells the administrator only half of what he must know before he has a rational basis for acting. Estimates of a program's cost are essential to the person who decides whether particular programs will create sufficient returns to justify the commitment of resources necessary to bring them into existence. Cost estimates are also necessary to help the official choose between alternative crime prevention strategies. In their simplest form, these statements are self-evident: it would certainly be worth one million dollars to cut Chicago's larceny rate in half, but not one billion; it would be folly to spend one million dollars on a program if the same results could be achieved by a different method for $500,000.

Yet the notion of designing research so as to compare the costs of alternative means of crime prevention (e.g., prisons versus police) has a degree of novelty. It is novel, however, only in this context. The comparison of the costs of alternative programs in order to arrive at marginal costs, which together with the marginal value of the revised output provide a basis for decision, is an elementary and basic mode of economic analysis. Indeed, the function of the concept of cost is precisely to enable "choices among alternatives according to some criterion of preference."[87]

But the reference to "some criterion of preference" points to a crucial problem in this area. In economics the cost of an event has been defined as "the highest-valued opportunity necessarily forsaken."[88] In this context valuation involves more than monetary worth or market value. The relative worth or utility of social services cannot be wholly computed in economic terms.

As Leslie Wilkins has pointed out in discussing social action relating to the prevention of crime and the treatment of offenders, "We must be careful about what we mean by cost in this connexion. This is not the simple accountancy term cost, but a concept of a social benefit cost."[89] And the problem here is

87. Alchian, "Cost," in 3 *International Encyclopedia of the Social Sciences* (1968) 411.

88. *Id.* at 404.

89. Wilkins, "Crime Prevention and Costs in National Planning: A Discussion of Concepts and Issues" (1967) 25 *Internat. Rev. Crim. Policy* 23.

that such values as humanity (i.e., the quality of being humane) and justice, and such disvalues as pain and suffering, belong to a different universe of discourse and have different logic from that of economic efficiency.

To put the problem in more specific terms, we need to briefly consider some of the many different types of cost which are incurred by law enforcement systems. The commitment of resources to publicity campaigns and to the administration of criminal justice in courts involves monetary costs and the use of personnel that could be deployed in other phases of crime prevention. The nonmonetary costs of publicity campaigns include the environment of fear or tension that such campaigns might produce and the possibility of a gradually diminishing willingness on the part of the public to pay attention to official pronouncements. The nonmonetary costs of a low commitment of resources to courts include delay, injustice, and the appearance of unfairness to those who come before the bar of justice.

By far the most expensive aspects of law enforcement are police and punishment facilities. An extra police officer assigned to a particular task will cost at a rough approximation from $10,000 to $25,000 per year. And giving the policeman this job means that one less policeman will be available for other duties. The nonmonetary costs of extra policing include the effect of a "police environment" on community atmosphere and on attitudes of individuals subjected to increased police contacts. The monetary costs of imprisonment to the prison administration are substantial: from $620 to $2,600 per prisoner per year in California, depending on conditions and methods of accounting.[90] Nonmonetary costs could include extra crime caused by the aggressiveness or inability to pursue gainful employment that could be side effects of protracted imprisonment. And, as discussed earlier, when extra punishment is administered for exclusively deterrent purposes, the harm suffered by the offender must also be considered as a cost by the official.

90. Lamson and Crowther, Memorandum, Assembly Office of Research, California Assembly, 1969 (unpublished). Supplementary data on costs were obtained from Mr. Lamson.

A rational crime control policy takes account of all program costs in determining whether programs are worth the resources necessary to administer them and in choosing between alternative methods of achieving crime prevention. But since all costs are not of the same type, difficult problems of comparison are inevitable. How much money is it worth to prevent ten rapes? How many fewer housebreakings justify keeping ten men in jail for two extra years? How many robberies equal one burglary? It is far easier to outline the types of cost that should be considered in evaluating alternative methods of crime control than to proclaim with any confidence the priorities to be accorded to different types of cost.[91]

The fact that some of these values cannot be computed, measured, or compared in terms of economic profit and loss does not mean that they have to be ignored. Nor does it mean that they cannot be comprehended in our calculations. The fact that qualities or properties are not quantifiable does not preclude rational analysis, evaluation, or ethical and aesthetic choices.

Moreover, the fact that qualities or properties are incommensurable does not mean that they are mutually exclusive. As Professor Galbraith has pointed out, it is possible to "defend low pecuniary interest on grounds of high moral principle."[92] And just as a work of art may be purchased both because it is cheap *and* because it is beautiful, so a method of crime control may be preferred because it is both humanitarian *and* involves a smaller or equal expenditure of resources than available alternatives.

It does not follow, therefore, that the existence of multiple and incommensurable criteria *necessarily* makes choice more difficult. For example, Wilkins says that "there is no evidence that humanitarian treatments are any less effective than severer forms of punishment,"[93] and that conclusion is at least possible. It may also happen—if infrequently—that a humanitarian treatment is cheaper than a harsher punishment (as in the case of probation versus imprisonment).

And even when there is no such convenient confluence, it is

91. See chap. 4, infra, at 207–8.
92. Galbraith. *The Liberal Hour* (1960) 13.
93. Wilkins, *supra* note 89.

important that the existence of many different types of cost be recognized. This recognition may often make the decision-making process more difficult. But in this context appreciation of the complexity of problems is to be preferred to easier solutions achieved through oversimplification.

Economists have in fact begun to enter the field of crime and punishment; principally by way of superimposing economic theory and econometric formulae on data derived from this area.[94] Although our economically oriented colleagues assure us that we pay them insufficient attention, elsewhere in this book we discuss some economic models for the empirical testing of propositions about deterrence.

For the present it is sufficient to point out that, possibly through lack of complete understanding, we are skeptical of economic exercises in determining the optimum enforcement of laws.[95] We cannot accept that the costs of crime have been completely delineated or put properly into perspective.[96] We approach in a gingerly fashion confident assertions about the production function of policing and punishing.[97] Yet we feel justified in embarking on a simplified model of the economy of punishment without subscribing to or endorsing that model's more sophisticated and, in our view, more dangerous descendents.

B Determining Costs in Crime Prevention

If the successful establishment of priorities in choosing among different types of costs proves elusive, a number of more modest points can be made about cost considerations in deterrence. Perhaps the most important point is the most basic: the study of costs in crime prevention is necessary for policy research

94. See Becker, "Crime and Punishment: An Economic Approach" (1968) 76 *J. Polit. Econ.* 169–217; Landes, "An Economic Analysis of the Courts" (1971) 14 *J. Law & Econ.*, and "Rules for an Optimal Bail System" (1970) mimeograph; Erlich, "Participation in Illegitimate Activities" (1970) mimeograph.

95. Stigler, "The Optimum Enforcement of Laws" (1970) 78 *J. Polit. Econ.* 526–36. See also Becker, *supra* note 94.

96. See Martin and Bradley, "Design of a Study of the Cost of Crime" (1964) 4 *Brit. J. Crim.* 591: "Crime . . . though frequently studied as a social and psychological phenomenon has rarely been considered in terms of its economic impact." Also Martin, "The Cost of Crime: Some Research Problems" (1965) 23 *Internat. Rev. Crim. Policy* 57–63.

97. See Erlich, *supra* note 94.

purposes as well as for accounting purposes. In fact, focusing on issues of cost might provide a useful starting point for framing the questions that evaluative research should answer if it is to provide policy guides in crime control.

An example of recent policy change might illustrate this last point. In California, between 1963 and 1968, the average time served by the prisoner released from the California Adult Authority increased from thirty to thirty-six months.[98] Whether this change was the result of a change in conscious policy on the part of the Adult Authority or sentencing judges, or an unplanned occurrence, it represents an objective shift in punishment policy that should be objectively analyzed. Since imprisonment is "perhaps the most costly form of penal measure,"[99] in terms both of cost to the national economy and of suffering on the part of offenders and their families, the California change is of much more than local interest. Incarceration rates, particularly high in the United States, are subject to wide variations throughout the world "without any established relationship between costs and benefit which the community pays and receives in relation to these differences."[100]

Are the longer prison sentences worthwhile? In order to provide a satisfactory answer to that question, research must seek to establish (1) the types and amount of program costs,

98. Personal communication from Robin Lamson, 6 November 1969. See also, Lamson and Crowther, *supra* note 90.

99. Wilkins, *supra* note 89, at 23.

100. *Id.* at 24. Wilkins gives a 1960 estimate of incarcerated population rates in certain developed countries per 100,000 inhabitants as follows:

United States of America	About 200
Finland	About 153
Denmark	About 73
Sweden	About 63
England and Wales	About 59
Norway	About 44

This variation in incarceration rates does not appear to be a Western world or developed country phenomenon, for Wilkins also cites rates for some Asian countries:

Hong Kong	162
India	89
Philippines	84
Ceylon	48

(2) the *nature* of the program's effect on crime; (3) the *extent* of program's effects, and (4) the cost and relative effectiveness of alternative methods of achieving the same objectives.

i Program Costs

As noted above, imprisonment generates a number of different types of cost: monetary and nonmonetary; direct (such as dollars expended by the state) and indirect (diminished ability of longer-term ex-prisoners to adjust when released); costs absorbed by the state and those absorbed by the inmates. Cost study begins with the enumeration of those costs easiest to quantify and determine—the direct monetary costs absorbed by the state. In California the cost of maintaining one extra prisoner for one year is $620 when there is surplus space available. The average Adult Authority prisoner population is 30,000.[101] The monetary cost of the extra time served amounts to about $9,000,000 over the period of thirty-six months (one-half man-year × 30,000 prisoners × $620).[102] These figures already exist or would be extremely easy to compile in most jurisdictions in the United States, but they usually command the attention of budgetary authorities for housekeeping purposes while failing to play an important role in basic decisions about crime control policy.

The statistics presented have already quantified a second type of cost produced by the extra punishment: the additional confinement absorbed by the present prison population, an average of six months for 30,000 men. Other types of possible cost, such as the effect of overcrowding and decreased ability on the part of ex-prisoners to adjust to outside life, cannot be estimated. And there is no way of adding up the costs to the state and the costs absorbed by the prisoners into a single index number.

But even this incomplete picture of program costs provides a useful point of departure. The utility of committing resources to crime control research should be judged against the total cost of crime control programs. As Wilkins says, "The measure-

101. See Lamson and Crowther, *supra* note 90.
102. *Ibid.*

ment of cost cannot be achieved without cost. The utility of data must be assessed against the cost of obtaining it."[103] It is clear that in this case the stakes are high. Because the stakes are so high, the need for evaluation extends not only to decisions about instituting new crime control programs or committing more resources to police or corrections, but also to existing patterns of resource allocation and strategies of control. So little is known about present programs that it would not be inaccurate to call most present crime policies expensive experiments that all too often do not permit adequate evaluation.

ii Nature of the Program's Effect on Crime

Thus far the analysis has considered only the liabilities incurred as a result of the change in sentence length. The motivation for longer sentences is the hope that they will reduce crime, and a necessary step in evaluation is determining whether this hope is being fulfilled. The extra prison sentences could be reducing crime in at least three ways: (1) the offenders might have committed crimes during those months if they had been released; (2) those prisoners serving the longer sentence could be persuaded that future efforts at crime are not worth the risk of penalties; and (3) some potential criminals on the outside could be deterred from committing crimes.

The longer sentences may have been motivated solely by a desire for a greater degree of marginal general deterrence. Like most crime control strategies, however, they may affect the crime rate in a number of ways. And any rational analysis of the results of the program must seek to account for all the different mechanisms that may have an effect on crime.

The different types of effect must be studied in different ways. In order to test hypotheses about the reduction of crime among convicts serving extra sentences, the records of these convicts after release should be compared to those of similar convicts who served shorter sentences. The test for marginal general deterrence would focus on the crime rate of the rest of the population. If an investigation revealed that no reduction in crime was being achieved by the shift in policy, the evaluation would be completed; if investigation revealed

103. Wilkins, *supra* note 89.

that the extra imprisonment was responsible for some decrease in criminal activity, evaluation of the program would just be starting.

iii Extent of Program Effects

The emphasis in the first question on the cost of a particular crime control measure shows that, to properly evaluate increased sentences, it is not sufficient to determine *whether* the program decreases crime. It is also necessary to ask, and this is the crucial question, *how much* of an effect is attributable to the new policy. At this point the official is asking about marginal changes in punishment rather than the difference between the threat of punishment and none, and he is interested in the quantity of an effect rather than its quality. Here the official and the theoretician may often part company, because the same set of findings may have strikingly different implications for researchers and policy planners.

For example, in the Chicago False Fire Alarm Project,[104] it appeared that eight-hours-a-day surveillance by teams of two firemen could reduce an individual school's false alarm rate if the surveillance resulted in apprehending a child pulling an alarm. However, after each of sixteen schools had been exposed to two man-weeks of surveillance, it turned out that apprehensions occurred at only four schools, and the effect of the apprehension on the false alarm rate was slight and transient, amounting to an expenditure of several hundred dollars for each false alarm prevented. Thus, while the test may have provided valuable information, and while surveillance makes sense in a limited number of circumstances, the fire department would not be seriously tempted to continue the program of regular school surveillance past the experimental period.

Another example comes from Professor Beutel's investigation of the administration of Nebraska's criminal laws dealing with the writing of bad checks.[105] His basic findings were that

104. See Center for Studies in Criminal Justice, University of Chicago Law School, "The Chicago False Fire Alarm Project" (1967) unpublished.
105. Beutel. *Some Potentialities of Experimental Jurisprudence as a New Branch of Social Science* (1957) 224–429.

in spite of an unusually severe penalty structure, Nebraska experienced about the same rate of bad-check writing as a similar state with less stringent policies,[106] and those areas of the state that punished particular types of bad checks more stringently than others did not have a lower rate of bad checks.[107] Since areas were compared that might have experienced different rates of bad check writing in the absence of the difference in punishment policy, it would be difficult to prove that the stringent Nebraska policy had no deterrent effect at all. However, since the cost of the Nebraska bad check policy was so great,[108] the small measure of deterrence that might have been missed by the study was of no practical importance.

Social scientists, although they have assessed the kind and sometimes even the extent of the consequences of preventive measures, have rarely accompanied their analyses by any assessment of cost. There is no reason why social scientists should not conduct their research in this way if they wish to.[109] But the study of countermeasures demands cost assessment before it can inform or influence policy.

iv The Availability of Alternative Means

Even programs with crime prevention results worth their cost should be subordinated to alternative programs that can achieve better results at the same cost, or similar results at lesser cost. And in this connection we repeat that the suffering of offenders should be regarded as a cost. So if similar results can be achieved by means of an alternative program which involves less offender suffering, then that alternative program should be preferred as being cheaper. The dollar spent in the prison system in pursuit of crime reduction is more usefully thought of as part of a budget for crime reduction than simply or exclusively as part of a prison system budget. Money spent

106. *Id.* at 355.
107. *Id.* at 351.
108. *Id.* at 406–7: According to Professor Beutel, the administration of bad check laws in Nebraska cost more than making all such checks good would have done.
109. See, e.g., Schwartz and Orleans, "On Legal Sanctions" (1967) 34 *U. Chi. L. Rev.* 274–300: This article reports the results of a field experiment on factors affecting compliance with federal income tax laws.

on prison sentences to reduce crime could also be spent on other changes within the prison system (such as better job training) aimed at reducing crime. The same funds could be spent through other agencies to achieve crime reduction—for example, through more intensive policing—and perhaps with greater success.

We would add that deterrence should not be regarded as having a preferred position in crime control policy independent of empirical evidence as to effectiveness. Decisions regarding priorities in this area of social practice should be made in the light of operational efficiency. Rational resource allocation in crime control, as the President's Commission on Law Enforcement and Administration of Justice pointed out,[110] cuts across departmental lines to seek the least-cost means to achieve the common goals of the different levels of the criminal justice system. We hear this chestnut of wisdom often; yet redundancy will be necessary until we act as if the principle is understood.

C Cost Models and Research Strategy

The evaluation model presented above includes questions that present research techniques often are not equipped to answer. But, in the absence of some answers, the perspective gained by structuring a model of crime-control research procedure can prove helpful. It would be difficult to design research that could determine with any confidence the extent to which the increase in California sentences has influenced the crime rate through marginal general deterrence. But even when the extent of crime prevention cannot be precisely estimated, cost studies can start official discussions about how much of an impact on crime would be sufficient to justify particular programs. Such discussions can simplify and help shape the design of research to suit official needs. As in Nebraska, once the cost of a program is recognized, the researcher can stop looking for needles in the haystack and confine his search to possible skyscrapers.

Finally, a checklist of the questions that comprehensive policy research must answer can be valuable for pointing out

110. U.S. President's Commission on Crime and the Administration of Justice, *The Challenge of Crime in a Free Society* (1967) 7.

areas of ignorance. Once missing links between particular research findings and our rather simple evaluative model are
established, those areas where findings cannot be translated
into policy mandates can be more clearly isolated.

SECTION 5 A POLITICAL ASPECT

There is a reciprocal relationship between punishment policy
and the system that administers it. Judges and juries may affect
punishments, but punishments may also affect judges and
juries. The prescription of harsh penalties may on occasion
create pressures and conflicts in society because of the character of the punishment, the crime, the victim, or because
of some interrelationship between these factors.

Such conflicts may be resolved in a number of ways. It is
often suggested that one result of the use of harsh punishments
is that those who administer them, and perhaps to a lesser
extent those who tolerate or approve them, adjust to the experience by becoming hardened and brutalized. Bernard Shaw
speaks of vengeful punishment as "a sport for which a taste
can be acquired . . . easily and rapidly."[111] And he suggests
that not only executions and floggings but also imprisonment
(as he observed it) were likely to "harden the authorities and
lower the standard of humanity all through our penal system."[112] Evidence for such assertions is commonly either not
produced or, when produced, of an anecdotal character. But
the suggestion at least has *prima facie* plausibility.

More frequently however, and with better documentation,
it is asserted that the employment of harsh penalties leads to
nullification of the law by virtue of the fact that, at various
levels or stages in the criminal justice process, there is a deliberate refusal fully to implement the statutes to which the
severe punishments are attached. Andenaes says in this connection: "Experience seems to show that excessively severe penalties may actually reduce the risk of conviction, thereby leading
to results contrary to their purpose. When penalties are not
reasonably attuned to the gravity of the violation, the public is
less inclined to inform the police, the prosecuting authori-

111. Shaw, *supra* note 42, at 44.
112. *Id.* at 59.

ties are less disposed to prosecute and juries are less apt to convict."[113]

The most commonly adduced example is of course that of capital punishment in late eighteenth- and early nineteenth-century England. Professor Jerome Hall describes the actions of judges in interpreting capital statutes at that time as constituting "a long series of technicalities in which they have effectively submerged statutory provisions of capital punishment."[114] Hall maintains that judges *invented* technicalities "in order to avoid infliction of the capital penalty."[115] In his *History of English Criminal Law,* Professor Radzinowicz cites a number of "leading judicial decisions" which, as he says, "clearly bear out"[116] Professor Hall's assertions.

Professor Radzinowicz goes further and demonstrates that many other factors too were "responsible for the virtual suspension of the operation of many capital statutes."[117] One of these was the frequency of recommendations by judges that the Crown make use of its prerogative of mercy.[118] Another was the common practice by juries of eliminating capital charges by understating the value of stolen property.[119] Another was the frequent commutation of death sentences by the Crown.[120] If one accepts that "a certain proportion of bills thrown out and of verdicts of acquittal"[121] were also due to belief in the disproportionate severity of many capital statutes, then it is clear that the extensive restriction of the operation of those statutes constituted a substantial degree of nullification.

It is possible, however, to point to less familiar and more recent examples of this process at work. In the 1970 crackdown referred to earlier the supervising judge of the Chicago Traffic Court announced that he had directed the judges under his control to impose a mandatory minimum seven-day jail

113. Andenaes, "The General Preventive Effects of Punishment" (1966) 114 *U. Pa. L. Rev.* 970.
114. Hall, *Theft, Law and Society* (1955) 87.
115. *Id.* at 92.
116. Radzinowicz, *A History of English Criminal Law* (1948) 86.
117. *Id.* at 95.
118. *Id.* at 113–14.
119. *Id.* at 94–97.
120. *Id.* at 112–22.
121. *Id.* at 97.

sentence on all Chicago drivers convicted of driving while under the influence of alcohol during the holiday period.

In the event, by no means all those convicted of drunk driving during the period the policy was enforced were sentenced to a seven-day jail sentence. An evaluation study of this program reveals that less than half those individuals went to jail. Moreover although the "seven-day" policy did increase the length of jail sentences imposed, approximately one-third of the jail sentences were of less than one week.[122] In a subsequent extension of this scheme the mandatory minimum was reduced to a two-day jail sentence in order to secure more compliance from the judges.

Another example of the judiciary's systematically exercising discretion in such a way as to mitigate the severity of the law may be found in an empirical study, conducted in the county of Los Angeles, of the enforcement and administration of the sections of the *California Penal Code* regulating adult homosexual behavior.[123] In California the designation of a felonious homosexual crime as either a misdemeanor or a felony ultimately depends upon the sentence imposed by the court.[124] It was found that, of a random sample of 493 defendants originally charged with, and later convicted of, felonious homosexuality in Los Angeles County in the years 1962–64, 95 percent received sentences which converted their offenses to misdemeanors.[125]

This systematic disposition of adult consensual homosexual offenders as misdemeanants by sentence has been attributed to three factors: "(1) Judicial recognition of the inefficacy of the criminal law as applied to adult consensual homosexuality; (2) Judicial acknowledgment of the inappropriateness of incarceration as a technique for proscribing homosexual behavior; and (3) Judicial evaluation of public consensual homosexuality activity as a nuisance rather than as a menace to the com-

---

122. Zimring, "Chicago's Crackdown on Drunk Driving" (1971) unpublished.
123. "Project: The Consenting Adult Homosexual and the Law: An Empirical Study of Enforcement and Administration in Los Angeles County" (1966) 13 *UCLA Law Rev.* 643–832.
124. *Id.* at 766.
125. *Id.* at 765 n. 10.

munity."[126] An overwhelming majority of the judges interviewed apparently were of the opinion "that very little homosexuality can be deterred."[127]

Juries may react similarly to severe laws. The California code prescribes exceptionally heavy penalties for the possession or sale of, or other involvement with, marijuana.[128] Apparently there are "signs that convictions in marijuana cases are becoming somewhat more difficult to obtain."[129] Two-thirds of those arrested for possession of the drug are "released, dismissed or acquitted."[130] Of course, this low ratio of arrest to conviction is not entirely, or even primarily, due to the failure of juries to convict. But it has been argued that, as with Prohibition, it is likely to become more and more difficult to get jurors to return criminal convictions—especially "10 to 15 years from now, when the population which today contains a high proportion of marijuana users [i.e., young people] begins to appear in increasing numbers on jury panels."[131]

Discretion of this nature may be exercised at earlier stages and lower levels in the criminal process. And in the case of both homosexual crimes and marijuana offenses, police discretion is said to be exercised in a manner which constitutes not merely selective but discriminatory enforcement. In the Los Angeles study of homosexual law enforcement it is suggested that there may be preferential treatment of some suspects "on the basis of the economic status or prominence of the suspects,"[132] and, moreover, that there may be considerable "discriminatory nonenforcement."[133] In the California Marijuana Study, it is asserted that college campuses and middle-class

126. *Id.* at 783.
127. *Id.* at 785–86.
128. Kadish and Paulsen, *Criminal Law and Its Processes*, (2d ed. 1969) 24–28. In this discussion of California's marijuana laws it is pointed out that Section 11530 of the Health and Safety Code provides that anyone convicted of possessing marijuana may be imprisoned for up to 10 years for a first offense, from 2 to 20 years (with a mandatory prison sentence) for a second offense, and for correspondingly longer periods of time for subsequent offenses.
129. *Id.* at 28.
130. *Id.* at 26.
131. *Id.* at 28.
132. *Supra* note 123 at 741.
133. *Id.* at 742.

marijuana users enjoy a large degree of immunity from marijuana arrests.[134]

The British Street Offenses Act of 1959, which drastically increased the penalties for soliciting by prostitutes, yields another instance of police discretion. The sharp fall in prostitutes' convictions for soliciting apparently demonstrated the efficacy of fines as a general deterrent.[135] Subsequently however, it appeared that "many police forces adopted a practice of cautioning women for soliciting on the first and even the second occasion; and since no central records of women so cautioned were left, a prostitute could usually escape prosecution by moving to another police district when she knew she could not expect another caution."[136]

Andenaes cites the policy of county attorneys and sheriffs in relation to the severe bad check laws in Nebraska, as described in Beutel's study of the operation of those laws.[137] Beutel concludes his examination of that policy as follows: "In all, the Nebraska picture is one of spotty performance by law enforcement officials, varying all the way from those who are frustrated by the enormity of enforcing the laws as written and consequently do nothing or as little as possible to those who try to enforce the statute literally but usually fail at re-election."[138] Beutel found that bad checks were rarer in Colorado, where the law was milder but enforcement was more uniform and effective.[139]

These and other studies suggest a number of general principles regarding the way in which increasing penalties for deterrent purposes may create pressures and conflicts. It may be said that escalating the level of punishment is most likely to be acceptable and effective when there is no tendency on the part of the public, jurors, judges, prosecutors, and police to identify with the people punished.

Where there is general moral condemnation of the behavior being penalized, it is relatively easy to enforce harsh penalties.

134. Kadish and Paulsen, *supra* note 123, at 27.
135. Walker, *Crime and Punishment in Britain* (1965) 241–42.
136. Walker, *Crime and Punishment in Britain* (2d ed. 1968) 241 n. 3.
137. Andenaes, *supra* note 113, at 970.
138. Beutel, *Experimental Jurisprudence* (1957) 366.
139. *Ibid.*

As a corollary to this, where there is general sympathy for and identification with offenders (as in the case of drunk driving in the United States), it will be more difficult to achieve effective enforcement of those penalties. Indeed in this context the level of law enforcement must be seen as a dependent variable, because such factors as sympathy with offenders may influence the kind of enforcement that a harsher penal policy will receive. Somewhat ironically, where there is widespread moral condemnation of a forbidden behavior, the enforcement of harsh penalties is likely to be both easiest and least necessary. On the other hand, where the behavior is not strongly condemned but widely tolerated, the enforcement of stringent penal provisions will be both most difficult and most necessary in order to educate the community and to reduce a high rate of crime.

There are a variety of reasons why the escalation of penalties is likely to produce social conflict and tensions. As already indicated, there may be general identification with offenders and/or the offense. But even where there is no identification, some proscribed behavior may be regarded with toleration or accepted as a "necessary evil" (e.g., prostitution). Furthermore, although the degree of such toleration will vary considerably from one culture to another, many societies have a tradition of minimal authoritative regulation of social life and are reluctant to enforce harsh penalties as a means to achieve social control.

Of tactics designed to enhance deterrence, perhaps none cause and exacerbate tension as much as increasing penalty levels.[140] Raising penalties may have untoward effects at all levels and stages of the criminal justice process. There is likely to be selective enforcement, as our examples indicate, of many different kinds. Indeed the result may well be a decrease in deterrent effect either generally or among the group which benefits most by the selectivity. Moreover, insofar as selective enforcement is discriminatory (i.e., based upon such consid-

---

140. One competing possibility would be situations in which there has been selective enforcement against low status groups in society and attempts are made to broaden law enforcement to include high status persons. See Zimring and Hawkins, "The Legal Threat as an Instrument of Social Change" (1971) 27 *J. Soc. Issues* 45–46.

erations as social prominence, economic status, or race), and this kind of differential selectivity is a corollary of a stringent penal policy, there may be an ethical argument for the employment of alternative means of enhancing deterrence, such as measures designed to increase the credibility of the threat of punishment.

In commenting on what has been called the "pouring panic of capital statutes"[141] in the eighteenth century, Professor Radzinowicz observes that any such expansion of the law designed "to enhance its severity" will "constitute an unsettling element in the administration of criminal justice."[142] This is undoubtedly true, and one of the principal reasons is a systematic or political one. Legislatures are generally concerned with the use of the criminal law at the strategic rather than the tactical level for they do not come in actual contact with the enemy. In eighteenth-century England, "as any new offense gained prominence, it was countered by a new capital statute."[143] And in the United States today, as Andenaes points out, "when the legislators . . . attempt to check any apparent rise in the crime they generally increase the severity of penalties."[144] But at the level of enforcement, the situation is radically different.

Although enforcement against all violators may be the official assumption of the system,[145] full enforcement is in fact quite impracticable[146] and selective enforcement is inevitable. Thus the police, while they do not make basic decisions about penal policy, have very wide discretion in regard to its application. The prosecutor also has discretion whether to prosecute or not. Grand juries may decline to indict, and trial juries may acquit the guilty. Trial judges may, in many jurisdictions, suspend either the imposition or the execution of sentence. Moreover, even "correctional bodies are given, by design or

141. Fox, *The English Prison and Borstal Systems* (1952) 22.
142. Radzinowicz, *supra* note 116 at 106.
143. Fox, *supra* note 141, at 22.
144. Andenaes, *supra* note 113, at 965.
145. Remington and Rosenblum, "The Criminal Law and the Legislative Process" 1960 *U. Ill. L. Forum* 496.
146. Goldstein and Goldstein, "Police Discretion Not to Invoke the Criminal Process: Low Visibility Decision in the Administration of Justice" (1960) 69 *Yale L. J.* 586–87.

default, responsibility for decisions which are of major importance."[147]

The widespread exercise of discretion, which constitutes an intrinsic limitation on the legislative process in this field, can of course be viewed as advantageous in that it provides "built-in checks and balances against the abuse of official power."[148] But it is notable that the smallest degree of discretion is exercised precisely at the level of those who have the closest and most continuous contact with the offender. Inevitably, tension and conflict arise. It is significant that leaders in the movement for penal reform are frequently penal administrators and prison wardens, and, on occasion, judges.

147. Remington and Rosenblum, *supra* note 145, at 483.
148. *Id.* at 497.

3   Definition

SECTION 1 TERMINOLOGY

It is essential, if analysis is to replace emotion in discussions of deterrence, to read some precision into the definitions of a few central terms.

A sign in the park reads

> *Walking On the Grass Is Prohibited*
> *$100 Fine*
> *Violators Will Be Prosecuted*

Smith and Jones pass the sign while taking a lunch-hour stroll on the park sidewalk. The sign announces a legal *threat*: the attempt of the *threatening agency* (here presumably the city authorities) to decrease the amount of *threatened behavior* (walking on the grass) by announcing that the agency will impose unpleasant consequences on those individuals who commit the threatened act. The sign conveys a *legal threat* because it is based on a rule of law issued by an agency of governmental authority.

Like most legal threats, this message is issued to citizens in general rather than to particular individuals. In this situation the *threatened consequences* include a fine and prosecution.

70

Smith and Jones are part of the *audience* of the threat. The agency probably considers them part of the threatened audience whether or not they actually read the sign, because they are two of the people the threat is aimed at influencing. However, if our interest is confined to how such announcements affect human behavior, membership in the threatened audience should be restricted to those individuals who are aware of a threat's existence.

The threat communicated to Smith and Jones may or may not affect their behavior. They may stay off the grass because neither had intended to walk there in any event. One or both may walk on the grass in spite of the threat. If the sign produces any change in the behavior of Smith and Jones, such as inducing them to keep off the grass, tempting them to walk on the grass in defiance of the order, or persuading them to walk in some other park during their lunch hour, the threat will have had a *channeling effect* on the behavior of one or more members of its audience, for the channeling effect of a threat is the totality of all changes in the behavior of its audience attributable to existence of a threat.[1] The term *Deterrence* is used more restrictively, applying only to cases where a threat causes individuals who would have committed the threatened behavior to refrain from doing so. *The net deterrent* effect of a particular threat is the total number of threatened behaviors it prevents less those it creates.[2]

There are a number of situations where threats may influence behavior in the direction desired by the threatening agency,

---

1. Let us assume a threat has the following effects on a three-actor audience:

No threat situation	*Threat situation*
A. Would have walked on grass	Did not walk on grass
B. Would not have walked on grass	Did not walk on grass
C. Would not have walked on grass	Did walk on grass

In this circumstance the *channeling effect* is *not* zero but $+1$ and -1.

2. In the situation referred to in note 1 *supra*, there is a *deterrent effect* of — 1 act committed (A) but no *net deterrent effect* because of other effect produced by the threat (C). Even though the absence of net change may provide a conclusive reason for refusing to employ the threat, nevertheless the existence of the *deterrent effect* should be recognized. This is only one example of the many situations in which the question whether deterrent effects are operative must be distinguished from the policy question whether a particular penalty should be employed. See chap. 2, sec. 3 *supra*.

but the result will be less than fully law-abiding conduct. The potential bank robber may respond to the threatened penalty for bank robbery by switching to burglary, heeding one threat only to disregard another. The presence of a police patrol may reduce the burglary rate in Manhattan at the expense of the Bronx. Or intensive law enforcement may persuade the mugger to reduce the level of his activities from five to three crimes a week. In each of these cases the mechanism of deterrence is observable, but the result of the threat is not law-abiding behavior on the part of the individual threatened. Yet in all of these cases, a deterrent effect as defined above will exist, at least on the Island of Manhattan. A more troublesome case is that where the posting of a 65 m.p.h. speed limit causes a driver to reduce his speed from 90 to 70 m.p.h. In this case, which can be called *partial deterrence*, no law violation will have been prevented by operation of the legal threat, but the speed reduction is still an important contribution toward the goal of the legal threat.

Another distinction which is of crucial importance relates to issues of *absolute deterrence* and *marginal deterrence*. If one is interested in comparing the rates of behavior that would result from a particular threat with the rates of behavior that could be expected if the threat were removed, it is the *absolute deterrent effect* of the threat that is at issue. If, on the other hand, one seeks to compare the effectiveness of one type of threat with that of a different threat (say, the threat of y years in prison with the threat of $y + 10$ years in prison), the *absolute deterrent effect* of a larger penalty is not the central issue; rather, such a comparison will throw light on the question whether the larger penalty functions as a *marginal deterrent*, reducing the rate of threatened behavior below that experienced under the lesser penalty.

A further distinction which is commonly drawn in the literature is that between *general deterrence* and *individual* or *special* deterrence. Bentham, for example, although he says "determent is equally applicable to the situation of the already-punished delinquent and that of other persons at large,"[3] distinguishes "particular prevention which applies to the delinquent himself;

3. Bentham, "Principles of Penal Law" in 1 *Works* (1843) 392.

and general prevention which is applicable to all members of the community without exception."[4] Curiously enough, many of those who do draw this distinction make no further use of it.[5] Rather than a dichotomy we see the special effects of punishment as one variable condition in deterrence. An act of punishment may be seen as an attempt to enhance deterrent threats not only for all potential criminals out in society but also for those actually punished by altering the way in which they will respond to such threats in the future. It is the latter which has been called individual or special deterrence. But insofar as this process works by making or attempting to make, individuals more sensitive to future threats because of present punishment, it is really not so much special or individual deterrence as it is a special effort to make individuals more sensitive to general deterrence.[6] Similarly, all that is involved in the com-

4. *Id.* at 396.

5. Thus Wechsler and Michael, in their "Rationale of the Law of Homicide" (1937) 37 *Colum. L. Rev.* 731 n. 127, draw what is essentially the same distinction in terms of "intimidating" and "deterring": "For convenience we use the former word to refer to the individual who has been subjected to treatment and the latter to refer to the general population." But having drawn the distinction they say: "By 'intimidating' we mean the same as 'deterring,' i.e., coercing an individual to refrain from the behavior in question because of his fear of the unattractive legal consequences." And they make no further reference to this distinction. Similarly Nigel Walker, in his *Crime and Punishment in Britain* (1965) 131, says: "Many forms of penal measure were originally designed with the aim of deterring either the offender himself or potential imitators, from committing another offence of the same kind. In most cases it is assumed that what discourages others from imitating the offender's example also discourages the offender himself from a repetition; but since there are obvious exceptions—for example, the death penalty, the punishment of the insane and the imprisonment of the destitute—it is necessary to distinguish the two aims under such labels as 'individual' and 'general' deterrence." Having drawn this "necessary" distinction, Walker does not refer to it again.

6. As Professor McTaggart put it, at the turn of the century, in his *Studies of Hegelian Cosmology* (1901) 145: "The pain and coercion involved in punishment present the law with much greater impressiveness [for the punished offender] than for the mass of people." And as Professor Andenaes has put it more recently in "General Prevention—Illusion or Reality" (1952) 43 *J. of Crim. Law, Criminology and Police Science* 197: "The *deterrent effect* which the law by itself has on every citizen *will be strengthened* in his case by the fact that he knows from personal experience that the law means what it says" (our italics). This assumption has been questioned. Thus Sir Lionel Fox, writing on the treatment of young offenders, in *The English Prison and Borstal Sys-*

mon practice of imposing progressively heavier sentences on recidivists, which has also been called special deterrence, is a more rigorous application, to a particular group, of the principle of general deterrence.[7]

SECTION 2 THE DETERRENT PROCESS

The definitions offered above describe deterrence only as a result—the number of offenses prevented—without providing any insight into how legal threats might achieve such results. Commentators have suggested various psychological processes by which the threat of punishment might result in deterrence. The mechanism most often referred to is *direct* or *simple* de-

---

tems (1952) 349, says: "It cannot be too strongly emphasized that to send a young person to prison for a short sentence is likely to make certain of one thing and one thing only—that by removal of the dread of the unknown *a great part of the deterrent effect* of prison for the future *will have been lost*" (our italics again). In something of a counterpoint three pages earlier (at 347) he has written: "It may be that for some, who come to it [i.e., prison] for the first time, this experience will at least have the effect of deterrence and to that extent serves its purpose." The truth is that the effect of the experience of punishment is likely to be highly variable. It is not possible to say much more than that those who have been punished may be assumed to have a knowledge of the nature of penal sanctions that is qualitatively different from the knowledge of those who have not. But see also chap. 4, sec. 2 *infra*.

7. Norval Morris, in "Impediments to Penal Reform" (1966) 33 *U. Chi. L. Rev.* 632, defines "special deterrence" as "the threat of further punishment of one who has already been convicted and punished for crime; it may be the same medicine that is threatened as a method of dissuading him from recidivism or it may be the threat of a larger or different dose." But "a larger or different dose" of deterrence is still deterrence, however different or "special" the patients may be. Leslie Wilkins, in *Evaluation of Penal Measures* (1969) (Appendix A: General prevention measures) 157, says that "deterrence of offenders from committing *further* crimes is quite a different matter from the deterrence of *others* from committing crimes in the first instance. In the former case the person who is required to learn conforming behavior is the person directly concerned in the action of society, whereas in the latter case what is done to one person is believed to have an effect upon others" (author's own italics). And in *Social Deviance* (1964) 203: "But action to deal with *known delinquents* is not *prevention of crime* but *prevention of recidivism* which may be a different type of problem" (author's italics again). Although it is undeniable that a different response may be expected from those who have actually experienced the threatened consequences (and there are many *other* variables which condition the effectiveness of threats), the threat mechanism, which is the essence of deterrence, remains the same. And the prevention of recidivism *is* the prevention of crime.

terrence, but a number of more subtle ways in which threat and punishment might reduce the number of offenses have also been suggested, and we shall attempt to distinguish and define them.

A Simple Deterrence

The theory of simple deterrence is that threats can reduce crime by causing a change of heart, induced by the unpleasantness of the specific consequences threatened. The *locus classicus* is of course Cesare Beccaria's seminal essay *On Crimes and Punishments*, where he defines "the political intent of punishments," as "to instill fear in other men."[8] Similarly, Bentham at one point defines deterrence in terms of "intimidation or terror of the law."[9] More recently, Professor Andenaes has referred to this aspect of deterrence as "mere deterrence"[10] and "the mere frightening or deterrent effect of punishment."[11]

Many individuals who are tempted by a particular form of threatened behavior will, according to this theory, refrain from committing the offense because the pleasure they might obtain is more than offset by the risk of great unpleasantness communicated by a legal threat. In this simple model of deterrence, the reaction is a very specific one—comparing *this* crime with *this* penalty for one particular moment—and the results of weighing the pros and cons of lawbreaking do not alter the individual's personality, or his sense of right and wrong, or his general propensity to obey the law. If the individual is to be kept law-abiding, the process of simple deterrence must confront him at every turn—making each form of forbidden conduct a risk not worth taking. Thus we find Bentham explaining that "the profit of the crime is the force which urges a man to delinquency: the pain of the punishment is the force employed to restrain him from it. If the first of these forces be the greater the crime will be committed; if the second, the crime will not be committed."[12]

8. Beccaria, *On Crimes and Punishments* (1764; trans. Paolucci, 1963) 30.
9. Bentham, *supra* note 3, at 396.
10. Andenaes, "The General Preventive Effects of Punishment" (1966) 114 *U. Pa. L. Rev.* 950.
11. Andenaes, *supra* note 6, at 176 and 179.
12. Bentham, *supra* note 3, at 399.

The imagery here is somewhat mechanical, but at other points the image of the potential criminal reacting to punishment threats is more like that of a potential customer peering at a price list, on which, Bentham insisted, "the value of the punishment must not be less, in any case, than what is sufficient to outweigh that of the profit of the offence."[13]

It is not altogether surprising that this model of man either as at the mercy of mechanical pushes and pulls or as "a lightning calculator of pleasures and pains," to use Thorsten Veblen's phrase, has been rejected as unsatisfactory by subsequent writers. Professor A. J. Ayer, in a critique of Bentham's system, has said that it is "based upon a false psychology."[14] And Professor H. L. A. Hart has remarked that "The old Benthamite confidence in fear of penalties threatened by the law as a powerful deterrent, has waned with the growing realisation that the part played by calculation of any sort in anti-social behavior has been exaggerated."[15] Indeed, some writers, convinced that the notion of simple deterrence is entirely dependent on the Benthamite model, have rejected it altogether.[16]

Others, however, while discarding the model, have recognized the plausibility of the notion that some people sometimes refrain from crime specifically in order to avoid unpleasantness.[17] In other words, they have recognized that the conceptual scheme of the classical theorist, even though it may be incompatible with some aspects of experience, is still compatible with others—although even simple deterrence is in fact considerably more complex than the classical theory suggests.

In some cases of simple deterrence, the emotional effect of the threat on the threatened audience may be minimal: the man dissuaded from parking his car in a tow-away zone may

13. *Ibid.*
14. Ayer, "The Principle of Utility," in Keeton and Schwarzenberger (eds.), *Jeremy Bentham and the Law* (1948) 255.
15. Hart, *Punishment and Responsibility* (1968) 1.
16. See, e.g., Barnes and Teeters, *New Horizons in Criminology* (1951) 337–38 and 375: "The claim for deterrence is belied by both history and logic.... [Bentham's] felicific calculus—the idea that to achieve the most pleasure and the least pain is the main object of an intelligent man—is no longer taken seriously as the sole key to human behavior."
17. See, e.g., Andenaes, *supra* note 6, at 176; and Morris, *supra* note 7, at 627.

suffer only the mildest regret that the threat of unpleasantness has made this convenience impractical. In other cases, simple deterrence will be achieved because the threat of consequences produces substantial anxiety or fear in potential deviants, even amounting to intimidation. Thus, depending on the nature of the threatened behavior and the threatened consequences, simple deterrence may be associated with different levels of emotional arousal. Within the simple model of deterrence, then, a number of different processes may be at work, producing different kinds of emotional effect that may condition different types of threat response.

Beyond the notion of simple deterrence, however, a number of less direct mechanisms through which the threat of punishment may induce compliance with the law have been suggested, and these more subtle processes may well be more important than simple deterrence in reinforcing patterns of law-abiding behavior. The search for these more subtle effects involves a wide range of behaviors. As Professor Packer puts it, "Our hypotheses about the operation of general deterrence should be broadened to include also the effect of punishment—and indeed, of all the institutions of criminal justice—on the totality of conscious and unconscious motivations that govern the behavior of men in society."[18] It is necessary, therefore, to consider other ways in which the threat and example of punishment may play a role in reducing crime. And among the preventive effects of punishment it is possible to distinguish its functions as an aid to moral education, as a habit-building mechanism, as a method of achieving respect for the law, and as a rationale for obedience.

B The Threat of Punishment as a Teacher of Right and Wrong

Simple deterrence is not the primary explanation of widespread patterns of conformity to most of our criminal laws. Even Bentham recognized that, apart from the behavior of those who were "only restrained by laws," some behavior was governed by "other tutelary motives such as benevolence, re-

18. Packer, *The Limits of the Criminal Sanction* (1968) 42.

ligion or honour."[19] The truth is, as Professor Toby has said, "that the socialization process keeps most people law-abiding, not the police."[20] And in recent years it has been suggested that the threat and example of punishment may play an important part in the socialization process as a teacher of right and wrong. This is what has been referred to as "the educative-moralizing function of the law"[21] or "the moral or socio-pedagogical influence of punishment."[22]

Discussion of the moral-educative effects of punishment in the English speaking world owes much to the work of Professor Andenaes, and we may appropriately and conveniently quote his definitions.

In Swedish discussion, the moralizing—in other words the *educational*—function has been greatly stressed. The idea is that punishment as a concrete expression of society's disapproval of an act helps to form and strengthen the public's moral code and thereby creates conscious and unconscious inhibitions against committing crimes.[23]

Punishment is a means of expressing social disapproval. In this way the criminal law and its enforcement supplement and enhance the moral influence acquired through education and other non-legal processes.[24]

As "a means of expressing social disapproval," punishment is a ritualistic device designed to influence persons by intimating symbolically society's moral condemnation, and penal provisions may be seen as symbolizing cherished values.[25]

When both this ritualistic aspect of punishment and the way in which the machinery of the traditional criminal legal process achieves "the dramatization of evil"[26] is recognized, it is not inappropriate to talk of punishment as educational. That punishment is effective in conveying social reprobation is

19. Bentham, *supra* note 3, at 399.
20. Toby, "Is Punishment Necessary?" (1964) 55 *J. Crim. Law, Criminology and Police Science* 334.
21. Tappan, *Crime, Justice, and Correction* (1960) 247.
22. Andenaes, *supra* note 10, at 949–50.
23. Andenaes, *supra* note 6, at 179.
24. Andenaes, *supra* note 10, at 950.
25. Andenaes, *The General Part of the Criminal Law of Norway* (1956) 78: "Penal provisions may symbolize values which various groups within the populace cherish."
26. Tannenbaum, *Crime and the Community* (1938) 19.

clearly reflected in the stigmatization and the loss of social status commonly involved in criminal punishment.[27]

From this point of view, a criminal trial followed by conviction and sentence can be seen as a public degradation ceremony, in which the public identity of the convicted individual is lowered on social scale. Such ceremonies have been described as "a secular form of communion" which helps to "reinforce group solidarity" and "bind persons to the collectivity."[28] Moreover, such ritualistic procedures have long been used in the sphere of education to foster commitment of values.[29]

That threat and punishment can be and are used as an educational technique is, of course, recognized even by those dubious about their value as an instrument of moral education. Professor H. L. A. Hart says that "there is very little evidence to support the idea that morality is *best* taught by fear of legal punishment" (our italics).[30] Similarly, Professor R. S. Peters, commenting on the argument that punishment might "help to mark out what is right and wrong and . . . help to stamp in desirable habits which will later make a solid foundation for a rational moral code," says that "whether punishment *often* has this effect on individuals is an empirical question" (our italics).[31]

The doubts expressed by Hart and Peters seem to arise in

27. See Martin, *Offenders as Employees* (1962) 39; McSally, "Finding Jobs for Released Offenders" (June 1960) 24 *Fed. Probation* 12; Schwartz and Skolnick, "Two Studies of Legal Stigma" (1962) 10 *Social Problems* 133. See also Goffman, *Stigma* (1963); Freidson, "Disability as Social Deviance," in *Sociology and Rehabilitation* (ed. Sussman, 1966) 71–79.

Because it relates to conduct, such evidence is more convincing than evidence derived from attitude studies, the results of which are derived from verbal responses: Walker and Argyle, "Does the Law Affect Moral Judgments?" (1964) 4 *Brit. J. Crim.* 570. This article reports an attitude survey, the results of which suggest that knowledge that a form of conduct or type of action is criminal appears to have little bearing on people's moral attitude toward the behavior in question. No matter how much people may disclaim censorious feelings, their conduct is apt to belie their professions.

28. Garfinkel, "Conditions of Successful Degradation Ceremonies" (1956) 61 *Am. J. Soc.* 421. See also Packer, *supra* note 18, at 43–44.

29. See Borstein, Peters, and Elvin, "The Role of Ritual in Education," in *Proceedings of the Royal Society* (1965) *passim*.

30. H. L. A. Hart. *Law, Liberty, and Morality* (1963) 58.

31. Peters, *Ethics and Education* (1966) 274.

part because of an apparent incongruity between the means and the end of punishment. Consider, for example, the question of capital punishment. In this connection, Hart is critical of James Fitzjames Stephen's celebrated dictum, "The fact that men are hanged for murder is one great reason why murder is considered so dreadful a crime."[32] Professor Andenaes also discusses this point: "It may be said that capital punishment for murder exerts a moral influence by indicating that life is the most highly protected value."[33] Beccaria, on the other hand, used the same example to draw the opposite conclusion: "The death penalty cannot be useful, because of the example of barbarity it gives men. . . . It seems to me absurd that the laws which are an expression of the public will, which detest and punish homicide, should themselves commit it."[34]

Because of its unique character, the death penalty may appear to belong in a different category from all other penalties, and the moral effect of that penalty may therefore seem not really relevant to a consideration of the educative-moralizing function of other penalties. But the truth is that Beccaria's argument can easily be applied to other penalties. For, as Professor Kenny pointed out in explaining the "special attractiveness" of the criminal law both for students and ordinary readers, "the vivid and violent nature of the events which criminal courts notice and repress" is matched by the character "of those by which they effect the repression."[35]

32. Hart, *supra* note 30, at 58. Stephen's idea was developed a little further in the Report of the Royal Commission on Capital Punishment 1939–53 (Cmd. 8932) ¶59: "We think it reasonable to suppose that the deterrent force of capital punishment operates not only by affecting the conscious thoughts of individuals tempted to commit murder but also by building up in the community, over a long period of time, a deep feeling of peculiar abhorrence for the crime of murder. 'The fact that men are hung for murder is one great reason why murder is considered so dreadful a crime.' This widely diffused effect on the moral consciousness of society is impossible to assess but it must be at least as important as any direct part which the death penalty may play as a deterrent in the calculations of potential murderers."

33. Andenaes, *supra* note 10, at 967. However, he expresses reservations on this point.

34. Beccaria, *supra* note 8, at 50.

35. Kenny, *Outlines of Criminal Law* (1929 ed.) 2. Kenny continues: "Forcible interferences with property and liberty, with person and life, are the causes which bring criminal law into operation; and its operations are themselves directed to the infliction of *similar acts of seizure, suffering, and slaughter.*"

The same point was made by Stephen: "Criminal law is itself a system of compulsion on the widest scale. It is a collection of threats of injury to life, liberty, and property if people do commit crime."[36] It might be said, therefore, that there is no reason to think that any other item from this collection of threats is more likely to engender respect for values than the threat of the death penalty. Indeed, it could be argued that the only sort of respect which systems of compulsion commonly inspire is precisely that which is implied in the concept of mere deterrence and no more.

The central weakness of the argument is that it does not meet the point developed above about the ritualistic aspect of punishment. What is called the educative-moralizing function of punishment is largely independent of the nature of the penalties employed. It is true that some penalties may be regarded as poetically appropriate (castration for dangerous sex offenders) or inappropriate (imprisonment in a wholly male institution for male homosexuals) for particular types of offenders and offenses. However, there is nothing intrinsic to any punishment which makes it either fitting or unfitting. Extrinsic factors deriving from the context in which punishment is used are determinative.

It is possible to distinguish at least three aspects of the operation of punishment in this didactic or educative role. In the first place, to put it in very simple terms, the association of forbidden behavior and bad consequences may lead individuals to view the behavior itself as bad. Thus, knowledge that people who steal are treated badly would lead to the association of wrongfulness with stealing, and ultimately to the conclusion that stealing is wrong. This is the point that the Report of the Royal Commission on Capital Punishment makes when it suggests that the use of capital punishment in the past may have created "a strong association between murder and the death penalty in the popular imagination."[37]

In the second place, punishment by a legal system will communicate to the individual that the legal system views the threatened behavior as wrong, and this information will also affect the moral attitudes of the individual. The internal reason-

---

36. Stephen, *History of the Criminal Law of England* (1883) 107.
37. Report of the Royal Commission, *supra* note 32, at ¶59.

ing would go: "The institutions I respect view this behavior as wrong; therefore, I should consider this behavior wrong."

For it is a mistake to think that the only sort of respect inspired by the criminal law is that which is implied in the concept of mere deterrence. The criminal law is more than a neutral system of compulsion; respect for legal authority is different from mere response to threats. To ignore this confuses authority with coercive power. Although coercive power may sometimes be a necessary condition for the exercise of authority and for securing obedience, respect for authority depends on recognition of its legitimacy.

It is not necessary to consider here the various principles of legitimacy upon which authority is said to depend, nor to discuss their sociological and ideological bases. It is sufficient to note that in any society, if it is to continue in existence, there must be a general acceptance of authoritative regulation as a means of achieving social control. This affirmative attitude toward obedience to rules may be a more powerful factor than the fear of punishment in securing conformity. Moreover, the respect, or deference, which the law attracts makes it possible for the law to exercise a socializing influence by securing society's acceptance of rules and regulations in areas where custom, tradition, morality, or religion provide no final guidance.

A striking example of the way in which respect for legal authority may operate can be found in Bruno Bettelheim's eyewitness account of the behavior of political prisoners in two German concentration camps.

In their behavior became apparent the dilemma of the politically uneducated German middle classes when confronted with the phenomenon of National socialism. They had no consistent philosophy which would protect their integrity as human beings. . . . They had obeyed the law handed down by the ruling classes, without ever questioning its wisdom. . . . They could not question the wisdom of law and of the police, so they accepted the behavior of the Gestapo as just. What was wrong was that they were made objects of a persecution which in itself must be right, since it was carried out by authorities.[38]

38. Bettelheim, "Individual and Mass Behavior in Extreme Situations" (1943) 38 *J. Abnormal and Soc. Psych.* 417 and 426. The two camps were Dachau and Buchenwald.

Some relatives of those in the camps

just would not believe that the prisoners in the camps had not committed outrageous crimes since the way they were punished permitted only this conclusion.[39]

In the third place, threat and punishment may aid moral education by serving as an attention-getting or attention-focusing mechanism. The threat of punishment for stealing forces the individual to think about the moral nature of stealing. Such reflections might lead to the conclusion that stealing is wrong because it causes other people to suffer and underlines the security of a system of private property. In this last aspect, which Professor Andenaes calls "punishment as an eye-opener,"[40] the threat of punishment provides only the occasion for reflection rather than any substantial moral precept.

Professor Geis cites the case of a vice-president of the General Electric Corporation sentenced to jail for antitrust violations, who told the U.S. Senate Subcommittee on Antitrust and Monopoly that "the consequences visited upon him represented the major reason for a re-evaluation of his actions." He said that "the taint of a jail sentence . . . had the effect of making people start looking at moral values a little bit."[41]

Professor Peters, although critical of the use of punishment as a means of moral education, admits that "isolated punishments of the 'sharp shock' variety . . . may function in a beneficial way by focusing awareness on social realities."[42] Such statements do not constitute evidence that punishment inevitably operates in the manner suggested, but they suggest that it might and in some circumstances does. The extent to which it does is, of course, an empirical question.

39. *Id*. at 441.
40. Andenaes, "Some Further Reflections on General Prevention," working paper, Center for Studies in Criminal Justice (1968).
41. Geis, "The Heavy Electrical Equipment Antitrust Cases of 1961," in Geis (ed.), *White-Collar Criminal* (1968) 114.
42. Peters, *supra* note 31, at 275. Peters also suggests that punishment which brings home to the offenders "imaginatively the consequences of actions as they effect other people" may have some "effectiveness . . . in moral education" (*id*. at 279). Here the emphasis is on the actuality of punishment "as an eye opener" rather than the threat and example of it. This aspect is dealt with in chap. 4, sec. 2 *infra*.

C Threat and Punishment as Habit Builders

Andenaes distinguishes three principal general preventive effects of punishment. "It may have a deterrent effect," he says, "it may strengthen moral inhibitions (a moralizing effect), and it may stimulate habitual law-abiding conduct."[43]

At another point he says that "with fear or moral influence as an intermediate link it is possible . . . perhaps to establish a condition of habitual lawfulness."[44] Others too have written about what has been called the habituative effect or function of punishment,[45] but Andenaes's treatment is the fullest and most explicit.

We find the clearest example of this in the military where extended inculcation of discipline and stern reaction against breach thereof can induce a purely automatic habitual response —not only where obeying specific orders is concerned, but also with regard to general orders and regulations.[46]

We have another example in the relationship between an occupying power and occupied population. The regulations set down by the occupier are not regarded by the people as morally binding; but by a combination of terror and habit formation a great measure of obedience can be elicited—at any rate in response to commands which do not conflict too greatly with national feelings.[47]

We are not ordinarily subject to the kind of discipline and close supervision found in the army,[48] nor to the terrorist tactics of an occupying power.[49] But if army techniques of social

43. Andenaes, *supra* note 6, at 180.
44. Andenaes, *supra* note 10, at 951.
45. Tappan, *supra* note 21, at 247: "The criminal and penal law, in providing standards of conduct and penalties, stimulates the habit of law-abiding conduct." Morris, *supra* note 7, at 631: "Punishment . . . sometimes has an habituative effect in conditioning human behaviour." Packer, *supra* note 18, at 43: "Every one of us is confronted daily by situations in which criminal behavior is a possible alternative. More frequently and more significantly, we automatically and without conscious cognition follow a pattern of learned behavior that excludes the criminal alternative without our even thinking about it."
46. Andenaes, *supra* note 6, at 179.
47. *Id.* at 179–80.
48. See Mattick, "Parolees in the Army During World War II" (1960) 24 *Fed. Probation* 54: "The Army provides a total environment . . . a disciplined, structured and predictable social environment."
49. See Olivecrona, *Law as Fact* (1938) 149: "Such a regime is characterised by the fact that fear of sanctions is the immediate and domi-

control are different from civilian ones, the difference is one of degree.

Drawing an example from ordinary life, Andenaes suggests that the Norwegian legislation dealing with drunk driving "has been instrumental in forming or sustaining the widespread conviction that it is wrong, or irresponsible, to place oneself behind the wheel when intoxicated."[50] He goes on: "When a man goes to party where alcoholic drinks are likely to be served, and if he is not fortunate enough to have a wife who drives but does not drink, will leave his car at home or he will limit his consumption to a minimum."[51]

It is precisely this kind of patterned behavior or tendency to behave automatically in a certain way which we ordinarily refer to as a habit. And there can be no doubt that such settled practices or customary manners of action are a powerful factor in preventing infringements of the law.[52]

It is clear that this sort of pattern is not confined to drunk driving. On his first few trips downtown, the threat of punishment may cause a man to refrain from speeding on his way to work. After a while, however, more than the simple deterrent effect may be at work, for he may have developed the habit of driving at a certain speed, and this habit provides additional insulation against future law violation.

Insofar as observation of the rules of the road becomes, as it does for many drivers, a matter of habit, the habituative effect of the law is a major factor in legal social control; for

---

nating motive for lawful conduct. It is well known how strict and unrelenting a terroristic regime must be if it is to be at all effective. Fear is insufficient as a barrier unless it is sustained by very drastic and unflinching menaces."

50. Andenaes, *supra* note 10, at 969: "The awareness of hazards of imprisonment for intoxicated driving is in our country a living reality to every driver, and for most people the risk seems too great."

51. *Ibid.*

52. This particular example refers to a motoring offense. But this is not to say that it can be regarded as of negligible importance. Motoring offences are among the "most deadly and destructive of all contemporary offences." Wootton, *Crime and the Criminal Law* (1963) 25. Walker, *supra* note 5, at 32–33: "Delinquent motorists overwhelmingly outnumber all other offences: two out of every three people found guilty in court are traffic offenders.... It is clear that anti-social use of vehicles is a much more important source of death, bereavement, physical suffering and disablement than any intentional forms of violence."

such habits are not acquired in infancy. Repeated observation of a rule which may initially be conscious and deliberate can induce an habitual disposition and ultimately automatic compliance.

The habituative effect of the law is not confined to the inculcation of new habits. It seems likely that over a very large area of conduct it may take the form of negative reinforcement in the inhibition of types of undesirable behavior which are already largely controlled by habit. For the principal importance of habit in relation to social control derives from the fixity of habit organization and the consequent relative dependability of human conduct. As Gardner Murphy puts it:

The genuine importance of habit as a social stabilizer appears then not to reside so much in . . . forming new habits as in the attitude of condemning what one has condemned since childhood.[53]

Since the family—at least in Western Europe and the United States—is "the most important of habit forming institutions,"[54] one might expect the direct influence of the criminal law on habit formation to be limited to behavior learned later in life, like driving motor vehicles. But one cannot rule out the possible indirect influence of the criminal law on what habits are formed in childhood.[55]

A good deal of adult habit formation may be governed by what Andenaes calls police regulations—"traffic ordinances, building codes, laws governing the sale of alcoholic beverages, regulations governing commerce, etc."[56] It seems likely that, in many cases of this kind, observance of the law eventually becomes a habit which is followed automatically without reflection. And although these regulations "play a modest role in the literature [they] have a good deal of practical importance. . . ."[57]

53. Murphy, "Habit," in 4 *Encyclopaedia of the Social Sciences* (ed. Seligman, 1937) 239.
54. *Id.* at 238.
55. Walker, "Morality and the Criminal Law" (1964) 11 *Howard L. J.* 214: "It is arguable that the criminal law may cause his parents to teach him [the child] rules which they would not otherwise have bothered about. . . . If so, the legislation of one generation might become the morality of the next."
56. Andenaes, *supra* note 6, at 182.
57. *Ibid.*

Finally it may be said that as the habit of obeying the law in particular situations develops over a period of time, the threat of punishment may initially produce a number of separate habits of compliance. But these in turn can result in a more generalized habit of obeying the law, so that ultimately we reach a position where, as Packer puts it, "we automatically and without conscious cognition follow a pattern of learned behavior that excludes the criminal alternative without our even thinking about it."[58]

D Threat and Punishment as Mechanisms for Building Respect for Law

If the commands of a legal system were not reinforced with the threat of punishment, many individuals would see no basis for believing that the legal system really meant what it said. For many the threat alone would probably be sufficient to ensure conformity. But, as Andenaes says, "it may be that some people are not particularly sensitive to an abstract threat of penalty."[59] For them the penalties must "be demonstrated in concrete sentences which they feel relevant to their own life situations."[60]

Another reason why the penalty provisions of the law require enforcement is that impunity can have demoralizing consequences. Even those who are themselves law-abiding can be demoralized by watching law breakers escape unpunished. As Alexander and Staub put it "in the case of escape from justice . . . every member of the community feels he was wronged."[61]

The imposition of punishment is a demonstration to society as a whole that that legal system is serious in its attempt to prohibit criminal behavior: punishment is the "convincer." The unpunished criminal is a direct challenge to the authority behind the law. "From this point of view the significance of the individual sentence, and the execution of it, lies in the support that these actions give to the law."[62]

58. Packer, *supra* note 18, at 43.
59. Andenaes, *supra* note 10, at 950.
60. *Ibid.*
61. Alexander and Staub, *The Criminal, the Judge, and the Public* (1956 ed.) 213.
62. *Ibid.*

*E Threat and Punishment as a Rationale
   for Conformity*

Temptation to break the law is often a disturbing experience. Even a man completely convinced that stealing is wrong may occasionally need help in fending off the temptation to break his own moral code. A person in this position may require additional pressure toward conformity, as a defense against pressures within him that are morally distressing; and the threat of punishment may provide that additional pressure when needed.

Alexander and Staub put this in psychoanalytic terms: "The greater the pressure coming from repressed impulses, the more aware becomes the Ego that it needs the institution of punishment as an intimidating example, acting against one's own primitive world of repressed instinctual drives."[63] Professor Sprott explains "our desire to punish" as in part due to "a tactical move on the part of our inhibitory system to ensure that an awful warning be presented to the less reputable parts of ourselves, which are aroused by the spectacle of someone doing what we would secretly like to do ourselves."[64]

Here, too, the mere threat of punishment may not be enough. The disturbing spectacle of crime being perpetrated may need to be neutralized by the reassuring example of punishment being imposed. Impunity may not only engender disrespect for legal authority but also undermine the authority of conscience.

Threat and punishment may provide both a rationale for conformity and an instrument for the rationalization of conforming conduct. In other words, they may provide an additional reason for obedience to law in circumstances in which individuals are subject to temptation. Such rationalization is just as likely to be influential in group decision-making processes. In view of the group nature of a good deal of criminal activity, especially among juveniles, this might be a significant factor in crime prevention on some occasions.

These, then, are some of the less direct ways in which the threat of punishment may have subtle but significant effects on the rate and quality of lawbreaking in society. Little is known about whether, when, and how much, these mechanisms

63. *Ibid.*
64. Sprott, "Sentencing Policy," in Halmos (ed.), *Sociological Studies in the British Penal Services* (1965) 32–33.

affect behavior.[65] If the threat of punishment plays a role in the development of morality and respect for law, it is far from the only force at work in that phase of socialization. And since the threat of punishment and other socialization processes are so closely interrelated, it is difficult to isolate the effects of threatened punishment for empirical study.

SECTION 3 RESEARCH IMPLICATIONS

No one doubts that threat and punishment exert some control over some types of crime. But to conceive the preventive effects of punishment as a matter of simple deterrence or intimidation in terms of the classical theorist's conceptual model is to oversimplify an extremely complex process. In the preceding discussion we have attempted to distinguish some of the more significant elements in that process. What are the implications of that discussion for research? Clearly there are many different facets to the study of the effects of threats on human behavior, and equally clearly there are many different ways in which they might be studied. The proper focus for deterrence research depends on which specific questions about penal policy are of central importance.

Consider the question of drunk driving. The offense might be punished at present with fines and expressions of social disapproval which are marginal at best. A legislator, examining this policy, would have a rather specific frame of reference when asking questions about the effects of threat and punishment. With the present penalty as a starting point, he would cast his eye part of the way up and part of the way down the scale of possible agency responses to drunk driving, and he would wish to know what effects particular changes might have on the drunk driving rate. He would probably not be interested in the effects of leaving drunk driving unpunished, because there are reasons other than deterrence for its punishment. He would not wish to know about all the consequences of harsh sanctions, because there are reasons

65. Some psychologists hold, for instance, that the threat of mild sanctions will prove more conducive to moral learning about the threatened behavior than the threat of severe sanctions, because the threat of severe sanctions produces avoidance of the threatened behavior without internal conflict, and such conflict is the occasion for much of moral learning. See, e.g., Turner and Wright, "Effects of Severity of Object" (1965) 2 *J. Pers. and Soc. Psych.* 128–32.

other than deterrence which render harsh sanctions for this crime undesirable and impractical.

Again, when a legislator enters the capital punishment controversy, his interests are narrowly specific. He wishes to know what differential effects can be expected when we substitute one severe sanction, life imprisonment, for an even more severe sanction, the death penalty. To start a dialogue with the legislator by detailing the effects that threat and punishment might have would be a mistake, for many of the issues relating to the effects of threats are irrelevant to the decision whether to shift from one heavy penalty to another.

It is difficult to suppose that a move between two such drastic sanctions would substantially change the educative effect of punishment. Educative considerations, however, would be highly relevant to a decision whether a certain type of behavior were to be punished or not, or to situations where substantial movements up or down the scale of agency responses were being contemplated. Should traffic offenders, now subject to light fines, be sent to prison? If the issue is whether the punishment for a specific major crime should be reduced or increased by a moderate amount, the most important question for research should be whether the higher penalty is a simple marginal deterrent, and by how much. The range of options presented by such a problem bears no apparent relation to the educative or moralizing effects of the institution of punishment. Thus, while threat and punishment may operate in ways that can be loosely categorized as deterrent at many levels, different types of penal-policy questions call for different operational definitions of the deterrent effect that evaluative research seeks to investigate.

When the treatment of whole categories of behavior as criminal is called into question, the scope of our analysis must be broadened to the "totality of conscious and unconscious motivations that govern the behavior of men in society."[66] We cannot be satisfied with the analysis of only the mechanisms of simple deterrence when our policy decisions may affect much more; but it would be equally indefensible to agonize over the effectiveness of punishment as a mechanism to induce respect for law when considering whether meat should be added to prison lunches.

66. Packer, *supra* note 18, at 42.

4   The Deterrent Effect

Deterrence is a function of the declaration of some harm, loss, deprivation, or pain that will follow noncompliance with commands. The central concept is that of threat, a transaction which involves two parties: a threatening agent or agency and a threatened audience. In chapter 2 we considered the rationale of deterrence and in particular its function as the motive and justification for crime control policies. The focus of inquiry was on the beliefs, attitudes, and behavior of officials, the threateners.

In this chapter the center of attention changes from the threateners to the threatened. For the degree to which threats can effectively be used as a means of inducing compliance to law is determined by the responses of threatened audiences of potential criminals.

The major portion of the analysis in section 1 is concerned with the *general* effects of threats: behavior that can be expected from people even if they are not caught and punished. Much of this discussion of general effects will also be relevant to the behavior of persons who are punished—what is sometimes called "special deterrence." The combination of actual punishment and the threat of further punishment raises some distinct issues which will be discussed in section 2.

SECTION 1 GENERAL DETERRENCE

In elucidating the concept of general deterrence and in exploring the nature and scope of the processes involved, we are seeking (1) generalizations that apply to all legal threat situations, and (2) explanations of significant differences observable in the effectiveness of various legal threats.

Since legal threats may vary greatly in form and content, and threat responses range from total absence of reaction to full compliance, it might seem that the differences between legal threats must assume much greater significance than any similarities we may find. Moreover, the amount of empirical investigation which has been done into the operation of legal threats is so limited that it must provide a somewhat exiguous basis for general inferences. But if present knowledge about the operation of *legal* threats is wanting, there have been findings in experimental psychology relating to the use of threats which are relevant to our concerns.

A Some Generalizations: Constraint and
  Psychological Reactance

One common element of all threats (whose defining characteristic is the announcement that unpleasant consequences will be attached to particular behavior) is that they provide their audiences with a reason for avoiding the threatened behavior. It is in the nature of a threat that it is designed as a barrier to commission of the forbidden behavior. Nevertheless, the way in which this barrier is viewed by the threatened audience will be subject to considerable variation. The power of the threat of unpleasant consequences as a reason for avoiding behavior is very far from constant or universal.

It may be asked, however, whether any generalizations can be made about the nature of the audience reaction to threats. At least two authoritative suggestions have been made, which are based on experimental investigations and seem to be applicable to at least a wide range of threat situations. The first generalization we shall consider comes from Kurt Lewin's treatment of the psychological situations of reward and punishment,[1] and the second is derived from J. W. Brehm's theory of psychological reactance.[2]

According to Kurt Lewin: *"Threat of punishment always and necessarily gives rise to the structure of a constrained situation."*[3] Lewin argues that there are a variety of barriers to deviant behavior: physical, social, and ideological, but these barriers may allow a good deal of freedom. The threat of punishment, however, always imposes some constraint. The threat of unpleasant consequences is a force which can operate where there is no physical obstacle to impede the threatened behavior, where social barriers such as are provided by a given social milieu (e.g., a family or school) are weak, and where no ideological or moral limits are set.

"The constrained aspect of the situation," Lewin maintains, "is prominent in proportion to the sharpness of the pressure. . . . The sharper the threatened punishment the greater, ordinarily, is the general restriction."[4] And when threats of punishment possess "a sufficient real firmness" and punishments are severe enough, "the milieu as a whole assumes the constrained character of a prison or reformatory marked by bars, locked rooms, and constant surveillance."[5] The prospect of punishment, in other words, can restrict freedom by the creation of an emotional barrier.

Nevertheless, although Lewin's statements are based on observation of human behavior, it is questionable whether they have universal validity. Indeed, it is unlikely that he intended them to be interpreted in that way. We should remember that his generalizations were derived from investigations in the field of child psychology and that the focus of the inquiry was the use of "the prospect of reward or punishment as a means of bringing about or suppressing certain definite behavior in the child."[6]

1. Lewin, "The Psychological Situations of Reward and Punishment," in *A Dynamic Theory of Personality* (1935) 114–70.
2. Brehm, *A Theory of Psychological Reactance* (1966).
3. Lewin, *supra* note 1, at 129.
4. *Ibid.*
5. *Ibid.*
6. *Id.* at 114.

It would certainly be unwise to assume that an atmosphere of constraint is an inevitable product of legal threats. It is difficult to understand how a threat could produce feelings of constraint among those not tempted to commit the threatened behavior unless the fact of the threat caused a significant re-evaluation of the behavior. And where members of an audience have considered behavior to be highly undesirable in the absence of threat, it seems unlikely that the addition of a threat would make much difference in the way they view the behavior.

Mention of the possibility that threats may cause reevaluation of behavior brings us to our second general hypothesis about threat situations. Lewin noted, but did not develop, the point that, as a result of the threat of punishment, sometimes "an originally neutral event first acquires positive attraction."[7] This notion accords with the common pattern of experience reflected in Mark Twain's assertion that Adam "did not want the apple for the apple's sake, he wanted it only because it was forbidden."[8] An explanatory hypothesis known as the theory of psychological reactance, which deals with this and other related behavioral phenomena, provides a second generalization about audience reaction to threats.

The theory has been briefly stated by Professor Brehm:

When a person believes himself free to engage in a given behavior, he will experience psychological reactance if that freedom is eliminated or threatened with elimination. Psychological reactance is defined as a motivational state directed toward the re-establishment of the threatened or eliminated freedom, and it should manifest itself in increased desire to engage in the relevant behavior.[9]

Professor Brehm cites a great deal of experimental evidence which, although it does not constitute unequivocal proof, strongly supports the conclusion that people are motivationally aroused by the elimination or threat of elimination of a behavioral freedom, and tend to show increased desire for the eliminated or threatened behavior.[10] In other words, it appears

7. *Id.* at 163.
8. Twain. *Pudd'nhead Wilson's Calendar* (1894), heading of chapter 2.
9. Brehm, *supra* note 2, at 15–16.
10. *Id.* at 123 and *passim*.

that the introduction of a threat as a barrier to committing a particular behavior is likely to cause members of a threatened audience to revise attitudes toward the desirability of the behavior. People who felt that the behavior was desirable in the absence of threat may come to consider it even more desirable, though the prospect of unpleasant consequences may persuade them to desist from it. Those who originally were neutral about the desirability of a threatened behavior may come to ascribe it some positive value, despite the unpleasantness of threatened consequences.

This initial reaction, however, is not necessarily sustained. Brehm points out that, "if there are penalties for engaging in a certain behavior, the individual must recognize those penalties and the chances that he will have to pay them."[11] Thus, while threats may initially lead to a higher valuation of the threatened behavior, persons who refrain because of the threat may afterward come to derogate the behavior and view it as less desirable.[12]

While there is confirmation of the existence of the "forbidden fruit" effect in a variety of situations where members of an audience were not previously disinclined toward the threatened behavior, the findings are by no means unequivocal or clearcut. For example, a "sour grapes" effect was noted in some experiments.[13] Also, where behavior has been considered undesirable before it was subjected to threat, very little in the way of reactance can be expected to occur.[14] As Professor Brehm puts it, "No general answers can be given at this time."[15]

What conclusions then can be drawn from the theories concerning the psychological dimensions of threats which we have briefly summarized above? It is clear that what does *not* emerge

11. *Id.* at 126–27.
12. *Ibid.* Brehm says in this connection, "Precisely what happens to the reactance, then, is not at all clear." But he suggests that "at least in some cases" where the individual decides to refrain from the behavior, he will react along the lines indicated above. In this connection he refers to Festinger's theory of cognitive dissonance. For this, see Festinger, *A Theory of Cognitive Dissonance* (1957), and Brehm and Cohen, *Explorations in Cognitive Dissonance* (1962). See also *Id.* at 36 on the "sour grapes" effect.
13. *Id.* at 36.
14. *Id.* at 3–4.
15. *Id.* at 127.

is the kind of simple model in which threats provide a barrier which is reinforced by constraint and automatic devaluation of the threatened behavior. Such a model, which would accord with the notion of simple deterrence subscribed to by the classical theorists but has long been considered inadequate, fails to account for many "nonobvious or paradoxical aspects of behavior."[16] Since feelings produced by threats may lead in opposite directions, leaving the forbidden behavior more dangerous at the same time that it is more attractive, no general statement can be made about which pull will be stronger.

Nevertheless, the studies we have considered cannot be considered unsatisfactory or unhelpful merely because they do not provide us with a general formulation that integrates all available information. On the contrary, they indicate significant psychological aspects which might otherwise be overlooked. It is important that we recognize, for example, that for those who are tempted to commit threatened acts, a threat may produce a reason for avoiding such an act which competes with a reason for performing it: the new attraction added by the threat itself.

Moreover, it may be predicted that whenever threats are directed at behavior which is to some degree attractive, the psychological elements we have been considering are likely to be present: constraint, psychological reactance, and conflict. The nature of the conflict resolution will be a function of a variety of factors, which are the subject of the rest of this section.

The crucial task in any discussion of the effectiveness of threats is the search for those variations in circumstance which account for the great differences among responses to, and results of, threats.

B Differences among Men

One natural place to search for the explanation of different patterns of response to threats is in personality, attitude, and status. We shall be concerned here only with those differences which have some bearing upon differential threat response. Explanations based on differences among men—unlike those

16. Brehm and Cohen, *supra* note 12, at viii.

based on variation in the nature of the threatened behavior—seek to establish general patterns of threat sensitivity that are characteristic of categories of individuals in a variety of situations.

If an individual's relative immunity to the threat of sanctions while filling out his income tax return is attributable to a personality characteristic, the same characteristic could determine his reaction to the temptation to steal or to exceed the speed limit. If differences among men were the only explanation of differential deterrability, society might possibly be divided into deterrable and nondeterrable segments.

Indeed, a number of writers do appear to hold that deterrence is irrelevant to large segments of the population. Alexander and Staub distinguish between a "very great" number of "neurotic criminals," who "cannot help doing" what they do, and a "very small" number of "normal criminals," who may be deterred by "the fear of painful consequences."[17] Jackson Toby, on the other hand, maintains that "the bulk of the population . . . have introjected the moral norms of their society [and] cannot commit crimes because their self-concepts will not permit them to do so."[18] Leslie Wilkins distinguishes between "criminals or would-be criminals" and "those of us who have never needed a deterrent."[19]

We shall be considering distinctions of this kind in more detail later in this subsection. For the moment it is sufficient to observe that general patterns of threat responsiveness based on personal differences will predict responses with only partial effectiveness.

Knowing that Joe Doe is relatively unconcerned about the threat of punishment for tax cheating, and that this lack of concern is related to a general tendency, will not tell us that he

17. Alexander and Staub, *The Criminal, the Judge, and the Public* (2d ed. 1956) 209–11. It should be noted that in the Preface of the second edition Alexander qualifies this to the extent that he acknowledges "the prevalence . . . in the United States" of "a large group of professional criminals" who are "normal, non-neurotic criminals." *Id.* at xi.

18. Toby, "Is Punishment Necessary?" 55 *J. Crim. Law, Criminology and Police Science* (hereafter cited as *J. Crim. L. C. and P. S.*) (1964) 333.

19. Wilkins, "Criminology, An Operational Research Approach," in Welford (ed.), *Society: Problems and Methods of Study* (1962) 323.

will be undeterred by the threat of punishment if confronted with the opportunity to commit armed robbery. Joe's insouciance may suggest that he is more likely than others without that attitude to be unimpressed with the threat of punishment for robbery. But his chances of being deterred in the second situation may still be overwhelmingly high. This preliminary point is crucial, for it imposes a substantial limitation upon the inferences that may be drawn from personality differences.

In the following pages we survey some of the differences among men which have been held to be important in relation to threat responses. We do not say that they are without importance in the explanation of differential threat responsiveness. It seems to us that from the standpoint of public policy their significance is limited. Such differences, being little amenable to change or manipulation, cannot often be exploited for the purpose of increasing the effectiveness of threats.

i Differences in Personality Type

Although there is a considerable literature on the subject of the relation between criminal conduct and personality, very little attention has been paid to the relation between deterrence and personality. The most recent attempt to consider the implications of personality theory for the study of crime and criminality, Professor H. J. Eysenck's *Crime and Personality*, has little to say about legal punishment, and in regard to deterrence offers merely the observation that "it is doubtful whether punishment acts as a very effective deterrent."[20] Personality theorists' interest in criminal behavior has been almost wholly confined to the causation rather than the prevention of crime. Indeed, most of the personality differences that are mentioned in connection with the effect of sanctions are based on quite simple distinctions not related to systematic explanations of human personality. Some of these distinctions, however, are of fundamental importance and will be considered here.

(a) The future versus the present. One such relatively simple distinction is between those individuals for whom the future plays an important part in present thinking, and those who are

20. Eysenck, *Crime and Personality* (1964) 147–48.

less "future-oriented." The future-oriented individual will be prepared to forego a gain today in order to enjoy a larger one next week. The present-oriented one will accept a lesser but more immediate reward.[21] In threat response, the converse of this effect is significant. Since the unpleasantness threatened will always come after the commission of the threatened behavior,[22] and is often quite distant in both time and probability from the temptation to act,[23] the less future-oriented person will be more willing to place a heavy mortgage on immediate gratification. The world of small children, Lewin notes, is "of small extent temporally and spatially" and not until "a sufficiently large temporal space" becomes psychologically real for the child "can the threat of punishment be effective."[24]

Failure to relate to the future is not confined to children. It has been suggested that members of some disadvantaged subcultures place less emphasis on future events than members of the middle class. Oscar Lewis, in *La Vida*, remarks that a "characteristic trait" in "a culture of poverty" is "a strong present-time orientation with relatively little ability to defer gratification and plan for the future."[25] This might seem to support the view that disadvantaged groups are generally less deterrable, and that their nondeterrability accounts, in part, for the higher rates of criminal behavior among some subcultures.

The problem with attributing higher crime rates to lesser deterrability, and lesser deterrability to the lack of emphasis on the future among some subcultures, is that of separating *cause* from *consequence*. The relative lack of emphasis on the future may simply be a reflection of the fact that people in some positions have less to look forward to than people in others. If a tendency to discount the future is the result of environmental

21. See Mischel, "Preference for Delayed Reinforcement: An Experimental Study of a Cultural Observation" (1958) 56 *J. Abnormal and Soc. Psych.* 57–61.

22. Eysenck, *supra* note 20, at 110: "The punishment, in the ordinary sense, always follows the crime."

23. Lewin, "The Psychological Situations of Reward and Punishment," in *A Dynamic Theory of Personality* (1935) at 163: "Punishment is psychologically farther off than satisfaction of the desire [so that] a certain intellectual maturity is a necessary condition of the effectiveness of threatened punishments."

24. *Ibid.* See also Mischel, *supra* note 21, at 60.

25. Lewis, *LaVida* (1966) xlviii; also Mischel, *supra* note 21.

conditions, then these environmental conditions and not any separate trait of personality may be responsible for a different view of threats among members of the culture of poverty.

Moreover, even if it is plausible to assume that a short-term view contributes to lessened degrees of threat responsiveness, it cannot be inferred that such a difference is responsible for the increased rate of crime observed among such groups. Too many variables—each a plausible explanation for higher rates of crime in its own right—intervene. For discounting the future may be the result of a number of other psychological and physical conditions, which may themselves account for the diminished effectiveness of threats.

One scholar who emphasizes the importance of this particular difference between men in relation to deterrence is Margery Fry. She speaks of "present-dwellers" and "future-dwellers." The present-dwellers' preoccupation is "limited to the recent past and the immediate future."[26] For them, she says, "the emotional force of present desire is overwhelming in contrast to the apprehension of future pain."[27] Such people, she maintains, "are unlikely to be restrained by apprehension from actions prompted by immediate lust or greed or anger."[28]

Miss Fry even goes so far as to suggest that the increase in crime which followed World War II might have been partly due to the fact that "many recruits to the population of present-dwellers were gained under war conditions."[29] Those were people who "found that the only way of surviving conditions which stretched endurance to the limit was to narrow down attention to the immediate claims of day to day, and even of hour to hour."[30] A long course in this frame of mind, she maintains, may result in the loss of "the habit of normal foresight."[31]

Among "future-dwellers" Miss Fry distinguishes between "those with apprehensive imagination" and "the optimistic apprehender."[32] Of the first category she remarks that "the

26. Fry, *Arms of the Law* (1951) 83.
27. *Ibid.*
28. *Ibid.*
29. *Ibid.*
30. *Id.* at 84.
31. *Ibid.*
32. *Id.* at 82–83.

existence of the penalties of law has perhaps more effect on this group of the population than any other."[33] But the second type, Miss Fry continues, "the self-confident and conceited future-dweller, is very well known amongst convicted prisoners."[34]

Having drawn these distinctions Miss Fry goes on to say that "obviously this division of people . . . is an unduly diagrammatic one."[35] This important point applies equally to our own scheme of classification. For convenience of exposition we deal with the distinction between optimism and pessimism separately in the subsection which immediately follows. But our method is no less arbitrary and "diagrammatic" than hers. And the neat demarcations which we draw in theory between different traits and characteristics are not intended to imply that no overlap occurs in practice.

(b) "Optimists" versus "pessimists." Unless members of a threatened audience are the kind of persons who choose to defy threats "with a policemen at their elbow," reacting to a threat may involve weighing the chances of being apprehended and punished. It might be assumed that people weighing the chances of being apprehended and punished would be influenced by the objective probability of being discovered. But, as Leslie Wilkins says, "It seems probable that in most serious offences the offender is not aware of the true probabilities of being caught."[36] Indeed, most potential lawbreakers do not have complete information about the risk of apprehension. It follows therefore that the subjective judgment, or "guess factor," will play an important role in the individual's estimate of his chances of escaping without apprehension and punishment.

Psychological research has established that even when it is possible for a person to know the objective probabilities of achieving a particular goal, a person's estimate of his own chances of success will often differ from objective probabilities.[37] It is thus plausible to suppose that optimists, who under-

---

33. *Id.* at 82.
34. *Ibid.*
35. *Id.* at 84.
36. Wilkins, *supra* note 19, at 324.
37. Cohen, *Chance, Skill and Luck* (1960) *passim.*

estimate the chances of being apprehended, will be less responsive to threats than pessimists, who overestimate them.

The worrier will tend to overestimate the objective probability of being caught, if he is not completely informed about the probability of apprehension, while the optimist will tend to underestimate apprehension chances. Even if both the worrier and the optimist knows what the chances are, in general, of being caught, the worrier will tend to feel that his personal chances of successful evasion are no better than anybody else's, and may be worse, while the optimist will feel that his personal chances of successfully escaping threatened consequences are much better than the general average. As a result, the optimist will prove to be a more difficult person to deter.

Two studies relevant to this distinction between optimists and pessimists were carried out recently in this country and in the United Kingdom. In the first, Daniel Claster asked a sample of delinquent boys and a sample of nondelinquent boys to estimate (1) *the general chances* of being apprehended and punished, and (2) *their personal chances* of being apprehended and punished, in relation to a variety of offenses.[38] The two samples gave similar answers about the general chances of being apprehended and convicted, and about their personal chances of being convicted of offenses if apprehended. But the delinquent boys perceived their personal chances of arrest if they committed crimes to be significantly lower than the personal chances estimated by nondelinquents.

These results might be considered as evidence of the delinquents' possessing, as Dr. Claster suggests, a "magical immunity mechanism"[39] that served to neutralize fear of punishment and made this group less susceptible to deterrence. It is curious, however, that the same mechanism did not appear to operate in relation to answers about chances of conviction after arrest.[40] Moreover, it is possible that the delinquents' estimates of personal apprehension chances were accurate and based on personal experience not possessed by the nondelinquent boys; or

38. Claster, "Comparison of Risk Perception between Delinquents and Non-Delinquents" (1967) 58 *J. Crim. L. C. and P. S.* 80.
39. *Id.* at 85.
40. *Id.*

alternatively that a low estimate of chances of apprehension served to rationalize their behavior in retrospect.

The second study was carried out by the British Government Social Survey among fifteen- to twenty-one-year-old youths. The youths were asked how they rated their chances of detection in relation to a number of offenses. In this case, also, it was found that those with more experience of committing offenses were more optimistic about their chances of immunity to detection.[41] And, as Nigel Walker pointed out in a review of the study, where it was possible to estimate the real probability of detection it appeared that "optimism meant realism."[42] So available data fall short of establishing that personality traits associated with differential estimates of risk play a significant role in responsiveness to threats.

But even if studies showed that a majority of criminals are more optimistic than the facts warrant, and less prone to worry than law-abiding citizens, there is still the problem mentioned earlier of separating cause from consequence. Dr. Claster describes the optimism expressed by delinquents as an "immunity mechanism" that "protects" delinquents from fear. Does this mechanism exist before a boy embarks on a delinquent career, or does it develop as a result of ignoring threats? For if it develops after deterrence has failed, it can hardly explain the initial failure.

A number of other questions arise in relation to the distinction between optimists and pessimists. It should be noted that the "optimist" who acquires that title because he tends to underestimate risks of apprehension is not necessarily a person with a generally roseate view of the world around him. If the hypothesis holds true that persons without a strong sense of a personal future doubt that the future is promising then the most threat-resistant personality of all would be a man who tended to underestimate risks, yet hold a generally *pessimistic* view of his chances for future success.

Again, one might ask whether what is characterized as optimism might not reflect a preference for risk taking rather than

41. Willcock and Stokes, *Deterrents and Incentives to Crime among Youths Ages 15–21* (1968).
42. Walker, *Sentencing in a Rational Society* (1969) 65.

a sanguine view of future prospects. Finally there is the political question: What would be the social policy significance of a confirmed finding that optimists were less deterrable than pessimists? It is extremely difficult to envisage any manner in which policies could offset or reverse or in any useful way take account of such a state of affairs.

(c) *Risk preference and risk avoidance.* In theory, at any rate, the optimist can be distinguished from the risk preferrer in that optimism gives rise to exaggerated estimates of the probability of success whereas risk preferral leads to incurring hazards even when both the subjective or objective probability of success may be relatively slight.

The risk preferrer is stimulated by and enjoys risk taking. The risk avoider finds risks distasteful and hazardous courses of action unwelcome. A risk preferrer could be pessimistic in that his estimates of chances of success were consistently low, while a risk avoider could be an optimist in that his estimates of the probability of success were consistently high. The distinction between the risk preferrer and risk avoider lies in the fact that, even if their perceptions of the probability of harm and opportunity for gain were the same, the former would be more likely to take a chance than the latter.

In the literature both of economics and of psychology the subject of risk taking has received attention. Economists have discussed such questions as the functional and dysfunctional aspects of risk taking in relation to the role of the entrepreneur and the speculator.[43] They have analyzed risk-taking behavior in terms of utility theory,[44] but they are not concerned with the personality correlates of that behavior.

Psychologists have displayed interest in behavior under conditions of risk, although little empirical research has been done on this subject. Such evidence as is available—drawn largely from studies of gambling—suggests that some behavior which might be regarded as reflecting irrational optimism may in fact

43. See, e.g., Willett, *The Economic Theory of Risk and Insurance* (1951).

44. See, e.g., Vickrey, "Measuring Marginal Utility by Reactions to Risk" (1945) 13 *Econometrica* 319–33; Friedman and Savage, "The Utility Analysis of Choices Involving Risk" (1948) 56 *J. Polit. Econ.* 279–304; Mosteller and Nogee, "An Experimental Measurement of Utility" (1951) 59 *J. Polit. Econ.* 371–404.

have a very different motivational basis. Some psychologists have suggested that for many persons gambling is an expressive activity enjoyed for its own sake rather than an instrumental activity aimed at economic gain.[45] Gamblers vary in the degree to which they take chances, but there are some who seem to prefer risks which generate a maximum of tension and anxiety.[46]

The psychoanalyst Edmund Bergler, who has written extensively on the psychology of gambling, argues that some gamblers are neurotics driven by latent rebellion "against logic, cleverness, moderation, morals and renunciation" and by "a deep unconscious feeling of guilt."[47] In such cases, according to this analysis, the gambler "really" wants to lose, and keeps going until he loses in order to obtain the requisite self-punishment.

More relevant to the distinction we are considering is some work done by John Cohen, who conducted a series of experiments at the University of Manchester to see whether any systematic tendencies could be discovered in forms of risk taking, guessing, predicting, and decision making.[48] An interesting finding emerged from an experimental study of the effects of alcohol on risk taking and incurring hazard in driving by a group of experienced bus drivers. Cohen found that, while the drivers took greater risks after alcohol and thus incurred a greater degree of hazard, the alcohol had the effect of inducing them to underestimate hazards rather than deliberately to incur greater risks.[49] In other words, while the drivers' optimism increased, their attitude to risk taking remained unchanged. But it should be noted that this experiment was

45. Royden, Suppes, and Walsh, "A Model for the Experimental Measurement of the Utility of Gambling" (1959) 4 *Behavioral Science* 11–18; Scodel, Ratoosh, and Minas, "Some Personality Correlates of Decision Making under Conditions of Risk" (1959) 4 *Behavioral Science* 19–28.
46. Atkinson, "Motivational Determinants of Risk-taking Behavior," in Atkinson (ed.) *Motives in Fantasy, Action, and Society* (1958) 322–39.
47. Bergler, "The Gambler: The Misunderstood Neurotic" (1943) 4 *J. Crim. Psychopathology* 385; See also Bergler, *The Psychology of Gambling* (1957).
48. Cohen, *supra* note 37 *passim*.
49. *Id.* at 142–56.

conducted with a homogeneous group of "very highly selected and exemplary drivers."[50]

Cohen deals only briefly with crime. Referring to "certain types of monetary offence" in cases where "the barrier between man and crime is not an inner moral revulsion but fear of an external penalty," he suggests that "the offender may differ from his law-abiding neighbour simply in being prepared to violate the law untroubled by the uncertainties which alone deter his neighbour."[51] Cohen does not, however, mention the possibility that the degree of uncertainty and risk might in some cases act as a stimulus to criminal behavior.

We cannot specifically affirm the relevance of risk preferral versus risk avoidance to differential deterrability. It is, however, clear that attitude to risk is a dimension of personality which can be distinguished from the optimism-pessimism continuum. And it is reasonable to assume that it conditions threat responsiveness.

(d) *Reflection versus impulse.* The distinction between reflective and impulsive acts and personalities is one that has generated comment from a number of criminal law scholars: "The longer an offence is premeditated," wrote Bentham, "the greater is the aggravation."[52] In support of this he argued that "the longer a man is governed by hostile feelings . . . the stronger proof he gives of perverse anti-social dispositions." He went on to say that "the punishment must be more severe. . . . Such characters must be restrained by greater terrors."[53]

Whether or not persons with "perverse anti-social dispositions" are more likely to be restrained by "greater terrors," we can assume that persons guided by impulse rather than judgment, premeditation, or reflection are by definition less likely to be restrained by threats because they are less likely to reflect on the consequences of their act. In fact, impulsiveness may be the sort of disposition which would qualify individuals for

50. *Id.* at 155.
51. *Id.* at 39.
52. Bentham, "Specimen of a Penal Code" 1 *Works* (1843) 165.
53. *Id.* at 167.

membership of what Wechsler and Michael, in their well-known article "A Rationale of the Law of Homicide," refer to as "the class of non-deterrable persons."[54]

In their discussion of the significance of the distinction between deliberation and impulse, however, Wechsler and Michael do not draw the conclusion that impulsive behavior is nondeterrable. Indeed, they see the distinction as primarily one of degree. "The less thorough the deliberation the more 'impulsive' the act."[55] Their view may be summarized briefly as follows: "The threat of unwelcome treatment at the hands of the law provides a competing motive." The influence of "the legally created motive" will, of course, vary. But "the creation of the motive *may* . . . lead . . . excitable men to control their excitement, whatever its cause." Wechsler and Michael conclude: "It cannot be denied in general that men may be led to control their passions by the threat of unpleasant treatment if they do not do so."[56]

Human beings cannot, of course, be divided into two discrete classes: the impulsive and the reflective. Some people are more apt to be moved by sudden impulse or swayed by emotion than others but they can hardly be wholly unreflective all the time. If they were, they would not live long enough to constitute a problem for law enforcement agencies. At the opposite extreme infinitely protracted reflection about possible consequences would result in a complete passivity. Most people are content with less thorough deliberation than that.

Yet there is plausibility in the notion that differences in the degree of men's reflectiveness before they enter into a course of action are important in explaining differential deterrability. Furthermore, threats seek to create a strong association between threatened behavior and threatened consequences in the mind of potential offenders, but the strength of such an association may depend in part on the time and thought that members of a threatened audience devote to the meaning and consequences of their acts. In this sense, the process of deterrence

54. Wechsler and Michael, "A Rationale of the Law of Homicide" (1937) 37 *Colum. L. Rev.* 759.
55. *Id.* at 734; See also *id.* at 1282–84.
56. *Id.* at 735–36.

by threat may be one of accretion.[57] The person who acts on impulse is less likely to spend time thinking of consequences, and if the association between act and consequence cannot be fully realized in the span of time consumed by his impulse decision, his actions will be insulated from the accretive or cumulative influence of punishment threats.

The distinction between impulsive and reflective persons is to some degree analogous to the distinction between present-oriented and future-oriented persons. Among other similarities both continua probably owe more to cultural than biological differences. The impulsive-reflective theory emphasizes the amount of time available for and devoted to reflection, rather than the relative value of present and future gratification. In practice, however, impulsive conduct and a lack of future orientation may most often occur together.[58] Here the problem of cause versus consequence recurs, for an impulsive life style may be the result, as well as part of the cause, of paying little heed to the threat of punishment.

(e) *Normality versus neurosis.* Some speculations about personality differences that may affect threat responsiveness grow out of more ambitious and systematic theories of human behavior. In particular, Alexander and Staub, to whose work we have already referred, suggest that "psychoanalytic criminology" based on "the teaching of Freud"[59] throws some light on the functioning of deterrence.

Alexander and Staub delimit "three large classes of criminals," whom they define as "the neurotic criminal," "the normal criminal," and "the criminal whose criminality is conditioned by some pathological process of organic nature."[60] The third group, which "includes but a very small minority of

57. The possibility that threat communication and influence may result from cumulative impact over time was noted in another connection, by Barmack and Payne, when observing that the delay between an experimental countermeasure and significant results may have been due to the fact "that the spread of *information* about the countermeasure is an accretive process which necessitates repeated announcements" (our italics). Barmack and Payne, "The Lackland Accident Countermeasure Experiment" (1961) 40 *Highway Research Board Proceedings* 513.

58. See Mischel, *supra* note 21, at 57, where the present-oriented subjects are also described as "impulsive."

59. Alexander and Staub, *supra* note 17, at xv.

60. *Id.* at 45.

criminals," is composed of persons "either retarded in their development because of defective biological growth or those whose psychological personality was destroyed by some organic processes (idiots, paretics, schizophrenics and epileptics)."[61]

In addition to these three classes Alexander and Staub refer to "a number of normal individuals who, under certain specific conditions, become *acute criminals*." These persons "cannot be fitted into any special typological scheme." The outstanding factor in the kind of crimes they commit is not "the peculiarity of the person who committed it, but the singularity of the circumstances which led to it."[62] The acute criminal, in short, seems to be a psychologically normal person who is driven to an isolated criminal act by abnormal pressure of circumstances.

In their discussion of what we may call the organic criminal and the acute criminal, Alexander and Staub make no specific reference to deterrence. Of the first, they claim that, "as a result of toxic or other organic destructive processes," the personality is "considerably damaged or totally paralyzed,"[63] implying that such individuals would be unresponsive to the threat of punishment. As for the acute offender, the effectiveness of threats would presumably be impaired because other barriers to criminal activity normally in operation would have been overpowered by the force of circumstances before he was confronted by the possibility of crime.

The authors confine their reflections on deterrence to the normal and the neurotic criminal. They first believed that normal criminals constituted only a very small group.[64] Subsequently, as a result of working with William Healy in Boston, they found that "normal non-neurotic criminals [were] common in the United States."[65]

The normal criminal is one "whose psychic organization is similar to that of the normal individual, except that he identified himself with criminal prototypes."[66] These individuals Alexander and Staub adjudge to be "psychically healthy" and "well adjusted to the criminal prototypes of their social con-

61. *Id.* at 44.
62. *Id.* at 45.
63. *Id.* at 119.
64. *Id.* at 211.
65. *Id.* at xi.
66. *Id.* at 45.

science and to their criminal environment."[67] They differ from normal individuals only in that they "belong to a social class that lives by different standards."[68] Alexander and Staub believed the "rational principle of intimidation and of prevention"[69] to be applicable to this class of offender. Not only did they regard "normal criminals" as susceptible to deterrence but they admitted that "only fear of painful consequences . . . may prevent their committing anti-social acts, or may at least reduce the number of the latter."[70]

With the neurotic criminal the position is rather different. On the basis of their German studies the authors state that "the number of neurotic criminals is very great,"[71] but William Healy assured them (and subsequent collaboration with Healy convinced them) that "the type of neurotic criminal which we described was relatively rare in the United States."[72] The neurotic criminal is one "whose hostile activity against society is a result of an intrapsychic conflict between the social and anti-social components of his personality; this conflict, like that of a psychoneurosis, comes from impressions of earliest childhood and from circumstances of later life."[73] His criminal behavior "is prompted first of all by unconscious motives, and therefore it is impossible for the conscious personality to take any part in it."[74]

The punishment with which an offender of this class is threatened "cannot intimidate him, and therefore cannot deter him from his behavior, because of the simple fact that unconsciously he feels the need of punishment and therefore welcomes the severity of the law; quite often he even actively seeks punishment."[75] The authors conclude that "the social advantages derived from the *general intimidation* (general prevention of crime) appear highly questionable."[76]

67. *Id.* at 43.
68. *Id.* at 43–44.
69. *Id.* at 211.
70. *Id.* at 210.
71. *Ibid.*
72. *Id.* at x.
73. *Id.* at 45.
74. *Id.* at 120.
75. *Id.* at 107.
76. *Ibid.*

We do not know whether Alexander and Staub, if they had fully revised their work, would have altered that conclusion in the light of their revised estimate of the numbers belonging to the categories of normal and neurotic offenders. But if the distinctions were valid, the question how many criminals would fall into each of these categories would clearly be an important one. It would also be of interest to know what types of crime the different personality types would be prone to commit. Answers to these questions would be useful both for testing the hypothesis that neurotic criminals are undeterrable and for gauging the potential value of this type of insight.

Since Alexander and Staub's conclusions were based on observations made among criminals rather than among the general population,[77] they do not imply that all neurotics are less deterrable than other personality types. The authors suggest, in fact, that the neurotic particularly "needs the institution of punishment as an intimidating example" to aid in the struggle against the "primitive world of repressed instinctual drives."[78]

A peculiar problem with much psychoanalytic criminology, and with Alexander and Staub's study in particular, is the evidential basis for the propositions advanced. In this instance the thesis is "illustrated by some especially striking case histories."[79] But these do not themselves constitute proof of the generalizations which they illustrate, and no other evidence is offered in support of the authors' contentions. In these circumstances one cannot rule out the possibility that an exercise in circular reasoning may be involved, in that the neurosis which is used as the explanation of the criminal behavior has been inferred from the criminal behavior which it is supposed to explain. And, in the absence of any independent evidence, the assertion that neurotic criminals are nondeterrable may merely reflect the fact that failure to be deterred was one of the characteristics which led to the diagnosis of neurosis.

(f) *Personality, criminality, and deterrence.* A number of other personality dimensions have been thought to be related

---

77. For an elaboration of the difficulties encountered in generalizing from a sample of imprisoned criminals to other groups, see the discussion of the Warden's Survey, *supra* chap. 2, sec. 1.

78. Alexander and Staub, *supra* note 17, at 215–16.

79. *Id.* at xvi.

to the propensity to commit crime. Ideas such as Lombroso's
theory of the born criminal type[80] are of only antiquarian interest now. But more sophisticated theories, to the effect that
some if not all offenders are predisposed to criminal behavior
because of their physical or psychological constitution, are
supported by evidence and have certainly not been conclusively refuted.

As one example we may mention William Sheldon's contention that not only is there a correspondence between body type
and personality type but that delinquents differ from non-
delinquents in their body types and related temperamental and
psychological traits and tendencies.[81] There is some support
for Sheldon's findings in the Gluecks' study of delinquent
youths[82] and in a more recent study by T.C.N. Gibbens of
English borstal boys.[83]

Another example may be found in the work of Professor
Eysenck. Eysenck's theory relies on modern learning theory
for its foundation and on experimental work in conditioning for
its details. He maintains that criminals are "people who have
inherited a central nervous system which conditions only rather
poorly, as well as an autonomic nervous system which tends to
over-react."[84] Eysenck's theory too is supported by the findings
of others.[85]

A third example is the typology put forward by Hewitt and
Jenkins in their *Fundamental Patterns of Maladjustment*. Based
on the psychiatric approach, it links behavior patterns with
specific personality structures but has reference also to socio-
cultural factors. Hewitt and Jenkins distinguish three major
types of maladjusted youth: the unsocialized aggressive delinquent, the socialized delinquent, and the overinhibited neu-

80. Lombroso and Ferrero, *Criminal Man* (1911).
81. Sheldon, *Varieties of Delinquent Youth* (1949).
82. S. and E. Glueck, *Unraveling Juvenile Delinquency* (1950).
83. Gibbens, *Psychiatric Studies of Borstal Lads* (1963).
84. Eysenck, *supra* note 20, at 163.
85. See, e.g., Trasler, *The Explanation of Delinquency* (1962); and
Franks, "Recidivism, Psychopathy and Delinquency" (1956) 6 *Brit. J.
Delinq.* 192–201; Franks, "Personality Factors and the Rate of Conditioning" (1957) 48 *Brit. J. Psychol.* 119–26; Franks, "Conditioning and
Abnormal Behavior" (1962), in Eysenck (ed.), *Handbook of Abnormal Psychology* (1961) 457–87.

rotic.[86] This typology too has found support from other researchers.[87]

The evidence for such theories as these is by no means conclusive, and even when the data are well established it is possible to question the validity of the inferences drawn. Sheldon and the Gluecks, for example, interpret the association between delinquency and a certain type of physique as evidence of an inherent tendency to delinquency in persons of that body type. But the association might merely reflect the fact that such a type of physique (in this case muscular and athletic) is well adapted to certain types of criminal activity.

Though concerned primarily with the causation of crime rather than its prevention, such theories, insofar as they are valid, may well have significant implications for deterrence studies. If they are correct, the theories we have mentioned will mean that a greater proportion of the crime-prone personality types will commit threatened behaviors a greater number of times than those individuals displaying different personality traits; even though the rate of deviance among the crime-prone may still be quite small.

Yet the higher rate of noncompliance noted in crime-prone groups is not necessarily tied to different patterns of threat response. For example, we do not know whether or not the differences between criminals and others in responsiveness to conditioning observed by Eysenck are related in any way to differential responsiveness to threats. It may simply be that pressures toward deviancy, or barriers (other than threat) to deviancy, are distributed unevenly among personality types. Isolating facets of personality that are associated with high involvement in criminal activity will tell us much about the types of people for whom the operation of threat and punishment is of the most critical importance for a legal system. But if crime-related personality traits are not accompanied by psychic mechanisms that affect threat responses, the crime-

86. Hewitt and Jenkins, *Fundamental Patterns of Maladjustment* (1947) 25–36.
87. See Jenkins, "Diagnosis, dynamics and treatment in child psychiatry" (1964) 18 *Psychiatric Research Report* (American Psychiatric Association) 91–120.

prone individual may still be just as susceptible to threats as anybody else.

For example, a disproportionate number of unsocialized aggressive personality types will commit aggravated assault each year. But the threat of punishment may be equally effective on unsocialized aggressive and inhibited neurotic personality types, as illustrated by table 1.

TABLE 1
Hypothetical Percentage Distribution of Inhibited and Aggressive Personality Types

	Inhibited	Aggressive
Would not have committed assault in any event	97	70
Would have committed assault but were deterred by threat of consequences	2	20
Committed assault in spite of threat of consequences	1	10
Total	100	100

Knowing only the proportion of apprehended offenders that are aggressive-personality types, we would be tempted to conclude that threats have a lesser effect on the behavior of aggressive personalities than on inhibited neurotic personalities. When we also know the percentage of persons of each type that would have committed the crime but were deterred, we find that threats were equally effective among both groups, deterring two out of three potential assaulters. And the deterrent effect among aggressives resulted in ten times as much crime prevention as among inhibited neurotics.

If a particular personality trait of the kind we have discussed earlier were associated with deterrability, it would give us the proportions summarized in table 2.

In this case, a difference in threat responsiveness appears to explain the difference in crime rate.

These hypothetical tables bring out some of the problems encountered when we try to relate personality traits to deterrability, and deterrability to differences in crime rates. In the

TABLE 2
Hypothetical Percentage Distribution of Future-Oriented and Non-Future-Oriented Personality Types

	Future-Oriented	Non-Future-Oriented
Would not have committed assault in any event	80	80
Would have committed assault but were deterred by threat of consequences	17	14
Committed assault in spite of threat of consequences	3	6
Total	100	100

first place, personality traits do not come one to a customer. And persons who differ in one personality trait may differ in others as well. Thus, if a greater proportion of aggressive persons than passive persons were lacking a significant sense of the future, table 1 would appear to show that aggressive persons were less deterrable than passive types, even though aggressiveness per se did not affect deterrability.[88]

A second problem is simply that the data presented in the tables are hypothetical. There is, unfortunately, no direct method of determining what proportion of a population, let alone what proportion of a particular group within a population, with a particular personality type, "would have committed assault but were deterred by threat of consequences." For this reason, the tables *serve as an illustration* of the distinction between crime-related and more specifically deterrence-related personality traits, rather than *indicating a method of researching* the influence of character traits.[89] But understanding the difference between data on crime proneness and data on deter-

88. Zeisel, *Say It with Figures* (5th ed. 1968) 132–46.
89. A further problem encountered when testing propositions about personality, deterrence, and crime is that often the number of personalities of each type in the population as a whole is not known. This is the issue in the current dispute over whether the XYY chromosome is related to violent crime. The problem is solved whenever control groups of members of a normal population are available.

rability—the difference between tables 1 and 2—can provide a helpful caution to those who would otherwise leap to conclusions about threat sensitivity from data on relative crime rates. Men commit the lion's share of armed robbery. Does this mean that the threat of punishment works less well among men than among women, or is more needed by men, or both? The problem is insoluble on the basis of crime statistics alone, but the illustration is useful if it tells us only that.

(g) *Crime, deterrence, and the stages of human development.* Many of the personality dimensions we have been discussing are products of a developmental process rather than inborn and immutable. This raises the possibility that, just as different individuals may vary in their sensitivity to sanction threats, one individual may be more or less susceptible to threats at different stages in his development. As an obvious point of departure, it is likely that a certain degree of ability to deal with abstractions is necessary to deterrability and that very small children lack this critical capacity. There may also be important differences between adolescent and adult modes of personality organization that bear on deterrence. The adolescent may typically have a less developed sense of the importance of the future than the adult and may be prone to making different kinds of guesses about the outcome of risks. Particular stages in adolescence may be associated with different reactions to authority, which in turn affect threat responses.

While some predictions about characteristic adolescent versus adult propensities can be said to have general application, the forms in which developmental processes affect individual character are significantly influenced by cultural conditions. Combined with the always difficult task of separating out differences in the pressures toward deviancy from differences in threat response, the task of isolating the types of developmental changes that affect deterrability seems more difficult in practice than in theory.

A basic objection to the entire discussion of the relation between personality traits and deterrence may be raised. It may be argued that, even if personality differences do influence deterrability, the existence of such an influence is not relevant to legal policy because a threat is usually issued generally. Since the audience of a threat is composed of a mix of personality types, "tailoring" threats to particular personality types is impossible.

In answer to this objection, two points can be made in favor of research into the relations between personality and deterrence. First, any knowledge that can be gained about the relation between threat response and personality type is potentially useful, even if all categories of crime are committed by a mixture of different personality types. If the deterrent threat issued to the community at large can be altered to exert greater influence over a particular personality type without impairing its effectiveness among others, the effectiveness of the threat will be strengthened. Even if threats to the community at large are not altered, the way in which threats are communicated to particular groups and individuals can be. Furthermore, if the general-deterrent threat of the law cannot be specially designed for particular types of offenders, there seems to be no reason why the form of individualized threats should not be tailored to individual personality differences.

A second answer to the objection that personality differences are not relevant to penal policy is that, while crime as a general category may be committed by the whole spectrum of personality types, some specific crimes may be committed much more often by particular personality types, and, with respect to those crimes, knowledge of the relation between personality type and threat responsiveness may be valuable. While larceny may be said to be the province of no single personality type, except perhaps the "larcenous personality," can the same be said for public exhibitionism or even violent assault? Even if no remedies exist for a threat immunity associated with particular personality types, when a certain personality type dominates the crime statistics and population of potential offenders in relation to one or two specific offenses, it would be useful to know that the deterrent threat is, for that reason, more or less likely to produce substantial benefits.

Yet it must be admitted that our present knowledge about differences in human personality and their bearing on criminal behavior is very limited. A recent edition of one authoritative textbook in criminology concludes: "Research studies conducted by scholars representing different schools of thought have found no trait of personality to be very closely associated with criminal or delinquent behavior. No consistent statistically significant differences between personality traits of delinquents and personality traits of nondelinquents have been found."[90] Moreover, even if more were known there would still remain the problem whether differential criminality is related in any way to differential deterrability. No significant contribution to the formulation of penal policy is to be expected in the immediate future. Hypotheses about the relation between deterrence and personality differences cannot be regarded as more than tentative. And further knowledge will probably prove more useful in the design of correctional procedures than in the realm of general deterrence.

ii Differences in Attitude

The term *attitude,* as Allport pointed out, has an extremely wide range of usage.[91] In the thirty-five years since he wrote, the range has become even wider. We shall not attempt to survey or analyze the many definitions of attitude to be found in the literature, but will simply present our own.

We use *attitude* to designate dispositions according to which an individual's beliefs, thoughts, feelings, and tendencies to action are organized with respect to various aspects of his environment.[92] By this formulation, some of the personality traits which we have considered in the immediately preceding subsection might well be called attitudes. This is not surprising in view of the ambiguity of both terms and their shared field of reference. For both *attitude* and *trait* are often used indistinguishably to refer to various components of personality.

According to our definition a particular attitude is an organization of interrelated beliefs, thoughts, feelings, and tendencies to action around a common focus. The particular attitudes with which we are concerned here are those which may have some bearing on the question why some men are deterred by legal threats and others are not. Of special significance are

90. Sutherland and Cressey, *Criminology* (8th ed. 1970) 170.

91. Allport, "Attitudes" (1935), in Murchison (ed.), *A Handbook of Social Psychology* 798–844.

92. Cf. "An attitude can be defined as an enduring organization of motivational, emotional, perceptual and cognitive processes with respect to some aspect of the individual's world." Krech and Crutchfield, *Theory and Problems of Psychology* (1948) 152.

attitudes connected with citizen and subject roles which are involved in the concept of socialization, and more specifically attitudes toward authority.

(a) *Socialization.* The process of socialization has been studied by anthropologists, psychologists, sociologists, and political scientists. It is generally recognized as an important tool of government and one of the most powerful agents of social control. Its role in the control of criminal behavior has been emphasized by many authorities. Professor Sprott says, "By and large most people are deterred by the effects of the socialization process which they have undergone and do not refer at all to the risks of legal punishment."[93] Jackson Toby maintains that deterrence is irrelevant to "the bulk of the population who have introjected the moral norms of their society," and that "only the unsocialized (and therefore amoral) individual . . . is deterred from expressing deviant impulses by a nice calculation of pleasures and punishments."[94] Orville Brim states that "one major cause" of deviance is "ineffective socialization of the individual."[95]

Although the importance of socialization is generally recognized, and some aspects of the process have been studied intensively, general understanding is limited. Within a society, the life experience and therefore the learning processes of individuals may vary greatly. Some men will grow to adulthood with strong loyalties to the social system, as well as to the smaller family, clan, institutional, and community groups in which they live most of their lives. Others develop strong loyalties to the smaller groups but are less committed to the larger social entity. Some may grow to reject both the ideology of their particular living groups and that of the larger social system.

There is no codified body of knowledge and no general theory which integrates the findings of the great variety of psychological and anthropological studies which have been

93. Sprott, "Sentencing Policy," in Halmos (ed.), *Sociological Studies in the British Penal Services* (1965) 36.
94. Toby, "Is Punishment Necessary?" 55 *J. Crim. L. C. and P. S.* (1964) 333.
95. Brim, "Adult Socialization" (1968), in Sills (ed.), 14 *International Encyclopedia of the Social Sciences* 561.

carried out in the field of differential development. It is sufficient for our purpose, however, to note that it takes place and
that it is generally deemed to be an important factor in relation
to social control.

The intensity of personal commitment to the values and
goals of a society is a significant predicator of law-abiding behavior for one reason that has nothing to do with simple deterrence: the strongly socialized individual will obey commands
out of a desire to do right, quite independent of the specific
consequences of wrongdoing. Further, a strongly socialized
individual is more likely to comply with threats because he is
more sensitive to the negative aspects of threatened consequences than his less socialized neighbor. Social disapproval,
which is an important part of most threatened consequences,
will be carefully avoided by the strongly socialized individual.

Because the desire to obey commands in order to do the
right thing, and a greater sensitivity to consequences involving
community disapproval, will commonly occur together, it is
extremely difficult to estimate how much of an observed difference between strongly and weakly socialized individuals is
attributable to the greater sensitivity of the former to the negative aspects of threatened consequences. Perhaps the crucial
test of such an effect would come in an area covered by a legal
threat where the chances of apprehension were known to be
nil. In such circumstances, the desire to be law-abiding for its
own sake would presumably still be operative, while a greater
sensitivity to the negative aspects of threatened consequences
would not.

Although no criminal behaviors exist in our society for which
the chances of apprehension are nil, behaviors for which the
chances are extremely low might serve as adequate substitutes.
It could also be argued that, since it is part of human nature
to avoid even low risks of very high costs, those who fear the
law's sanctions most will be influenced by that fear even where
the risk is statistically minimal. Sensitivity to sanctions may
influence rates of compliance even in such areas as the requirement (once difficult to enforce) that interest and dividends
be reported on individual income tax forms.

In the absence of conclusive data, a plausible explanation is
that, where a threatened behavior is considered to be a serious

breach of society's moral code, the higher rate of compliant behavior on the part of the strongly socialized citizen can be attributed mainly to his sense of right and wrong rather than to his special sensitivity to the negative aspects of threatened consequences. When a threatened behavior is considered a less drastic breach of the moral code, his threat sensitivity may play a greater role.

How much of a role such factors play, either in absolute or in relative terms, cannot now be estimated. But that they are crucial to much of social behavior is unquestionable. Despite theoretically conflicting interpretations of the genesis of differential social attitudes, it is clear that what makes up those attitudes—the basic beliefs and dispositions regarding such matters as national loyalty, the legitimacy of institutions, and traditional values—are of fundamental significance in the preservation of social order. Not least important among these predispositions are orientations toward authority, which have been the subject of some study and require separate consideration here.

(b) *Attitudes toward authority: the "authoritarian personality."* One of the most widely recognized and influential conceptions relating attitude to social behavior centers on the "authoritarian personality." Some well-known studies begun during the mid-1940s suggest that the authoritarian personality, said to be the result of strict parental control in childhood, predisposes subjects to obedience to authority because compliance fulfills a deep personality need.[96] Persons of this type, some writers believe, identify with authority more intensely than others and thus find it easier than others to obey orders and comply with the demands of the authorities. Although there is a considerable literature on this topic, there is no consensus about the nature of the relation between the authoritarian per-

96. Adorno et al., *The Authoritarian Personality* (1950) *passim*; see also Christie and Jahoda, *Studies in the Scope and Method of "The Authoritarian Personality"* (1954); Sanford, "The Approach of the Authoritarian Personality," in McCary (ed.), *Psychology of Personality* (1956); Kirscht and Dillehay, *Dimensions of Authoritarianism* (1967); Hoffman, "Some Psychodynamic Factors in Compulsive Conformity" (1953) 48 *J. Abnormal and Soc. Psych.* 383–93; Mussen and Kaggan, "Group Conformity and Perceptions of Parents" (1958) 29 *Child Development* 57–60; Steiner and Johnson, "Authoritarianism and Conformity" (1963) 26 *Sociometry* 21–34.

sonality and the tendency to conform. This type of person will, however, be more likely to refrain from committing a particular behavior because it is threatened than would be a person whose attitude toward authority is either more ambivalent or more flexible. The person who obeys orders because he feels an inner need to do so will obey whether or not he considers the threatened behavior seriously wrong and largely independent of his chances of being apprehended. While someone with less respect for authority may see an element of challenge in a threat and be tempted to try to "get away with something," the authoritarian personality will comply with the threat and will be more likely to change his opinion of the rightness or wrongness of the behavior solely because it is threatened.

There is some overlap between the theory linking compliance to strong socialization and the theory linking compliance to the authoritarian personality; but there are important differences also. The authoritarian personality is not necessarily strongly socialized. He is more likely to express racial and religious prejudice than the nonauthoritarian, even though these prejudices are not officially condoned.[97] The authoritarian is no more likely to hold strong moral views about the rightness or wrongness of conduct than the nonauthoritarian, and his opinion, if not firmly held, is easier to change.[98] Finally, the authoritarian is likely to respond with obedience not only to legal commands but to orders from those in most high-status positions. Such a tendency could lead to cooperation, for example, with occupying powers or other high-status individuals in positions of power whose authority does not stem from the social value system native to the authoritarian.

Some confirmation of the theory that particular types of parental discipline produce personality patterns which are reflected in social and political behavior may be found in a comparative study made of two African tribal groups. In one group the children were strictly subordinated to the adults, and in the other they were treated much more permissively. It was

97. *Id.*
98. Crutchfield, "Conformity and Character" (1955) 10 *Am. Psychologist* 191.

found that the former group was much more compliant and deferential to the British colonial authority than the latter.[99]

It might be questioned whether in our society the much greater complexity of social organization would not preclude any such direct reflection of parental discipline. Certainly the available evidence is circumstantial, and the authoritarian personality cannot confidently be linked to possible differences in response to threats. The study of authoritarian attitude patterns has been limited to finding differences of attitude among different groups, and relating one type of attitude to other attitudes or to attitude change. Attitude surveys elicit only verbal responses, and it is important to distinguish between expressions of sentiment and tendencies to act. For any firm conclusion about differential deterrability to be drawn, evidence relating to more concrete behavioral response would be required.

(c) *Attitudes toward authority: the "anti-authoritarian personality."* Of special interest to the student of criminal sanctions is the possible existence of a segment of the population that rebels against the whole concept of obeying orders and rejects authority in any form. The term *anti-authoritarian* rather than *nonauthoritarian* characterizes this attitude. Insofar as there is an identifiable revolutionary youth movement in our society it may be that some members of it are dedicated to the total rejection of all authoritative regulation. Norman Cohn, in his brilliant study of revolutionary millenarianism and mystical anarchism *The Pursuit of the Millennium*[100] maintains that the ideal of emancipation from society is still with us and has a powerful appeal to "certain politically marginal elements in technologically advanced societies—chiefly young or unemployed workers and a small minority of intellectuals and students."[101]

There is certainly evidence of forms of anti-authoritarianism[102] which appear to involve the rejection of the prevailing

99. LeVine, "The Internalization of Political Values in Stateless Societies" 19 *Human Organization* 51–58.

100. Cohn, *The Pursuit of the Millennium* (1970 ed.).

101. *Ibid.*

102. Berger, "Hippie Morality—More Old Than New" (1970), in Gagnon and Simon (eds.), *The Sexual Scene* 59–73.

political, economic, and social institutions in favor of some not altogether clearly defined situation in which completely autonomous individuals are able to express themselves fully and develop their own personalities without interference from institutional authority.[103] While this may not represent a full commitment to the sort of philosophical anarchism exemplified in the writings of Godwin, Proudhon, and Kropotkin,[104] it does in some cases take the form of deliberate defiance of the law and provocation, which can result in "rather severe sanctions [being] involved against the offenders."[105]

A person with this sort of attitude toward authority would be likely to view each new threat as an invitation to defiance. The psychological prediction that threats create an atmosphere of constraint, and make the threatened behavior initially more attractive, applies to this group with special force. Indeed, the attractiveness of a forbidden behavior to an anti-authoritarian may increase as the consequences of apprehension are escalated, because the greater penalty is evidence of a greater challenge attached to the legal threat.

But if confronted with any forms of consequence except some expressions of social disapproval, the anti-authoritarian probably will show no special appetite for unpleasantness. For this reason, it is likely that the probability of apprehension and the magnitude of unpleasantness threatened will serve as behavioral controls, either by keeping anti-authoritarian sentiments from expressing themselves in conduct or by determining what types of conduct (presumably those threatened less severely or with less credibility) will be chosen for expressing antisocial drives. Moreover, for this group the chances of apprehension and the extent of unpleasantness threatened may be of particular importance in determining threat response, because there are very few other barriers to committing the threatened acts.

The anti-authoritarian personality serves as an example of

---

103. *Id.* at 61.

104. Godwin, *Enquiry Concerning Political Justice and Its Influence on Morals and Happiness* (1946 ed.); Proudhon, *What Is Property?* (1876 ed.); Kropotkin, *Mutual Aid: A Factor of Evolution* (1955 ed.); Woodcock, *Anarchism: A History of Libertarian Ideas and Movements* (1962).

105. Berger, *supra* note 102, at 69.

the special role that relatively small groups may have in criminal studies. In normal times, the anti-authoritarian personality would not be of great interest to the psychologist trying to explain the outcome of presidential elections, because this group is so small. But recurrent and serious criminality is the product of a relatively small segment of the community. And if small subgroups are disproportionately represented in the ranks of criminals and potential criminals, they may account for a major share of crime.[106] If the socialization process keeps most people law-abiding, the effectiveness of simple deterrent threats must be judged in terms of that part of the population which remains potentially criminal after socialization has done its work. In many cases, this residue may consist of small groups who differ substantially from the rest of the population in many respects.

iii Differences in Status

"Social status," Barbara Wootton says in *Social Science and Social Pathology*, "is a vague enough concept at the best of times."[107] She goes on, "It is not, therefore, surprising that such material as is forthcoming on this subject [i.e., "the causes or characteristic features of crime and delinquency"] is almost too diverse and sketchy to allow of any conclusions being reached."[108] At another point she says, "We are completely in the dark as to the contribution which particular social classes make to particular categories of crime."[109]

Yet anyone with any familiarity with the evidence knows that one of the most dramatic relationships one finds in studying samples of people arrested and imprisoned is that which exists between social status and crime. Despite her skepticism, Miss Wootton concludes her analysis of the evidence presented in twenty-one selected studies by acknowledging that, on the definitions used in the studies, "those who find themselves in trouble with the criminal law on either side of the Atlantic are predominantly drawn from the lower social classes."[110]

106. See Zimring and Hawkins, "Deterrence and Marginal Groups" (1968) 5 *J. Research in Crime and Delinq.* 100–114.
107. Wootton, *Social Science and Social Pathology* (1959) 100.
108. *Ibid.*
109. *Id.* at 48.
110. *Id.* at 107.

The truth is, as Donald West says, "All investigators are agreed that persons from the lowest social class are over-represented, and persons from the middle classes under-represented, in samples of delinquents brought to justice."[111] Or, to cite a more recent text, "There is no doubt that the incidence of official delinquency is higher in the lower than in the middle and upper classes."[112] Known criminals in our society have less education, lower social standing, less opportunity to become socially mobile, and less money than non-offenders. As a corollary, all that is known about crime in our society suggests that the well-placed and well-off commit not only fewer but less serious offenses.

This is not to deny that law enforcement is biased and selective in that socially disadvantaged persons are more likely to be apprehended and prosecuted than those in higher socioeconomic groups.[113] But while various forms of bias built into the reporting of crime and the enforcement of criminal laws may account for some of the difference noted between classes, it would be extremely fanciful to argue that all of this difference can be attributed to bias.[114]

111. West, *The Young Offender* (1967) 56; West cites a variety of studies in support of this assertion, including Little and Ntsekke, "Social Class Background of Young Offenders" (1959) 10 *Brit. J. Delinq.* 130–35; Gibbens, *supra* note 83, at 62; Rose, *Five Hundred Borstal Boys* (1954); Morris, *The Criminal Area* (1957) 166; Mannheim et al., "Magisterial Policy in the London Juvenile Courts" (1957) 8 *Brit. J. Delinq.* 13–33.

112. Hood and Sparks, *Key Issues in Criminology* (1970) 54–61. Hood and Sparks also cite a number of relevant studies including Douglas et al., "Delinquency and Social Class" (1966) 6 *Brit. J. Crim.* 294–320; Gold, "Undetected Delinquent Behavior" (1966) 3 *J. Research in Crime and Delinq.* 27–46; Reiss and Rhodes, "The Distribution of Juvenile Delinquency in the Social Class Structure" (1961) 26 *Am. Soc. Rev.* 720–32.

113. Porterfield, "Delinquency and Its Outcome in Court and College" (1943) *Am. J. Soc.* 199–208; Akers, "Socio-economic Status and Delinquent Behavior" (1964) *J. Research in Crime and Delinq.* 38–46; Short and Nye, "Extent of Unrecorded Juvenile Delinquency" (1958) *J. Crim. L. C. and P. S.* 296–302; Dentler and Monroe, "Social Correlates of Early Adolescent Theft" (1961) 26 *Am. Soc. Rev.* 733–43; Vaz, "Self-reported Delinquency and Socio-economic Status" (1966) 8 *Can. J. Correction* 20–27; Voss, "Socio-economic Status and Reported Delinquent Behavior (1966) 13 *Social Problems* 314–24.

114. See West *supra* note 111, at 55–60; Hood and Sparks, *supra* note 112, at 54–61; Gold, *supra* note 112; Reiss and Rhodes, *supra* note 112.

There are more plausible explanations of most of the difference in criminality noted between economic and social classes. In the first place, for a great variety of reasons low-status cultures are more supportive of criminal behavior than high-status cultures. In the second place, crime is relatively less attractive to the man who has legitimate means available to satisfy most of his desires.[115] To the poor man, who lacks status and has achieved fewer of his wants, the prospects for future achievement through legitimate channels seem remote.[116] Criminal means to achieve some of the things all men desire will seem rational to the poor far more often than to the wealthy, and social frustration, resentment, and the temptation to rebel will be felt more frequently and intensely by those with less to show for adherence to the predominant system of values.

If differences in culture and in perceived opportunity through legitimate means were the complete explanation for the relation between crime and social and economic status, there would be no basis for concluding that low-status groups are any less amenable to the influence of threat and punishment than high-status ones. As noted above in the discussion of crime and personality traits, finding that one group is tempted by criminal alternatives more often than another does not show that such a group is less sensitive to threats. There are, however, reasons for believing that some relation does exist between social standing and the effectiveness of threats.

First, it seems likely that those who attain high status will possess many of the characteristics that may be associated with maximum threat influence, such as a sense of the significance of the future and strong loyalty to a social system that has been responsible for much of their success. By the same token, lower-status groups will contain a disproportionate number of more socially alienated, less consistently socialized, and more present-oriented people. If this theory holds true, an association between deterrability and social status will exist which can be attributed to causes apart from the difference in status.

115. Cloward and Ohlin, *Delinquency and Opportunity* (1961).
116. It should be noted that the great majority of offenses are offenses against property. If we regard robbery as a property offense rather than as an offense against the person, the U.S. crime figures for 1969 were: property offenses, 4,632,270 = 93 percent; offenses against the person, 358,477 = 7 percent.

A second possibility is that personal success makes an individual more susceptible to the influence of threats because success determines the amount of investment in society an individual puts at risk when committing a threatened behavior. In this sense it could be said that the man who has everything also has everything to lose, as well as little to gain, from the commission of forbidden acts. The other side of the coin is equally important: "Deterrence does not threaten those whose lot in life is already miserable beyond the point of hope."[117]

It follows that those with a greater stake in life's continuing as it has been will have more to fear from the legal threat of unpleasantness and social disapproval. But this observation cannot be made into a complete repudiation of the possibility of deterrence among low-status groups, because bad conditions can always get worse. Even the poorest and least free in our society have life itself and some measure of personal freedom at stake when considering the prospect of criminal acts. Very few men have ever indicated a preference for prison over the worst of our slums, and the prospect of social stigma would not be welcomed by most of those with the lowest stake in maintaining the status quo.

Further, it cannot be said that threat responsiveness and investment in the status quo rise and fall together in any sort of calibrated, arithmetic progression, particularly since a person's opinion of the worth of his present life opportunities, rather than status as an objective fact, is the significant factor in predicting response to threats. Those with extremely high positions in life may feel they have stronger motives for obeying the law than have any other groups. But there is no reason to suppose that a lower-middle-class person would consider his investment in the social system any less worth protecting than that of a wealthier neighbor. The "investment" theory of deterrence is stated most powerfully when it is put forward as a contrast between the great mass of people with much to lose and those with little or nothing to lose if apprehended for law violation.

C Types of Threatened Behavior

Professor Andenaes has frequently emphasized that "any realistic discussion" of the effectiveness of legal threats must

117. Packer. *The Limits of the Criminal Sanction* (1968) 45.

be based on recognition of relevant "differences between types of offenses."[118] "Simple common sense," he says, "indicates that a threat of punishment does not play the same role in offenses as different as murder, rape, tax-evasion, shoplifting, or illegal parking."[119] Although Andenaes has developed this point more fully than any other scholar, many others have observed that the threat of consequences is likely to operate more effectively in controlling some types of conduct than others.

Thus, Bloch and Geis in *Man, Crime, and Society* say that "a major difficulty in the deterrence dispute has been the inability to differentiate among different types of offenders."[120] They go on to suggest that there are some types of criminal behavior—*crime passionel* murders are cited as an example—in regard to which "the penalty involved is probably of little, if any, consequence.[121]

William Chambliss has stressed "the importance of looking at types of offenses" when considering "the effectiveness of legal sanctions."[122] He too cites murder, which he says is "usually shrouded with a great deal of emotional involvement on the part of the offender," as being an instance in which "one might well expect punishment to be less effective precisely because such offenses are less dictated by 'rational' considerations of gain or loss."[123]

Leslie Wilkins in *Social Deviance* also refers to the fact that "the pressures to be offset are not invariant." He points out that "the average housewife does not need to be deterred from poisoning her husband, but possibly does need a deterrent to shoplifting! Perhaps the average motorist does not need a deterrent to stealing cars, but the majority seem to be in need of a deterrent to speeding or parking in unsuitable places."[124]

118. Andenaes, "The General Preventive Effects of Punishment" (1966) 114 *U. Pa. L. Rev.* 957–58. See also Andenaes (a) "Deterrence and Specific Offences" (1971) 38 *U. Chi. L. Rev.* 537–53; (b) "General Prevention—Illusion or Reality?" (1952) 43 *J. Crim. L.C. and P.S.* 176–90; and (c) *The General Part of the Criminal Law of Norway* (1965) 72–73.

119. Andenaes, *supra* note 118 (a), at 2.

120. Bloch and Geis, *Man, Crime, and Society* (2d ed. 1970) 444.

121. *Id.* at 444–45.

122. Chambliss, "Types of Deviance and the Effectiveness of Legal Sanctions" 1967 *Wisc. L. Rev.* 707.

123. *Id.* at 706–07.

124. Wilkins, *Social Deviance* (1964) 118–19.

Evidence on the number of potential criminals of any kind who are deterred by threats is sparse. But it is reasonable to assume that the jealous husband bent on homicide is less likely to be deterred by legal threat than the housewife considering pilferage as a method of reducing her grocery bill, or the bank clerk who views embezzlement as a method of securing funds to indulge in speculation. Moreover, variations in the content of legal threats may also have greater or lesser impact, depending on the nature of the crime. The rate of illegal parking is likely to be more sensitive to changes in the credibility and severity of threats than the rate of incest.

That deterrent threats function differently with respect to various threatened behaviors should come as no surprise, since crime is a separate and unitary class of behavior only in the legal sense. The concept of crime covers a wide and heterogeneous range of behaviors which have in common only the fact that they have been declared to be contrary to the criminal law. In all other respects, classes of criminal activity differ from each other as widely and significantly as any kind of criminal behavior can be said to differ from lawful conduct.

Although recognition of differences between types of offense is essential to any attempt to explain why legal threats function with varying degrees of effectiveness, recognition alone does not advance us very far. What is required is analysis directed at distinguishing those elements which determine differential threat responsiveness. For this purpose it is necessary to go further than identification and enumeration, or the drawing of broad distinctions such as those between crimes against the person and crimes against property, or between "crimes of passion" and "crimes of gain," or between offenses which are *mala per se* and *mala quia prohibita*.[125]

One difficulty is that the universe of possibly significant differences seems almost infinite. Anything that differentiates one type of crime from another may also conceivably affect deterrability and, if it does, may help to explain differential threat effectiveness. But even if comprehensiveness is unattainable, it is necessary at least to attempt a systematic ordering of the

125. Andenaes mentions the latter distinction as "a fundamental one." But he goes on to say that "there are variations within each of these two main groups." *Supra*, note 118 (a), at 957.

factors involved. The scheme proposed here is a relatively simple one, and, while it is inevitably incomplete, we believe that it encompasses most of the differences that have been noted as significant in the literature. It is based on four overlapping dimensions of difference which appear to be especially relevant to the explanation of the variable effectiveness of legal threats. It comprises differences in

i. the kinds of people drawn to different types of criminal activity

ii. the barriers, other than legal threats, that may condition the rate of a particular crime

iii. levels of motivation typically associated with different types of crime

iv. the emotional context of decisions to commit crimes.

i Differences among Potential Criminals

"It is important" say Hood and Sparks, "to distinguish between different types of potential offender, when assessing the deterrent effect of punishment. . . . Before we can even begin to measure the general-deterrent effect of specific penalties, we must thus identify with some precision the potential offenders to whom those threatened penalties apply."[126] Hood and Sparks add that, while "this can in principle be done . . . it may be very difficult in practice."[127]

In practice it has not been attempted. Not that the type classification of offenders or offenses is a novel idea. Indeed, the fact that the concept of crime covers a heterogeneity of behavior has led a number of criminologists to concentrate on particular types of crime and to develop typologies both of offenders and offenses.[128] But although a great variety of typologies exists, they have been developed either for etiological or for treatment purposes.

This is not to say that typologies developed for such purposes would be of no value in assessing deterrent effectiveness. Modes of classification designed for explanatory research

126. Hood and Sparks, *supra* note 112, at 174.
127. *Ibid.*
128. See *Id.* at 110–40 for an excellent survey of such typologies.

or theory will not, of couse, necessarily be useful in allocating offenders to treatment categories.[129] At the same time, such studies of specific types of crime as Cressey's research on embezzlement,[130] Lemert's studies of Check forgers,[131] Sutherland's work on professional theft[132] and white collar crime,[133] and Camp's study of bank robbery[134] indicate that there are significant differences in terms of class, personality and other factors between these classes of offenders. And it is not unreasonable to assume that social and personality differences influence susceptibility to the influence of threats.

The analysis of criminal careers or criminal behavior systems could conceivably reveal that the background dimensions which determine patterns of criminal behavior are significantly related also to threat responsiveness. Insofar as this is a reasonable hypothesis then differences in the type of potential criminal are one possible source of the variance in threat effectiveness noted by type of crime.

ii Differences in Barriers Other than Threats

There are a number of reasons, other than the threat of legal consequences, which cause people to refrain from homicide, including personal abhorrence of killing, commitment to religious and ethical value systems according to which such behavior is reprehensible, and other "extralegal restraints upon the commission of crime."[135] But apart from the legal consequences, there are few reasons to refrain from parking in a prohibited zone when there is something to be gained from parking there. This point may be illustrated by a hypothetical table comparing the behavior of persons tempted to commit homicide with those tempted to park illegally.

---

129. *Id.* at 124.
130. Cressey, *Other People's Money* (1953).
131. Lemert, "An Isolation and Closure Theory of Naive Check Forgery" (1953) 44 *J. Crim. L.C. and P.S.* 296–307, and "The Behavior System of the Systematic Check Forger" (1958) 6 *Social Problems* 141–49.
132. Sutherland, *The Professional Thief* (1937).
133. Sutherland, *White-collar Crime* (1950).
134. Camp, "Nothing to Lose: A Study of Bank Robbery in America" (1967) Ph.D. diss. Yale University. Cited by Bloch and Geis, *supra* note 120, at 289–90.
135. Andenaes *supra* note 118 (a), at 538.

TABLE 3

Hypothetical Distribution of 1,000 Persons Tempted to Commit Homicide and Illegal Parking

	Homicide	Parking
Restrained from offense as result of other barriers	990	50
Would have committed offense but were deterred by legal threat	5	800
Committed offense	5	150
Total	1,000	1,000

In Table 3, the complex of legal and social controls was more successful in restraining potential killers than in preventing illegal parking: a total of 5 persons committed homicide, compared with 150 parking violators. But the legal threat deterred only half of the potential homicides that were not prevented by other considerations, while deterring more than 80 percent of potential parking violators.

In the case of illegal parking, there is nothing unusual about the 800 persons who were restrained from considering this course of conduct only as the result of deterrence, or the 150 who were not restrained at all. There are very few social forces operating to make people fear or abhor such minor deviations from social norms. On the other hand, the small minority of people who continue to contemplate homicide, in spite of its being generally condemned and regarded with abhorrence, are clearly a special group, either very powerfully motivated toward homicide or insensitive to social values, or both.

Moreover, the characteristics that set this group apart from others may make them less responsive to the threat of consequences. Andenaes's generalization, "The more rational and normally motivated a specific violation may appear, the greater the importance of criminal sanctions as means of sustaining lawfulness,"[136] reflects the fact that our criteria of rationality and normality customarily include respect for and adherence to generally accepted social values.

136. *Id.* at 958.

Thus, while it may be true, as Norval Morris asserts, that "the effectiveness of deterrence varies in inverse proportion to the moral seriousness of the crime,"[137] the increased effectiveness of deterrence noted in relation to minor offenses may be due to the impact of threats on persons for whom a deterrent threat is not necessary to prevent more serious criminality. In other words, the apparent relative ineffectiveness of threats in relation to more serious offenses may be a function of the existence of powerful pre-barriers preventing breaches of the more basic provisions of the criminal law governing the protection of life, physical safety, and property.

iii Differences in Levels of Motivation

The literature of motivation provides an impressive array of theories, constructs, research methodologies, and empirical findings.[138] But we are not concerned here to discuss theories of motivation or analyze motivational processes. We make no attempt to use the technical terminology of experimental or social psychology. Our terms are those employed routinely in everyday life, and no special connotations are intended. The point which we wish to make is a relatively simple one.

For the individual who does not need a deterrent, the threat of consequences can be received and digested without tension or conflict, but in such cases processes other than threat will be responsible for conformity to legal commands. The notion of deterrence suggests that threats play a dynamic role in the behavior of some people, establishing barriers to conduct that would not exist without the threat and causing tendencies to violate the law to be replaced by patterns of conformity. Threats produce a motivational conflict between the reasons for avoiding threatened behavior provided by the threat and the motives for committing that behavior which lead to the need for external controls.

Discussing the credibility and severity of a threat helps to predict threat response by providing information about only one side of such a conflict: the drives to avoid criminal be-

137. Morris, *The Habitual Criminal* (1951) 13.
138. For a survey of the literature of motivation see Murphy, "Social Motivation," in Lindzey (ed.), 2 *Handbook of Social Psychology* (1954) 601–33.

havior that emanate from a particular threat. It is equally important to know what kind of drives, and of what intensity, are responsible for pressures toward deviation, for the balance between what is lost if crimes are committed and what will be lost if they are not committed will vary with the importance of the drives toward particular criminal acts. Thus, the same type of threat operating on the same person may be sufficiently influential to deter behavior that is weakly motivated but will fail to deter behavior that is strongly motivated.

The strength of a person's motivation toward a particular crime would appear to be a function of the importance of the drive he seeks to satisfy by criminal means and the availability of alternative means for satisfying the same drive. The strength of the drive that motivates criminal behavior has an obvious effect on amenability to deterrence: the man who steals because he is hungry or addicted to drugs is less likely to be deterred than the woman who shoplifts as a result of whim or the parking violator who is trying to save money or time. For certain people in certain situations, the drive toward committing a crime may be so strong that no threat will stop them.

When other means exist to satisfy the drives that lead to crime, deterrence is more effective. The man who can either steal or work to eat is surely more likely to be responsive to legal threats directed against stealing than the man who has to steal to eat.

Different types of crime may be associated with different levels of motivation, and this could account for some of the variation in the success of legal threats. Possessing and taking illegal drugs is, for the addicted person, the only available means of fulfilling strong drives. Andenaes speaks of "the overwhelming motivating power of the addiction."[139] To the extent that drug taking is preponderantly the behavior of addicts, the threat of consequences is likely to have less effect on the rate of this crime than on others.[140]

For the drug addict, shoplifting may be one of many means of obtaining money to support his habit; for other shoplifters the crime may be the result of a weakly motivated desire for

---

139. Andenaes, *supra* note 118 (a), at 539.
140. Chambliss, *supra* note 122, at 707–08.

more of the better things of life. The legal threat can operate with greater force on the weakly motivated shoplifter and result in keeping many members of this group law-abiding. If the drug addict has legal alternative means to obtain money, the threat aimed at shoplifting may deter him from shoplifting even though he continues to violate the law by taking drugs.

If, however, the drug addict's only alternative means of obtaining money for drugs are illegal, the credibility and severity of a threat directed at shoplifting may motivate him to use other illegal means of obtaining money. Insofar as a large number of potential shoplifters either are weakly motivated toward the drives for which they might steal or have alternative means of drive satisfaction available, the threat of consequences will be more likely to have a significant influence on the rate of this crime.

iv Differences in the Emotional Context

Andenaes remarks that it "is an old proposition" that "carefully planned acts are more easily deterred than those that result from a sudden, emotional impulse."[141] "Sudden emotional impulse" could be subsumed under the heading "Levels of Motivation." But it also connotes a particular context and raises some issues which deserve separate treatment, although the distinction may in some cases be only a matter of perspective.

The context in which decisions to commit or refrain from crime are made will presumably have some bearing on the relative influence of threats in the decisional process. Decisions that are made very quickly, as a reaction to a sudden impulse, may be less susceptible to the influence of threats than decisions that are arrived at over longer periods of time. Decisions about criminal conduct that are made when a person is in circumstances which provoke great emotional arousal may be less amenable to threats than decisions that occur when the potential criminal is less aroused, because very high degrees of emotional arousal may eclipse thoughts of future consequences by riveting all of the potential criminal's attention on his present situation.

---

141. Andenaes, *supra* note 118 (a), at 539.

Examples of crimes committed in such circumstances would be homicide or assault occurring as a result of a domestic quarrel or rape in cases of extreme sexual provocation. Here it is the particular situation which prevails over threat influence rather than just the motivational level of the individual as in the drug addiction example cited above. And insofar as particular types of crime are associated with highly emotive decisional environments, such differences in the emotional context of crime could help to explain why some threats are more effective than others.

A somewhat analogous context is that in which a lower level of inhibition prevails. The threat of consequences would appear to be less effective when decisions about criminal conduct are made under the influence of drugs or alcohol. The ineffectiveness of threat may in some cases be due to the increased affect and more uninhibited emotional expression resulting from drug or alcohol consumption. The presumed effect of alcohol becomes important if alcohol is more often associated with particular types of crime, such as homicide or violent assault, than with others.

The relation of context to threat effectiveness becomes important if it is determined that some crimes (such as homicide and certain sex offenses) are usually associated with such emotional contexts while others (such as illegal parking or shoplifting) are rarely so related. But the relation between emotional context and a specific type of crime will never be a complete one. There are, to be sure, coolly calculating potential killers and highly emotional shoplifters.

The association of particular emotional contexts with crime, or the association, dealt with in the preceding subsection, of particular levels of motivation with crime, will prove helpful in distinguishing between the different types of offender represented in the same offense group as well as in distinguishing between types of offenses. For example, the distinction between the amateur and the professional shoplifter may be as important in predicting threat responses as any distinction between shoplifters as a group and pickpockets.[142] But if a particular level of motivation is more often associated with one crime

---

142. See Cameron, *The Booster and the Snitch* (1966).

than another, the relation between motivation and crime need not be complete to explain differences in the impact of legal threats.

v Conclusion

As we indicated earlier, our classification of factors that might be associated with differences in the efficacy of threats is inevitably incomplete. To give only one example of a case we have not discussed, the presence of a group at the scene of a crime may affect threat responsiveness. And insofar as some types of crime (e.g., juvenile vandalism) are frequently group phenomena, this may be of considerable significance. Nevertheless, our scheme does appear to be consistent with predictions made by others about deterrent effectiveness in different types of crime. Professor Morris's prediction that deterrence is inversely related to the moral seriousness of the threatened behavior is explicable on the basis that minor crimes are more weakly motivated, are associated with lesser degrees of emotional arousal, are committed by broader cross sections of the population, and are characterized by fewer pre-barriers other than legal threats. Similarly, Professor Andenaes's observation that the more rational and normally motivated a crime, the greater is the importance of criminal sanctions as a means of preventing it, can be explained by the fact that there are pre-barriers to abnormal crimes in the form of moral and social inhibitions which keep most people from committing them.

The observation that crimes committed for material gain are more susceptible to deterrence than crimes of passion such as homicide and assault can be viewed as consistent with the analysis above (though, of course, not validated) because crimes of passion are associated with higher levels of emotional arousal, and there are more likely to be substitute methods of obtaining money (either lawfully or unlawfully) than substitute means for achieving the ends sought in aggressive crimes. It may also be the case that many potential property criminals are not powerfully motivated.

Our analysis is largely consistent with the theory advanced by Professor Chambliss that *instrumental* crime is more susceptible to deterrence than *expressive* crime.[143] Instrumental crime is defined as crime which "is instrumental to the attainment of some other goal,"[144] whereas an act of expressive crime "is committed because it is pleasurable in and of itself."[145]

Chambliss cites murder and drug addiction as being at one extreme of his typology and parking law violations as being at the other—"probably no one violates parking laws simply because it is pleasurable to do so."[146] In the light of this distinction Chambliss argues that expressive acts are "quite resistant to punishment as a deterrent," while instrumental acts "are more likely to be influenced by the threat or imposition of punishment."[147] As suggested above, this prediction will largely hold true, because there are more likely to be substitutes for instrumental behavior (where other means may be available for the attainment of an end which is external to the criminal act) than for expressive behavior (where the act itself is what the potential criminal wants).

However, the distinction between instrumental and expressive crime would not seem to be as clear where no substitute exists for a specific criminal means of obtaining an end. A pregnant woman seeking an abortion is trying to commit an instrumental act,[148] but this is her only means of avoiding childbirth. The nonsubstitutable nature of the act would suggest that the act would be difficult to deter, while its instrumental nature would tend in the opposite direction. With respect to a financially motivated doctor who is tempted to perform abortions, on the other hand, both the emphasis on available substitutes and the distinction between instrumental and expressive behavior would suggest that deterrence is more likely.

Suggesting that deterrence may be more difficult in some situations than in others is not the same as saying that deter-

143. Chambliss, *supra* note 122, at 708. See, for criticism of this distinction, Andenaes, *supra* note 118 (a), at 538–39.
144. Chambliss, *supra* note 122, at 708.
145. *Ibid.*
146. *Ibid.*
147. *Id.* at 712.
148. We owe this point to Professor Andenaes.

rence does not function at all for particular offenses. Even under unfavorable conditions, the threat of consequences may influence many people most of the time. Similarly, the fact that deterrence is more difficult with respect to some offenses does not mean that changes in the credibility or severity of threats will not result in marginal deterrence in these cases. But it does appear that marginal deterrent effects of changes in the conditions of a legal threat will be greatest when the conditions for deterrence are most favorable.

Increasing the perceived credibility of the threats relating to homicide and illegal parking may thus reduce the proportion of potential offenders of both kinds who become actual offenders. But similar changes in the content of the two threats will achieve a more dramatic increase in deterrence among weakly than among strongly motivated persons; in situations where the degree of emotional arousal associated with decisions about crime is low rather than high; and where the threat is the only major barrier to crime.

Because the classification of offense types in accordance with the likelihood of deterrence cannot produce positive statements about the presence or absence of a deterrent effect, it cannot be directly translated into policy. Even if marginal increments in the credibility of threats aimed at illegal parking will reduce that rate more substantially than would a similar measure against homicide, the social importance of preventing homicide may dictate that resources would be more wisely invested in deterring homicide. And the fact that legal threats operate with less effect on some types of potential criminals does not mean that other forms of social control will achieve better results.

For this reason it seems to us that Professor Chambliss is going considerably farther than the evidence warrants when, on the basis of his analysis, he suggests:

A truly rational system of justice is one that will maximize its effectiveness by imposing criminal sanctions where these act as an effective deterrent, and at the same time develop alternatives to punishment where it is found to be ineffective. The implication of this foregoing analysis would be that the legal system will have little effect in reducing the frequency of such things as excessive drinking, drug use, most murders, most sex offenses and aggravated assault. For these behaviors, alternative mechanisms of social control must be instituted.[149]

Unfortunately, even if predictions about the conditions that mitigate or strengthen deterrence in particular types of offense were completely accurate (and there is little present basis for this conclusion), such predictions could only provide statements about the relative likelihood of deterrence; and these would be insufficient foundations for ordering priorities in penal policy. Much more specific empirical research is necessary to determine whether particular countermeasures achieve a degree of deterrence sufficient to justify their costs.

Although we have been concerned here with differences between types of offense, exclusive stress on the nature of the offense can be misleading. It is one thing to say that an act like homicide is "quite resistant to punishment as a deterrent,"[150] for such an act may well be relatively insensitive to modest changes in penalty when the pre-barriers other than threat are strong and the consequences are both severe—the death penalty or life imprisonment. It is quite another thing to suggest that the homicide rate would be unaffected by a sharp decline in the penalty imposed when the pre-barriers other than threat are relatively weak, for example, in a "culture of violence." While the degree of marginal deterrence achieved by the higher penalty might still be less than in the case of parking offenses it does not follow that such a consideration should determine policy.

D Threat as Communication

The deterrent effect is sought by means of the multiple threats of punishment embodied in the criminal law, both through penalties provided for infringement and through examples supplied by law enforcement. It follows that communication can be of decisive importance in this process. For the effective operation of deterrence as a means of social control

---

149. Chambliss, *supra* note 122, at 714.
150. *Id.* at 712.

must depend, among other things, on the effective communication of threats of punishment and their concrete exemplifications to the public.[151]

Both the extent of communication and the way in which threats are communicated may affect the willingness of people to comply with their terms. Indeed, the deterrence threat may perhaps best be viewed as a form of advertising. Our analysis accordingly takes in both aspects of threat communication: the message and the medium.

i Public knowledge as a Threshold Requirement

Four conditions must be fulfilled if threats are to be effective as a means of crime control. First, unless members of an audience know that a behavior is prohibited, the prohibition cannot affect their conduct. Second, unless it is known that those who commit the prohibited behavior may be punished, the threat of punishment will not affect the rate of that behavior. Third, unless differences in the level of threatened punishment are perceived, increases in penalty can have no marginal deterrent effect. Fourth, if variations in rates of detection are to serve as marginal deterrents, knowledge of those variations must be transmitted in some fashion to potential offenders.

Only a very limited amount of research has been done into the extent of public knowledge of the existence and terms of legal threats. Accordingly, very little is known about the extent of such knowledge or about the sources from which people obtain what information they have. It is reasonable to suppose that most people have a fair idea of where the boundary between criminal and noncriminal behavior is drawn. However, many people do not know that some forms of behavior, which are not viewed as major infractions of the community's moral

---

151. Cf. "Punishment must be inefficacious ... where the penal provision ... is not conveyed to the notice of the person on whom it is intended to operate, as from want of due promulgation." Bentham, "Principles of Penal Law" 1 *Works* (1843) 397; and "A deterrent may be seen as something which changes the 'pay-off' of the criminal strategy ... and it is expected to change would-be offenders' assessment of the pay-off by action on *other* offenders. ... If the action taken in respect of *other* persons and *other* crimes is to influence the strategy of would-be offenders, an essential requirement is the *communication* of such action to those whom it is desired to deter" (author's italics). Wilkins, *supra* note 19, at 324.

code, are unlawful, and even greater numbers of people appear to be unaware when changes in the scope of the criminal law take place.

An example of widespread ignorance of a criminal law that has been on the books for many years was discovered through a survey of public knowledge of crime and penalties in Nebraska, where writing checks with insufficient funds on deposit to cover them constitutes a misdemeanor.[152] In a public opinion poll, 41 percent of Nebraska adult males declared that this behavior would not be criminal if arrangements to meet the obligation were eventually made.[153] Another public opinion poll, taken after England had abolished the prohibition against attempted suicide, showed that 76 percent of those polled were unaware that such a change in the law had taken place.[154] Both these cases may be considered exceptional however—the Nebraska case because the law was rarely enforced and the English one because of the unique character of the offense.

It is highly unlikely that public ignorance of the existence of legal prohibitions is widespread with respect to most forms of serious criminality. What is much more likely is that people are not informed about the specific penalties provided. Surveys in California[155] and Nebraska[156] have established that the public knows little about the legislatively proscribed minimum and maximum penalties for a variety of crimes. In California, only inmates of adult correctional facilities were able to give the correct answer more than a quarter of the time to a number of multiple-choice possibilities. Public knowledge of changes in the minimum and maximum punishments provided by law was also found to be quite low.[157]

Some years ago, Professor Ball, in an article "The Deter-

152. See Nebraska Revised Statutes §28–1213, 1943.
153. Poll conducted in 1968–69 by the Center for Studies in Criminal Justice at the University of Chicago, in collaboration with Professors Harvey Perlman and Allan Booth of the University of Nebraska.
154. See Walker and Argyle, "Does the Law Affect Moral Judgments?" (1964) 4 *Brit. J. Crim.* 572; see also Walker, "Morality and the Criminal Law" (1964) 11 *Howard Journal* 214.
155. Social Psychiatry Research Associates, *Public Knowledge of Criminal Penalties: A Research Report* (1968).
156. Poll 1968–69, *supra* note 153.
157. *Supra* note 5.

rence Concept in Criminology and Law," wrote that "the deterrent effect of the law obviously depends upon the individual's knowledge of the law and the punishment prescribed. . . . The same is the case with respect to particular penalties."[158]

But findings of the type cited above do not indicate that deterrence is not possible among those who do not know the specific penalty provided for violations of criminal law. As long as it is widely known that behavior is punished, this information alone could have a significant deterrent effect. It has even been suggested by Norval Morris that a threat which produces uncertainty about what penalties are imposed for violation may be a more effective deterrent than complete knowledge about sanctions.[159] And Leslie Wilkins has asked whether an offender may not be deterred "only because he has beliefs about what might happen to him which are incorrect."[160] In any event it seems probable that vague forebodings will provide a sufficient basis for deterrence for most people at most times when the possibility of criminal behavior is considered. Nevertheless, if people are insensitive to *shifts* in the level of punishment threatened for particular acts, *increasing* punishment levels will not increase the deterrent effectiveness of threats.

At the same time, the finding that most people do not know specific provisions in the penal code cannot be considered conclusive evidence that higher penalties do not produce marginal general deterrence for two reasons. In the first place, higher penalties might affect perceptions without engendering precise knowledge. And in the second place, even if only 10 percent of a population knows the specific penalty for a crime, that 10 percent could include the overwhelming majority of those for whom the threat of punishment is necessary.

Higher penalties *might* lead those who cannot correctly estimate the penalty for an offense to think it higher than they would if the penalty were not increased. Comparison could be made between areas where the penalties differ widely, to see whether public estimates of the severity of punishment also

158. Ball, "The Deterrence Concept in Criminology and Law" (1955) 46 *J. Crim. L.C. and P.S.* 351.
159. Morris, *supra* note 137, at 12.
160. Wilkins, *supra* note 124, at 119.

differ. And in order to determine whether the potential criminal is more likely to know specific penalty levels than the average citizen, high-risk groups could be asked about penalty levels, and their answers could be compared with answers given by the general public. For a number of reasons, neither strategy would produce incontrovertible propositions on the subject, but both methods show promise of increasing knowledge.[161]

To date, no comparison of public penalty estimates in high- and low-penalty areas has been made, but preliminary studies have investigated whether high-risk groups are better informed than the general public. In California it was found that Adult Authority prison inmates, the highest-risk group of all, showed a remarkably high level of knowledge about maximum and minimum penalties for most types of serious crime and were sensitive to changes in penalties.[162] In addition, college students were able to reply correctly more often than any other group that the legally prescribed penalties for possession of marijuana had not been changed recently.[163]

On the other hand, inmates of Youth Authority penal facilities were not better informed than the general public, even though the former group was much more likely to commit crime in the future. (At the same time it is reasonable to presume that these juveniles would be aware of juvenile court policy.) Equally revealing is the fact that students from high schools in high-delinquency areas knew just as little about minimum and maximum adult penalties as students from high schools in low-delinquency areas.[164]

---

161. See chap. 5, *infra.*
162. The California data show the following contrast in percentage of sample with correct answers (*supra* note 155):

	Public	Prisoners
First-degree robbery	8%	85%
Assault	35%	59%
Rape with injury	16%	43%
Forgery	17%	50%

163. 65 percent of the college students correctly answered that no change in penalty had occurred, compared to 47 percent of adult prisoners and 38 percent of high school students in a low-delinquency area, the second and third highest correct-answer groups on this question. Unpublished data taken from the California poll, conducted by Social Psychiatry Research Associates (1968) *supra* note 155.
164. *Supra* note 155.

With the exception of college students' awareness of marijuana penalties, it would thus appear that many potential offenders have levels of information as low as those demonstrated by the general public; but the firsthand experience with punishment in adult prison facilities is a great teacher.[165] The exception is significant, however, in that it reflects the importance of salience in penalty knowledge. The California and Nebraska data also show that a greater proportion of the general public gave correct answers about drunk driving than about any other crime.[166]

Sophistication is another important factor, for not only are high school students more ignorant of penalties than are college students, but they are *equally* ignorant of penalties whether they come from high- or low-delinquency areas. The fact that the differences between groups are sharp suggests that peer group contact is important insofar as it intensifies salience and provides a medium for word-of-mouth communication.

On the basis of the available information, the following tentative hypotheses may be advanced. Unless he is sophisticated, a person who is more likely to commit crimes at some future time does not have much more general knowledge about penalties than the rest of the population. At the same time, the more likely a person is to commit a crime, the more likely he is to know the penalty for that particular crime as opposed to other crimes. Lastly, prison inmates know more about the penalties provided by the criminal law than the general public.

These tentative findings cast some doubt on the breadth, although not the substantiality, of any marginal general deterrent effect attributable to higher minimum and maximum sentencing provisions alone. More important, perhaps, for present purposes, such findings show that communication of threats is neither automatic nor complete in the criminal justice system. Variations in the way threats are communicated may lead to different levels of public awareness, and this in turn may affect the likelihood and degree of deterrence.

If information is to play a role in deterring individuals from criminal conduct, they must have access to it and must remem-

165. *Ibid.*
166. *Supra* notes 153 and 155.

ber it at the time that decisions about criminal conduct are made. With this task as a goal, effective communication will require that the message be delivered in ways that will make members of the threatened audience pay attention and remember the information being conveyed; and, if possible, that the information contained in the threat be associated with the threatened behavior in the minds of the audience so that their recollection of the terms of the threat will be greatest when it is most needed—at the time when criminal alternatives are considered.

Passing a new law will, by itself, have no effect on the perception of those whose conduct the law seeks to alter. Formal and informal channels of communication—including newspaper and television accounts of the new threat and stories of those punished for lawbreaking—will bring the message to members of the threatened audience. The California prison survey suggests that word of mouth, in many circumstances, is the most successful means of communication; and also that membership of a group that is aware of the penalties is necessary for communications. One research finding indicates that, in order to reach and influence most members of the threatened audience, the threat will have to be repeated a number of times, with each repetition not only increasing the number of people exposed to the threat but heightening the comprehension of those who have been previously exposed.[167]

In many situations, authorities seek to capture the attention of a threatened audience by using examples of those punished for law violations. Judges sentence offenders with the object that potential criminals will hear of the sentence and that this

---

167. See Barmack and Payne, "The Lackland Accident Countermeasure Experiment" (1961) 40 *Highway Research Board Proceedings*, 513 (1961). The Lackland experiment is one of the few investigations of propaganda techniques used to alter conduct in a field setting. The authors report a three-month lag between the introduction of the countermeasure (an information and persuasion campaign with some changes in the threatened consequences for accident records) and signs of a significant effect. One explanation of this lag is that "the spread of information about the countermeasure is an accretive process which necessitates repeated announcements . . . and word-of-mouth communication until a substantial majority of the population becomes aware of the countermeasure."

message will result in general deterrence.[168] In recent years, the administration of some punishments, notably the death penalty, has galvanized public attention. In other countries, the names and punishments meted out to tax offenders are published both as a punishment for violation and as a mechanism for drawing the attention of the community to the existence of punishment for the violation. While the aim of such practices is to enhance deterrence by drawing the attention of members of the threatened audience to the punishment precept, there is little hard evidence to indicate that they have succeeded.

Two studies of the homicide rate just before and just after death sentences in Philadelphia and executions in California do not provide evidence of any net reduction in homicide rate that could be attributed to publicity about the penalties.[169] Other programs for drawing attention to punishment have not been evaluated. The capital punishment case may be exceptional, because with this type of crime the emotional arousal and power of suggestion associated with the death penalty and with the offense of homicide may actually create homicidal tensions at the same time as it may deter some potential offenders.[170] In other cases, drawing attention to episodes of punishment may have counterdeterrent effects on those individuals who imagined the penalty to be worse than it was. More often, however, it would seem likely that publicity of this kind, if it has any effect, will tend in the direction of enhancing deterrence.

168. A federal judge in Chicago was quoted by the *Chicago Sun Times* in 1967 as stating, at the time of sentence, that the penalty he regularly fixes for draft-law violators has recently been increased as the result of increased violation. An even more explicit case of a court's sentencing offenders on the assumption that potential offenders were listening closely was one chapter of the story of the Great Train Robbery in Great Britain. See 80 *Law Qtly Rev.* (1964) 473.

169. See the studies of Savitz and Graves, reprinted in Bedau (ed.), *The Death Penalty in America* 1967 at 315–32.

170. In Dr. Graves's study, the homicide rate before executions was reported to be above average, while the rate just after executions was reported to be below average, consistent with the theory that increased arousal attributable to the atmosphere leading up to the execution could have affected the rate of homicide. See *id.*, at 329. Given the great number of factors that could influence the apparent findings, the study must be viewed as merely suggestive.

A special problem in the communication of information about threat and punishment is that of bringing such considerations to the attention of potential law violators at the time that decisions about law violation are to be made. The moment of truth in the life of a potential delinquent will seldom take place in the local law library. A threatening agency must either try to get its message through at the time when such decisions are made, or seek to plant the association between crime and punishment so firmly in the minds of potential offenders that the thought of penalties will automatically accompany any consideration of the threatened behavior.

On occasion, it is possible to place reminders of prohibition and penalty at the scene. Speed limit signs and other posted notices in public places both serve as notice that certain behavior is forbidden and act as reminders that unpleasant consequences will accompany apprehension. The recent campaign in Michigan to post signs that read *Drunk drivers go to jail* made explicit this second function of on-site legal commands.

Most legal threats, however, cannot be directly inserted by the threatening agency at the site of possible law violation. And an attempt to create automatic association between crime and penalty among those tempted to transgress is likely to produce more consumer resistance than even the most unpalatable of commercial products. It might perhaps best be compared to the task of getting people to associate candy with dentists.

ii Threat as Persuasive Appeal

The communication involved in a threat is not merely the disinterested dissemination of information or factual material; it is designed to produce a response in terms of attitude and behavior. So if the first task of a threatening agency is the communication of information, its second task is persuasion. Every threat is, in effect, an agency appeal designed to reduce the quantity of threatened behavior. And since "information alone seldom provides sufficient impetus to change attitudes or actions toward a given object,"[171] it is important to consider those aspects of the communication process which relate spe-

171. Leventhal, Singer, and Jones, "Effects of Fear and Specificity of Recommendation upon Attitudes and Behavior" (1965) 2 *J. Pers. and Soc. Psych.* 20.

cifically to the arousal of motives and the formation and modification of attitudes.

Psychologists have used the expression *threat appeal* to refer to those contents of a persuasive communication which allude to or describe unfavorable consequences that are alleged to result from failure to adopt the communicator's recommendations.[172] In view of the nature of the legal threat it is not surprising that notices often consist of no more than heavy emphasis on the unpleasant consequences of being caught.

Emphasis is confined in most cases to the maximum penalty possible for an offense, and appeals frequently read like that cited above relating to the consequences of drunk driving. Other examples might be *Littering is punishable by $500 fine*, or perhaps *False statements on this document constitute perjury and are punishable by imprisonment*.

Another very common technique involves emphasizing the probability that violation will lead to apprehension. An agency will often tell members of the threatened audience about the means available for detecting violations; two frequent instances of this type of threat appeal are *Speed timed by radar*, and *Our cameras are making a confidential record of this transaction*. Similarly, private detective agencies and security organizations, in apparent pursuit of general deterrence as well as more conventional advertising, will frequently post notices in conspicuous places to the effect that they service a particular premises.

Persuasive techniques employed are not confined to the use of "threat appeal." Sometimes, although much less commonly, agency appeals try to diminish the attractiveness of threatened behaviors, or seek to secure compliance by means of appeals to the honesty, patriotism, or civic pride of the threatened audience. Recent examples of this approach are *Every litter bit hurts*, and *Only you can prevent forest fires*. Most commonly appeals of this nature are used as an adjunct to the threat of sanctions rather than as a substitute for the threat. Some campaigns for tax compliance mounted by the Internal

172. Hovland, Janis, and Kelley. *Communication and Persuasion* (1953) 60.

Revenue Service, for example, combine appeals to duty or conscience with threat of sanction.[173]

But for the most part the emphasis has always been on "threat appeal." Insofar as threat appeals are sometimes used to arouse fear, we may question whether fear arousal can contribute to the overall effectiveness of the communication and, in particular, to its deterrent effect. Sometimes "dire consequences are emphasized to the point where the audience becomes extremely apprehensive and upset."[174] Thus, in the belief that "shaking up" an audience will focus attention on the foolishness and dangerousness of bad driving, many local traffic courts and traffic safety programs show films that depict violence on the highway in the most graphic of terms.[175]

The use of threat appeals designed to arouse fear is employed in publicity campaigns by health authorities and road safety organizations as well as by politicians, both in support of national defense programs and as a feature of antiwar propaganda. The fact that it "is a prominent feature of many mass communications"[176] has led a number of researchers —though not in the field of law—to investigate the conditions under which such messages persuade.

The pioneer study of the effect of fear-arousing communications was published by Janis and Feshbach in 1953.[177] In that study, randomly selected groups of Connecticut high school students heard three different types of lecture on dental hygiene. One group heard a lecture designed to have a strong fear appeal, with frequent references to pain, harm to the teeth, and diseased gums. The second group heard a milder presentation

173. Schwartz and Orleans, "On Legal Sanctions" (1967) 34 *U. Chi. L. Rev.* 274–300, report a field experiment on motivational factors affecting compliance with federal income tax laws in which an attempt was made to distinguish and compare the effects of sanction threats and appeals to conscience.

174. Hovland, Janis, and Kelley, *supra* note 172, at 60.

175. The advertising description of one such film, *Signal 30*, stresses the blood-and-gore aspects (in color) as educational. The picture has been used in a number of driver-improvement courses administered by traffic courts.

176. Hovland, Janis, and Kelley *supra* note 172, at 61.

177. Janis and Feshbach, "Effects of Fear-Arousing Communications" (1953) 48 *J. Abnormal and Soc. Psych.* 78–92.

with less emphasis on the consequence of tooth neglect and only a moderate degree of fear appeal. The third group heard a lecture in which most of the threat material was replaced by neutral informative material which focused on other reasons why dental hygiene was a good idea.

The results of the experiment indicated that the group exposed to the strong fear appeal felt much more worried about the condition of their teeth than the other two groups. Those subjected to the moderate appeal tended to feel more worried then the minimal group. Subsequently, however, the students were questioned in order to discover to what extent they were following the specific recommendations relating to dental hygiene which all three forms of the talk contained. It was found that the greatest amount of conformity was produced by the communication containing the least amount of fear-arousing material.

When a similar experiment was repeated with different subjects, no significant difference was found between the effects of the three different threat intensities.[178] Other experiments with the fear-arousing content of appeals dealing with such things as the use of automobile seat belts[179] and the taking of inoculations[180] have produced a variety of results which, while not necessarily inconsistent with one another, do not furnish us with any firmly established general conclusions about the effectiveness of threat appeals in persuasive communications.

It has been found that fear at relatively low levels may produce increased attitude change,[181] whereas high fear levels may increase resistance to persuasion.[182] It has also been found that fear-arousing appeals may motivate effort to avoid the anxiety-evoking thoughts induced by them[183] and even lead

178. Moltz and Thistlethwaite, "Attitude Modification and Anxiety Reduction" (1955) 50 *J. Abnormal and Soc. Psych.* 231–37.

179. Berkowitz and Cottingham, "The Interest Value and Relevance of Fear Arousing Communications" (1960) 60 *J. Abnormal and Soc. Psych.* 37–43.

180. Leventhal, Singer, and Jones, *supra* note 171.

181. Berkowitz and Cottingham, *supra* note 179.

182. Janis and Terwilliger, "An Experimental Study of Psychological Resistances to Fear Arousing Communications" (1962) 65 *J. Abnormal and Soc. Psych.* 403–10.

183. Hovland, Janis, and Kelley, *supra* note 172, at 78–79.

to deliberate rejection "motivated by aggression."[184] Another finding is that the effects of fear dissipate rapidly with the passage of time.[185]

One explanation for the variety of unintended effects that have been recorded is that the communication stimuli interact in the process of communication with various predisposing factors in the audience. Thus, it appears that fear-arousing approaches may have opposite effects upon attitude change depending on a subject's initial position and predispositions, and may in some cases strengthen "incorrect" responses more than "correct" responses.[186]

While much suggestive material has emerged from studies of the conditions under which fear-arousing appeals are effective or ineffective, it is not possible to extrapolate from them to the operation of legal threats. This is of course partly because findings to date are too inconclusive, but it is also because the appeals and audiences used for experimental purposes differ very greatly from those involved in most legal threats. In the first place, the exposure of individuals in real-life situations to communications is both voluntary and likely to be highly selective. In the second place, the legal threat is made by an agency with the power to create unpleasantness, unlike the persuader in the dental hygiene lecture who has no power to make his prophecies come true. Carl Hovland and his Yale associates suggest in this connection that "where the communicator has the *power* to administer severe punishments and the audience has already learned not to ignore his threats, strong fear appeals are likely to induce a high degree of conformity"[187] (our italics).

That suggestion, however, was made in reference to prisoners in German concentration camps who, "presumably as a consequence of repeated threats of severe deprivation and torture," began to manifest various signs of "identification with

184. *Id.* at 79 and 86.

185. Leventhal and Niles, "Persistence of Influence for Varying Durations of Exposure to Threat Stimuli" (1965) 16 *Psychological Reports* 223–33.

186. Weiss et al., "Argument Strength, Delay of Argument, and Anxiety in the 'Conditioning' and 'Selective Learning' of Attitudes" (1963) 67 *J. Abnormal and Soc. Psych.* 157–65.

187. Hovland, Janis, and Kelley *supra* note 172, at 82.

the aggressor."[188] This too can hardly be regarded as directly relevant to the behavior of ordinary citizens facing the somewhat milder threat appeals to be encountered in a free society.

What can be said is that fear arousal may not be a consistently successful method of securing compliance. Moreover, viewed collectively, these studies do make a strong case for testing the effectiveness of fear-arousing appeals in criminal law and related areas.[189] With the development of new techniques and methods in the rapidly expanding field of communications research it should be possible to devise methods of obtaining relevant knowledge from systematic studies.

iii Personalizing Threats

In the model of simple deterrence which is implicit in the writings of Bentham and others of the so-called classical school of criminology[190] it is assumed that the threat of punishment should be issued to society in general by its embodiment in the criminal law and the examples supplied by its enforcement. Yet that threat and the appeal to refrain from criminal conduct can be issued in many different ways: to society in general; to particular groups; to an audience that has been physically assembled to hear about a threat; or even to individuals, by means of letters or personal interviews.

Personal interviews, being expensive, will typically occur only among special high-risk groups (usually prior offenders) or in experiments designed to establish whether different types of communication affect behavior. But there is some basis for believing that the more personalized a particular communication may be, the greater its chances of affecting behavior.

Since the advent of the computer, some commercial firms

---

188. *Ibid.*
189. Perhaps the best place to start such an investigation would be in the related areas of traffic safety and traffic law. The National Safety Council has conducted holiday safety campaigns for some time that stress the number of deaths expected in a given holiday period, and these campaigns have been criticized in recent years. Traffic courts use fear-arousing materials as a part of driver education programs which they compel some offenders to attend. Large numbers of drivers are exposed to such appeals, and the stakes in the traffic safety area are higher than anywhere else in the criminal justice system in terms of lives lost and property damage.
190. Vold, *Theoretical Criminology* (1958) 14–24.

go to great lengths to personalize advertising appeals—printing the name and address of the recipient on the outside of the envelope in a mailing campaign and addressing the recipient by name a number of times in the course of presenting their appeal.[191] With respect to threats, this type of practice might influence behavior by producing the impression among members of an audience that somebody is watching them personally.

An interesting finding emerged from a study dealing with the Driver Improvement Meetings program in California. Under this program offenders were sent personal letters beginning, "The records of the Department of Motor Vehicles show that you may be a negligent operator as defined by law," mentioning the possibility of license suspension or revocation and inviting attendance at a Driver Improvement Meeting. The program proved an effective means of reducing traffic convictions among persons eligible for it, but was equally effective for those who merely received the notice but failed to appear at the meeting.[192]

Field experiments designed to test the effects of particular types of appeals have employed personalized letters and interviews with mixed success. In one comparative test, referred to above, of normative appeals (*Paying taxes helps your country*) and threatening appeals (*Computers can catch you*), both appeals being issued by a nongovernmental agency, there was a significant increase in the amount of income reported and the amount of taxes actually paid by subjects of both appeals.[193] This tax experiment can hardly be viewed as conclusive evidence that personalized appeals have more influence than general appeals, since no controlled comparisons were made with similar groups that had been exposed to nonpersonalized appeals with the same content. But the results obtained in this experiment suggest that the effects of personalization should be tested. And the possibility that personalization contributed

191. Publishers Clearing House, a magazine sales firm, used name and local residence references twice in the same page of one 1969 contest promotion letter. Reader's Digest used six different references to the recipient's name and address, besides referring to two other local residents by name, in a 1969 contest promotion.
192. Coppin, Marsh, and Peck. *A Re-evaluation of Group Driver Improvement Meetings* (1965) 15–20.
193. Schwartz and Orleans, *supra* note 173.

to the effect of the experiment is an obstacle to any conclusion that less personalized appeals of the same type as those used in the tax study would have had the same effects.

Most forms of communication are far less costly than personal interviews. In cases where deficiencies of information or attention may impair the efficacy of threats, correcting these deficiencies will usually prove less expensive than other changes designed to increase threat effectiveness. To the extent that changes in communication can improve the effectiveness of threats, and that extent is presently unknown, a failure to take communication into account will result in employing more costly methods of reducing crime than are necessary.

iv Conclusion

It is not suggested that a complete understanding of the effects of threats on behavior is attainable by considering the legal system as a branch of the advertising profession; nor is there much danger that considering threat as communication will lead to overemphasis by officials on this aspect of deterrence. Nevertheless, the communication of legal threats is analogous to the advertising function in that it must compete for attention, must convey information, and must, if it is to serve its purpose, persuade.

A variety of special problems arise in the field of deterrence which have no exact counterpart in other areas. In particular, decisions about communications are necessarily dependent upon other deterrence variables. Thus, the decision whether to emphasize the nature of the penalty or the probability of apprehension must depend upon which is the most effective deterrent. So in order to determine what to stress in the communications process we have to know what deters.

Not only do legal threats have to compete with other types of communication; they have also to compete with each other. The most effective use of communication resources in this field will depend on a variety of factors, including the differential sensitivity of behaviors to threat, priorities in crime prevention, and the effectiveness of various types of threat.

Finally, and here the analogy with advertising is clear, attention has to be paid to demographic factors. In some cases optimal effectiveness might be achieved by the widest possible dissemination of a threat. This might apply to noncompliance with certain federal income tax laws, for example. In regard to other types of offense it is likely that communication through more specific channels to particular marginal groups of potential offenders would be more effective.[194]

In the last analysis, variation in the substance of threats is probably more important than variation in form. But to conceive threat as communication makes explicit the fact that the perceptions of an audience, rather than the threat as intended by the agency, will determine the degree to which legal threats will achieve desired goals. Similarly, a communication perspective clarifies the role that assumptions about public knowledge play in predictions about the outcome of threats which stress variations in the probability of apprehension and the severity of consequences. For example, later in the text we confront the assertion that increasing the probability of apprehension serves as a more effective marginal general deterrent to crime than increasing the severity of threatened consequences. Whatever might be the theoretical justification for this generalization, evidence in its support will be limited to the effect of actual increases or decreases in the severity of penalties. If penalty knowledge is usually more limited than knowledge of the number of police or means of apprehension, then the actual deterrent effect of increases in severity may be lower than the potential effects, and failures of communication may be mistaken for indications that perceived severity is not a significant variable. Extensive publicity and increased severity of sanctions may conjointly achieve substantial marginal general deterrence. And the impression that penalties are high may be easier to maintain, even if untrue, than the impression that chances of apprehension are great. This may be the case, for instance, in low-apprehension offenses like drunk driving and tax cheating, when a substantial proportion of the population will have experience with chances of apprehension (they drove after drinking) but not with penalties (they were not apprehended). We raise this possibility as one illustration of the way in which communication issues should be considered in interpreting data as well as in the design of crime control policy.

194. Zimring and Hawkins, "Deterrence and Marginal Groups" (1968) 5 *J. Research in Crime and Delinq.* 100–114.

E Probability, Applicability, and Credibility

We have considered public knowledge of the existence of a legal threat as a necessary condition of efficacy. But two further conditions must also be fulfilled: (1) members of the threatened audience must believe that the agency intends the threat to be applicable to them, and (2) they must believe that the agency is capable of enforcing the threat. These conditions we shall refer to as the *applicability* and the *credibility* of threats.

i Applicability

Members of an audience will not fear the imposition of threatened consequences unless they are persuaded that the threat is meant to apply to them. When they are not so persuaded, they will enjoy a feeling of immunity which is much more basic and fundamental than would be derived from a perceived failure of enforcement. For an exemption which is seen as an expression of a threatening agency's policy provides a degree of assurance much greater than the merely contingent immunity which is the unintended result of deficiencies in the law enforcement practice.

If a certain type of behavior, although actually prohibited by statute, has not been prosecuted and appears to have been tolerated by the authorities for a period of time, the public may come to believe that the threatening agency does not seriously intend the legal threat. We shall refer to this type of exemption from prosecution as a *general immunity*.

In other cases there may be a pattern of selective enforcement in which the discrimination relates not to a class of behavior but to a class of persons. When a threat is issued to society in general, but only certain classes are caught and punished, members of a class that goes unpunished may come to regard themselves as members of an elite who are exempted from the threat. They may recognize the threat as genuine but feel that it is directed at others and not to them. In other words, they will regard themselves as enjoying a *status immunity*.

In these two cases, because the immunity is interpreted as an expression of the threatening agency's will rather than a reflection of its inability, not only will the threat be inoperative as a simple deterrent, but any moral or educative force it might have possessed will be neturalized by the absence of enforcement. In the first example the public may cease to regard the behavior as wrong. In the second, those who are exempt from arrest and prosecutions are likely, if somewhat less so than in the first example, to cease to regard the behavior as wrong, at least for members of the elite group to which they belong.

A study by Professor Chambliss of penalty and enforcement practices in regard to parking regulations at a midwestern university[195] provides an illustration of apparent status immunity. Campus police for some time had ticketed all cars found in *No parking* zones, but nothing had been done to collect the fines from faculty members who had been ticketed but did not voluntarily pay. When the parking problem grew worse, the university publicized a new policy, increasing the fine for multiple offenders and announcing that parking fines would henceforth be deducted from faculty paychecks. After the new policy was announced, the rate of prohibited parking by faculty members decreased. But this decrease was largely confined to those who had been the most persistent offenders before the change— those who had not in fact paid the fines under the old system.[196] Thus, it seems likely that the announcement that faculty members would be fined, rather than the increase in fine, was responsible for most of the decrease in prohibited parking. Before the change in policy, nonpaying faculty members could reason that their cars received tickets because the police could not distinguish them from student cars, and that the nonenforcement of the fines showed that the university did not mean the parking restrictions to apply to them. For such a group, the new policy might have been the first notice that *their* parking behavior was *really forbidden*.

In much the same way, when laws against gambling or holding unlicensed parades are not enforced against church bingo or parading Elks, those groups may continue to violate such laws without fear of apprehension and without notice that their behavior is considered wrongful by the threatening agency. In

195. Chambliss, "The Deterrent Influence of Punishment" (1966) 12 *Crime and Delinq.* 70–75.
196. *Id.* at 72 and 75.

these circumstances, the threat of consequences may not produce even the moral impetus to abide by the law that might accompany knowledge that the conduct was considered wrongful.

It is important to distinguish between the kinds of general and status *immunity* which appear to be guaranteed by law enforcement policy and the *impunity* which may be enjoyed by offenders because of sporadic or inefficient law enforcement. In the first case, those threatened do not believe that the threatening agency wishes to apprehend and punish them. So not only do they have no fear of the threatened consequences, but they do not regard their behavior as criminal. In effect, there is nullification of the law both in that it is inoperative and because the negative social connotations normally conveyed by a prohibition are canceled.

The situation is very different where the threatening agency actively seeks to apprehend and punish offenders but is unable to do so in all cases. For in this case it is not the agency's will but rather its ability which is in question. Even though the chances of impunity for some offenses may be very great indeed, the law is not thereby regarded as abrogated. And the deterrent efficacy of the threat of punishment, although diminished, will rarely be extinguished.

ii Credibility

Nevertheless, if audience members are to be deterred from committing a threatened behavior because they fear the imposition of consequences, they must believe that the threatening agency is capable of catching and punishing some offenders. This does not mean that there must be no unsolved crimes. It has been estimated that in England and Wales offenders in general have three chances in four of committing a single major offense without detection.[197] Yet even a level of general impunity of this order does not mean that the threat of punishment will be inoperative.

It seems likely that for most people at most times, especially with respect to serious crimes, the threshold at which a deterrent effect may be produced will be the perception merely that they *might* be caught. In most cases the unpleasantness of the

197. McClintock, et al. *Crime in England and Wales* (1968) 120–25.

consequences of apprehension will be sufficient to outweigh the attractiveness of the criminal behavior. Even a small chance of highly unpleasant consequences is something which most people do not like to risk.[198]

This is not to say that variations in the perceived probability of apprehension will not have an effect on *whether* people violate and *how often* they violate the law; in the criminological literature there can be found considerable support for the view that increasing the risk of punishment will increase the degree of deterrence. But most of the authorities confine themselves to statements of a highly general character.

"It has been affirmed and reaffirmed," says Professor Radzinowicz, "by leading penal experts and criminologists in virtually every country and ever since the beginning of the nineteenth century, that if punishment could be made certain almost all crime would be eliminated."[199] Most often this consensus is expressed in statements to the effect that "the degree of risk of detection and conviction is of paramount importance to the preventive effects of the penal law."[200] Some writers express a faith in the marginal deterrent effect of comprehensive enforcement, while doubting that increased penalties pay similar dividends. Dr. Temple declares: "The effectiveness of a deterrent is derived less from its severity than from its certainty."[201]

Although the objective probability that commission of a crime will lead to imposition of consequences is of unquestioned importance to deterrence and will help explain why some threats operate more effectively than others, an exclusive emphasis on objective probability may be misleading for two reasons. In the first place, if audience members perceive that a threat applies to them, the moral message that the behavior is forbidden can influence law-abiding people to refrain from crime even if the probability of apprehension is quite low. Pro-

---

198. See Edwards, "Information Processing, Decision Making, and Highway Safety," in O'Day (ed.), *Driver Behavior: Cause and Effect* (1968) 165–80.
199. Radzinowicz, Preface to McClintock and Gibson, *Robbery in London* (1961) x.
200. Andenaes, *supra* note 118, at 960.
201. Temple, *The Ethics of Penal Action* (1934) 33.

fessor Andenaes has argued that despite "the high rate of illegal abortions, there are probably few areas where so little enforcement creates so much prevention as in the field of abortion."[202] This occurs, he says, not only because "the medical profession on the whole is quite susceptible to the threat of law and the censure of society," but also because this "is an area of the law in which the law may itself have a moral impact. If abortions were legalized women would find it easier to overcome the feeling of guilt that now often accompanies the act."[203]

In the second place, to cite Andenaes again, "the decisive factor in creating the deterrent effect is, of course, not the objective risk of detection but the risk of it as it is calculated by the potential criminal."[204] In other words, predictions about the effectiveness of threats that are based on objective probabilities of apprehension may be inaccurate, because subjective judgments about personal chances of being caught, rather than the cold mathematics of crime, will determine how an individual responds to the threat of consequences—and the relationship between such judgments and objective probabilities is imperfect. "It seems reasonably safe to assume that for most serious offences the offender does not know the true probability of being caught . . . ," says Leslie Wilkins. "May not some people over-estimate the risk? . . . It is certain that people's actions are determined by what they believe to be true rather than by what is in fact true. There may be little association between fact and belief."[205]

We have to recognize that many factors other than objective probability, such as personal feelings of optimism or pessimism, or propaganda about the chances of apprehension, may play an important role in personal judgments about the element of risk in relation to a specific crime.[206] Emphasis on the objective probabilities of apprehension may make us unaware of how and when changes in enforcement affect the perceptions of a threatened audience. For such changes may have a gradual

202. Andenaes, *supra* note 118 (a), at 545.
203. *Ibid.*
204. Andenaes, *supra* note 118, at 963.
205. Wilkins, *supra* note 124, at 119.
206. See the discussion and references cited *supra* chap. 4, sec. 1, subsec. B (i), (ii), and (iii); and also *infra* chap. 4, sec. 1, subsec. G (i).

rather than immediate effect on subjective judgments about risk, and changes in the objective chances of apprehension, insofar as they have an effect on people's perceptions, may affect some people differently than others.

iii Certainty and Credibility

Stimuli that may condition the perceived credibility of legal threats include

1. Publicity about crime detection rates;
2. Publicity about the apprehension or conviction of criminals (e.g., *Round up of drug sellers underway* or *Bank cashier jailed for embezzlement*)
3. Publicity about new enforcement methods (e.g., *Computers enlisted in war against false alarms*)
4. Direct or word-of-mouth experience of enforcement presence (e.g., more policemen on the street)
5. Direct or word-of-mouth experience of actual enforcement (e.g., being checked or arrested by police)

Of all these influences, it seems probable that direct personal experience, when it occurs, will have the most potent effect on perceptions of credibility. If a man drives under the influence of alcohol and is apprehended by the police, the experience is likely to increase his estimate of the risk of apprehension he will incur if he repeats such conduct. A similar change in perception can be expected if a person is stopped by police in a check for drunk driving but gets off because he is not under the influence of alcohol at the time.

News that friends or relatives have been apprehended or inspected will have a similar effect, though probably to a lesser degree than first-person experience. By the same token, committing a crime without being apprehended, or knowing of people who commit offenses without detection, will lower personal estimates of the risks involved in a particular crime.

A Swedish survey of drivers provides evidence which, while not wholly conclusive, suggests that personal experience with apprehension machinery not only increases perceived risk of apprehension, but decreases the rate of drunk driving among those who have been exposed to such experience. In that survey, drivers who reported having been stopped and screened by

Swedish traffic control police had less subsequent drunk driving than unchecked drivers.[207]

There is rather less reason to assume that personal experience with increases in the number of police, and nothing more, will reduce crime. It is true that in New York City the rate of street crime decreased after the saturation of a small high-crime-rate area with extra police.[208] But because the New York experiment, while increasing the presence of enforcement personnel, also succeeded in increasing the objective likelihood of detection, this study does not necessarily show that enforcement presence has an independent influence on the credibility of threats.[209]

Overall, there will be a direct relation between increased objective probability of apprehension and increases in the perceived credibility of threats that result from personal experience with apprehension machinery. The number of persons exposed to apprehension will increase and decrease as the degree of detection increases and decreases. For the whole of a particular audience, then, changes in perceived credibility based on personal experience will occur only as a result of changes in the actual probability of apprehension.

With respect to police presence, the relation is somewhat less direct. In rare cases the probability of apprehension may change without any corresponding change in the degree of police presence or in methods of detection. More commonly, increased police presence will increase the probability of apprehending offenders. But it will not usually be on a one-to-one basis. Doubling the police presence in a community (and thereby doubling exposure to police) will not necessarily double the number of arrests or the clearance rate for street crimes. Yet the objective probability of apprehension will tend to increase or decrease along with variations in the presence of enforcement machinery.

---

207. Klette, "On the Functioning of the Swedish Legislation Concerning Drunken Driving" (1966) unpublished. The evidence is not wholly conclusive because it may be that those checked and released, while more likely to be drivers, were less likely to be drunk than other drivers.

208. New York City Police Department, *Operation 25* (1955).

209. *Id.* at 9–15.

There is of course no necessary relation between publicity about new methods of enforcement or about the prosecution of violators and increases in the actual probability of apprehension. Insofar as such publicity affects subjective judgments about risk of apprehension made by potential criminals, it represents an opportunity to increase threat credibility without increasing enforcement. As Leslie Wilkins says, "It may be possible to change behavior in desired directions, not only by changing situations, but by changing *beliefs* about situations."[210]

Such opportunities, however, will be limited by the effects of personal experience. Where potential criminals are likely to gain personal experience of apprehension risks, either through committing crimes and escaping without detection or through personal knowledge of the successful criminality of others, such experience or knowledge will, over time, erode the foundation of credibility. In such circumstances a publicity campaign might increase the perceived credibility of the legal threat in the short run, but perceptions of risk would decrease as personal experience accumulated. Audience members exposed to publicity campaigns, and subsequently persuaded that the risk of detection was not as represented, might discount future announcements of breakthroughs in crime prevention. If so, publicity without substance may decrease the credibility of legal threats in general among some potential criminals.

In situations where many potential criminals have no personal experience of enforcement machinery, general publicity campaigns are likely to exert greater influence on public perceptions of the risk of detection. Such campaigns may persuade large segments of the population that the risks of crime are greater than they actually are. Very few citizens have any personal knowledge or experience which would lead them to question the Shakesperean maxim that "Truth will come to light; murder cannot be hid long."[211] Indeed, law-abiding members of society will spend most of their lives dependent on secondary sources for their impressions of the efficiency of criminal law enforcement in respect of most categories of crime.

210. Wilkins, *supra* note 124, at 119.
211. Shakespeare, *Merchant of Venice*, act 2, sc. 1. Cf. also "For murder though it have no tongue will speak with most miraculous organ," *Hamlet*, act 2, sc. 2.

Andenaes is probably correct in suggesting that "many law abiding people . . . are deterred because of an over-estimation of the risks."[212] He goes on to say that "if it were possible to convince people that crime does not pay, this assumption might act as a deterrent even if the risks, viewed objectively, remained unchanged."[213] And it seems likely that, in an area where the crime rate is low and examples of undetected crime are not widely known, the facade of enforcement may be able to establish permanent impressions of threat credibility in excess of actual clearance rates.

The fact that law-abiding members of society depend heavily on secondary sources for perceptions of threat credibility does not, by itself, mean that publicity campaigns that affect such perceptions will decrease the crime rate. For widely represented among such groups are people who do not need a deterrent, or who can be deterred on the basis of some slight chance of apprehension. It is only when potential criminals are not heavily exposed to personal experience that second- and thirdhand impressions of the credibility of threats will have a permanent influence on the perceptions of those for whom the credible legal threat is most necessary.

An important distinction is that between the effect of credibility on the numbers of persons deterred, and the effect of credibility on movements in crime rates. Variations in detection rates might not affect very many people but at the same time might have a considerable effect on a crime rate.

We have to remember that "the number of persons frequently committing serious offenses is relatively low."[214] But if variations in the credibility of threats can influence the number of persons participating in robbery, or can influence the frequency of robberies committed by those participating, it can have a significant effect on the robbery rate.[215] In these circumstances, it may be that changes in the credibility of threats can be an

212. Andenaes, *supra* note 118, at 963.
213. *Ibid.*
214. Hood and Sparks, *supra* note 112, at 175.
215. Moreover, if the increase in the credibility of threats is a function of an actual increase in the apprehension of offenders, then the latter will have a preventive effect which is quite independent of deterrence.

important factor in the control of serious crime without affecting the perceptions of a great number of people.

For this reason we doubt the validity of Nigel Walker's view that to improve law enforcement by increasing the probability of detection is "one of the commonest platitudes on the subject of law enforcement."[216] Walker cites the finding of the British Government Social Survey on deterrents to crime among fifteen- to twenty-one-year-old youths (the age group with the highest rates of serious crime) to which we referred earlier.[217] It was found that the great majority of those questioned greatly overestimated their chances of being caught, although there was a more "realistic minority" with "more experience . . . of committing offences."[218] Walker suggests that this finding throws doubt on the idea that by increasing the *objective* probability of detection we can improve crime prevention.

So far as shop-breaking (and most other acquisitive crimes) are concerned this is a visionary's hope. The clear-up rate is so low that it is over-estimated by all but a small minority. To alter the estimates of the realistic minority would require an enormous increase in police efficiency; and to raise still further the over-estimates of the majority seems almost out of the question.[219]

On this, two comments seem appropriate. First, with regard to most serious crimes it is not "the over-estimates of the majority" but the apparently more realistic estimates of the minority which are important. Second, the assertion that only "an enormous increase in police efficiency" would be effective in altering the minority's estimates is supported by no evidence whatsoever.

iv Some Evidence

There is evidence that the perceived credibility of a threat serves to condition its deterrent effectiveness, but there are indications that the process is more complex than many early writers believed. In Denmark an unusual opportunity to study

216. Walker, *supra* note 42, at 65.
217. Willcock and Stokes, *supra* note 41.
218. Walker, *supra* note 42, at 30.
219. *Ibid.*

the effects of decreasing the apparent probability of apprehension occurred when the German occupation government arrested the Copenhagen police force en masse during the Second World War. Reacting to the emergency, citizen groups in Copenhagen established vigilante groups and increased the penalties threatened for major crimes. During this policeless period, the rates of many crimes where the offender could not be identified by the victim (such as robbery, burglary, and larceny) increased approximately tenfold. Other crimes, where the offender could be identified without police work, did not increase in frequency to any spectacular degree.[220] It is unknown to what extent the large increases in crime were due to the same number of criminals committing many more crimes or to a greater number of people deciding to commit crimes.

In Detroit, police dissatisfaction with wages and working conditions led to a more restricted form of "police holiday." During a period lasting at least seven months in 1967, the same number of police continued on traffic patrol but issued about half as many tickets to motorists for moving violations. If Detroit's motor vehicle accident rate is an index of the number of traffic offenses committed, the number of actual violations did not increase, because the accident rate actually declined.[221] It is far from clear, of course, that accident rates are an accurate index of rates of traffic law violation.[222] But the fact

220. See Trolle, *Syv Maaneder Uden Politi* ("Seven months without police") (1945); Hurwitz, *Criminology* (1952) 303; Andenaes, *supra* note 118 (b), at 186–88; Andenaes, *supra* note 118, at 962.

221. Detroit Police reports for 1966–67 show the following comparison in moving violations:

	1966	1967	% Change
Jan.–April	163,873	152,423	−7
May–Dec.	265,234	128,617	−52

Statistics on fatal accidents, obtained from the Detroit Police Traffic Division, show no trend upward during late 1967:

	1966	1967	% Change
Jan.–April	79	62	−22
May–Dec.	160	155	−3

Total accident figures decreased dramatically after April of 1967:

	1966	1967	% Change
Jan.–April	26,121	23,973	−8
May–Dec.	63,119	45,101	−29

However, this decrease might be another result of a slowdown in police reporting.

222. For a description of efforts to investigate the relation between accidents and violations in California, see Coppin and Peck, *The 1964 California Driver Record Study* (1967).

that accident rates did not rise at all is some indication that Detroit's police holiday did not have a spectacular effect on the rate of traffic violations.

Detroit's experience differed from Copenhagen's in that the same number of police remained on the street in Detroit. Thus, the cues (mainly police presence) that many citizens had of the extent of traffic enforcement went unchanged, though the objective probabilities had changed markedly. Even if the citizens' awareness of the lower level of enforcement had been total, there would have been no reason to expect a dramatic increase in traffic violations. The number of traffic violations may largely be a function of the number of miles driven, and the diminution in enforcement would not be likely significantly to affect that total.

In Copenhagen, by contrast, the rise in the crime rate might even have reflected some overestimate of the actual increase in impunity rates, because the traditional police presence had been completely eliminated. The increase in such offenses as robbery and burglary probably also reflected the fact that the "demand" for apparently risk-free opportunities to commit those offenses is much more elastic than the "demand" for traffic violations. It is likely too that potential robbers and burglars are more interested in, and aware of, variations in law enforcement practice and the unusual opportunity situation than are potential traffic violators.

The British experience with the Road Safety Act of 1967 shows how a change in the perceived credibility of a new legal policy may differ somewhat from the objective change in risks of apprehension. Immediately after the much publicized act went into effect, creating a new offense—driving with an undue proportion of alcohol in the blood—and equipping the police with portable "breath test" kits with which to screen suspected drunk drivers, the rate of nighttime traffic fatalities dropped sharply, indicating a substantial decrease in the rate of drunk driving.[223] As time passed, the rate of traffic fatalities increased

223. See Great Britain, Ministry of Transport, Press Notice No. 892, 19 Dec. 1967; No. 7, 8 Feb. 1968. As Andenaes points out, the fact that the reduction after the new law was greater for serious accidents than for less serious accidents is in harmony with the findings of previous traffic research, which shows that, when drivers with blood alcohol levels over .08 percent (the prescribed limit under the 1967 act) have accidents, they tend to be more severe than the average accident.

somewhat from the low levels experienced right after the law went into effect,[224] which may indicate that drivers had re-evaluated the impact of the change in enforcement on their personal chances of being apprehended for drunk driving.

In this case the introduction of the new law was heralded by a large and costly publicity campaign, which began two weeks before the law came into force and ran for over three months. Andenaes raises the question whether this publicity may not have created in many drivers exaggerated ideas of the risk of detection, followed with the passage of time by "a more real-istic assessment of the risk."[225] He also suggests that the "high degree of risk awareness" created by the new law may have be-come dulled when the publicity slackened.[226] Either of these interpretations, if proved correct, would establish the role of subjective factors in the deterrent effect of the Road Safety Act.

A somewhat more ambiguous indication that increases in certainty of apprehension deter crime is the finding that states with a higher number of prison admissions relative to the num-ber of reported offenses tend to have a lower crime rate. Whether this means that crime is deterred by more efficient police work, or simply that it is easier to apprehend a greater percentage of criminals when the crime rate is low, is unclear. Only the former interpretation would be evidence of the mar-ginal deterrent effect of increases in threat credibility.

Professor Tittle, who reports the finding that higher pro-portionate enforcement is correlated with lower crime rates, proposes one test of whether low crime rates are a cause or an effect of relatively high probabilities of apprehension. He ob-tained the correlation between probability of apprehension and the ratio of police to population, and found that as probability of apprehension tends to increase, the ratio of police employees

---

Andenaes, *supra* note 118 (a), where he cites Borkenstein et al., *The Role of Drinking Driver in Traffic Accidents* (1964) 176–77.

224. The British Ministry of Transport reports that October–May serious and fatal nighttime accidents decreased 37 percent in the months following the effective date of the law, but increased 20 percent from a much lower base in the period October 1968 through May 1969. Per-sonal communication from J. Betts to Franklin Zimring, October 1969.

225. Andenaes, *supra* note 118 (a), at 551.

226. *Ibid.*

to population tends to decrease (the correlation obtained was −.53).[227]

The data do not, however, negate the possibility that greater probability of apprehension is the result of lower crime rates making police work easier. This is because the police burden may best be seen as the ratio of police to crimes rather than to population. A high-crime area may have a high ratio of police to population and a low ratio of police to crimes; while a less crime-prone area may have fewer police per thousand citizens but more police per thousand crimes. There is also the disquieting possibility that apparent "certainty" is achieved by differences in reporting practices.

v Concluding note

It should be added that all the evidence referred to above relates to general tendencies and patterns, and many fundamental questions remain unanswered. Credibility is a matter of cues and of their perception by subjects. These cues may be various, including such things as the visibility of police patrols, news stories, or reports from friends and acquaintances. We do not know how these stimuli operate in the context of credibility. Some questions to which we do not have answers are:

1. Are changes in the perceived credibility of threats significantly related to the nature and magnitude of the penalties involved? For example, do variations in risk of severe penalties, such as the death penalty and life imprisonment, function in this context in the same way as variations in the risk of encountering fines? To what extent in each case does the analogy with the price system apply? And insofar as it does apply, what are the various elasticities of response over the range of penalties?

2. Is there a point of diminishing returns in the provision of threatening cues or signals by the authorities? Where the police:citizen ratio is high, would not an increase in police manpower to the point of saturation achieve

227. Tittle, "Crime Rates and Legal Sanctions" (1969) 16 *Social Problems* 409–23.

only a relatively small marginal increment in deterrence?

3. How long does it take, with respect to various crimes and different circumstances and settings, for changes in enforcement to operate as cues and cause changes in public perceptions? Is it not likely that a considerable variation in temporal patterns must prevail?

4. Is the best way to achieve an increase in the credibility of legal threats always by increasing the probability of apprehension? Or may it not be that an increase in appropriate publicity will achieve the same effect more economically? Since a gaming house might attract more players by means of promotion than by increasing players' chances of winning, is it not possible that a law enforcement agency might deter more offenders by publicity than by increasing offenders' chances of apprehension?

The last question raises a more general issue relating to credibility. Extensive publicity may, of course, tend to undermine the credibility of legal threats when there has been no change in the substance of law enforcement. But dramatic increases in the efficiency of law enforcement will fail to achieve maximum impact without extensive publicity. For some potential offenders, personal experience of the enforcement of a law will not occur until months or years after a change in enforcement takes place. And such an experience may be the result of law violation that could have been prevented. The credibility of legal threats is enhanced more quickly, and among a greater number of potential offenders, if publicity accompanies increases in the ability of a legal system to apprehend offenders.

F Types of Threatened Consequences

The prospect of unpleasant consequences is the fuel which powers the machinery of deterrence. It follows that analysis of the deterrent effect and variations in that effect must include consideration of the role of the threatened consequences.

Consideration of the threatened consequences must comprehend at least three fundamental questions. In this subsection we shall deal with two of them. First, we shall try to define the scope of threatened consequences, that is, the range of occurrences that can properly be regarded as part of the consequences implied by a legal threat. Second, we shall deal with the nature of these consequences, that is, we shall attempt to distinguish the different kinds of unpleasantness which function as threat elements. In subsection G we shall consider the effects of variations in the severity of consequences.

i The Scope of Threatened Consequences

If one were to ask a judge to describe the penalty for driving while intoxicated, he would probably confine his answer to the fine or sentence of imprisonment provided in the penal code of his jurisdiction. If the question were rephrased as "Why would people wish to avoid being apprehended and convicted for this offense?" it is likely that he might respond more fully. He might then mention the unpleasantness associated with arrest and trial for driving while intoxicated—a process that many people would regard with more apprehension than the actual sentence of the court. He might also indicate that jail is an experience most people would wish to avoid. Finally, he would be likely to mention the effect of conviction and jailing, not only on the defendant's standing in his community, but also on other persons who are of particular, and in some cases intimate, importance to the offender.

In discussing the threat of punishment we have to consider not only what is explicit in the threat but also many other elements which are only implicit but may nevertheless exercise a deterrent influence as great as, or greater than, the penalty provided by law. Indeed, we must, as Andenaes points out, "necessarily consider the total social consequences, of which the penalty is but a part."[228]

While court sentences are usually expressed in the general terms laid down in penal codes, the real nature of penalties is determined by a variety of factors including statutory rules, penal regulations, administrative discretions, and material circumstances which govern their actual execution. To give an example, all that is explicit in a sentence of imprisonment in most cases is confinement in prison.[229] As Fox puts it, "the treatment the prisoner will receive may be said to be implicit

228. Andenaes, *supra* note 118, at 964.
229. Fox. *The English Prison and Borstal Systems* (1952) 16.

in the sentence, but all that is explicit in deprivation of liberty."[230] Yet the conditions of incarceration may vary from squalid and insanitary promiscuity under a punitive disciplinary regime to comparative comfort in an atmosphere of benign permissiveness.

We must recognize that there are other aspects of the administration of criminal justice which, while forming no part of the formally prescribed punishment, must nevertheless be regarded as part of the threatened consequences. Thus, in the case of driving while intoxicated the whole process of apprehension and detention is unpleasant. There is no doubt both that it is intended to be unpleasant and that members of the threatened audience recognize this. It would be illogical to restrict the definition of threatened consequences in such a way as to exclude such aspects of the enforcement process which are integral parts of the system and may often be as significant as the formally prescribed punishments themselves.[231]

Official *actions* can set off societal *reactions* that may provide potential offenders with more reason to avoid conviction than the officially imposed unpleasantness of punishment. "A trusted cashier committing embezzlement, a minister who evades payment of his taxes, a teacher making sexual advances towards minors and a civil servant who accepts bribes have a fear of detection which is more closely linked with the dread of public scandal and subsequent social ruin than with apprehensions of legal punishment."[232]

Because such reactions emanate from sources other than the threatening agency and may not be an intended result of punishment, they cannot strictly be considered part of the consequences threatened by the agency for offenses. However, these secondary reactions cannot be ignored if the effectiveness of particular threatened consequences is to be understood. For example, the social disapproval that jail might occasion will surely have different degrees of influence on skid row drunks

---

230. *Ibid.*
231. With regard to shoplifters, for example, Cameron found that the process of apprehension and interrogation alone served as an effective spur to future conformity. See *supra* note 142, at 151.
232. Andenaes, *supra* note 118, at 964.

and potential antitrust violators.[233] Similarly, such considerations will operate with more force on certain types of shoplifters than on others.[234]

The effectiveness of the threat of jail, then, will be dependent both upon societal attitudes to those who are jailed and upon the jailed individual's reaction to those attitudes. At the same time, such variations in attitude and response clearly come outside the boundary of legal punishment, and the formal definition of legal consequences cannot include such unofficial community responses. From the viewpoint of formal logic our definition of the scope of threatened consequences may not be entirely satisfactory, but it is the only definition that suits our purpose. Any serious study of the effects of legal consequences must encompass all the meanings that the threat of consequences may convey to members of a threatened audience.

ii Types of Unpleasantness

The many different types of unpleasantness conveyed by threats may condition different patterns of threat response and thus be related to variations in threat effectiveness. The major forms of unpleasantness conveyed by threats which we shall discuss here are economic deprivation, loss of privileges, confinement, physical punishment, and social stigma.

(a) *Economic deprivation.* Financial penalties in the form of fines or the confiscation of property are as old as the criminal law. Indeed, in the form of restitution or composition they could be said to be even older. Schafer states: "not only in the time of the Greeks, but in still earlier ages . . . for injuries both to person and property, restitution or reparation in some form was the chief and often the only element of punishment."[235] Yet, although the fine is of all penal sanctions "nu-

233. Cf: Lovald and Stub, "The Revolving Door: Reactions of Chronic Drunkenness Offenders to Court Sanctions" (1968) 59 *J. Crim. L.C. and P.S.* 525–30; and Geis, "The Heavy Electrical Equipment Antitrust Cases of 1961," in Geis (ed.), *White-Collar Criminal* (1968) 103–18.

234. Cameron, *supra* note 142, at 164: "The contrast in behavior between the pilferer and the recognized and self-admitted thief is striking."

235. Schafer. *Restitution to Victims of Crime* (1960) 3–7.

merically the most important, the cheapest, [and] by no means the least effective," it is also "probably the least studied."[236]

The threat of economic disadvantage through such mechanisms as fines or lost deposits is still widely used in the regulation of minor offenses; and large fines are provided as optional forms of punishment for more serious offenses. In addition, the award of money damages as punishment or compensation in civil cases is often seen as an attempt by the legal system to deter antisocial but noncriminal behavior through the threat of economic deprivation. "In a materialistic age dominated by property and motoring crime," says Alec Samuels, "economic sanctions seem likely to continue to grow in size and importance."[237]

When the main force of a deterrent threat is the unpleasantness of a fine or cost, the operation of the legal threat appears to be similar to that of a price system. The measure of threatened punishment can be rather precisely calibrated by dollar amounts. Samuels points out that "the tariff can be readily applied by the court, without time or effort being required, it gives the appearance of consistency, and often satisfies the rough sense of equality of treatment expected by the offenders."[238] At the same time, both the offender and the authorities may come to view the fine as the "price" of the threatened behavior. It has been argued that this may cause those who have paid the price to feel no moral compunction about their offense,[239] and may also cause those who collect the fine to attach less moral significance to the offense being punished than if other forms of punishment had been used.

In one sense, the salience of economic threats increases with wealth: the threat of economic deprivation only operates on those who have economic resources to lose, and the raising of a fine threat is of significance only to those who have sufficient resources to pay the lower fine. In another sense, the significance of a fine threat is inversely proportional to financial means, for the threat of a $10 fine would seem more severe

236. Samuels, "The Fine: The Principles" (1970) *Crim. L. Rev.* 272.
237. *Ibid.*
238. *Id.* at 204–5.
239. *Id.* 202: "The inadequate fine may be taken as license to commit an offence for a fee."

to a man with only $100 than to a man with $1,000. The
threat of small fines would thus seem more important to less
wealthy members of an audience, while the threat of very large
fines would have more influence on those with the means to
pay them than on those without.

Economic deprivations can be used—with poetic appropriateness—to threaten activities that are motivated by the desire
for economic gain,[240] but fines are in fact threatened for prac-
tically every type of offense.[241] In some countries they are used
quite extensively for crimes of violence and sexual offenses.[242]

Nevertheless, principles of deterrence no more sophisticated
than those of Jeremy Bentham, and some common sense, would
suggest an upper limit to the kind of offense for which most
people can be effectively threatened by means of fines. Alec
Samuels, with such a limit in mind, distinguishes between "adequate" and "inadequate" fines.[243]

If we ask what the criteria of adequacy are in relation to
fines, it seems that three conditions must be fulfilled. First, the
fine must be at least sufficient to outweigh the value of the
behavior or, as Bentham phrased it, "the profit of the offence."[244] Second, it must be sufficient to allow for the fact
that, in considering the present value of the prospect of future
loss, a discount is commonly implicit in the postponement of
consequences. Third, it must be sufficient to offset the perceived
chances of nonapprehension. At the same time it is presumed
that any other disadvantages threatened, such as the psychic
costs of apprehension and conviction and the stigma involved,
will work conjointly with the fine threat to deter.

Bentham reminds us, however, that the fine "is not furnished
with any of those symbolical helps to exemplarity"[245] which

240. *Id.* at 203. Samuels speaks of "the really heavy fine" being
"appropriate . . . where the object is to prevent the acquisition of a financial profit from the offence."

241. *Id.* at 202.

242. For crimes of violence in Britain see McClintock and Gibson,
supra note 199, at 73–85, and McClintock, *Crimes of Violence* (1963)
137–77, where it is reported that about a third of violent offenders are
fined. For sexual offenses see Radzinowicz (ed.), *Sexual Offences* (1957)
218–35, where it is shown that over 40 percent of such offenders were
fined.

243. Samuels, *supra* note 236, at 202.

244. Bentham, *supra* note 151, at 469.

245. *Ibid.*

attach to other forms of punishment, and that it is in fact "attended with a less degree of infamy than any other."[246] And if, as the evidence suggests, the incentive toward serious crime is found disproportionately in the lower socioeconomic levels of society, then it is evident that there are serious limitations on the use of the fine, because for all but minor offenses the adequate fine will necessarily be a fairly substantial amount of money. For this reason the social control of most forms of criminality rarely depends on the fine alone.

Though studies have shown the threat of small fines to be effective in reducing the frequency of some types of behavior, the studies to date have dealt with relatively minor offenses that are not strongly motivated, and there is no reason to suppose that economic threats are of any unique efficacy.[247] However, economic deprivation is one form of punishment that promises a direct gain to the punishing agency in the form of the money taken from offenders by the act of punishment. As Bentham put it, "pecuniary forfeiture" possesses "the striking advantage of being convertible to profit."[248] By contrast, most other forms of punishment result in considerable costs— to punishing agencies.[249] In this respect the existence of fines may serve as an incentive to criminal law enforcement, where the costs of other forms of punishment may operate as a brake on thorough enforcement.[250]

(*b*) *Loss of privileges.* Another form of punishment which has a long history is the deprivation of various rights and privileges. Von Hentig talks of "derogatory punishments"[251] and

246. *Id.* at 460.

247. For a summary statement on the efficacy of fines "in terms of reconviction rates" see Samuels, *supra* note 236, at 206–7. Studies to date of fine threats have related to illegal parking traffic offenses and noncriminal conduct, and the effect of fine threats on major crimes has not been studied.

248. Bentham, *supra* note 151, at 468.

249. Professor Schelling, in "An Essay on Bargaining" (1956) 41. *Am. Econ. Rev.* 282, defines a threat as the announcement of "an act that one party would have no incentive to perform, but that is designed to deter through its promise of mutual harm."

250. The incentive to enforcement presented by fine systems is clearly evident where it produces minimum ticket quotas for parking and traffic police.

251. Von Hentig, *Punishment* (1937) 226–31.

Sutherland and Cressey of "social degradation."[252] Both include not only such things as "the deprivation of civic rights"[253] or "loss of rights of citizenship"[254] but also methods of punishment like "being pilloried and ducked"[255] or "branding on the left cheek,"[256] which are really degradation ceremonies or methods of stigmatization, a topic with which we deal separately below.

In many situations, conviction for a serious offense will result in the offender's losing privileges normally available to most members of society. The principal rights which at present may be lost in various states in this country as a result of the commission of major crime have been summarized recently as follows:

(a) The right to vote is lost by conviction of almost all felonies in all states except Indiana, Massachusetts, New Hampshire and Vermont.

(b) The right to hold public office is lost in most states. Public offices are generally restricted to electors, and therefore the loss of suffrage carries with it the loss of the right to hold office. In addition, certain other restrictions are specified in some states such as incapacity to serve on a jury or to testify as a witness.

(c) The right to practice certain professions or occupations. In addition, in a few states the convicted felon loses the right to make a contract, to marry, or to migrate to a foreign country."[257]

In most cases, the deprivations listed are probably not among the main reasons why a potential offender would wish to avoid conviction for major crimes. But there are other disabilities imposed as a result of conviction, such as the loss of driving privileges, which both numerically and socially are at least as important as those listed.

Thus, for some offenses of minor and intermediate severity, the disability or loss of privilege may be the most unpleasant of consequences threatened, and will be specifically related to

252. Sutherland and Cressey, *supra* note 90, at 308–9.
253. Von Hentig, *supra* note 251, at 230.
254. Sutherland and Cressey, *supra* note 90, at 309.
255. Von Hentig, *supra* note 251, at 229.
256. Sutherland and Cressey, *supra* note 90, at 309.
257. *Ibid.*

the offense (as when serious or persistent traffic violations lead to the revocation of the offender's license to drive). By contrast, with more serious offenses, the loss of privileges will be a relatively minor part of the total punishment and will not necessarily be related to the offense leading to the loss (as when convicted felons are deprived of voting rights, eligibility for public office, or the opportunity lawfully to possess a firearm).

When the lost privilege relates specifically to the offense leading to punishment, as in the driving example, the threat of consequences may be of special significance to potential offenders because this group is more likely than others to attach importance to the privilege. Thus, the propensity of persistent traffic offenders to commit such offenses is some evidence either of frequent driving or of the special emotional significance of driving for this particular group. The loss of privileges that are not specifically related to the offense, particularly when attached to conviction for major crimes, may have less significance for potential criminals than for most other citizens. It seems likely, for example, that the average citizen places more value on the right to vote or run for public office than does the potential armed robber.

The loss of privileges unrelated to the offense has not generally been discussed or evaluated as a deterrent mechanism when attached to other major penalties for serious crimes. This is true, for example, of the ban on the lawful possession of firearms by felons,[258] which, while not designed as a deterrent to potential felons becoming actual felons, is viewed as a means of preventing convicted felons from obtaining guns that might be used in future crimes. But in most areas of the United States firearms remain readily available to convicted felons through unlawful channels.[259]

The loss of driving privileges for persistent or serious traffic violations is intended both as a general deterrent addressed to all potential traffic violators, and as a mechanism to reduce driving (and therefore the risk of violations) among persistent offenders who have such privileges revoked. The effect of such

258. 18 U.S.C. (1968) 924(c).
259. See Newton and Zimring, *Firearms and Violence in American Life* (1969) chaps. 1 and 12–14.

threats on the general rate of traffic violations has not been studied, but there has been a considerable discussion and some evaluation of license revocation. It has been argued that the essentially deterrent thrust of revocation (since revocation generally does not make it physically more difficult for an individual to gain access to a car) is more effective than fines on persistent traffic offenders.[260] Professor Packer has, however, expressed some doubts about the efficacy of revocation as a means of treating traffic offenders, since the practice employs a weak threat of detection where the incentive to drive without a license is strong.[261] Because "delinquent motorists overwhelmingly outnumber all other offences"[262] and also because a general problem regarding the use of loss of privileges is involved, Professor Packer's argument on this topic should be examined. "Unfortunately," he says,

> we have no assurance that license suspension or revocation would be an effective sanction. Failing some dramatic technological advance that would make it possible to identify unlicensed drivers without stopping and questioning them, there is every reason to believe that large numbers of people would simply accept the risk of being caught and would continue to drive. The use of criminal punishment would simply be postponed one step rather than avoided. There would be, if anything, a decrease in the deterrent efficacy of the law, because an unlicensed driver is less likely to be apprehended than one who is drunk.[263]

The main thrust of Packer's argument deals with revocation as a deterrent to future violations by those who have had their licenses revoked, and not with the general deterrent efficacy of the threat of revocation: "The apparatus of the criminal law, for all its terror, usually produces a less onerous punishment than license revocation would be perceived as being."[264] The difficulty of apprehension might dilute the public perception of the disadvantages of revocation but would probably not eliminate it.

---

260. Middendorf, *The Effectiveness of Punishment, Especially in Relation to Traffic Offenses* (1967) 106.
261. Packer, *supra* note 117, at 255.
262. Walker, *Crime and Punishment in Britain* (2d ed. 1968) 32.
263. Packer, *supra* note 117. at 255.
264. *Ibid.*

With respect to the credibility of license revocation, the quoted statement produces a rare opportunity to disagree with Professor Packer's analysis. A driver who is both drunk and driving without a license is no less likely to be apprehended than one who is merely drunk, and far easier to convict of a traffic violation. The penalties for driving after license revocation appear to be the highest meted out to traffic offenders of any kind, according to a study of sentencing in the Detroit traffic court.[265] And the driver without a license can be apprehended for this offense whenever he is stopped by a police officer, not merely when he is drunk. General traffic violations of the kind that betray the unlicensed driver occur far more often than drunk arrests. Thus, while many people, perhaps even a majority of the class, may continue to drive after suspension or revocation, the revocation procedure and enforcement are not so toothless as to preclude deterrent effectiveness.

Professor Cramton, another scholar who has written on this topic, doubts the effectiveness of license revocation in the more limited area of drunk driving because many offenders in this class are addicted to alcohol.[266] But this does not necessarily mean that they are also addicted to driving.

The criticism of license revocation as a special deterrent points up a general problem regarding the use of loss of privileges as a means of deterring further offenses. The real meaning of loss of privileges (unless highly reliable means for monitoring the use of the privileges exist) is the addition of a further legal threat to an existing one, where the punished group has already ignored the existing threat.[267] The same type of criticism could be leveled at the threat of lost privileges as a marginal general deterrent, because in order to outperform the threat of fines or jail sentences, the loss of privileges would have to influence the behavior of some people who are not impressed by the threat of other sanctions.

There is no reason to reject out of hand the notion that some drivers will take the threat of revocation more seriously

265. Zimring, "Punishment Theory and Traffic Offenders" (1966) unpublished.

266. Cramton, "Driver Behavior and Legal Sanctions: A Study of Deterrence" (1969) 67 *U. Mich. L. Rev.* 421ff.

267. For this reason Von Hentig refers to these measures as "secondary punishments." *Supra* note 251.

than the threat of other punishment. Thus, if driving without a license is either more severely threatened than other traffic crimes or easier to detect, revocation may prove more effective than alternative sanctions as a general deterrent to traffic violation, and even as a special threat to already convicted traffic offenders. Moreover the loss of a driving license has both a physical and a symbolic palpability that other threats do not possess.

Whether or not the loss of privileges or rights can operate effectively in this way, in this and other areas, is of course an empirical question. As is the case in so many controversies in this field, a feasible program of further research is the surest method of assessing both the pitfalls and the potential of loss of privileges as a deterrent measure.

(c) *Confinement.* Penal confinement, ranging from a few days to the remainder of an offender's life, is one of the many alternative sanctions for minor offenses and, in most countries, the usual punishment threatened for major crimes. Imprisonment has been called "a comparatively modern method of dealing with offenders,"[268] and it was not until the early nineteenth century that it came to be used as the principal method for dealing with serious offenders.

Apart from stigmatization, which will be discussed more generally under a separate heading, there is much in penal confinement to inspire apprehension, including loss of freedom to act and make choices, deprivation of the opportunity to make money, sexual deprivation, invasion of privacy, rigid discipline, and living conditions far below the ordinary standards of society.

Prison life also has characteristics that might offset its manifest disadvantages for some people. Indeed, the question "How agreeable can we allow imprisonment to become?" (for "undoubtedly the more comfortable it becomes the less will be its deterrent effect")[269] has been seriously discussed recently. Chief Justice Cornelius of the Supreme Court of Pakistan has written:

268. Sutherland and Cressey, *supra* note 90, at 311–12.
269. Törnqvist, "Correction and the Prevention of Crime," in Christiansen (ed.), 1 *Scandinavian Studies in Criminology* (1965) 196.

At a time when the common person all over the world is finding it increasingly difficult to provide subsistence for himself, there is something of an absurdity involved in the consideration that he can procure such subsistence and a good many amenities and facilities besides (such as medical care) by simply committing crime. The possibility is exploited by individuals in every country.[270]

Sir Lionel Fox, commenting some twenty years ago on "the traditional stories of people who so much prefer prison to the workhouse or regularly winter in their favorite prison," remarked that although "there may well be such people . . . the Report of the Casual Poor Law Committee, 1930, found little factual foundation for these stories." He added that prison reception records demonstrated "that the class from which they are likely to be drawn is nowadays minimal in the prison population."[271] Still, "it is not impossible that there are poor people who commit crimes in order to achieve a better life in prison,"[272] and the quality of a person's life style in society may have some bearing on the extent to which imprisonment is considered undesirable. The relative deprivation of confinement should be greatest in cases where the contrast between life on the outside and the prospect of prison is most extreme. For some individuals the opportunity to escape from the often agonizing responsibility to make any decisions about the course of his daily life and from the burden of fending for himself may be welcomed.[273] Nevertheless, for most people the disadvantages of penal confinement are likely to outweigh the advantages by an overwhelming margin. It is only among those who have been rendered dependent by previous exposure to imprisonment that any inclination toward a prison environment has been noted in the United States.[274]

270. Cornelius, "Crime and the Punishment of Crime" (1966) 6 *Excerpta Criminologica* 10.

271. Fox, *supra* note 299, at 134–35.

272. Middendorf, *supra* note 260, at 67.

273. See Morris, *supra* note 137, chap. 6, for a description of some personality types apparently better suited to the discipline and dependency of prison life than to the rigors of life in society.

274. See Clemmer, "Observations on Imprisonment as a Source of Criminality" (1950) 41 *J. Crim. L.C. and P.S.* 311, for a discussion of the role which experience with prison might play in developing patterns of dependency.

It has been said to be "implicit in the nature of imprisonment that it does not fall equally on all subjected to it."[275] The contrast in living conditions between prior life and prison existence was particularly noteworthy, for example, in the case of James R. Hoffa, former president of the International Brotherhood of Teamsters.[276] The same prison conditions provoke little comment when notorious criminals of lesser wealth serve their sentences. Yet, as one of this century's great prison administrators pointed out, those conditions are "at a level which most prisoners used to a modicum of material comfort or refinement find at the least austere."[277]

It is easy to underestimate the contrast between life in society and penal confinement. The most disadvantaged of our citizens stands to lose his personal freedom through penal confinement; and his ability to distinguish between life in prison and life in society may be considerably greater than that of more dispassionate observers. Sir Alexander Maxwell thus defines the essence of imprisonment:

The right of citizens to freedom from restraint is a precious right, and the loss of that right is a severe deprivation. If anyone is illegally held in captivity by some other person or persons, he suffers a grave injury, for which the courts will award him heavy damages, however considerately he may have been treated by his captors. When an offender is held in legal custody, he suffers a grave punishment, however free from punitive conditions his treatment may be.[278]

With the lack of freedom as the common denominator of penal confinement, the prospect of prison may well function with equal effectiveness as a disincentive among both poor and rich. For if "the essence of imprisonment is deprivation of personal liberty,"[279] the unattractiveness of prison as a general deterrent may be relatively unaffected by changes in the material conditions of penal confinement. If so, conjugal visits,[280]

275. Fox, *supra* note 229, at 132–33.
276. Lewis Wolfson the financier and Bobby Baker are more recent examples of the same phenomenon.
277. Fox, *supra* note 229, at 134.
278. Maxwell, *The Institutional Treatment of Offenders* (1943) 39–40.
279. Fox, *supra* note 229, at 131.
280. But cf. the view of the great French criminological pioneer Gabriel Tarde, who lived in Paris, that "it is less a deprivation of liberty

protein diets, and television privileges can be added or sub-
tracted from the basic environment of penal confinement
without affecting the fundamental and most hated ingredient
of prison life which is loss of freedom.

Perceptions of prison life held by those who have been in
prison and those who have not would be worthy of comparative
study by psychologists, but they have not as yet received much
attention. It seems likely, for instance, that particular features
of prison life do not necessarily have the general deterrent effects sometimes attributed to them. Asking what kinds of
things might make a person want to avoid imprisonment is
different from asking what might make him want to get out
once he is in prison.

It would be of interest, and some importance, to determine
whether potential criminals view penal confinement primarily
as a period of days or years, or as a series of deprivations with
the period of time of secondary importance. It would be natural,
and is probably common, for legislators to assume that twenty
years in prison is twice as severe a punishment, and twice as
effective a deterrent, as ten years. But many potential criminals
(particularly those without any experience of confinement)
may view the prospect of prison in a different light. Apart
from normal tendencies to discount future pain and pleasure,
the *intensity* of confinement as an experience, rather than the
length of the experience, might dominate the consciousness of
most potential offenders, with only those who are case-hardened
to the deprivations of prison life measuring the unpleasantness
of possible future confinement in a temporal frame.

(*d*) *Pain and death.* Every healthy organism seeks to protect itself from unpleasant physical sensations, and also to
stay alive. As long as deterrence has been a goal of criminal
sanctions, legal systems have sought to mobilize the drives to
avoid pain and death as a means to prevent or reduce crime.
Sometimes both corporal punishment and the death penalty
have been employed in conjunction. As late as the nineteenth
century the punishment for treason in England consisted of

---

than a deprivation of physical love which makes the malefactor dread
imprisonment." *Penal Philosophy* (1890, trans. Howell 1912) 492.

hanging, cutting down while the prisoner was still alive, disemboweling, cutting off the head, and quartering the body. It is notable that the use of corporal punishments has in general "increased and decreased in prevalence with the death penalty."[281]

The imposition of physical punishment can be regarded as a basic or primitive criminal sanction for at least three reasons. First, the drive to avoid pain and preserve life is a common denominator for all men. Second, the imposition of physical punishment requires less advanced technology and fewer resources than the imposition of penal confinement over a period of time. Third, the drive to avoid physical punishment or death need not be based on any feelings of loyalty toward the agency threatening this type of consequence, whereas the drive to avoid being branded deviant is based on some respect for the society and for the social institution responsible for making the condemnatory judgment.

It has also been suggested that the imposition of physical punishment is primitive in a pejorative sense, because such punishment shows little regard for the interests of the offender, and brutalizes both those who inflict it and society at large. Some have maintained that brutal punishment impedes the moral development of societies that resort to it, and may undermine the moralizing effects of punishment. Thus, while it can be argued that the willful taking of life merits capital punishment, there are those who see a peculiar inconsistency in society's showing its abhorrence of killing by taking the life of the offender.[282]

Governmental agencies will commonly resort to physical punishment in situations where alternative means of deterrence may not be readily available. The threat of physical punishment is used extensively, for example, when the threatening agency does not command the loyalty of its audience, as in the case of occupying powers trying to secure the obedience of an enemy population, or of governments attempting to sub-

281. Sutherland and Cressey, *supra* note 90, at 308.
282. Beccaria, *On Crimes and Punishments* (1764 trans. Paolucci 1963) 50: "The death penalty cannot be useful, because of the example of barbarity it gives men. . . . It seems to me absurd that the laws, which are an expression of the public will, which detest and punish homicide, should themselves commit it."

due internal rebellion. In most Western nations the use of physical punishment is generally restricted to offenses that are considered particularly reprehensible, or to offenders for whom other methods are considered likely to be ineffective—as, for instance, persons already confined in penal institutions.[283]

Because the drive to avoid pain is basic to all men, and the drive to preserve life is not only basic but paramount,[284] there is some reason to regard the threat of pain or death as likely to produce the broadest and most extensive of deterrent effects. But there is surprisingly little in present research to indicate that either corporal or capital punishment has any unique deterrent efficacy when other harsh measures, such as long-term imprisonment, are also available.[285] Modern discussions of corporal punishment have discarded the notion that it has salutary effects on those actually punished.[286]

There are some exotic physical punishments for which a high degree of deterrent effectiveness has been claimed. Thus, Chief Justice Cornelius, whom we cited earlier on the subject of the attractions of imprisonment for "the common person all over the world," says of Saudi Arabia: "In that country . . . the punishment for theft is the cutting off of hands, which punishment is very promptly and publicly administered, and has proved to be an extremely effective deterrent against that form of crime.[287]

Two points here have to be borne in mind. First, it is important to distinguish between the deterrence of crime and its prevention, for this particular penal method also involves

283. As was the case in the United Kingdom with regard to corporal punishment between 1948 and 1967.

284. Stephen, "Capital Punishment" (1864) 69 *Fraser's Magazine* 753: "All that a man has will he give for his life. Any secondary punishment, however terrible, there is hope; but death is death; its terrors cannot be described more forcibly."

285. See *Corporal Punishment: Report of the Advisory Council on the Treatment of Offenders.* Cmnd. 1213 (1960) 15: "The available statistics . . . suggest . . . that corporal punishment was not an especially effective deterrent immediately before its abolition, and they show that its abolition did not result in an increase in the offences for which it was previously imposed." But the report states that the figures do not provide "a basis for any firm conclusions."

286. See *id.* at 17: "The weight of the evidence that we have received is to the effect that corporal punishment does not lead to reformation."

287. Cornelius, *supra* note 270, at 11.

physical incapacitation. Second, and particularly in the light of our own rather squeamish discussion, earlier in this book, of the ethics of deterrent punishment, somewhat higher standards of evidence are required than Cornelius offers before one can draw confident conclusions about the efficacy of maim as an instrument of social control. All that Cornelius offers in support of his assertions is the observation that "no one from Pakistan who visits Saudi Arabia for the Pilgrimage ever returns without a strong impression of the very high degree of security of property which prevails in that country"; to which he adds, "One and all put it down to the fact that the punishment for theft is the cutting off of hands."[288]

Research into the comparative effectiveness of capital punishment and protracted imprisonment as deterrents to criminal homicide is abundant. Studies have compared homicide rates of neighboring states with similar social environments but contrasting penalties for homicide, and have concluded that executions have no discernible effect on homicide rates.[289] Research efforts have focused on the same jurisdiction before and after the death penalty was either introduced or abolished, without finding any change in the rate of homicide that could be attributable to change in penal policy.[290] Other strategies of research have been used and have produced no evidence of the special effectiveness of the threat of death but rather carry some weight as to the opposite conclusion.[291]

Even if the threat of death for murder has no marginal deterrent value when compared with protracted imprisonment, it still might be true that capital punishment would serve as an effective marginal deterrent for other types of crime more susceptible to the influence of variations in threatened punishment. It might also be true that the death penalty would function as

288. *Ibid.* See also the discussion of "Tiger Prevention," *supra* chap. 2, sec. 2, subsec. B (ii).

289. See the papers collected in Bedau, *The Death Penalty in America* (1967 ed.) 258–332.

290. Sellin, "Death and Imprisonment as Deterrents to Murder," in Bedau *supra* note 289, at 274–84.

291. Sellin, "Does the Death Penalty Protect Municipal Police?"; Campion, "Does the Death Penalty Protect State Police?"; Savitz, "The Deterrent Effect of Capital Punishment in Philadelphia"; Graves, "The Deterrent Effect of Capital Punishment in California"; all in Bedau, *supra* note 289, at 284–332.

an effective marginal deterrent to homicide when compared with much lower terms of imprisonment or lesser penal measures. What the available studies do establish, however, is that the uniqueness of even the most extreme of physical punishments as a means of securing obedience to law cannot be assumed.

In the case of both the death penalty and forms of physical punishment like maim, the lack of evidence that they are more effective than other severe sanctions may have somewhat equivocal policy implications. If one regards them as more punitive than any appropriate available alternatives, the lack of evidence might be adduced against their employment. But if one regards them as more clement,[292] their use may be advocated just because they are not proved ineffective. Here a distinction must be drawn between maim, where no real evidence is available, and the death penalty, where the apparent lack of marginal effect in relation to homicide is better established.

(e) *Stigmatization.* The discovery that a person has committed a crime can change the community standing of an individual because social feelings about the crime will attach to social judgments about the criminal. In addition, the consequences of apprehension for criminal behavior may carry with them significant measures of social reprobation. Imprisonment involves demotion to the socially depressed and disapproved status of prisoner or convict, and the label is likely to remain longer than the sentence of imprisonment.[293]

The fact "that social standing is injured by punishment,"[294] and the "danger of exclusion from the group,"[295] are, according to Lewin, two of the most potent elements in the threat of punishment. Andenaes put it this way: "That the offender is subjected to the rejection and contempt of society serves as a deterrent; the thought of the shame of being caught and of the subsequent conviction is for many stronger than the thought

292. See, e.g., Barzun, "In Favor of Capital Punishment" (1962) 31 *The American Scholar* 181–91, where it is argued that "imprisonment is worse than death."
293. See the references given *supra* in chap. 3, note 27.
294. Lewin, *supra* note 1, at 138.
295. *Id.* at 127.

of the punishment itself."[296] Thus, the possibility that criminal activity might lead to stigmatization, a process that involves both reduction in status and elements of symbolic and actual exclusion from the group, may serve as a deterrent to crime.

This possibility has long been recognized and acted upon in the form of what Bentham refers to as "punishments belonging to the moral sanction," "the punishment of infamy," and "ignominious punishments."[297] The ducking stool, the stocks, and the pillory were "not only instruments of corporal punishment but were used to reduce the status of the offender as well."[298] Some types of trial-and-punishment proceedings were specifically designed to reduce prestige and bring down the wrath of society on the offender. We have spoken earlier of a criminal trial followed by conviction and sentence as being a public degradation ceremony in which the public identity of the convicted individual is lowered on the social scale.[299] The publication of the names of guilty offenders is an example of this approach.

Stigmatization may attach to knowledge that an offender has been apprehended for a particular crime, or punished in a particular way, without any efforts on the part of the punishing agency. Bentham talks of "punishments belonging to the moral sanction itself" as existing "independently of any employment of [moral sanction] by the magistrate."[300] Indeed, stigmatization may cling to punishment and conviction even when the legal system tries to discourage it. Andenaes remarks, "It often seems to be the fact that the individual was punished which is considered disgraceful rather than the commission of the crime itself."[301] And if social stigmatization can exist independently of legal efforts to achieve or accentuate it, the prospect of stigmatization must be recognized as likely in some cases to be a formidable element of the message communicated by many legal threats.

Some evidence that this may be the case can be derived from

---

296. Andenaes, *supra* note 118 (b), at 78.
297. Bentham, *supra* note 151, at 453–67.
298. Sutherland and Cressey, *supra* note 90, at 308.
299. See *supra* chap. 3, sec. 2, subsec. B.
300. Bentham, *supra* note 151, at 456.
301. Andenaes, *supra* note 118 (b), at 78–79.

the British Government Social Survey on deterrents to crime among fifteen- to twenty-one-year-old youths to which we have made a number of references.[302] The youths were given in ran-

TABLE 4
Ranking of Eight Deterrents

	Percentages (rounded)	Mean Rank
1. What my *family* would think about it	49	2.38
2. The chances of losing my job	22	2.96
3. Publicity or shame of having to appear in court	12	3.88
4. The punishment I might get	10	4.40
5. What my *girlfriend* would think	6	4.72
6. Whether I should get fair treatment in court	2	6.07
7. What my *mates* would think	1	6.08
8. What might happen to me between being found out and appearing in court	2	6.20

dom order eight cards each of which described a possible consequence of arrest, and were asked to rank them in order of importance. Table 4 indicates their response in terms of the percentage placing each item first.[303] A striking feature of these results is that if we add together the figures for items 1, 3, 5, and 7, all of which relate to the possibility of unofficial disapproval, we get a total of 68 percent who regarded one or the other aspect of such disapproval as the most important deterrent consideration. Since the nature of the offense involved was apparently not specified, we cannot generalize confidently, for it seems probable that this would affect the ranking of the deterrents. Nevertheless, it seems reasonable to conclude that the prospect of "losing a part of that share which he would otherwise possess of the esteem or love of such members of the community as the several incidents of his life may

302. Willcock and Stokes, *supra* note 41.
303. *Id.* at 76, table 44.

lead him to have to do with" does, as Bentham said, "possess a degree of force which cannot be despised by any individual."[304]

The prospect of stigmatization functions differently from the threat of other types of consequences (such as pain or confinement) because it is of special importance to those who attach significance to the judgments of others, and because the sting of community attitudes is difficult to administer to offenders in calibrated doses. Among members of a threatened audience, the fear of stigmatization will generally be greatest among those who are most socialized and presumably least in need of a deterrent. According to Lewin, among those who do *not* respect "the ideology, that is, the moral limitations of the group, threats of punishment frequently become ineffective" because "exclusion from the group" is not seen as a significant penalty.[305]

When stigma does attach to an individual as the result of punishment for a serious crime, it is more likely to be a total destruction of reputation than a small step down the ladder of repute. And when an offender has been stigmatized once, the effects of this process are likely to stay with him for many years. Having earned the status of criminal, the offender will have less incentive to avoid further consequences that bring with them the threat of stigma. As Lewin puts it, "Once punishment loses . . . its aspect of disgrace the strength of its negative valence decreases considerably. There then stands behind the threat only the specific unpleasantness of the punishment."[306]

If the threat of particular consequences functions as a deterrent because it carries with it the prospect of stigma as well as other deprivations, it is essential to recognize that variations in the severity of the penalty are not necessarily accompanied by upward or downward shifts of similar magnitude in the stigma value of punishment. Doubling a prison sentence from five to ten years is not likely to double the social consequences of conviction.

The expression "branded a criminal" derives from the practice of using actual physical stigmata as a means of reducing

304. Bentham, *supra* note 151, at 453 and 458.
305. Lewin, *supra* note 1, at 127.
306. *Id.* at 138.

the social status of offenders. It is said to have been abandoned in eighteenth-century England because it "had not had its desired effect of deterring offenders from the further committing of crimes and offenses but, on the contrary, such offenders, being rendered thereby unfit to be entrusted in any service or employment to get their livelihood in any honest and lawful way, became the more desperate."[307]

Insofar as stigmatization may cause a permanent reduction in status and perhaps encourage membership of a criminal subculture, its effectiveness as an element in the threat of punishment may still be purchased at a price. As Andenaes says, stigmatization of the offender "conflicts with another purpose of punishment, since it makes more difficult the offender's reacceptance into society. . . . Both purely humanitarian and social considerations make it clear that the one who has served his sentence should be helped to his feet again."[308]

G Variations in the Severity of Consequences

The last of the three questions we raised about the role of the threatened consequences in the operation of deterrence is rather more complex than has sometimes been thought. For this reason and because the issues are of a somewhat different character from those discussed above it merits separate treatment.

i The Basic Issue

Since the power of a legal threat to function as a simple deterrent comes from the unpleasantness of the consequences threatened, one natural strategy for increasing the deterrent efficacy of threats would appear to be an increase in the severity of those consequences. It seems reasonable to conclude, to us as to Andenaes, "that as a general rule, though not without exceptions, the general preventive effect of the criminal law increases with the growing severity of penalties."[309] The theory of increased penalties as a marginal deterrent is simple and straightforward: all other things being equal, an increase in

307. Pike, 2 *A History of Crime in England* (1873–1876) 280; cited in Sutherland and Cressey, *supra* note 90, at 309.
308. Andenaes, *supra* note 118 (b), at 78–79.
309. Andenaes, *supra* note 118, at 970.

the severity of consequences threatened should reduce the number of people willing to run the risk of committing a particular criminal act, in much the same way that increases in the price of a product will decrease the public demand for it.

The analogy with the price system has long enjoyed popularity with theorists. More than eighty years ago, Gabriel Tarde wrote: "The same thing applies, it seems to me, to the effect of penalties upon criminality as applies to the effect of prices on consumption."[310] More recently Professor Stigler has argued that "the offender is deterred by the expected punishment, which is (as a first approximation) the probability of punishment times the punishment—$100 if the probability of conviction is 1/10 and the fine $1,000. Hence, increasing the punishment would seem always to increase the deterrence."[311]

If variations in the severity of threatened consequences were indistinguishable in effect from variations in price, there would be reason to assume that all increases in severity would tend to reduce the number of threatened behaviors committed. But, as Tarde pointed out, "The consumption of the article does not decrease in proportion to the rise in its purchase price. Sometimes it drops far more rapidly than the price rises; . . . sometimes it drops very much more slowly."[312] And the analogy is an incomplete one. An important difference between penalty and price is that a potential buyer will presumably know the price of a product before making a purchase decision. No such assumption can be made about the potential criminal's knowledge of the consequences threatened for a particular behavior. Ignorance about penalties, which is widespread among potential criminals,[313] may lead to irrational conduct and negate the possibility that change in penalties will operate as a marginal deterrent for the ignorant.

A second difference is that the price of a product is a sure condition of purchase, while the incidence of consequences threatened for an offense will be only occasional. This factor, by itself, would not necessarily impair the marginal deterrent

310. Tarde, *supra* note 280, at 482.
311. Stigler, "The Optimum Enforcement of Laws" (1970) 78 *J. Polit. Econ.* 527.
312. Tarde, *supra* note 280, at 482.
313. See *supra* sec. 1, subsec. D, notes 5–6 and accompanying text.

effect of increases in the severity of penalties in cases where the risk of apprehension remains constant. If potential offenders believe that their chances of apprehension cannot be ignored, the risk of a high penalty provides more incentive to avoid crime than the risk of a low penalty. Indeed, the low risk of a high penalty (say 1/100 x $1,000) may, for some people, be more worthy of avoiding than a higher risk of a lower penalty (say 1/10 x $100) because the realization of the first risk would mean personal catastrophe. However, given the offenders' vagueness about penalty and the further complication of risk, it would take a rather large increase in penalty before potential offenders perceived a real change in "cost."

The uncertainty involved in penalty is not a matter of objective probabilities but rather of subjective perceptions. We have already noted, in our discussion of the credibility of threats, some reasons for discouraging overemphasis on the objective probabilities of apprehension. It is not the actual degree of risk, but the way in which people perceive and respond to risk that is crucial.

Some authorities suggest that potential criminals make serious attempts to assess that risk. The California Youth and Adult Corrections Agency reports: "There is evidence from many sources that the certainty of the punishment is less significant as deterrent than the certainty of detection. Potential criminals do seem to calculate the chances of being apprehended."[314] On the other hand, it has been held that, when considering chances of impunity, deliquents "have a stronger tendency than other men to dwell exclusively on the favorable instances."[315]

Clearly, estimates of the chances of apprehension may vary enormously. If the chances of apprehension were generally regarded as extremely high, then increases in the severity of penalties should significantly reduce crime rates. But if potential offenders find in the uncertainty of apprehension a reason for believing that they will not be caught, they will be immune to the influence of severer penalties. And this conviction of per-

314. California State Assembly Office of Research, *Crime and Penalties in California* (1968) 23.
315. Chadwick, "Preventive Police" (1829) 1 *London Review* 301–2. Cited by Radzinowicz, *supra* note 199, at xiii.

sonal immunity may be widespread among those for whom severe penalties are supposed to operate as a marginal deterrent.

If the threatened consequences are so high at the outset that only the foolhardy would find it worthwhile to run the risk of apprehension and punishment, the marginal deterrent effect of increased severity might well be minimal, for the foolhardy are a majority of the critical audience of a penalty change.

ii Some Evidence

A number of studies dealing with the impact of penalty increases on crime rates underscore the point that the use of simple price system models is not completely satisfactory. The attempts to ascertain whether the death penalty reduces homicide more than protracted imprisonment, which we mentioned earlier, support the conclusion that the introduction or elimination of the death penalty has no discernible effect on homicide rates.

Furthermore, studies in single jurisdictions, before and after upward shifts in penalties provided for rape,[316] marijuana possession,[317] and assaults on police officers,[318] have found no changes in the trend of crime rates that could be attributed to the penalty changes. However, it must be noted that the studies of crime trends in a single jurisdiction are less reliable than the series of studies on capital punishment and homicide.[319]

Two studies of a rarely enforced Nebraska law providing much stiffer maximum sentences for bad checks over $35 than for bad checks under that amount failed to find any difference in the frequency of the larger bad checks that could be attributed to the difference in threatened consequences.[320] Cham-

316. Schwartz, "The Effect in Philadelphia of Pennsylvania's Increased Penalties for Rape and Attempted Rape" (1968) 59 *J. Crim. L.C. and P.S.* 509–15.

317. California State Assembly Office of Research, *Crime and Penalties in California* (1968) 12. The California statistics on marijuana deal only with the number of reported arrests because no reliable estimates of the gross number of crimes are available for this crime.

318. *Id.* at 10–12.

319. See *infra* chap. 5.

320. See Beutel, *Experimental Jurisprudence* (1957) 224–420. In 1967, a study supported by the Center for Studies in Criminal Justice at the University of Chicago used different methods to come to the same conclusion. See Zimring, "Bad Checks in Nebraska: A Study in Complex Threats" (1968) unpublished.

bliss, it is true, found that parking offenses decreased after increases in the fines threatened for persistent offenders. But it seems likely that other changes in policy toward parking offenders accounted for the major share of the decrease.[321]

Rusche and Kirchheimer confronted the issue of marginal deterrence in a broader framework by analyzing rates of a number of different crimes in England, France, Italy, and Germany from 1910 to 1928.[322] In England, the authors noted a small decrease in crime together with a trend toward greater leniency. In France, rates of most crimes remained stable while punishment levels decreased.[323] In Italy and Germany, punishment for major crimes increased, but the crime rate fluctuated without any apparent relation to punishment levels.[324] The authors of this study recognized that the countries being compared differed substantially in attributes other than punishment policy, so that it was impossible to draw positive conclusions about the effect of higher penalties on crime rates. But the figures from the study "provide no basis for assuming that the policy of punishment affects criminality."[325]

Gibbs[326] and Tittle[327] analyzed crime statistics and punishment data from the various states in the United States in an effort to determine whether variations in the probability of apprehension or the severity of punishment were related to variations in the rate of particular crimes. The Gibbs study related only to homicide, while the Tittle study involved homicide, rape, burglary, robbery, sex offenses, and auto theft.

For homicide, highter-than-average severity of sentences was significantly correlated with lower-than-average crime rates when figures for all states were analyzed without distinctions based on region of the country.[328] For the other offenses, no significant correlation between severity of sentences and crime

321. Chambliss, *supra* note 195, at 70.
322. Rusche and Kirchheimer, *Punishment and Social Structure*, (1939) 193–205.
323. *Id*. at 193–200.
324. *Id*. at 200–205.
325. *Id*. at 200.
326. Gibbs, "Crime, Punishment and Deterrence" (1968) 48 *Southwestern Soc. Sci. Qtly* 515–30.
327. Tittle, "Crime Rates and Legal Sanctions" (1969) 16 *Social Problems* 409–13.
328. *Id*. at 415.

rates was found, which apparently lead to the remarkable conclusion that severity of sentence influenced the rates of one crime thought to be the least deterrable of offenses, but did not similarly affect such traditional property crimes as larceny and burglary.[329]

However, when severity of punishment and crime rates were compared by grouping states into regions, states with higher-than-average penalties apparently did no better in relation to homicide than those with lower penalties. Nor did they in regard to the other categories of crime where nationwide totals had also shown no apparent relation.[330] Thus, regional differences in crime that are unrelated to severity of punishment appear to have been responsible for the nationwide correlation between punishment levels and crime.[331] A more detailed sta-

329. *Id.* at 415–17.

330. The procedure followed to control for regional effects in Professor Tittle's data were (1) the division of the country into five regions—East, South, Border, Midwest, and West; (2) the calculation for each region of the mean rate of the particular crime and the mean length of sentence for that crime; (3) the rating of each state as above or below the average for its region in rate of particular crime and in severity of sanction. It was found that while, for instance, the correlation between average prison sentence and homicide rate for the nation as a whole was −.46, in only 21 of the 46 states for which data were available did a state with higher than regional-average penalties show a lower than regional-average rate or, to the same effect, did a state with lower than regional-average penalties experience a higher than regional-average homicide rate. At the same time, in 25 of the 46 states, mean sentences and mean crime rates were both either higher or lower than the regional average. The authors conducted this analysis of the data with Professor Tittle's assistance.

331. The principal problem with using an undifferentiated national sample of states is that areas, such as the Deep South, that have very high rates of homicide appear to regard intraracial killing as less serious than do other areas of the country. Thus, the South, with a rate of homicide of .09 per thousand during the period studied, compared with .03 for the Midwest and .02 for the East, had an average prison sentence of 89.6 months for homicide, compared with 199.4 for the Midwest and 214.5 for the East, appearing to suggest that higher penalties create less homicide. But when we ask whether those states with higher penalties in the South do any better than their neighbors, the data suggest they do not. The five Southern states with lower than mean sentences for homicide have slightly lower homicide rates than the four higher than mean punishment states. The relation between severity and rate, undoubtedly present in the nation as a whole, is apparently not a causal one. See note 328 *supra* for data on all 46 states controlled for region, and *supra* sec. 1, subsec. E (iii), for a discussion of the relation

tistical analysis of similar data is in progress, and the preliminary findings suggest that greater sentence severity is associated with lower crime rates while not isolating as yet the
question of general deterrence.[332]

iii Some Conclusions

The studies carried out to date illustrate some of the difficulties involved in evaluating the impact of severity of consequences on crime rates. Comparative studies are unreliable
because factors other than the crime rate may cause crime
rates to differ; and areas that differ in punishment policy may
also differ in these other factors. Studying the crime rate before and after a change in penalty is useful, but it is difficult
to determine what the crime rate would have been in the period
following the change if the change had not occurred; trends
before the change are of some assistance but trends themselves
may change. Moreover, with the exception of some studies on
capital punishment, the quality of research on the issue of
severity of penalties is generally spotty. In spite of the methodological problems, however, existing studies do tentatively support a number of conclusions.

First, cross-cultural and interstate comparisons of sentence
severity and the crime rate show that moderate variations in
the severity of punishment for serious crime are probably not
a major factor in explaining the differences in crime rate that
are observed in different jurisdictions. While such studies are
far from perfect, they do help to set an upper limit to the
amount of variation in the crime rate that might be attributable to punishment policy.

Second, specific investigations of the use of capital punishment for homicide, and those of upward shifts in the minimum
and maximum terms of imprisonment for other major crimes,
have produced mainly negative conclusions. It would be tempting to generalize from these specific case studies that increases
in severity are of little use as marginal deterrents, but such a
generalization would be unwarranted on the evidence.

---

between probability of punishment and crime rates and Tittle's treatment of this topic.
332. Ehrlich, "Participation in Illegitimate Activities: An Economic
Analysis" (1970) unpublished.

Many of the studies of upward shifts in penalty, such as those of the change in punishment for possession of marijuana and assault on police officers in California, do not rule out the possibility that increased penalties did have a marginal deterrent effect.[333] Moreover, a number of these studies—including the California studies, the Nebraska bad check sounding, and probably the Philadelphia rape analysis—focused on changes of penalty where public knowledge of penalties was low and where changes in actual sentencing practice may not have occurred.[334]

More favorable conditions could, conceivably, lead to different results. It is also important to note that all of these studies involved moderate shifts in legislatively prescribed punishments for offenses that were already severely punished. It cannot be concluded that larger increases in penalty would in no circumstances have an effect on crime rates, particularly when the base penalty for an offense is quite low. There is no justification for generalizing about the effects of increased fines for parking offenses on the basis of data relating to the use of the death penalty for homicide; at least no theory has been validated which would justify such inferences.

But available data do suggest that increases in legislatively provided penalties for major crimes have little impact as a marginal general deterrent in many situations where officials place great faith in such increases. This finding could be adduced in support of experimental downward shifts in maximum threatened punishment for major crimes where present penalty levels

333. The California marijuana study, *supra* note 314, presents the weakest evidence, because it rests on arrest rates rather than changes in the crime rate. Moreover, because trends can change, all the single-jurisdiction studies leave open the possibility that a shift in penalty may be evidence that conditions exist which might cause a change in trend. However, conclusions based on the cumulative evidence of a number of single-jurisdiction "before and after" studies, which all fail to reveal changes that could be attributed to the change in punishment policy, are less vulnerable to attack than conclusions based on individual studies. And when comparative and retrospective techniques are combined and frequently repeated, as was the case in the capital punishment studies, the use of imperfect research technique can lead to the construction of an impressive case for or against marginal deterrence in a particular comparison of penalty threats.

334. See *supra* note 155 for data on California. The Nebraska data are discussed *supra* in sec. 1, subsec. D (i).

reflect deterrent intentions that may not be producing results. We must bear in mind for later consideration the difference between the maximum penalty threatened and the average penalty imposed. Nowhere is this more important than in America, where relatively few serious offenders are convicted and there are very wide variations in the penalties imposed.

The failure, if failure it be, of many increases in severity of consequences to function as a significant marginal deterrent to major crimes is not wholly incomprehensible. We attribute it, in part, to the widespread lack of information about penalties among many classes of potential criminals, to the persistent optimism of many potential offenders, and to the fact that increases in a punishment that conveys stigma do not necessarily result in increased stigmatization.

Increased penalties are probably more or less significant depending on the size of the penalty increase relative to the size of base penalty. Raising a threatened prison sentence from five to seven years will have less impact than raising a threatened penalty from one month to one year, although the former shift represents more than twice as much additional punishment.

In either case, if the higher penalty threat is to have a marginal deterrent effect, it will do so by persuading those who would commit crimes if confronted with the old threat to refrain from them because of the increase. In the case of the five-year base penalty, any marginal general deterrence will have to occur among people who were willing to risk five years in prison, and this group is confronted with only a 40 percent increase in threatened penalty. But when a penalty is raised from one month to one year, the relative increase is 1,100 percent, and the population among whom marginal general deterrence must operate is not necessarily as intransigent as that to which the five-year base penalty would apply.

There may, of course, be people in the group of potential offenders threatened by the one-month penalty for whom the increase in penalty from one to twelve months will have no effect. But, since the base penalty is lower, there may be a larger number of people willing to risk the month in jail who are not as strongly motivated or as difficult to influence as those willing to risk five years. When the large relative increase in punishment is put into effect, it may function as a marginal

deterrent by substantially reducing the number of crimes committed by these less motivated or more responsive potential
offenders.

If the relative magnitude of increases in marginal deterrence
is important, upward shifts will result in diminishing marginal
returns as the base penalty increases. This does not mean, of
course, that increases in threatened penalties will fail to produce any marginal deterrence when base penalties are large.
Such increases could, indeed, produce relatively small deterrent returns that are still of great social importance.

Thus, the diminishing effects of increases in severity in weed-
ing out potential criminals is no reason for rejecting increases
in relatively high base penalties as proper policy in all cases.
But where the escalation in threatened consequence fails to
produce a discernible marginal effect on the crime rate, or
where the possible return is too small to justify the costs, the
policy implications of research findings are clear. It should be
added, however, and we shall return to this point, that most of
the studies considered deal with threat announcements that
may or may not have been realized in practice.

iv The Uses of Variation in Severity:
   The Fortress and the Stepladder

If potential criminals are responsive to variations in the severity of threatened consequences, how can the legal system
make the best use of those variations to achieve social defense?
One answer is that, since the goal of all legal threats is to keep
the population law-abiding, the widest possible distinction between criminal and noncriminal behavior should be created by
threatening all types of serious crime with penalties which are
as severe as possible.

The aim of this strategy is to create a fortress around criminal activity by using the full power of threatened consequences
to keep potential criminals from becoming actual criminals. In
eighteenth- and nineteenth-century Europe, penal practice appears to have been informed by this idea. In England, which
seems to have led the way in this as in other fields, there were
by the end of the eighteenth century over two hundred statutes
imposing capital punishment. In 1810, Sir Samuel Romilly said
in the House of Commons: "There is probably no other coun-

try in the world in which so many and so great a variety of human actions are punishable with loss of life as in England."[335]

Another possible strategy would be to threaten all serious crimes with major penalties, but to employ a considerable amount of variation in threatened penalties to emphasize distinctions between *types of crime*. The rationale behind this approach was expressed by Beccaria: "There must . . . be a proper proportion between crimes and punishments. . . . If an equal punishment be ordained for two crimes that do not equally injure society, men will not be any more deterred from committing the greater crime, if they find a greater advantage associated with it."[336] And Bentham gave a particular example of the necessity for establishing "a proportion between crimes and punishments": "If the punishment is the same for simple theft, as for theft and murder, you give the thieves a motive for committing murder, because this crime adds to the facility of committing the former, and the chance of impunity when it is committed."[337]

This theory also sees the institution of punishment, with its threats of conviction and imprisonment, as a mechanism for trying to keep all of the population law-abiding. But at the same time it seeks to use variations in the severity of major penalties to create a stepladder effect, threatening those crimes which are considered most serious with substantially greater consequences than other less serious, but still major, infractions of the criminal code. While simple larceny, burglary, robbery, and armed robbery are all serious threats to the security of property in society, it is nonetheless true that they are not regarded as equally serious crimes.

The fortress approach attempts to secure greater conformity to law by laying down high penalties for serious crimes of all kinds. The stepladder approach is based on recognition that "it is impossible to prevent all disorders in the universal conflict of human passions";[338] in other words, that total conformity to the law is not obtainable. Therefore, insofar as "a

335. Radzinowicz, 1 *A History of English Criminal Law* (1948) 3.
336. Beccaria, *supra* note 282, at 63.
337. Bentham, *supra* note 151, at 400.
338. Beccaria, *supra* note 282, at 63.

scale of disorders is distinguishable,"[339] we should, according to this view, make the distinction between penalties for different types of crime as great as possible, in order to ensure that crimes "be less frequent in proportion to the harm they cause society"[340] and thus to minimize the harm caused by criminal conduct. There are ethical reasons to punish crimes in proportion to their seriousness that function whether or not particular offenses are potential substitutes for each other. But the argument that more serious punishments should be saved for more serious offenses in order to reduce the rate of the latter must be based either on the notion that penal resources (including the moral force of punishments) are scarce or on the hypothesis that criminals may substitute one offense for another.

All existing punishment policies and penalty structures tend to be combinations of both fortress and stepladder strategies. But because the range of penalty options in society is not infinite and is usually limited by considerations other than deterrence, there is commonly tension between one or the other of these two strategies in crime control policy. "The great inconvenience resulting from the infliction of great punishments for small offences," Bentham said, is "that the power of increasing them in proportion to the magnitude of the offence is thereby lost."[341] Since the range of punishment options is limited, and since increases in threatened consequences are more significant when base penalties are low, the greatest contrast between types of crime is achieved when base penalties are lowest.

The nature of the difference and the basis of the conflict between the two approaches can, perhaps, best be brought out by means of an illustration. Table 1 compares hypothetical penalty structures, both of which are mixes of fortress and stepladder strategies, for a variety of property crimes.

The table assumes that the legal system has an equal stake in differentiating between property offenses at each point on the ascending scale, which is probably not true. But it demonstrates that schedule *B* can maintain 200 percent increases in penalty between classes of property offense without running

339. *Id.* at 64.
340. *Id.* at 62.
341. Bentham, *supra* note 151, at 400.

TABLE 5: *Two Hypothetical Penalty Structures*

	Schedule A		Schedule B	
	Years in Prison	% Increase from Penalty for Next Most Serious Crime	Years in Prison	% Increase from Penalty for Next Most Serious Crime
Larceny	5	...	1	...
Burglary	10	100	3	200
Robbery	20	100	9	200
Armed robbery	40	100	27	200
Robbery plus murder	*Life*	...	*Life*	...

out of punishment options, while schedule *A* can only maintain 100 percent increases.

Moreover, while schedule *B* confronts the practical problem of whether life imprisonment really exceeds twenty-seven years by any significant degree, when differentiating armed robbery from robbery plus murder, schedule *A* encounters this problem much earlier, because assumptions about longevity are involved in the distinction between robbery and armed robbery. It would probably be wise in both sentence structures to increase the contrast between penalties for armed robbery and robbery plus murder. But this could only be done by decreasing the gap between penalties for other crimes of graduated seriousness, or by lowering the base penalty for larceny.

Our hypothetical schedules and most of the discussion assume fixed statutory penalties. In the real world, however, we have to take account of maximum and minimum sentences, plea bargaining, and a host of other uncertainties. This kind of uncertainty, which is particularly associated with current trends in correctional practice, lends an equivocal character to real penalty structures.

The ambiguity of penalty structure could be seen as helping to resolve the conflict between fortress and stepladder considerations as they compete for the finite range of punishment options. It could be argued that the maximum penalty available for all serious crimes could be fairly high as long as the minimum were considerably lower. The possibility of the higher penalty could then function as a deterrent for the less serious crime, and the ambiguity surrounding the level of punishment could bring home to the offender the fact that aggravating circumstances or further criminality would generate the risk of sharply escalated levels of punishment.

Having raised this possibility we must confront another level of empirical question, Is not the chance of leniency built into ambiguous penalty structure itself a significant step away from the fortress strategy? To the extent that chances of leniency become a means by which the sanguine potential offender downgrades his estimate of consequences upon conviction, the ambiguity does not resolve the basic conflict between the fortress and stepladder strategies. For where there is a downgrading in deterrence, fortress values are sacrificed to stepladder possibilities, and the conflict is decided in favor of the stepladder. We call this "another level of empirical question" incidentally, because its reality as an issue of fact depends on the assumption that a good many variations in threatened consequences can act as marginal deterrents.

Whether social policy is better served by fortress or stepladder emphasis depends not only on the degree to which each strategy is effective in particular situations but also on questions about relative values that empirical research cannot answer. If an increase in the penalty for burglary succeeds in reducing the rate of that crime, this does not mean that all who have been deterred from burglary now obey the law. Many may have taken up other forms of crime, where the rewards are higher or the risks and penalties are lower. It may be easier to scale down the dangerousness of crime than to completely eliminate criminal tendencies among an audience of people who would violate laws at a given base penalty.

We are here confronted with problems which involve both facts and values. Judgments about the adoption of either the fortress or the stepladder approach have to be made in the light not only of the actual effects of increases in severity of punishment on potential criminals, but also of the relative importance of various crimes. That this is the case can be seen clearly if we assume that schedule *A* in table 5 produces 20 percent less larceny and 5 percent more burglary, robbery, and armed robbery than schedule *B* by keeping 1,000 additional potential criminals law-abiding. At the same time it eliminates the contrast between penalties that may have kept some thieves from more serious crime in schedule *B*.

The decision to be made is the sort of multidimensional one that we discussed earlier in this work.[342] For any judgment about the relative desirability of the two approaches will necessarily involve determining how many extra larcenies it is worth to society to prevent the added danger of one robbery. Empirical research may help to measure the effects of penal policy and to define the particular types of harm generated by each type of offense. But policy making has also to take account of those other dimensions which Beccaria designated by the expression "the public good."[343]

v Concluding Note

Professor Andenaes concludes his article "Deterrence and Specific Offenses" with the statement, "He who invests in increased severity has to calculate with diminishing returns."[344] By this Professor Andenaes may mean that, as a matter of simple mathematics, increasing punishment by a given amount has less of a proportional effect as one proceeds up the ladder of possible punishment levels. Thus the addition of 1 year to a 1-year sentence represents a 100 percent increase; whereas the addition of 1 year to a 10-year sentence represents only a 10 percent increase. But the applicability of this insight is limited. For moving from a 1-year to a 2-year sentence would not necessarily have less effect than moving from a 10-year to a 20-year sentence. Yet if that is what Professor Andenaes means, the assertion is a reasonable one, and there is some evidence to support it.

Nevertheless, there is a possibility that, while potential offenders may not make fine discriminations regarding the severity of threats within penalty categories, there may be thresholds which are psychologically important. Those who would accept with equanimity the prospect of an increased fine might nevertheless be alarmed by the possibility of imprisonment.

342. See discussion *supra* in chap. 2, sec. 4.
343. Beccaria, *supra* note 282, at 62.
344. Andenaes, *supra* note 118 (a), at 553.

Those for whom short terms of imprisonment would be acceptable as the risk taken for engaging in an illicit but profitable enterprise might feel differently about long sentences.

If the incomplete data available on the effect of modest changes up and down the scale of penalties correctly reflect reality, then the perceived disadvantages of increased penalties within certain penalty categories or within limited ranges of punitive severity, (e.g., an increase of from 10 to 30 days in jail or from 3 to 5 years in prison) may be relatively slight and often ephemeral, at least where the risk of punishment is perceived as small.

But there is no reason to believe that great increases in the severity of sanctions would not have marginal deterrent effects. Movements from fines to jail, or from county jail to state penitentiary, in that they involve crossing a "threshold," might produce increasing rather than diminishing returns. Yet, it is more likely that many increments in severity within politically acceptable limits are either unperceived or unpersuasive. In the world of political reality, penalty changes tend to be modest and confined to movements within thresholds.

These propositions of course are no more than hypotheses. They are poised somewhat insecurely on a narrow factual base and are liable to be toppled by the first stiff breeze of empirical evidence to the contrary. But there are peculiar difficulties about gathering the necessary evidence.

One of the principal difficulties is that of distinguishing quantum jumps across "thresholds" from other movements in penalties, and of finding enough of them to study. For if the categories of penalty are large, there will be few quantum jumps. A major problem here is that we are dealing with factors that are not subject to precise quantitative assessment. Those who will invest in psychological speculations of this nature certainly have to expect diminishing returns in terms of hard data.

H Group Processes and Group Morality: Some Comments on Juvenile Gangs and Conscientious Objection

In this section we deal with matters which, while important, really belong to the periphery of our central problem. They are, however, close to the heart of other people's concerns, and there is a considerable literature both theoretical and empirical dealing with topics which are discussed here. We are inclined to agree with Hood and Sparks that "empirical research designed to explore the structure, values, norms and the social dynamics of the group relationships which produce delinquency"[345] may be of vital importance. The inadequacy of our treatment of these and other issues touched on in the section, when it is not due to lack of competence, derives from the fact that our concern with them is here limited to their implications for and bearing upon the question of deterrence, a facet of group processes that is largely unresearched.

i Group Processes and Individual Propensities

(a) Introduction: the gang as a deterrence problem. It is only relatively recently that sociologists, psychologists, and anthropologists have focused scientific attention on the study of groups, group behavior and group processes. The importance of primary groups in the development of personality and attitudes was recognized earlier in the century by sociologists like Georg Simmel[346] and Charles Cooley[347] and psychologists like William James.[348] But the great majority of the research findings in this field have been published since 1950.[349]

Although Thrasher's classic study of the gang as a type of human group appeared in 1927[350] and Shaw and McKay's demonstration of the extent to which juvenile crime is a group activity appeared in 1931,[351] full recognition of the importance of group process variables in relation to crime and delinquency has been much more recent.[352] Nowadays it is widely maintained that "delinquency is not just a conglomeration of indi-

345. Hood and Sparks, *supra* note 112, at 109.
346. Simmel, *The Sociology of Georg Simmel* (1950).
347. Cooley, *Two Major Works: Social Organization and Human Nature and Social Order* (1956).
348. James, *Principles of Psychology* (1890) and *Talks to Teachers on Psychology* (1899).
349. For summaries of the literature, see Hare, *Handbook of Small Group Research* (1962), and McGrath and Altman, *Small Group Research: A Synthesis and Critique* (1966).
350. Thrasher, *The Gang* (1927).
351. Shaw and McKay, *Social Factors in Juvenile Delinquency* (1931).
352. For reviews of the literature on groups and gangs, see Geis, *Juvenile Gangs* (1965), and LaMar Empey, "Delinquency Theory and Recent Research" (1967) *J. Research in Crime and Deling.* 28–42.

vidual acts"[353] but rather that it is "mainly the product of the interaction between members of groups."[354]

Nevertheless, although there is "much support for theories which emphasize the importance of status and membership of groups for adolescents"[355] a great deal of what has been written about juvenile gangs has consisted of speculation and not infrequently "dramatisation of their real patterns of association."[356] Professor Geis, in his review of the historical and current literature on gangs, points out that "research is still in a very tentative stage, with numerous contradictory findings and unexplored questions."[357]

Confirmation of Geis's assessment can be found in a more recent review of the available literature by Hood and Sparks. "Criminologists are now faced with a number of rival theories,"[358] they write. "It seems as if theory has outstripped research and that what is needed is more detailed investigations to establish more precisely what behavior is characteristically committed by delinquent groups, what the nature and structure of peer groups are, what social bonds exist within the group and what values, beliefs and norms members share."[359]

Despite the fact that Cloward and Ohlin,[360] Cohen and Short,[361] Sykes and Matza,[362] Klein and Crawford,[363] and individual researchers like Miller[364] and Yablonsky[365] disagree

353. Hood and Sparks, *supra* note 112, at 80.
354. *Id.* at 108.
355. *Id.* at 109.
356. Walker, *supra* note 262, at 96.
357. Geis, *supra* note 352, at 2.
358. Hood and Sparks, *supra* note 112, at 86.
359. *Ibid.*
360. Cloward and Ohlin, *supra* note 115.
361. Cohen and Short, "Research in Delinquent Subcultures" (1968) 14 *J. of Soc. Issues* 20–37. See also Cohen, *Delinquent Boys: The Culture of the Gang* (1955).
362. Sykes and Matza: "Techniques of Neutralization: A Theory of Delinquency" (1957) 22 *Am. Soc. Rev.* 664–70; Matza and Sykes, "Juvenile Delinquency and Subterranean Values" (1961) 26 *Am. Soc. Rev.* 712–19.
363. Klein and Crawford, "Groups, Gangs, and Cohesiveness" (1967) 4 *J. Research in Crime and Delinq.* 63–75.
364. Miller, "Lower Class Culture as a Generating Milieu of Gang Delinquency" (1958) 14 *J. Soc. Issues* 5–19; Miller, "Violent Crimes in City Gangs" (1966) 364 *Annals of A.A.P.S.S.* 96–112; Miller, "Theft Behavior in City Gangs," in Klein (ed.), *Juvenile Gangs in Context* (1967) 25–37.
365. Yablonsky, *The Violent Gang* (1962).

about the nature of deliquent groups and the reasons for their existence, there seems to be general agreement that "the vast majority of early and mid-adolescent delinquency is carried out in groups."[366]

Most of the research studies performed in this area have been primarily concerned with the etiology of group delinquency. Much of the literature is concerned with what Sykes and Matza in a celebrated article called "techniques of neutralization";[367] that is, "rationalizations" or "justifications of deviant behavior" whereby "social controls that serve to check or inhibit deviant motivational patterns are rendered inoperative."[368] The literature does not deal with response to threats, being, as Cloward and Ohlin point out, "concerned almost exclusively with the moral judgments of delinquents and the way in which offenders handle guilt problems."[369]

Small family and peer groups shape and modify the attitudes and values that are of crucial importance in predicting how an individual will respond to a threat. But the study of delinquent groups makes it clear that beyond this basic degree of group influence there are a number of special circumstances and situations in which group pressures may determine threat responses.

The fact that research has not been directed specifically at this aspect of group behavior means that we can only offer hypotheses. But they are hypotheses derived from the available evidence rather than from *a priori* theories. And while we cannot claim that they are fully confirmed by the evidence, at least they are not in conflict with it.

One scholar who has dealt specifically with response to threats in a group context is David Matza. He maintains that two of the principal ways in which the normal "apprehensive component of infraction" is handled by "subcultural delinquents" are by the imputation of incompetence to law enforcement agents and by derogating the consequences of con-

---

366. Hood and Sparks, *supra* note 112, at 87, and LaMar Empey *supra* note 352.
367. Sykes and Matza, *supra* note 362.
368. *Ibid.*
369. Cloward and Ohlin, *supra* note 115, at 137.

viction.[370] "Delinquents," Matza maintains, "in fact do evade apprehension the vast majority of the time. Since the theory of police incompetence and delinquent potency is tenable . . . it serves as a major means of discounting apprehensiveness."[371]

The other means of dealing with apprehensiveness, the process of derogating or devaluing the consequences of conviction is, according to Matza, aided by the fact that "the official system normally begins by responding to the delinquent with light sanctions and slowly and gradually proceeds to weighter punishments."[372] "The subcultural delinquent," he says, "is inadvertently assisted in discounting the apprehensiveness connected with infraction by being gradually hardened to the more severe forms of sanction. Consequently, the apprehensiveness may be managed."[373]

A point made by Cloward and Ohlin is relevant here: that the accounts given by Cohen, and by Sykes and Matza, "do not differentiate sufficiently between the problems of members of delinquent subcultures and those of solitary delinquents."[374] And it seems reasonably certain that the techniques described by Matza are not confined to group members or to group situations; nor, probably, would he claim that they were.

(b) *Group pressures and deterrence.* In considering the way in which group pressures may moderate individual propensities, it is necessary to distinguish between situations in which group values include respect for the law and disapproval of criminal conduct, and those in which group values are in conflict with those that underlie the legal threat. In both cases a person may often be forced to make a decision about his response to a threat that might become visible to other members of his group. Strong pressures to conform to group expectations will be generated by the prospect that his decision will become known. A number of studies of the operation of group factors upon conformity, which compare responses made un-

---

370. Matza, *Delinquency and Drift* (1964) 186–87.
371. *Id.* at 187.
372. *Ibid.*
373. *Id.* at 188.
374. Cloward and Ohlin, *supra* note 115, at 137.

der public and private conditions, show clearly that conformity is much greater in the public context.[375]

When an individual member of a law-abiding group must make a decision about responding to a legal threat, his fear of disapproval by the group will supply him with an additional reason to heed the threat. In some cases, the deviant act itself might be visible to the group if committed, as when obedience to the law demands certain public gestures, or disobedience involves a conspicuous change in the individual's life style. In most other cases, the danger of deviant conduct's becoming visible to group members will come from the risk of detection or formal punishment.[376] In such situations, the risk of detection includes the risk of visibility, and the prospect of visibility is one of the significant forms of unpleasantness an individual may seek to avoid.

But when group values are in conflict with those that underlie the legal threat, as in the juvenile gang, the visibility of an individual's response to a threat results in pressure to defy the threat in order to preserve or secure standing with the group. Against the prospect that deviant behavior will result in punishment, the threatened individual must balance the likelihood that failure to defy a threat will lower his standing among the group and result in his being branded disloyal or cowardly. There are probably also some situations where failure to conform to the group expectation is threatened with more tangible discomforts.

The label of coward is likely to be particularly feared in youthful groups where courage, daring, and risk-facing capacity are valued. Indeed, this appears to be one of the principal ways in which group pressures may diminish the effectiveness of threats. Matza maintains that in those circumstances only a minority of youths will be "in the language of their companions, chicken, and in the language of classical criminology, deterred."[377] When the group rather than the individual is the

---

375. Deutsch and Gerard, "A Study of Normative and Informational Social Influences upon Individual Judgment" (1955) 51 *J. Abnormal and Soc. Psych.* 629–36, and Thibaut and Strickland "Psychological Set and Social Conformity" (1956) 25 *J. Personality* 115–29.

376. Andenaes, *supra* note 118, at 961.

377. Matza, *supra* note 370, at 186.

relevant unit of criminal participation it is particularly likely that the desire to conform and the necessity for making public responses may make individuals willing to risk unpleasantness that would be sufficient to deter them if each alone were responsible for the decision. If the fear of consequences is not regarded as respectable in a group, those who feel fear may be unwilling to make it known. Indeed, it becomes impossible to begin out loud the sort of dialogue which might lead away from criminality.

When fears are suppressed (rather than expressed) in favor of such values as "toughness" and "coolness,"[378] not only is their influence on the individual's behavior diminished but the group itself is insulated from them. Another factor, too, may help to make group members impervious to influences which might have deterred them as individuals—the *immediacy* of group pressures. This may be a powerful element in overwhelming ordinary tendencies toward caution in regard to participation in criminal activity.

It is because of the need to conform and the immediacy of group pressure that it is much easier to secure the compliance of a misbehaving child when this process is not visible to his deviant peers than when it is. In this respect, the evidence suggests that the child is the father of the man.

Observers fail to agree whether or not members of delinquent groups feel guilty about their delinquent acts. But a number of independent studies suggest that whatever group members' *private* feelings, they are at least *publicly* committed to delinquent norms and defiance of conventional values.[379] Commitment to delinquent values by a group not only takes the sting out of threat but may even result in inversion of the symbolic values of the sanction system and in their appropriation to serve opposite ends.

"In the identity system of the gang world," writes Carl Werthman, "repudiation increases with the fatefulness of the

---

378. Short, "Gang Delinquency and Anomie," in Clinard (ed.) *Anomie and Deviant Behavior* (1964).

379. See, e.g., Short and Strodtbeck, *Group Process and Gang Delinquency* (1965); and Schwendinger and Schwendinger, "Delinquent Stereotypes of Probable Victims," in Klein (ed.), *supra* note 364, at 91–105.

situation in which a boy is willing to take a risk, and thus the boys who have been sent to the more important prisons can flaunt this fact that they have paid and were willing to pay a more significant price for maintaining identity on the streets."[380]

Werthman quotes a gang member who says, "The stud who's been in jail expects you to respect him when he comes back. You know, before he goes in you respect him and he respects you, but when he comes back he expects you to respect him more."[381] Being punished may even become a status symbol. As Werthman puts it, "To the extent that boys do not drop out of gangs as they move through this sanction system, the fatefulness of their acts increases, and they tend to constitute an increasingly select elite."[382]

Researchers may, of course, encounter responses which are conditioned by precisely the group pressures being investigated. Fear of sanctions may be screened out of dialogue, if not out of action, by gang values. Nevertheless, it seems possible that threats of punishment, so far from being disincentives to crime, may in these circumstances even function as incentives to it.

Because much, perhaps even most, of juvenile crime is group activity,[383] group processes such as we have described, may be of crucial importance. Indeed, it seems likely that an understanding of group processes is an essential precondition to understanding some patterns of difference in threat response. It seems unquestionable that "generally speaking the imputation of legitimacy to a model of conduct that is widely disapproved requires continual reassurance from others in order to persist."[384] Similarly, there is little doubt that group membership, by providing an alternative "status universe,"[385] an alternative style of life, and an alternative system of values and norms, may profoundly moderate individual responses to threats

380. Werthman, "The Function of Social Definitions in the Development of Delinquent Careers," in U.S. President's Crime Commission Task Force Report, *Juvenile Delinquency and Youth Crime* (1967) 168.
381. *Ibid.*
382. *Id.* at 167–68.
383. LaMar Empey, *supra* note 352.
384. Cloward and Ohlin, *supra* note 115, at 138.
385. Short, Introduction to the abridged ed. of Thrasher, *The Gang* (1963).

and provide a measure of invulnerability to them. The operation of deterrence is greatly complicated when group pressures may not only inhibit the expression of the fear of sanctions but also in some instances convert stigmata into status symbols.

ii Conscientious Objection and Deterrence

We have considered briefly the way group processes may affect audience propensities to obey or defy threats with particular reference to the problem of what have been "delinquency-carrying groups" and "subcultural delinquency."[386] But not all subcultures are delinquent, and there are groups which, despite the fact that some of their norms deviate from the dominant social norms of broader society in ways which bring them into conflict with the law, would not be ordinarily described as criminal.

Whether or not the evidence justifies the belief that juvenile delinquency is the product of a subculture with deviant norms, there is no doubt that it is possible to find "examples of rather special kinds of crime inspired by membership of rather special kinds of groups."[387] And the sentiments and attitudes of such groups may have a profound effect on the nature of particular law enforcement problems and the effects of attempts at deterrence.

Vold, for instance, cites conscientious objection to military service as an example of "crime as minority group behavior."[388] The behavior of "the convinced pacifist who rejects the moral justification for his conviction or who constructs a rationale of his own course of action such that he can remain loyal and faithful to his minority group ideology" demonstrates, according to Vold, "the simple, stubborn fact that minority group members whose criminal behavior has been consistent with minority group views, are not changed easily by coercive measures applied by the majority group."[369] We shall therefore consider conscientious objection as a special case of the general phenomenon of group response to deterrence.

386. Bordua, "Delinquent Subcultures: Sociological Interpretations of Gang Delinquency" (1961) 338 *Annals of A.A.P.S.S.* 120.
387. Walker, *supra* note 262, at 97.
388. Vold, *supra* note 190, at 209–14.
389. *Id.* at 212–13.

When society as a whole views a particular criminal act as morally wrong, those who commit that act will consider it either morally wrong, morally neutral, or permissible because it is the means to an end that is judged to be morally acceptable. Only in the last of these conditions will the threat of consequences go against the moral sensibilities of the threatened audience. Moreover a sense of moral objection to the threat might not occur even then unless alternative means to the same end are not available.

There are, however, a few cases where the community threatens activity that members of the threatened audience regard as morally imperative. In the United States the laws against polygamy as applied to the Mormons,[390] laws prohibiting civil rights demonstrations in the South,[391] and various provisions of the Selective Service Act as applied against pacifists serve as outstanding examples. If the members of a threatened audience are otherwise in accord with the legal system, the criminalization of morally valued activity will set the stage for conflict between general feelings of loyalty toward society and allegiance to the particular behavior.

Often this conflict will be between an individual's loyalty to the all-inclusive society and his loyalty to the particular subculture that subscribes to the criminalized conduct. In some cases, as with the Selective Service Act since 1965, the moral value placed on the criminal conduct may be largely the product of individual feelings, and a group will have grown around the belief rather than vice versa. But in either case the group will provide moral support and an alternative focus for loyalty which will reinforce the strength of the conflict.

In cases of conflict where loyalty to the parent society emerges a clear victor, the moral value of the criminalized act will usually fade and will not permanently complicate the task of predicting how the threat's audience will respond to its terms. But if members of a threatened audience retain the strong opinion that the threatened behavior is morally right, to predict their response to the terms of the threat may be complicated, and the existence of that particular threat may

390. See *Reynolds v. United States*, 98 U.S. 145 (1878); *Mormon Church v. United States*, 136 U.S. 1 (1890).
391. See *Cox v. Louisiana*, 379 U.S. 536 (1965).

lead to more basic attitude and behavior changes on the part of some conscientious objectors. Those who retain their former attitudes about the threatened behavior will continue to have strong drives toward committing it but will be confronted with the prospect of social stigma and other types of punishment if apprehended.

While a normal response to unpleasant consequences is to avoid them, the moral value placed on the act *may* cause the moral quality of some or all punishment threats to be inverted. This is by no means inevitable nor will this response necessarily take the form of complete devaluation or revaluation of all such threats. In fact it is quite probable that responses may be differentiated in a variety of ways.

Five aspects of disobedience to law are normally considered to have negative value: resistance to enforcement of the law, the commission of criminal acts, arrest, conviction, and imprisonment. If moral value is placed on behavior which has been criminalized, attitudes toward resistance to the law and commission of the act will often be inverted. Sometimes, though less often, there will be a total suspension of negative evaluation in respect of arrest, conviction, and imprisonment. It is of course possible that individual judgments relating to all five aspects may be inverted. It is also possible that all five will still be considered worthy of avoidance because of their stigma value even though the individual considers the legal prohibition immoral.

It is important both to distinguish and to understand the intimate relationship between, on the one hand, *an individual* changing *his* views about the moral significance of criminal acts and their consequences, and, on the other hand, *people around him* changing *their* views. If both the individual and those important to him view a criminal behavior as morally imperative, the social stigma attached to persons apprehended for committing the threatened behavior may be viewed by those who value the behavior as evidence of righteousness.[392]

For the offender, pain and deprivation suffered on account of having committed the morally valued act will still be worthy

392. An allusion to the inverted moral quality of imprisonment can be found in the title of Martin Luther King's "Letter from a Birmingham Jail."

of avoidance but can be seen as a sacrifice for the moral value of the offense. If others agree with him, they may see the pain and deprivation as symbols of the sincerity of personal convictions and evidence of strength of character. And if the views of those others are important to the offender, the affirmative significance of punishment on his standing within the group will offset the powerful psychological forces that influence individuals to avoid painful consequences.[393] Thus, if a group of those who place moral value on threatened behavior exists to give support to the individual confronted with the choice of compliance or punishment, individuals are far more likely to invert the moral quality of punishment and actively rebel against the criminalization of the morally valued act. People operating without the support of such groups have, in some circumstances, defied such threats, and history pays special recognition to some members of this class. Moreover, it is possible that people placing moral value on a particular form of threatened behavior will coalesce to provide support for inversion of consequences and defiance of the law. The formation and activities of such a group would appear to be the basis of the prosecution case in the recent Boston trial for conspiracy of members of an ad hoc antidraft movement.[394]

The threat of punishment of behavior judged to have moral value may sometimes result in more generalized opposition to the legal system, and in a greater variety of criminal activities on the part of individuals who rebel at the enforcement of what they consider an unjust law. The loss of respect would sometimes appear to lower barriers to the commission of other types of criminal behavior and could result in higher rates of many types of crime, particularly if other crimes can be related to the ideological goals that underlie the initial rebellion.

Some traces of this tendency can be seen in the recent behavior of some "revolutionary" militants in the antiwar and civil rights movements. In their case, feelings of frustration and anger over a series of laws thought to be unjust appear to have been generalized over a period of time into a loss of

393. Cf. the way in which members of adolescent groups or a delinquent subculture can gain status by enduring punishment. See *supra* note 380.

394. See *United States v. Spock*, 416 Fed. 2d 165 (1st Cir. 1969).

respect for the legal system. This has then led to the advocacy of a greater variety of illegal tactics. Yet this pattern of reaction is by no means general. Those whose instincts are law-abiding are unlikely to defy or fail to support prohibitions on theft or drunk driving just because they think the laws relating to military service are unfair.

Indeed, the behavior of a large number of groups morally opposed to particular laws is surprisingly law-abiding. The Jehovah's Witnesses, the Quakers, and, more recently, the vast bulk of those in the pacifist and civil rights movements of the 1960s do not generalize defiance of one law into other types of criminal conduct. Members of such groups are very rarely involved in criminal conduct for which no personal moral justification exists. Opposition to particular laws on moral grounds appears most often in groups that have strongly developed moral codes and tightly knit group structures.

For them the process of inversion is self-limiting because it takes place only when the group's moral judgment is contrary to that of the legal system. For all other types of crime, the moral quality of the threat of punishment will not be inverted, and both the group sense of morality and a legal threat will stand as barriers to the commission of crime. Their crime rates are in fact very low. It is only when such a group becomes totally revolutionary that opposition to particular laws becomes a general moral license to crime, and even then group behavior may be restricted by the constraints of "revolutionary morality."[395] Indeed, for many revolutionary groups the motives which inspire their revolt may also make them more law-abiding in general.

When authorities are frustrated by conscientious objection to a particular legal prohibition, they sometimes increase the penalties threatened for violation. As noted before, some of the sting of threatened consequences will be removed by the process of inversion. But such increases in penalty may still provide members of the threatened audience with reasons for

395. Common criminals have seldom become heroic figures in ideological movements, and rather stern moral codes have usually been incorporated in revolutionary ideologies. To this effect, Lenin is reputed to have remarked contemptuously that if the German socialists were to board buses in order to nationalize them, they would first pay the fare.

refraining from the threatened behavior. Whether penalty increases will reduce the rate of the particular threatened behavior through increased fear of punishment more than it will increase defiance by solidifying opposition is an empirical question; results vary from case to case.

In interpreting the effects of penalty changes in this area we must recognize the probability that, in relation to laws covering military service, for example, only some of the offenders will have moral scruples supporting the commission of offenses. If we ignore the possibility that two or more marginal groups are involved, we may make the mistake of considering only the reaction of the morally committed group. Moreover, if we regard any changes in the crime rate as simply a reflection of the deterrent effect of the law on the behavior of that group, we may be completely misinterpreting the situation.

If the penalties for refusal to serve in the army were relatively slight, the number of conscientious law violators would be likely to be joined by a great number of nonconscientious violators. On the other hand, if the penalties were a great deal more severe and levels of detection very much higher, the proportion of conscientious violators to total violators would probably be very much greater. And in predicting the effect of the escalation of penalty threats in that situation we would expect the complicating factors involved in conscientious objection to play a more significant role.

When most offenders are conscientious objectors, harsher penalties may reduce the rate of deviancy but increase the resistance and hostility of those who remain defiant. In all but the most highly polarized of social climates, harsher penalties may also recruit new sympathizers to the cause of the conscientious objectors by providing offenders with a public audience for their claims of conscience or charges of oppression. This pattern of response was one aftermath of the harsh official and unofficial punishments meted out to civil rights demonstrators in the South in the early 1960s.

Less powerful side effects can occur when legal threats are attached to behavior that has been customary but not supported by strong moral feelings. Resistance to the prohibition of alcoholic beverages, for example, may be widespread when the use of alcohol has been an accepted custom, but such resistance will seldom initially assume the character of a crusade. Nevertheless, the behavior which threats seek to restrain will have acquired positive social meaning for members of a threatened audience far more often than in the case of traditional crimes.[396] Further, when the law seeks to restrain customary behavior, those whose responses are most important in the prediction of rates of compliance will be, not individuals, but groups among whom the forbidden behavior has been customary.[397]

Here too, if the group involved sees itself as suffering from poverty and discrimination, and particularly if this is the result of differentiation directly related to group membership, it may be that resistance to the prohibition of the custom will be generalized into a rejection of the entire value matrix of the legal system. As long as the group adhering to a particular custom is not thought of as unambiguously deviant, the attempt to maintain customary behavior may attract the sympathy and moral support of members of the community who do not identify with the custom but have no strong scruples against it.

Quite apart from special cases of this nature, it may be said that when harsh penalties are used to suppress customary behaviors, or when the prohibition of a behavior is perceived by a group as an attempt to persecute the group rather than deal with the behavior, moral indignation and many of its consequences may appear, complicating the task of predicting the effect of threat and punishment.

The extent to which crime in general and juvenile delinquency especially are the product of cohesive groups which follow deviant subcultural norms may well have been exaggerated. And it would be a mistake to assume that such groups exercise a major influence on threat response over the whole range of criminal behavior. But, as Nigel Walker points out, "It is a rare individual . . . who can do without the approval

396. See, for discussion of the use of the law to restrain customary behavior, Zimring and Hawkins, "The Legal Thrust as an Instrument of Social Change" (1971) 27 *J. Soc. Issues*, 33–48.

397. Cf.: Stjernquist, "How are Changes in Social Behavior Developed by Means of Legislation?" in *Legal Essays: A Tribute to Frede Castberg* (1963), and Massell, "Law as an Instrument of Revolutionary Change in a Traditional Milieu: The Case of Soviet Central Asia" (1968) 2 *Law and Society Rev.* 179–228.

of any of his fellow men; and even those who are impelled to adopt means to their goal that are officially disapproved will choose, if they can, means that have the approval of at least some minority."[398] Insofar as this is true, groups or associations will be formed which may affect reactions to legal threats in the ways we have indicated.

SECTION 2 THE INDIVIDUAL EFFECTS OF PUNISHMENT

A Introduction

"Future research," it has been said recently, "should make distinctions between general deterrence (the impact of punishment on potential offenders in the population) and specific deterrence (the impact of punishment on the offender) . . . since the two kinds of deterrence imply widely divergent mechanisms of control."[399] Throughout the literature there are frequent references to the necessity for distinguishing between general deterrence and what is variously called "specific"[400] or "individual"[401] or "special"[402] deterrence.

In section 1 of this chapter we have briefly indicated that we consider this nomenclature to be inappropriate. It is necessary to clarify our approach. We agree with Professor Hart that "the distinction between the efficacy of (1) the threat of punishment and (2) the actual punishment should be remembered . . .";[403] and with Andenaes that it is "necessary to make a distinction between the effects of a *threat of punishment* and the effects of *actual punishment* on the punished individual.[404] But it serves no useful purpose, indeed it obfuscates that distinction, to talk as though both the threat and the actuality were members of a single category or class; or alternatively

398. Walker, *supra* note 262, at 100.
399. Chiricos and Waldo, "Punishment and Crime: An Examination of Some Empirical Evidence" (1970) 18 *Social Problems* 215.
400. *Ibid.*
401. Walker, *supra* note 262, at 131.
402. Morris, "Impediments to Penal Reform" (1966) 33 *U. Chi. L. Rev.* 632.
403. Hart, "Murder and the Principles of Punishment" (1957) 52 *Northwestern U. L. Rev.* 452.
404. Andenaes, "Does Punishment Deter Crime?" (1968) 11 *Crim. L. Qtly* 78.

as though the former comprised a genus to which the latter belonged.

To talk of "the impact of punishment on potential offenders" and "the impact of punishment on the offender" as "two kinds of deterrence" is rather like saying that a storm warning and a storm are two different kinds of disturbance. The use of the expression "the impact of punishment" twice in one sentence to denote two quite separate and distinct processes generates a confusion of categories and obscures an important distinction.

One scholar who avoids this particular confusion is Professor Ewing, who uses the term *deterrent* "to cover only the effects on persons other than the offender, the latter effects falling under the heading of 'reformatory.' "[405] For, he says, if the punishment has so changed the offender "as to make him unwilling to commit the act even when he has no fear of punishment, then he is not 'deterred' but 'reformed.' "[406]

But it has to be said that not all those who are punished are necessarily "reformed" in the sense in which Ewing uses that term. In some cases it may be merely that they are made more sensitive to future threats of punishment. In other cases they may become less sensitive to those threats. The effects of the experience of punishment may, as we have pointed out earlier, be highly varied.[407]

It is clearly misleading, however, to use the term *special deterrence* of those who, after being subjected to punishment, become more responsive to threats of punishment. For no singular or unique "mechanism of control" of a different character from the process of general deterrence is involved. The experience of punishment is merely one of an enormous variety of factors which condition threat responsiveness. Moreover, few individuals have not at some time in their lives experienced punishment of some kind.

Apprehension and punishment may, it is true, produce significant changes in the attitudes and circumstances of offenders. Those changes may well affect the propensity of such persons

405. Ewing, *The Morality of Punishment* (repr. 1970) 63.
406. *Id.* at 64.
407. See *supra* chap. 3, note 6.

to commit crimes and their susceptibility to legal threats. Those who have been subjected to legal consequences, large or small, may react differently to legal threats of all kinds, and particularly to legal threats concerning the behavior that led to previous punishment. For this reason, a separate discussion of some issues relating to the individual effects of punishment is appropriate.

We begin with an attempt to define the issues involved. We then consider the measurement of effects in this area and of some empirical studies which relate to this question of the effectiveness of punishment. We deal next with the general issue of research in this area. Finally, we offer some tentative conclusions.

Consideration of the possible responses of previously punished offenders to legal threats involves recognition of all of the variables mentioned in the previous discussion of general deterrence as well as to the fact that apprehension and punishment may affect the offender's attitudes to both crime and the threat of punishment. Apprehension for committing a crime may cause offenders to revise upward their estimate of the probability of being apprehended again. It may also involve a public exposure of the individual's crime that can either sensitize him to the moral gravity of his act or harden his opposition to community judgments.

Some attitude changes of punished offenders are closely related to the effect of threats, and others are not, but all are important in relation to defining the role of punishment itself in crime prevention. Punishment effects that might condition future criminality include changes in the following:

1. The offender's attitude toward threatened consequences
2. The offender's attitude toward the threatened behavior
3. The offender's attitude toward society
4. The offender's ability to live with the law

i Changes in the Offender's Attitude toward Punishment

"*Prima facie*" Andenaes says, "it seems natural to expect that the experience of punishment would normally strengthen fear. The abstract threat of the law has come to life, and the offender visualizes the consequences more clearly than he did before. . . . The actual experience is much stronger than the theoretical knowledge."[408] But he goes on to say, "We cannot, however, take for granted that the experience of punishment always tends to strengthen the offender's fear of the law. It may work the other way."[409]

Such evidence as is available suggests that experience with punishment may in fact produce in its subjects both kinds of changes in attitudes toward punishment. Lewin, to whose research on the effects of punishment we have previously referred, has found significant changes in both directions. On one hand, he finds that when punishment has been previously administered, the negative valence of the punishment (to its subject) is very strong.[410] One reason for this effect, he asserts, is that punishment leads to an "increase in the degree of reality of the punishment"[411] by acquainting the subject directly with the sting of unpleasantness.

On the other hand, Lewin says that the experience of punishment may make subjects "become callous to the punishment and thus less sensitive to threats."[412] The prospect of a particular punishment may have lost its uniqueness and unfamiliarity to the punished subject. Such loss of effect would be likely to occur when a punishment derived most of its negative value from stigma. Once a person has lost a considerable amount of standing in the community, "he will have less to fear from a new conviction since his reputation is already tarnished."[413] Moreover, in some cases, exposure to stigmatization will cause an individual to react defensively to rejecting the values of the group that rebukes him. Thus Lewin predicts that "severe punishment is apt to lead to a revolution in the child's ideology."[414]

Punishment may either increase or decrease the anxiety its subjects experience about future punishment. It seems more likely that anxiety will be increased when highly socialized

408. Andenaes, *supra* note 404, at 88–89.
409. *Id.* at 90.
410. Lewin, *supra* note 1, at 134–35.
411. *Id.* at 162.
412. *Id.* at 137.
413. Andenaes, *supra* note 404, at 90.
414. Lewin, *supra* note 1, at 138.

persons are subjected to minor punishments. On the other hand, callousness toward punishment will probably be increased when less socialized persons experience penal measures that depend on the existence of strong feelings of social loyalty. Familiarity with punishment may also diminish the effectiveness of threats which derive their potency from fear of the unknown. The offender, says Andenaes, may have "had exaggerated ideas of the consequences of being caught and now draws the conclusion that it was not as bad as he had imagined."[415]

Little research has been done on the effects of punishment on attitudes toward punishment. Cameron, in her study of shoplifting, found that the often-punished "professional" shoplifter appears to take arrest and the prospect of conviction and punishment in his stride. "He does, of course, make every effort possible to talk his way out of the situation. But once he finds that this is impossible, he accepts jail and its inconveniences as a normal hazard of the trade."[416] The arrested amateur shoplifter, on the other hand, frequently displays considerable alarm and awareness of the seriousness of being caught.[417]

The greater sensitivity of the less experienced amateur might be a function of higher degrees of socialization, or of having more to lose in the way of community standing. Whatever the reasons, it is notable that the newly apprehended shoplifter appears to refrain from future shoplifting even in the absence of prosecution. Amongst those who "are apprehended and interrogated by the store police but set free without formal charge there is very little or no recidivism."[418]

Another study sought to determine whether prison inmates were more or less sensitive to variations in the threat of censure than college students. Projective tests were administered which involved making predictions about whether a hypothetical bank teller would embezzle funds.[419] Sensitivity to the risk of censure and other factors were measured by the vari-

415. Andenaes, *supra* note 404, at 90.
416. Cameron, *supra* note 142, 162.
417. *Id.* at 162–63.
418. *Id.* at 151.
419. Retting, "Ethical Risk Sensitivity in Male Prisoners" (1964) 4 *Brit. J. Crim.* 582–90.

ations in prediction that occurred when the risk of apprehension and other conditions were altered. Curiously, the study appears to give some support both to the theory that prisoners are more sensitive to the risk of censure-bearing punishment than to other factors *and* to the theory that the prisoners have less "ethical risk sensitivity" than college students. Prisoners showed more sensitivity to variations in what was termed the risk of censure than to factors such as variations in the amount that could be gained; but at the same time they showed less sensitivity to censure in general than the college students.[420]

The results of this particular study cannot be taken as evidence that the experience of imprisonment has an effect one way or the other on sensitivity to censure. In the first place, the prisoners may quite well have had very different value orientations from the college students long before they ever went to prison. Second, the prisoners may have been more interested in projecting a socially acceptable image when filling out the questionnaires than in candidly disclosing the factors which would influence their personal conduct when confronted with an opportunity to commit crimes.[421]

ii Changes in Attitude toward the Threatened Behavior

When punishment is considered a possibility by members of a threatened audience who have not experienced it, it is "psychologically farther off than [the] desired goal"[422] attainable by committing the threatened behavior. Once punishment is administered, the increased reality of the punishment experience may lead to changes in the subject's evaluation of the behavior that led to his discomfort. The experience of punishment may act as a "moral eye-opener," bringing home to the offender the fact that his behavior is considered seriously wrong and thereby reducing the probability that the offense will be repeated. Indeed, apprehension alone may in some cases be sufficient to achieve this. Speaking of the arrested amateur shoplifter, Andenaes says, "Before arrest most shoplifters do not think of themselves as thieves, but this is brought home to them through arrest and investigation."[423]

420. *Id.* at 587–88.
421. This possibility is discussed *infra* in chap. 5, sec. 6, subsec. C.
422. Lewin, *supra note* 1, at 163.
423. Andenaes, *supra* note 404, at 89.

Failing such a moral revelation, the experience of punishment may make clearer to the offender the disadvantages that accompany the offense and by association give him less favorable feelings toward the behavior. On the other hand, as with the threat of punishment discussed earlier,[424] so also the experience of punishment may cause offenders to experience conflict about the wisdom of their behavior. In some cases it may lead them to rationalize that, after all, the opportunity to commit the threatened act was worth the punishment. In the process of such rationalization, the threatened behavior may acquire a value to subjects higher than it had prior to punishment.[425]

This tendency to revalue behavior that has involved discomfort, in order to rationalize decisions, has been noted in laboratory experiments in "forced compliance," where the measure of sacrifice or discomfort was small. In one case, girls who were forced to undergo an unpleasant "initiation" in order to hear a recording designed to be dull and uninteresting rated the recording more interesting than girls who were subject only to a mild "initiation."[426] But it is not clear that more severe punishment would lead to a greater degree of the "it was worth it" effect. The whole process of rationalization might break down where the unpleasantness suffered was too great to permit a realistic judgment that the act was worth the punishment.

Nevertheless, because those caught and punished for committing offenses know that apprehension is generally uncertain, punished offenders can usually find alternative ways to rationalize their behavior without revaluing the threatened behavior. Thus the offender can say to himself, "I shouldn't have been caught," or, more ominously, "Next time I won't be caught." He can then continue to see his initial offense as justified because the unpleasantness suffered was simply the result of bad luck and not a necessary consequence of his action.

In the criminal process at the present time, penalty structures are probably high enough to make it difficult for most

424. See *supra* sec. 1, subsec. A.
425. See Festinger and Aronson, "The Arousal and Reduction of Dissonance in Social Contexts," in Cartwright and Zander (eds.), *Group Dynamics Research and Theory* (1960).
426. Aronson and Mills, "The Effects of Severity of Initiation on Liking for a Group" (1959) 59 *J. Abnormal Soc. Psych.* 177–81.

punished offenders to conclude that their criminal conduct was worth the price they paid. Moreover, punishment may often create negative associations with particular forms of threatened behavior, and with lawbreaking in general. For most offenders these should outweigh any tendency to view the pleasures of criminal conduct through rose-colored glasses. But punishment is unlikely to lead to significant changes in attitude in all cases, and changes in attitude will not necessarily be reflected in changed patterns of behavior. The persistence of the problem of recidivism indicates that the experience of punishment is not uniformly effective in this respect.

The attractiveness of criminal behavior can probably best be diminished when the consequences of apprehension activate latent moral judgments in the offender (as in the case of the amateur shoplifter). It is also likely to be diminished where drives toward the threatened behavior are initially weak. But when the drive to commit an offense is strong and the reality of punishment does not bring the offender's moral sensibilities to bear on his criminal propensities, the likelihood of attitude change will be considerably less.

ii Changes in Attitude toward Society

When the imposition of consequences for violation of a law is an important event in a man's life, it may lead to changes in his attitudes toward society that influence his future behavior. This possibility has long been recognized by penologists and by those who administer penal facilities throughout the world. It has led to the advocacy and sometimes the adoption of reform or rehabilitation as one goal of correctional administration.

The theory of reform or rehabilitation suggests that some forms of threatened consequences afford the opportunity to reorient the values of their subjects by discouraging commitment to antisocial values and encouraging loyalty to prevailing social norms. It differs from narrower theories which view punishment as a means of discouraging criminal conduct merely by associating unpleasantness with criminality in the mind of the offender.

But it is misleading to talk about *the* theory in this context. Nigel Walker points out: "As soon as the aim of reformation is extended beyond individual deterrence, theories about the way it is to be attained begin to multiply."[427] And it is difficult to disagree with his verdict that "the variety of these theories and the rapidity with which fashions in them change is a sure index of the failure of any one of them to yield spectacular results."[428] There is in fact a considerable literature dealing with the possibility that the experience of punishment leads to *less* favorable attitudes toward social norms on the part of punished offenders. Certainly the punishment process often generates hostility on the part of its subjects and creates some pressure to reject prevailing norms in order to protect self-esteem when punishment has conveyed a rejection of the offender by the social order.

While the effects of noninstitutional treatment on the beliefs, attitudes, and values of offenders has received some attention, most of the work done in this field has dealt with the effects of imprisonment on offenders' attitudes.[429] Unfortunately, since Donald Clemmer's pioneer study which appeared in 1940,[430] the research has yielded conflicting and inconclusive results.

It has traditionally been assumed that, since prison subjects the offender to constant association with others who have antisocial values and criminal skills, the net result of the punishment experience on an offender's attitudes may be an increased identification with deviant values. But more recent research suggests that in some cases the opposite may happen.[431] There is no consensus about the nature or extent of the effects of imprisonment on attitudes. As Hood and Sparks point out, "No research . . . has yet been done" which "connects the prisoner's experiences inside the prison, with his conduct after discharge."[432]

427. Walker, *supra* note 262, at 134.
428. *Ibid.*
429. For a useful recent survey of this topic, see Hood and Sparks, *supra* note 112, chap. 8: "The Impact of Imprisonment," 215–34.
430. Clemmer, *The Prison Community* (1940).
431. See Garabedian, "Social Roles in a Correctional Community" (1964) 55 *J. Crim. L.C. and P.S.* 338–47, and "Social Roles and the Processes of Socialization in the Prison" (1963) 11 *Social Problems* 139; Garrity, "The Prison as a Rehabilitation Agency," in Cressey (ed.), *The Prison: The Studies in Institutional Organization and Change* (1961).
432. Hood and Sparks, *supra* note 112, at 229.

However, the task of isolating the factors that determine whether, and in what circumstances, experience with punishment will produce greater or lesser loyalty toward prevailing social norms is one which lies beyond the scope of this discussion. It is sufficient for present purposes to note that either the rehabilitation or the further alienation of offenders as a result of punishment will have a significant impact on their future conduct.

iv Changes in Ability to Function

Some types of threatened consequences will affect the ability of offenders to live comfortably within the law. Social stigma and punishment-induced feelings of dependency can limit the opportunities available to punished offenders and impair their capacity to take advantage of such opportunities as remain. We have already mentioned the problems some ex-prisoners face in attempting to re-establish themselves in society.[433] And while stigmatization is undoubtedly more severe in the case of imprisonment it is not confined to that type of punishment.

On the other hand, job training and the treatment of physical and mental conditions in a prison setting can make the punished offender more capable of functioning effectively in society than he had been prior to serving his sentence. What Grunhut calls "training for work and training by work"[434] as one of the principal elements in prison rehabilitative programs is widely accepted by correctional administrators throughout the world today. The British Criminal Justice Act of 1948 provides that rules should be made for "the training of prisoners" and states that "The purposes of training in the treatment of convicted prisoners shall be to establish in them the will to lead a good and useful life on discharge, and *to fit them to do so.*"[435]

No research, however, has been done to determine to what extent various forms of punishment or punishment regimes render offenders either less or better able to adjust to society and conform to the law. We shall consider such research as has been done that is relevant to this question in the next two

433. See *supra* chap. 3, note 27.
434. Grunhut, *Penal Reform* (1948) 209.
435. Fox, *supra* note 229, at 73.

subsections. All that can be said at this point is that, if the propensity to commit crimes is related to opportunities to obtain gratification through legitimate means, the changes in status and ability that different punishment regimes may produce will affect recidivism rates among punished offenders.

B Some Studies

Although, as Hood and Sparks point out, "the effects of penal measures on the behavior of those not actually subjected to them . . . have been almost completely ignored by researchers,"[436] there has been "a great deal of research"[437] on the effectiveness of penal measures on "offenders actually dealt with by the courts."[438] These two authors go on to say, however, that "our knowledge is still limited and rudimentary"; and they cite approvingly Leslie Wilkin's verdict that we are still only at a stage where "the nature of our ignorance is beginning to be revealed."[439]

But we are not here concerned with *all* the effects of punishment on offenders, which may include incapacitation, reform, and rehabilitation as well as intimidation. Our basic question is, in Andenaes's words, "How does the experience of actual punishment influence the deterrent effect of the threat—a deterrent effect which has proved, in this case, insufficient to prevent the offence?"[440]

To consider "the effects of actual punishment under the aspect of deterrence alone"[441] presents a number of difficulties. Not least of these is the fact that the measure of the effectiveness of punishment and treatments which has been used by most researchers, i.e., "the conduct of offenders in a period after the completion of their sentences,"[442] does not discriminate between the variety of effects which punishment may have on individuals.

Moreover, almost all studies of the effectiveness of punishment have used the absence of reconviction as their principal

436. Hood and Sparks, *supra* note 112, at 172.
437. *Id.* at 171.
438. *Id.* at 172.
439. *Id.* at 171.
440. Andenaes, *supra* note 404, at 88.
441. *Id.* at 91.
442. Hood and Sparks, *supra* note 112, at 175.

if not their sole criterion of success. Researchers "have generally not distinguished between the deterrent and reformative aspects of individual prevention [but] have been content merely to count the numbers of offenders who have apparently succeeded in staying out of trouble for a fairly short period afterwards—without investigating the extent to which those offenders were actually 'reformed' by the treatment or punishment they received."[443] Andenaes writes: "If the prisoner does not relapse into crime we will not be able to tell whether this is due to a deterrent or a reformative effect of the prison, or if it might not have happened if no prison sentence had been imposed."[444] Hood and Sparks remind us of "the perennial problem that offenders may commit crimes during the follow-up period but may never be caught."[445] And in view of the fact that "most researchers have found that an offender's chances of recidivism are greater . . . the younger he is,"[446] we have to allow for the possibility that some "successes" may be attributable merely to the fact that the offenders have grown older and passed out of the more crime-prone age group.

"What we can measure," Andenaes concludes, "is how offenders perform after punishment, expressed in figures of recidivism."[447] But it is important to recognize that any difference in threat response between previously punished offenders and the rest of the members of a threatened audience could result from the fact that apprehended and punished offenders, particularly serious offenders, are a special high-risk group, independent of their experience with the legal system. Indeed, recognition of the fact that apprehended offenders are a special group in the population, apart from whatever effects apprehension and punishment might have, is a necessary beginning to any discussion of the effects of punishment on offenders.

When half of all those who have been convicted of larceny are arrested for larceny a second time, while less than one percent of all other members of a threatened audience are ever apprehended, some might be tempted to conclude that the apprehension and punishment of thieves does not deter them

443. *Id.* at 172.
444. Andenaes, *supra* note 404, at 92.
445. Hood and Sparks, *supra* note 112, at 177.
446. *Id.* at 180.
447. Andenaes, *supra* note 404, at 92.

from further offenses. To the extent that this inference rests on a comparison with the criminality of the general population, it is of course, invalid, because those punished for larceny are a specially selected group of property criminals, while the vast majority of the population never has and never will commit a serious property offense.

If such a comparison is invalid, the only data available on the effect of conviction and punishment on larceny offenders is that half are subsequently reconvicted. We cannot say that being convicted and punished had no effect on criminal propensities, because convicted thieves are a group that might otherwise have committed more crimes. It also cannot be said that this percentage is lower than it would be in the absence of punishment, since we cannot assume that all those who commit larceny once will do so again, or that all those who have been apprehended for larceny once will be caught in the future if they do repeat their crime.

The fact that those subjected to punishment are a high-risk group of potential future offenders establishes the importance of studying the reactions of this group to punishment and the threat of punishment. This is because apprehended offenders will be responsible for a far larger per capita amount of crime than the rest of the population, although the share of crime that can be attributed to previously punished individuals will vary with the type of crime.

According to an FBI study known as the Careers in Crime Program, those who have been arrested for some major crime are much more likely than the rest of the population to become involved in other forms of serious crime later in their careers.[448] There is also an English study of serious motoring offenders which suggests that such offenders have much higher than average involvement with nontraffic offenses.[449] It is necessary to add, however, that the data provided in both studies have subsequently been subjected to critical scrutiny which throws doubt on the validity of some of the interpretations offered.[450]

---

448. FBI, *Uniform Crime Reports* (1967) 34–44; (1968) 35–41; (1969) 34–40.

449. Willett, *The Criminal on the Road* (1964) 214–20.

450. See Ward, "Careers in Crime: The FBI Story" (1970) 7 *J. Research in Crime and Delinq.* 207–18; and Carr-Hill and Steer, "The Motoring Offender—Who is He?" (1967) *Crim. L. Rev.* 214–24.

Of particular interest in this context is the claim of the FBI study that it "has demonstrated the potential statistical use of criminal history information to measure success or failure of the criminal justice system."[451] "The key to the effectiveness of the system," states the report, "is in knowing what happened to the people who were handled or treated by the criminal justice process, specifically, whether they were deterred from further criminal acts and/or rehabilitated."[452]

More specifically, the study deals with the effects of what is called "leniency." It is pointed out that, in relation to "criminal repeaters," "leniency in the form of probation, suspended sentence, parole and conditional release had been afforded to 55 percent of the offenders. After the first leniency, this group averaged more than 5 new arrests."[453] The implication is that these forms of treatment which "represent a lesser punitive action than incarceration"[454] actually increase criminality.

Another recent study, however, dealing with juvenile delinquency and the "aftermath of apprehension," explicitly repudiates the suggestion that "lenient treatment is at fault."[455] The authors conclude "that what legal authorities now commonly do upon apprehending a juvenile for his delinquent behavior is worse than not apprehending him at all."[456] They claim to have demonstrated "that apprehension itself encourages rather than deters further delinquency."[457] As for "the deterrent effect of being caught and punished," they say that "there is no evidence substantiating such a deterrent effect."[458] On the contrary, "according to the findings of this study" the "non-apprehension of juvenile offenders" would be "likely to effect a reduction in their delinquency."[459]

Unfortunately both of these studies are subject to serious methodological deficiencies. The FBI Careers in Crime study has been critically analyzed by Paul Ward, who points out

451. *Supra* note 448 (1969) at 35.
452. *Ibid.*
453. *Supra* note 448 (1967) at 35.
454. *Ibid.*
455. Gold and Williams, "National Study of the Aftermath of Apprehension" (1969) 3 *Prospectus* 11.
456. *Id.* at 3.
457. *Ibid.*
458. *Id.* at 11.
459. *Ibid.*

that it suffers both from biased sampling which results in a systematic overestimate of the recidivism rate and also the inclusion among "offenders" of persons arrested but subsequently acquitted or having the case against them dismissed. He argues also that the suggestion that "lenient" methods of treatment are ineffective is not supported by the evidence provided and that a much more sophisticated analysis of the data would be required to reach any conclusion at all on that question. Hans Zeisel further suggests that the samples used by the FBI were hopelessly biased.[460]

The juvenile justice system study has been the subject of a critique by Professor Richard B. Stuart who indicates three methodological defects in it. First, he points out that the authors in selecting their criteria for cohort matching ignored three factors which, the evidence of other investigations suggests, "might have been major sources of variance in the results as obtained."[461] Second, he questions whether the apprehended delinquents and the controls were properly matched on the dimension of "seriousness of offenses."[462] Third, he questions the selection of a .10 level of statistical significance for the results rather than the more stringent .05 level.[463]

Somewhat removed from the studies just noted are some hundreds of studies dealing with the effects of punishment on animals or other intrahuman subjects. Two recent articles have considered the implications these laboratory studies might have for the punitive treatment of criminals.

Pran Chopra, in "Punishment and the Control of Human Behavior," maintains that we have "now probably reached the stage where extrapolations of findings to the human condition could have some meaning."[464] Accordingly he makes some suggestions as to the way in which those findings "may be applied to the actual problem of controlling illegal behav-

460. Ward, *supra* note 450. Zeisel, unpublished manuscript, University of Chicago, 1972.

461. Stuart, "Aftermath of Apprehension: Social Scientist's Response" (1969) 3 *Prospectus* 14–15.

462. *Id.* at 15.

463. *Id.* at 15–16.

464. Chopra, "Punishment and the Control of Human Behaviour" (1969) 2 *Austr., N.Z., J. Crim.* 150.

iour."[465] For example, he maintains that in the case of "illegal road behaviour" such as speeding and drunk driving we should not only make the punishment for the first infringement, "intense in its own right," but should "also make this penalty a discriminative stimulus for the maximum punishment available."[466] In this way we should avoid "the use of a graded hierarchy of punishment which is usually sequentially applied"[467]—a procedure which Chopra says "allows a maximization of recovery effects and is conducive to the development of avoidance behaviours rather than the suppression of a reference behaviour."[468]

Professor Singer, in "Psychological Studies of Punishment," also makes "suggestions for improving the effectiveness of criminal punishments" which he describes as "extrapolations from extensive laboratory research, involving both animals and humans, the results of which constitute our current basic scientific knowledge about punishment."[469] He states that "the empirical facts . . . are quite clear. Punishment can effectively suppress behavior, provided it is sufficiently severe."[470] From the experimental results he draws such conclusions as that "for maximum punishment effectiveness we should not permit parole,"[471] and that in the case of recidivism, if the initial punishment is "mild," we should "make repeated punishments not only progressively more severe but progressively much more severe."[472]

A number of comments are relevant both to the experimental studies and the extrapolations from them. The principal point is that the word *punishment* is used of processes which bear very little relation to the operation of the penal system. For, in the first place, the vast majority of the experimental subjects are rats, cats, dogs, monkeys, goldfish, and pigeons

465. *Ibid.*
466. *Id.* at 153.
467. *Ibid.*
468. *Ibid.*
469. Singer, "Psychological Studies of Punishment" (1970) 58 *Calif. L. Rev.* 435–36.
470. *Id.* at 415.
471. *Id.* at 422.
472. *Id.* at 422–23.

rather than human beings. In the second place, almost "the entire literature on punishment is based on . . . the electric shock."[473] These considerations place a substantial barrier in the way of deriving penological principles from what are called "the basic laws of punishment."[474]

One of the major criticisms made by experimental psychologists of "the punishment of crime" is that it is deficient as a form of aversive conditioning. It is, as Professor Eysenck says, "a very haphazard affair."[475] Both Mr. Chopra and Professor Singer speak of the necessity for increasing the certainty and diminishing the delay involved in the institution of punishment. "Extensive experimental investigation of the delay of punishment," says Singer, "has shown that effectiveness of punishment diminishes as it is administered from zero to five seconds after a behavior."[476] And although he makes suggestions for having "the legal process . . . speeded up,"[477] it is clear that the basic difference is not merely quantitative but qualitative.

Indeed, the only experience that fits the time dimensions required by the experimental psychologists would appear to be that of apprehension, although the "aftermath of apprehension" study does not support the notion that this experience operates as a notably effective deterrent.

Another critical aspect of the experimental studies of punishment which does not apply to the penal system is that aversive conditioning is based on repeatedly punishing repeated behaviors in a relatively short period of time. We know of no research in punishment that demonstrates a habitual act being punished only once and the habit being thus extinguished. But the fact that punishment is not aversive conditioning does not mean that it may not be effective. There are a variety of ways of controlling human behavior which bear no resemblance to the techniques employed by experimental psychologists. Moreover, within the institution of punishment there is no reason why the use of aversion therapy programs—such as have in

473. Campbell and Masterson, "Psychophysics of Punishment," in Campbell and Church (eds.), *Punishment and Aversive Behavior* (1969) 3.
474. Singer, *supra* note 469, at 408.
475. Eysenck, *supra* note 20, at 110.
476. Singer, *supra* note 469, at 418.
477. *Id.* at 420.

the past been employed in the treatment of drug addiction, alcoholism, and sexual perversions—should not continue to be used with appropriate safeguards and subject to constitutional limitations.

Unfortunately, none of the studies available provide us with any information about the way in which actual punishment affects future threat response. Professor Singer says that "to be effective in suppressing behaviour punishment must be unpleasant, and it must create some fractional unpleasantness in future situations."[478] But there is nothing in the studies we have been discussing to tell us to what extent it may or may not do this in the case of legal punishment.

C Research into the Effects of Punishment

The principal method used by researchers to test the effects of punishment on individual offenders is the study of subsequent criminality among punished offenders. But, as we have pointed out, such studies do not discriminate between the various effects which punishment may have. Their results will reflect not only the effects of punishment on threat responsiveness but also many other positive and negative influences that punishment may have had on subsequent behavior. This is because any particular form of punishment will invariably produce a mixture of effects.

It would be possible to test higher versus lower prison sentences, or prison sentences versus probation, by randomly varying the penalties given to convicted offenders. Or it would be possible to simulate this experiment by using base expectancy tables. But if prison sentences reduce subsequent criminality more than probation, does this mean that imprisonment increases responsiveness to threats or rather that it creates more opportunity for rehabilitation? If prison and probation lead to similar results, does this mean that imprisonment does not produce greater sensitivity to threats or rather that the negative aspects of imprisonment cancel out any increased responsiveness that might otherwise have influenced behavior?

When there are differences in recidivism rates, is it possible to determine to what extent they are due to changes in attitude

478. *Id.* at 426.

toward the threatened behavior or how far they are attributable to changes in attitude toward punishment? At times it may be possible experimentally to vary one or two separate factors of possible importance in predicting future criminality. But when large variations in punishment policy are tested (as when sentences that involve penal confinement are compared with those that do not), it will be an extremely complex task to unravel the different types of variable that might explain differences in recidivism. For the most part it will be possible only to test the relative effectiveness of different types of treatment, not the differential effectiveness of individual elements of treatment.

In policy terms, the problem of unraveling the various effects of different types of punishment is more apparent than real. The crucial question is always whether a program has a desirable net effect on future criminality, not whether some aspects of punishment that are inextricably bound up with forces pulling in the opposite direction or operating in different ways would tend to reduce crime if they could be isolated. Professor Tappan has argued that we are mistaken in contrasting deterrence and rehabilitation as though they were "incompatibly opposed" elements of punishment. "Rehabilitation and persuasive or intimidative measures are not distinct," he says. "It is submitted that a major component of rehabilitation—of change toward conformity—is a normally fearful facing of the reality that crime involves unpleasant consequences."[479]

Certainly, where punishment effects *can* be isolated by the varying of penal sentences, they can be tested individually to determine whether their presence has any effect on recidivism. If a set of punishment components cannot be separated, the only significant question is the effect of the set as a whole, rather than the effect of certain parts, and variations in punishment will provide the opportunity for such a test.

In one respect, the study of the effects of punishment on those punished is easier than the study of general deterrence, because one can expose different groups to different treatments, using methods that control for variations other than punishments that might undermine the significance of results. Once punishment groups have been selected and treated, keep-

479. Tappan, *Crime, Justice, and Correction* (1960) 258.

ing track of their criminal records will provide much more reliable guidance to the student of punishment effects than can be obtained by studying general deterrence through analysis of movements in the total crime rate.

It is difficult to institute more than one legal threat for a particular behavior in a jurisdiction. But different types of threatened consequences can be imposed on convicted offenders in ways that may generate knowledge about the relative effects of different types of punishment. It will not be possible by means of such studies to determine the amount of threat responsiveness generated by a particular punishment. But they may tell us about the much more important marginal effects that particular policies might have.

The major barrier to controlled study of different punishment regimes, other than inertia, is the objection that such methods require treating groups of similar offenders in different ways— a practice that many see as ethically obnoxious.[480] Yet detailed study of present patterns of sentencing in our criminal courts supports the conclusion that the variation in punishment meted out for the same offenses and same types of offenders by different judges is already extreme[481] and produces many of the costs associated with unequal treatment without any of the benefits of controlled study.

Moreover, as Professor Singer says in this connection, "One can also question whether it is ethical to continue to inflict punitive treatments when we have no knowledge that they help anyone and when we in fact suspect that in their present form they actually harm the offender and society."[482] This is essentially the question of the obligation to do research dealt with earlier in this work.[483] But it raises the additional and substantial problem that experimentation necessitates unequal and possibly inequitable treatment in some cases.

A large number of studies dealing with the subsequent criminal records of released prisoners bear on the marginal individual effects of increased severity of sentences. Simple recidi-

480. For a full discussion of this issue, see Morris, *supra* note 402, at 645–55.
481. See Green, *Judicial Attitudes in Sentencing* (1961) 67–71.
482. Singer, *supra* note 469, at 439.
483. See chap. 3, sec. 3, *supra*.

vism comparisons have tended to show that, among persons convicted of the same crimes, those treated more leniently have lower rates of subsequent criminality than those punished more severely.[484] But when such comparisons are controlled for differences in the offender groups other than type of punishment, "the dominant feature of the results is that the overall differences between various methods of treatment are small or nonexistent."[485]

If the overall rates of recidivism do not vary with severity of punishment, some prediction studies provide evidence that this apparent lack of difference could be the result of more severe punishment producing significant positive effects in some types of offender and significant negative effects on others that tend to balance out.[486] Moreover, it is one thing to say that severe punishment is ineffective in actually reducing recidivism and quite another to suggest that punishment does not produce effects on the individuals punished. The inconclusive or negative results of studies of the effects of increases or decreases in length of penal confinement have no impact on the argument that the experience of apprehension, conviction, and punishment may have a powerful restraining influence on those who encounter them. The FBI Careers in Crime study dealing with more than 17,000 persons released in 1963, to which we have already referred, found that, while more lenient penalties were associated with lower rates of rearrest, those who had been acquitted or had charges against them dismissed experienced a 91 percent rearrest rate within four years, compared to a rearrest rate of less than 60 percent for persons convicted and punished.[487] This finding is at best more suggestive than conclusive, and at worst it is misleading, because the FBI study did not relate release and rearrest data to specific types of crime or age and because of possible bias in the sample.[488] But this type of finding, and the shoplifting study discussed

484. See e.g., California Department of Corrections, "Parole Outcome and Time Served for First Releases Committed for Robbery and Burglary—1965 Releases" (1968) unpublished.

485. Andenaes *supra* note 404, at 93.

486. See Warren, "The Case for Differential Treatment of Delinquents" (1969) 47 *Annals of A.A.P.S.S.* 48.

487. *Supra* note 448 (1967) at 37.

488. Ward, *supra* note 52.

earlier,[489] suggest that apprehension and conviction may substantially reduce subsequent criminality.

Taken as a whole, studies of recidivism establish that those subjected to punishment for major crimes commit many more crimes after their release than other groups in the population, but fewer perhaps than they would if they had not been caught. Those studies that suggest the lack of a marginal individual effect associated with longer prison sentences would provide a justification for official experiments in the reduction of punishment for major crimes. When findings on the lack of marginal individual effects are collated with the few studies relating to the marginal general effects of increases in threatened punishment for major crime, they remove some of the barriers to downward shifts in punishment that are based on hypotheses regarding substantial marginal deterrence to future crime.

D Conclusions

In dealing with the effects of penal measures on those subjected to them we are not dealing with a unitary phenomenon. In the first place, penal measures vary both in their nature or quality and in the intensity or quantity of their application.[490] In the second place, the groups subjected to those measures are likely to be composed of different types of person, who may well react differentially to the experience of punishment depending on the nature of the offense.[491]

It is not possible, therefore, validly to extrapolate from findings regarding variations in response to a measure such as imprisonment to other forms of punishment. Most of the available studies in this field deal with the response of serious offenders to major penalties, and the findings are likely to be specific to particular audiences of potential offenders. But there is no reason why research on the effectiveness of punishment and treatment in relation to offenders should be restricted in this way.

Indeed, perhaps the principal conclusion is a practical one. It is that many offenses which are not considered very serious present considerable opportunities for research and experiment

489. Cameron, *supra* note 142.
490. See sec. 1, subsecs. F and G, *supra*.
491. See Zimring and Hawkins, *supra* note 106.

which have been almost wholly ignored. To give an example, the aggregate social costs of such offenses as shoplifting and traffic violations are enormous, yet both are regarded with some degree of toleration. The fact that such offenses are not subject to serious condemnation and that public attitudes regarding the "appropriate" penalties are not rigid means that opportunities for experiment both in relation to the levels and types of penalties and levels and techniques of enforcement are much greater than for major crimes. We shall later return to the possibilities for research in such areas as these.[492]

In the light of the paucity of available evidence it is difficult to offer firm conclusions regarding the way in which punishment will affect punished offenders' responses to legal threats. Many of the changes that punishment can produce are not directly related to the effect of threats on future conduct. If rehabilitation reduces recidivism because many former offenders wish to conform to prevailing social norms, it would be unwise to attribute this improvement wholly to greater sensitivity to threats or to assume that punishment per se is responsible for the decrease in subsequent criminality.

We can offer only some tentative suggestions. There is no doubt that the "actual experience" of punishment is, in some sense, "much stronger than the theoretical knowledge"[493] and that even apprehension and investigation alone may in some cases have a "dramatic impact."[494] But in what specific respects is threat responsiveness likely to be changed as a result of punishment?

It seems likely that there are two aspects of punishment, commonly mentioned in the literature as important in relation to general deterrence, which may assume much more importance when the offender has experienced punishment. Indeed it is questionable whether the emphasis commonly laid on them is justified except in relation to the punished offender.

The first of these is what Beccaria called "promptness of punishment."[495] It is referred to throughout the literature as being of major importance in relation to deterrence. To take

---

492. See chap. 6 *infra*.
493. Andenaes, *supra* note 404, at 89.
494. *Id.* at 90.
495. Beccaria, *supra* note 282, at 55.

first the earliest, and then some of the latest examples. Beccaria says "Of utmost importance is it, therefore, that the crime and the punishment be intimately linked together, if it be desirable that, in crude, vulgar minds, the seductive picture of a particularly advantageous crime should immediately call up the associated idea of punishment. Long delay always produces the effect of further separating these two ideas; thus, though the punishment of a crime may make an impression, it will be less as a punishment than as a spectacle."[496]

More recently, Hall Williams, writing of the "celerity of punishment," says, "One important factor in deterrence is the risk of being caught and swiftly dealt with."[497] Pan Chopra, in the article cited earlier, writes, "The ideal punishment situation is one in which the misbehavior is invariably detected and reliably evokes appropriate and immediate punishment."[498] Professor Singer declares, "Delay of punishment is of paramount importance and is probably largely responsible for the apparent ineffectiveness of our current punitive systems."[499] Professor C. R. Jeffery says, "A consequence must be applied immediately if it is to be effective; . . . Punishment decreases a response rate only if it is . . . applied near the time of the occurrence of the forbidden act."[500]

It should be noted that with the exception of Beccaria every one of these writers refers specifically to what Hall Williams calls "individual deterrence," that is, "the effectiveness of punishment as a deterrent on the individual offender."[501] For the individual who has actually experienced swift apprehension and punishment, the experience is likely to be a more significant influence than for those for whom it has only been "a spectacle." However, for a person who has had no experience of apprehension or punishment it is improbable that consideration of the speed at which law enforcement operations might take place would condition his response to the threat of punishment to any important extent. Without actual experience it would be

496. *Id.* at 57.
497. Hall Williams, *The English Penal System in Transition* (1970) 6.
498. Chopra, *supra* note 464, at 156.
499. Singer, *supra* note 469, at 420.
500. Jeffery, "Criminal Behavior and Learning Theory" (1965) 5 *J. Crim. L.C. and P.S.* 299–300.
501. Hall Williams, *supra* note 497, at 5.

unlikely to occupy a prominent place in his mind even if he were actually contemplating the possibility of criminal activity.

The other aspect of the threat of punishment which is likely to be of much greater importance to the offender who has already experienced punishment than to the one who has not, is the "principle of less eligibility,"[502] or what Bentham called the "Rule of Severity."[503] This principle, originally derived from the English Poor Law and later applied to the penal system, was defined by Bentham as follows: "Saving the regard due to life, health, and bodily ease, the ordinary condition of a convict doomed to a punishment, which few or none but individuals of the poorest class are apt to incur, ought not to be made more eligible than that of the poorest class of subjects in a state of innocence and liberty."[504]

This principle finds its expression in imprisonment in the way in which "the loss of liberty is aggravated by the physical discomforts and inconveniences of prison, the separation from families and friends, and the monotony of food, work, and recreation."[505] As Fox says, the principle "is deeply ingrained in common thought about the treatment of convicted prisoners." Moreover, it "has not been specifically rejected by any English prison administration."[506] While for those who have experienced imprisonment the conditions of confinement will probably appear as a significant implicit constituent of the threat of punishment, those who have not done so will in most cases be unlikely to consider them specifically or be influenced by them to any great extent.

Thus in respect both to the timing of punishment and to the details of it, it seems plausible to assume that experience of punishment will condition future threat responsiveness. It is important to add, however, that in neither case will it necessarily be in the direction of increased sensitivity to threats.

502. Mannheim, *The Dilemma of Penal Reform* (1939) 56.
503. Bentham, "Panopticon or The Inspection House: Postscript Part II" 4 *Works* (1843) 122.
504. *Id.* at 122–23.
505. Walker, *supra* note 262, at 131.
506. Fox, *supra* note 229, at 133.

5   The Strategy of Research

SECTION 1 INTRODUCTION TO RESEARCH
        STRATEGY
The case for serious research into the effects of threats was poignantly made by Michael and Adler, writing nearly forty years ago:

> We have no knowledge of the influence of any mode of treatment, existing or proposed, upon the behavior of actual and potential offenders. We do not know whether or to what degree any mode of treatment possessed reformative or deterrence efficacy. . . . We do not know whether or to what degree any preventive program, existing or proposed, is efficient as a preventive device.[1]

The intervening years have brought some progress, but clearly not enough. It is far from an easy task to outline the methods by which the effects of legal threats can be assessed. The criminologist who sets out to study those effects in a realistic social setting inherits a world and a criminal law he never made. Because he is rarely able to control punishment policy for experimental purposes (and the exceptions to this rule will be

1. Michael and Adler, *Crime, Law, and Social Science* (1933) 228.

discussed later), he must attempt to retain as much reality as possible in his imperfect experimental design.

The laboratory analogy, popular in other areas of social science,[2] is not widely used in criminological research. Perhaps it is just as well. For it is difficult to reproduce in the laboratory emotional stimuli as massive[3] or conditions as complex[4] as the threat of death or protracted imprisonment. Nor is it easy to understand the relation between the emotional level of a laboratory experiment and that involved in the threats attached to prohibitions of criminal behavior in the real world.[5] The basic task of the researcher, then, is to devise methods of channeling comparative and historical data about movements in the crime rate into designs that simulate the experiment that is so rarely possible.

It should be made clear at the outset that no collaboration between historian and statistician can produce information as significant as that which can be obtained from the controlled experiment. Much effort, ingenuity, and intelligence can be devoted to such questions as whether governments with severely repressive criminal sanctions achieve compliance rates higher than those observed under more lenient regimes.[6] But, as earlier discussions have indicated, it is one thing to note the difference or the lack of difference over time, or between areas, in

2. For laboratory experiments in other field concerned with similar questions see Hovland, Janis, and Kelley, *Communication and Persuasion* (1953), and Cartwright and Zander (eds.), *Group Dynamics, Research, and Theory* (3d ed., 1968).

3. For a survey of laboratory studies in which problems of social control were investigated, and an attempt at the assessment of their implications for real life situations, see Walters, "Implications of Laboratory Studies of Aggression for the Control and Regulation of Violence" (1966) 364 *Annals of A.A.P.S.S.* 60–72.

4. The space and time dimensions of real world threat situations present a great obstacle to experiment. While research has been done both into effects of verbally presented threats and into punished and rewarded behavior, these two variables have, to our knowledge, never been combined in a laboratory experiment.

5. For some of the conflict generated by laboratory studies, compare Walters, *supra* note 3, with Cohen and Brehm, *Explorations in Cognitive Dissonance* (1962), and Janis and Feshbach, "Effects of Fear-Arousing Communications" (1953) 48 *J. Abnormal and Soc. Psych.* 78–92.

6. Rusche and Kirchheimer, *Punishment and Social Structure* (1939) chap. 12 *passim*.

a crime rate and the conditions of threat and punishment that may accompany it, and quite another thing to establish a *causal* relation between a crime control policy and an observed crime rate.

If a crime rate increases after the introduction of severer penalties to deal with it, how is one to know whether the increase might not have been greater if no change in punishment policy had occurred? If a crime rate decreases after the change in punishment, how is one to know whether, had the change not occurred, the crime rate might not have been as low or lower? If one state punishes a particular crime more severely than does another, and yet experiences a higher rate of such crimes, can we assume a nexus of cause and effect between a more severe punishment policy and a higher crime rate? Too many other differences between the two states impeach the validity of such a conclusion.

Indeed, how can we rebut the inference that any cause-effect relation between crime and punishment operates in a direction counter to that which we might feel inclined to suppose. In other words, how can we refute the suggestion that the nature and extent of the crime problem determine the punishment policy rather than the other way around?

It is precisely because of the intractable problems that arise when serious students attempt to assess the effects of crime control policies through nonexperimental methods that we have to consider at some length the problem of methods of researching deterrence. This chapter, therefore, surveys the various methods that have been used for assessing the effects of legal threats upon crime rates. In the main, the survey will be limited to English-language research.

Before embarking on this enterprise, we must first answer a question: Why discuss the methodology of nonexperimental research in the context of deterrence when we ourselves have no special competence in this matter and when the problem of drawing inferences in this area is not peculiar to deterrence studies? The answer is simply that methodological problems are of tremendous importance in acquiring knowledge of deterrence. Moreover, there are some peculiar difficulties in deterrence research—problems relating to the nature of crime itself and to the nature of crime rates. A collateral advantage of this discussion may be that it will render more intelligible both our earlier reservations about, and our earlier enthusiasms for, studies which have been done in this field by others. Finally, being laymen ourselves, we claim to do no more than provide a laymen's guide to methodology.

Our second preliminary comment, notwithstanding the ancient and convenient tradition of caveat emptor, is that discussions of the methodology of research are inevitably duller than substantive speculation or conclusions about the state of the universe. We have no cure for the monotony of methodological discourse; we merely plead that the critical importance of methods of research in deterrence requires the serious and protracted attention of students of crime control policy.

Unfortunately, without the classic scientific insurance of controls, single observations of crime control policies and crime rates, of whatever form, have limited utility. The reader will quickly note that our analysis of each of these nonexperimental research approaches implies a criticism of the unwarranted ease with which generalizations have been drawn from often insufficient data.

Our third preliminary point is that, while the single application of any particular nonexperimental method in deterrence research may mean little, the cumulative import of many different imperfect approaches to the same question may be of critical significance. In an age where the term "synergism" has become a somewhat dubious slogan, it remains true that a series of imperfect exercises *can* sometimes produce reliable conclusions because each different but imperfect method may remove an element of doubt left by its predecessor.[7]

If a before-and-after study of change in crime control policy fails to persuade us that any change in the crime rate is attributable to the change in policy, can we as easily dismiss ten such before-and-after exercises that emanate from wholly different environments but all point to the same conclusion? If solely retrospective research contains within it the basis for suspecting a systematic bias, may not the addition of comparative researches, themselves imperfect, act to still anxieties?

7. See Zeisel, *Say it with Figures* (5th ed. 1968) 190–99, on "the confluence of proof."

At the outset, then, it is our belief that research in deterrence should be both purposefully repetitive in topic and selective in method. If a single question cannot be investigated through a perfect controlled experiment (which it seldom can), then this shortcoming must be compensated for by the adopting of a variety of approaches rather than a single method. Where possible, a nonexperimental assessment of a particular crime control policy should be implemented two or more times rather than once.

SECTION 2 COMPARATIVE RESEARCH
A Introduction

The ideal method of determining whether a particular punishment has an effect on the rate of crime would be a controlled experiment.

An example of a controlled experiment can be drawn from agriculture. A hundred small parcels of land are randomly assigned to a test group and to a control group. Each group of parcels is similarly cultivated, and planted with the same type of grain seed. One group of parcels is fertilized, and the other is not. Each group is then inspected to determine whether the fertilized parcels yield a greater harvest per acre than the unfertilized ones. The same type of random experiment can, of course, be used to test one type of fertilizer against another. Similarly we can test the extent to which different concentrations of the same type of fertilizer may have differential effects on crop yield.

In the assessment of crime control policy the procedure would take the following form. One hundred subjects, or one hundred areas, would be randomly divided into two groups, which would be treated alike in every respect but one. The exception would be that the first group, the "test group," would be exposed to the policy the investigators were seeking to assess, and the second, the "control group," would not be. The two groups would then be observed to determine whether the crime rate in the test group differed from that of the control group.

Ordinarily, a controlled experiment is beyond the reach of a criminologist seeking to investigate punishment policy, because he is unable to randomly assign regimes of punishment between individuals in the same jurisdiction, although experimenting between units is not out of the question. However, one strategy which can be adopted as a substitute for, and is a natural analogue of, the controlled experiment is the comparison of areas with different punishment policies in an attempt to determine whether differences in punishment policy cause differences in crime rates.

For example, those interested in whether the threat of capital punishment operates as a more effective deterrent to criminal homicide than the threat of protracted imprisonment might compare the rate of homicide in two contiguous jurisdictions, one with and one without capital punishment. The results of one such comparison are shown in table 6, which is based on data derived from Thorsten Sellin's report on the death penalty for the Model Penal Code Project of the American Law Institute.[8]

TABLE 6
Average Rate of Homicide per 100,000 Population (Sixteen Year Average 1940 to 1955)

Michigan (without Death Penalty) 3.49	Indiana (with Death Penalty) 3.50

While a comparison of this sort is certainly *evidence to the effect that* capital punishment was not a major influence on crime trends, the drawing of conclusions about cause and effect from a simple comparison between two different areas involves substantial risks. In the first place, rather than comparing one group of fifty different individual units under test conditions with a second equally large group under control conditions, as in the fertilizer example, the crime rate in one political unit was compared with the crime rate in only one other unit. Whatever safety exists in large numbers, and this is a topic we presently treat in some detail, a comparison of two single jurisdictions does not provide that safety.

Second, as visitors to and residents of either state might testify, Michigan and Indiana are different, not only in their

8. Sellin, *The Death Penalty* (1959) 28.

punishment policies, which formed the basis for the comparison, but also in a great many other respects. Any difference in crime rate might stem from any of these factors other than punishment policy. Indeed, the very fact that the two areas differed in punishment policy might be some evidence that they differed in other respects which had some influence on their crime rates.

In the controlled experiment which was discussed above, the danger that differences other than those the experimenter is seeking to test may produce differences in the crime rate or crop harvest is effectively dealt with. The random assignment of a large number of units to the test and the control categories creates a statistical insurance policy against other differences existing between them prior to the beginning of the experiment.

This is not to say that one of the fifty experimental plots of land being tested in the fertilizer experiment may not be greatly different from another in the control group. But the *random* assignment of large numbers of units tends to cancel out the differences that exist between individual pieces of land and creates a situation in which the risk of differences not attributable to the presence or absence of treatment is quite small, and whatever risk occurs can be calculated with some precision.

When the investigator cannot randomly assign the units he is comparing, no such safeguard exists. Thus, in the comparison of areas with and without a particular punishment policy, the units will have *classified themselves* with respect to the categories into which they fall. And the dangers attendant on self-selection open a methodological Pandora's box.

When two jurisdictions have independently arrived at dissimilar punishment policies with respect to one crime, it is probable that the scale of punishments each has established for other crimes will be dissimilar in some respects. Yet a particular penalty's relation to the penalties for potential substitute forms of criminality is one important measure of the severity of the penalty. A comparative study may involve two penalties that appear to be different but in context are quite similar, or two penalties that appear to be similar but in the context of other penalties are in fact quite different.

Moreover, the selection of a particular penalty for a crime may be related to many other conditions affecting the administration of criminal justice in an area, including methods of enforcement, efficiency of apprehension, and other factors. And beyond the so-called *internal* variables, that is to say, those relating to the mechanics of criminal justice, punishment policy may be associated with other factors that can have an effect on the rate of crime—including race, class, income, weather, cultural values, degrees of industrialization, birth and death rates, age distribution, the distribution of wealth, median living space per resident, and so on.

Our list of possible variables is hopelessly incomplete, but the point is made. Areas being compared which have decided on a different policy by methods other than random assignment in an experimental context may differ significantly from each other. And the possibility that such differences will be related to the difference that observers are attempting to test remains an omnipresent threat to the validity of any inferences that observers might draw.

Confronted with the undeniable possibilities of error involved in comparative exercises, researchers can react in one of three ways. First, they may consider that, while the dangers we refer to exist in theory, the probability of their being misled by them is small in most situations. Moreover, it could be argued that these dangers are better ignored in the interest of gaining knowledge than elevated to a dominant status by rigorous insistence on impossible methodological purism.

Unfortunately, despite its rhetorical charm, this approach often provides a quick side trip down the road of imprecision. For while comparison under some circumstances may produce results dramatic enough to discount the possibility that they have been produced by extraneous influence (e.g., in the case of smoking and lung cancer), it is more likely that freewheeling assumptions about the similarity of units being compared will be seriously misleading. We shall provide a number of examples of this phenomenon.

A second possible reaction is an out-of-hand rejection of the comparative method. Because the random experiment can never be exactly simulated in that factors other than the one we seek to select as the independent variable may produce apparent differences or conceal real ones, the comparative method may be viewed as inherently suspect. The weakness of this position, more popular with the critic than with the researcher charged with the responsibility for evaluation in an area of social importance, is that all the other methods available to the criminological researcher also have significant imperfections.

The third reaction is to attempt to find ways of controlling for some of the more obvious pitfalls of comparative research and, using such controls, to draw only the most conservative of conclusions from comparative studies. With the reservation that the basic limits of reliability must always be kept in mind, we adopt the third posture as the only realistic alternative under present conditions. And in the light of that conclusion, it becomes necessary to review a number of strategies for minimizing the danger of false inferences from comparative studies. In the course of the review we shall discuss some of the research in the deterrent effect of sanctions that has emerged in recent years.

B Controls for Comparative Research: Multiple-Unit Comparison

When crime rates in Michigan are compared with those in Indiana, the danger that differences other than differences in punishment policy will influence the conclusions of comparative research is twofold. First, differences between the two areas that operate *independently* of any difference in punishment policy may influence the crime rate. Second, factors that are functionally related to punishment policy may also influence the crime rate and thereby give rise to spurious conclusions. Thus, if public attitudes or the magnitude of the crime problem are related in a systematic way to the punishment policy selected by a jurisdiction, it may be that these factors rather than the policy that results from them will themselves have an influence on the crime rate. For instance, observers who note that Maine has both substantially higher prison sentences for criminal homicide than Georgia and substantially lower rates of criminal homicide might be tempted to conclude that the higher penalty is the cause of the lower rate.

Yet one factor that might condition the difference between Maine's punishment policy for homicide and that of Georgia could be the fact that social feelings against homicide are stronger in Maine than in Georgia. In this case, the very strength of social feelings against homicide in Maine rather than the peculiarity of Maine's punishment policy could account for the fact that the homicide rate in Maine is so low by comparison. This is one example of a situation in which differences in punishment policy coincide with differences in the crime rate, but where it might be a mistake to assume that the relationship between punishment policy and the crime rate is causal.

By the same token, two jurisdictions may have similar crime rates but widely different punishment policies, and this situation may lead to false conclusions regarding the deterrent effect of criminal sanctions. Assume, for example, that those countries with the most serious crime problems punish crimes more severely than those with less serious crime problems. Or, on the other hand, assume that countries with more severe punishment policies have crime rates no greater than those with more lenient policies. The conclusion here might be that punishment policy has no effect on the crime rate, when in fact the severity of a regime of punishment may have canceled out the differences in crime rates one would otherwise expect to observe between the two areas.[9]

9. It may be worthwhile to distinguish two different types of danger involved in drawing inferences about the relation between crime rates and punishment policies. There is, on the one hand, the danger of drawing false *affirmative* conclusions about the effects of punishment, and assuming a causal connection when areas which differ in penal policy differ also in crime rates. The trouble here is that there may be some other explanation of the difference in crime rates. On the other hand, there is the danger of drawing false *negative* conclusions and assuming that there is no causal connection when areas which differ in punishment policy exhibit similar crime rates. The difficulty in this case is that there may be other factors present which operate counter to punishment policy and conceal the effects which that policy may have had. Having distinguished between the false *affirmative* and false *negative* inference and recognized that both are dangerous, can it be said that one is more dangerous than the other? Our answer would be that the negative inference is less likely to be false because differences that coincidentally and precisely cancel each other out are likely to occur less often than unanticipated differences other than the presumed independent variable. It is particularly unlikely that superficial similarity will hide differences of large magnitude that are produced by punishment policy. However, when comparison does reveal some difference in rate, but the difference is too small to discount the chance that it is a random variation, there is a considerable danger of false negative inference. When, for instance, following some countermeasure, the rate of homicide drops from 12

The distinction between confounding factors in comparative study that are *not* related to differences in punishment policy and confounding factors that *are* so related becomes apparent when we consider the first basic method of control. That method is multiple-unit comparison. Imagine that, instead of studying the two areas in our earlier example, Michigan and Indiana, the comparative researcher obtains data from fifty different areas, thirty of which exhibit one pattern of punishment policy and twenty of which exhibit another. Or let us say, and this hypothesis is more in line with the reality of multiple-unit comparisons, the researcher attempts to compare crime rate differentials in fifty areas that can be ranged on a continuum of punishment policy from the least to the most extreme. In this case we observe a strategy that corrects for one of the two major sources of error in comparative study but fails to compensate for the other.

We are interested, let us say, in whether the severity of the average sentence meted out for criminal homicide has an effect on the number of homicides experienced in a particular jurisdiction. There are fifty states in the United States, each with an average sentence of imprisonment for criminal homicide. Comparing the average criminal homicide rate in those states in the lower half of average criminal homicide sentences with the average criminal homicide rate for those states in the higher half, it is possible to control for all those differences between areas that are not functionally related to differences in punishment policy.

Thus, while individual areas may differ in some respect that is not related to differences in punishment policy but still influences the crime rate, the very act of expanding the range of comparison to fifty different units will tend to even out those differences that do not have some systematic relation to punishment policy. But if there is some definite relation between factors that influence the crime rate and punishment policy, a multiple-unit comparison will fail to eliminate the confound-

cases to 9, it is perfectly correct for a social scientist to point out that such variations can frequently occur even if the countermeasure has no effect. But the insignificance of the decline does not disprove deterrence in that setting, and to claim that the countermeasure "failed" is as unwarranted as claiming that it "succeeded."

ing effects of these *related* factors and the influencê which they, rather than punishment policy, have on a crime rate.

Examples of multiple-unit comparisons failing to control for systematic differences between the areas being compared that are *not* caused by differences in punishment policy are relatively easy to find. Take for instance, the studies by Professors Gibbs and Tittle, which have already been referred to earlier in this book.[10] Both scholars analyzed crime statistics and punishment data from the various states in the United States in an effort to determine whether variations in the probability of apprehension or the severity of punishment were related to variations in the rate of particular crimes.

In the Gibbs study only the rate of homicide was examined. Professor Tittle examined homicide, rape, burglary, robbery, sex offenses, and auto theft rates together with average severity of sentences. In regard to homicide, higher-than-average severity of sentence was significantly correlated with lower-than-average crime rates when figures for all states were analyzed.

Use of data from a large number of units should have, and may have, effectively protected these studies from the confounding influence of differences in social climate that were randomly associated with punishment policy. But one hypothesis suggests a systematic relation between punishment policy with respect to homicide on the one hand, and factors that might have an independent influence on the crime rate on the other. The hypothesis is that areas with strong social feelings against homicide will tend to punish this crime more severely than areas without such strong feelings; and that these feelings, operating independently of any variation in punishment policy, will themselves have a significant influence on the crime rate.

In the case of Professor Tittle's study, there was a means of testing one version of this hypothesis against the general conclusion that severity of sanctions depresses the homicide rate. The penalties for homicide vary markedly in different regions of the United States, and so does the rate of criminal homicide. Professor Tittle's data run parallel to those of Professor Gibbs, and indicate that nationally—that is to say, without regional

10. Gibbs, "Crime, Punishment, and Deterrence" (1968) 48 *Southwestern Social Science Quarterly* 515–30; Tittle, "Crime Rates and Legal Sanctions" (1969) 16 *Social Problems* 409–23.

controls—those areas with the highest penalties for homicide tend to have the lowest rates of that offense. Table 7 sets forth these data.

TABLE 7
Homicide Rates of States of the Union by Higher and Lower than National Average Homicide Penalties

	High-Penalty States	Low-Penalty States
Higher than national average rate	24%	54%
Lower than national average rate	76%	46%
Total	100%	100%

Since the range of punishment policies within each region of the United States is quite substantial, we can test whether variations in punishment policy (rather than variations in social conditions) are affecting the crime rate by comparing rates *within* each region rather than between regions. Table 8 makes this comparison in a rather crude manner, by separating the various states of the union into regions and determining for each state whether its homicide rate, compared to the average of its region, is related to the degree of punishment for homicide when that figure is compared to a regional average.

As table 8 shows, there is no apparent relation within regions

TABLE 8
Homicide Rates of States of the Union by Higher and Lower than Average Homicide Penalties Compared on a Regional Basis

	Higher than Regional Average Penalties	Lower than Regional Average Penalties
Higher than regional average rate	50%	41%
Lower than regional average rate	50%	59%
Total	100%	100%

between severity of average sanctions for homicide and a particular state's homicide rate. We may mention here a more recent study using similar data to those of Gibbs and Tittle but extending the analysis both by examining the relations for three points in time rather than for a single time period only, and by relating *changes* in rates of crime to *prior changes* in the certainty and severity of punishment. The findings of this study do not support Professor Tittle's conclusion that rates of homicide and severity of punishment are inversely related.[11]

In the Gibbs and Tittle studies, effects were attributed to differences in punishment policy when they might have been caused by differences in regional location of states that differed in punishment policy. In this respect, Professors Gibbs and Tittle are not alone. Alan Krug, for example, attempted to discover whether gun licensing and registration laws influence the homicide rate of various states in the Union.[12] Like Professors Gibbs and Tittle, he used an undifferentiated national sample, rather than a region-by-region comparison of states with different firearms control policies. As a result, Mr. Krug found that states with gun laws, and in the category he included all the states in the South, actually had slightly higher homicide rates than states without gun laws. However, when Southern states are excluded from his analysis, the data tend toward precisely the opposite conclusion. A comparison in such crude terms, of course, cannot be thought of as a conclusive indication that gun laws are the cause of a lower homicide rate.[13]

Thus far in our consideration of multiple-unit comparisons we have focused on the comparison of various states within the United States and the possible problems associated with such comparisons. Multiple-unit comparisons can use even larger and more diverse units of comparison such as nations or

11. Chiricos and Waldo, "Punishment and Crime: An Examination of Some Empirical Evidence" (1970) 18 *Social Problems* 200–17.
12. Krug, "The Relationship between Firearms Licensing and Crime Rates" (reproducing 113 Cong. Rec. H9366 [daily ed. July 25, 1967]), in *The True Facts on Firearm Legislation—Three Statistical Studies* (1968).
13. Zimring, "Games with Guns and Statistics" 1968 *Wisconsin L. Rev.* 1113–26.

smaller units such as communities. In each case, however, the possibility of a systematic relation between the nature of a punishment policy and other factors that might influence the rate of conduct being studied remains a serious obstacle to confident conclusions.

For example, a comparison of punishment policy and crime rates published thirty years ago[14] showed that England and France in the early years of this century had both milder punishments for most crimes and more pronounced tendencies toward diminishing crime rates than did Italy and Germany during the same period. In this study the authors recognized the confounding effects that differences other than those in punishment policy might have had on variations in the rates of crime, and they drew the conservative conclusion that the data they had examined provided no evidence to support the hypothesis that punishment policy influenced the crime rate.

We may thus repeat our initial caution: While the use of multiple-unit comparisons provides insurance against one danger of comparative study—that of random variation—it provides no protection against the false conclusions that may be drawn when punishment policy is systematically related to variations in other phenomena that may influence the crime rate. We therefore turn to a second possible measure of protection.

C Controls for Comparative Research: Matching

By matching we mean the selection for comparison of areas that, although different in punishment policy, are as similar to each other in all other respects as is possible. An example of matching is found in Thorsten Sellin's now classic exploration of the comparative effects of the death penalty and protracted imprisonment as a deterrent to homicide.[15]

Facing the task of trying to extract some meaning from data on punishment policy and homicide rates from the various states in the United States, Professor Sellin could have relied, but did not do so, on the types of multiple-unit comparisons used by Professors Gibbs and Tittle and also by Mr. Alan Krug, many years later.[16] If he had done so, his results would

14. Rusche and Kirchheimer, *supra* note 6.
15. Sellin, *supra* note 8.
16. Gibbs, *supra* note 10; Tittle, *supra* note 10; Krug, *supra* note 12.

have appeared somewhat anomalous. For homicide rates vary in a distinctive regional pattern. At the same time, all the jurisdictions in the South had capital punishment for homicide. Thus Professor Sellin might have found in his earlier studies, what was found by other researchers somewhat later, that the homicide rate was significantly higher, by a margin of approximately 40 percent, in jurisdictions with capital punishment than in those without. As already indicated, such a finding tells us nothing about the effect of the use of capital punishment on homicide.

Professor Sellin adopted a more precise method of comparing states within the Union. Groups of contiguous states were matched wherever at least one of the states in a group differed from the others in the group in maximum penalties for homicide. The rates of homicide in states with capital punishment were compared with those in states without capital punishment only within these clusters of similar jurisdictions. The results of such inquiries are shown in table 9 which represents an adaptation of the data provided in Sellin's study.[17]

The conclusion drawn from these matched group comparisons was that capital punishment does not appear to have any influence on the reported rate of homicide.[18] And since the conclusion was based on a deliberate attempt to eliminate differences other than those in punishment policy that might influence the crime rate, it is more reliable than nonmatched interstate comparisons.

Despite conscientious attempts to control differences between areas, the comparative researcher who seeks to control differences other than the supposed independent and dependent variables he is attempting to study will encounter two difficulties. First, there are a great many differences between jurisdictions that may have influence on whatever the researcher is attempting to use as a dependent variable. Thus, he may never be sure that, in the course of trying to match similar areas, he has isolated every important difference other than the one selected for study, and has canceled it out by a process of

17. Sellin, *supra* note 8: The table is adapted from the tables provided at 23–24.
18. *Id.* at 34: "The inevitable conclusion is that executions have no discernible effect on homicide death rates."

TABLE 9
Comparative Crude Homicide Death Rates in States with and States without the Death Penalty—Average Annual Rate 1940–55 (Death penalty states are marked D)

Midwest

Matched Group 1			Matched Group 2			Matched Group 3		
Michigan	D Indiana	D Ohio	Minnesota	Wisconsin	D Iowa	North Dakota	D South Dakota	D Nebraska
3.5	3.5	3.5	1.4	1.2	1.4	1.0	1.5	1.8

New England

Matched Group 1		Matched Group 2		
Maine	D New Hampshire	D Vermont	Rhode Island	D Massachusetts	D Connecticut
1.5	.9	1.0	1.3	1.2	1.7

matching. The possibility that there are unknown variables which may invalidate the presumed similarity of areas being compared always threatens the confidence with which he can draw conclusions from multiple-unit comparisons of matched jurisdictions.

Second, even if all of the relevant variables other than those being studied can be successfully identified, it may not be possible to find jurisdictions that differ with respect to the variables being studied but are entirely similar to each other in other respects. Indeed if, as we have supposed, differences in punishment policy are systematically related to other variables that influence rates of crime, it may not be possible to find areas that differ in this one respect that do not differ in what may be related respects. In these circumstances, simple matching techniques are least likely to succeed. Matching will most probably succeed when the punishment policies under study are truly idiosyncratic and thus unrelated to other major variations between areas.

In practice, the closer a comparison comes to an ideal matching exercise, the more distant becomes the probability that overlooked or uncontrolled-for differences between comparison units will have an invalidating influence. The major inconsistencies in the conclusions of simple multiple-unit comparisons, like those discussed earlier, do not occur to the same extent in the cluster comparisons done by Professor Sellin and shown in table 4.

Moreover, the application of Professor Sellin's cluster comparisons over a large number of clusters of states lends even greater credibility to the conclusions he drew. Because his comparisons were repeated a number of times and yielded a consistent lack of significant difference in each repetition, the imperfections inherently associated with matching techniques would be important only to the extent that we might suspect a consistent and systematic relation between the presence or absence of the punishment policy variable he was studying and other factors that might influence the crime rate.

D Controls for Comparative Research:
Multiple-Correlation Analysis

One promising technique for simulating conditions of similarity between units being compared, when similar units for comparison cannot be found in the real world, is that of multi-variate correlation analysis. The uses and limitations of multi-variate analytical techniques can best be introduced by means of a simplified example.

If we knew that there were only two other variables, besides crime control policy, that affected a crime rate, and these variables were per capita income and the age distribution of the population, it might not be possible to find five, let alone fifty, areas in which these two factors were the same and crime control policies differed. However, it might be possible to find fifty areas in which statistical data would be available both on the two factors besides crime control policy that we knew influenced the crime rate, and on the nature of crime control policy and the crime rate itself.

With these data we could perform two statistical operations that would enable us to simulate a comparison of areas similar to each other in all respects except punishment policy. The first operation consists of estimating the relation between the two nonpunishment policy variables and the crime rate. Then, having found a value for each of these or for the two of them jointly, we can employ statistical correlation techniques, first to find the simple correlation between the variations in punishment policy and crime rate, and second to find what the simple correlation between crime rate and punishment policy would be in the absence of whatever relation does exist between other significant variables, the crime rate, and punishment policy.

For example, assume that we can find the correlation between the crime rate and the seriousness of sanctions administered for convicted felons. Assume also that we know how closely variations in punishment policy and variations in age distribution of the population are related. It is then possible to estimate what the statistical relation between punishment policy and the crime rate *would be* if differences between the states in income and age distribution did not exist. When we perform such an operation, we have an indication of the independent relation between punishment policy and the crime rate.

One problem, of course, is that of determining when the process of isolation has in fact progressed to the extent that the assumption that all significant variables are accounted for is justified. Very few, if any, studies done on the impact of criminal law variations on crime rates give us reason to believe that most of the many factors which should be included in such a statistical analysis are present and accounted for.

Multivariate correlation techniques are further limited by the fact that they can only test the separate effect of punishment policy if, and to the extent that, punishment policy varies independently of other factors that may be related both to variations in punishment policy and to the crime rate. If, for example, mean number of years of schooling and punishment policy were both inversely related to a crime rate and were always observed rising and falling together, the observer could not distinguish effects due to variations in years of schooling. Only to the extent that some independent variation is found can partial correlation techniques assist comparative research by artificially creating matching situations where the units being compared with respect to one variable are closely similar to each other with respect to all other variables.

Nevertheless, such statistical techniques are of value, not only in conducting comparative criminological research, but also in testing the validity of comparisons drawn from prior research that has failed to take account of significant variables. As long as their limitations are kept well in mind, the use of these techniques will be beneficial. Only when the statistical complexity of such methods lulls the researcher into a false sense that all relevant variables have been accounted for, or that natural variations are in fact present, does multiple-correlation analysis become more dangerous than helpful.

E Controls for Comparative Research:
Independent Evidence

The danger that false inferences may be drawn from comparisons will always exist, though in varying degrees. However, it is sometimes possible to find independent evidence which may provide corroboration for, or run counter to, a comparative inference.

It may be possible to test the validity of such an inference by examining the evidence of studies which run parallel to the basic comparative exercise. An example of this may be found in Thorsten Sellin's study "Police Safety" made in the course of his researches into the deterrent effectiveness of the death penalty.[19] Sellin set out "to test the claims of the police that the death penalty makes the lives of policemen safer."[20] He compared the data on killings of police in death penalty states and abolition states "of quite similar traditions, populations, and culture . . . bordering on one another."[21] He found it "impossible to conclude that the states which had no death penalty had thereby made the policeman's lot more hazardous." He found also that "the same differences observable in the general homicide rates of the various states were reflected in the rate of police killings."[22]

This parallel finding confirmed the conclusions of the earlier general comparative study. But it is conceivable that in other instances differences would emerge which might throw doubt on the validity of the original conclusions. Thus, if the figures for homicides arising out of robberies or other felonies were examined separately, significant differences might be found.

A basic theme in our discussion of the strategy of research in deterrence is that, though individual methods are imperfect, the employment of a variety of different methods to investigate a particular question may prove salutary. The imperfections of individual methods may to a large extent be canceled out when different, if equally imperfect, methods are used in independent assessments of a hypothesis.

In our prior discussion of Sellin's study of the death penalty and homicide rates, we mentioned the large number of different comparisons of clusters of similar states within the United States that formed the basis of Sellin's conclusion. Undoubtedly, the replication of a comparative method of analysis provides one helpful corrective or safeguard. However, because the danger exists that *punishment policy may be systematically related to other variables that affect a crime rate*, it would also seem wise to test the results generated by comparative research by using other *equally imperfect, but differently imperfect,* methods of research.

Thus, Sellin and his associates conducted, in addition to the

19. *Id.* at 52–63.
20. *Id.* at 53.
21. *Ibid.*
22. *Id.* at 57.

comparative researches previously mentioned, a number of other studies designed to determine whether the death penalty exercised any influence on the rates of capital crimes. In particular they examined "the rates of capital crimes in specific states or countries that have experimented with abolition in order to observe the effect of the abolition or the introduction of capital punishment on such rates."[23]

As we shall presently demonstrate, such retrospective studies, too, involve a host of problems no less imposing than, but of a different character from, those that have been discussed in relation to comparative study. In many cases, research using other than comparative methods can provide a means of assessing the validity of a comparative finding, so that the combination of two or more imperfect research approaches may reveal a relatively clear picture about the relation of the variables being studied to rates of crime.

SECTION 3 RETROSPECTIVE RESEARCH
A Introduction

At first glance, what we call retrospective studies—studies comparing crime rates in particular jurisdictions before and after changes in punishment policy—seem to be an improvement on the classical model of the controlled experiment discussed earlier. In the controlled experiment, the researcher depends on the mystical power of probability theory to guarantee that the two groups he randomly assigns into different categories are in fact similar to each other in all respects other than that of the independent variable to be tested. In a retrospective study, which focuses on change in what is assumed to be the dependent variable over a period of time, the apparent improvement on the experimental method is that the "test" unit is not merely similar to the "control" unit. It is in fact the very same person or area or country, different only with respect to a change in time and a change in punishment policy.

And if before-and-after studies seem an attractive methodological possibility, they are also an almost inevitable technique for assessing the effectiveness of crime control policies. Nothing could be more natural, for the observer or the administrator,

23. *Id.* at 63.

than the attempt to assess the impact of a change in policy by studying crime rates before and after that change was instituted. For this reason, retrospective comparisons of crime rates are by far the most common type of assessment of crime control strategy that students of the deterrent effect will encounter.

Before-and-after studies, however, contain many traps for the unwary. In the first place, if state or country A is studied before and after a particular change in punishment policy, "A before" and "A after" may very well be different from one another. The first reason is that the passage of time itself, except perhaps in cases of total social stagnation, inevitably involves change. In a country and in a decade where rapid and substantial change over time has become the rule, this point should be easy to appreciate. Figures 1 and 2 adapted

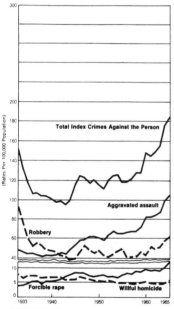

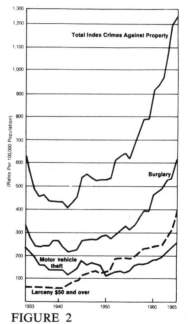

FIGURE 1
Index Crime Trends, 1933–1965: Reported Crimes against the Person
(Note: The scale for willful homicide and forcible rape is enlarged to show trend)

FIGURE 2
Index Crime Trends, 1933–1965: Reported Crimes against Property
(Note: The scale for this figure is not comparable with that used in figure 1)

from the *Report of the U.S. President's Commission on Law Enforcement and Administration of Justice* (1967) present long-range trends in respect of the seven index offenses for the period 1933–65.[24] As the figures show, differences in crime alone, independent of special changes that may or may not be attributable to changes in punishment policy, can be of substantial magnitude. But changes in crime trends which are attributable merely to the passage of time are not the only factor from which invalid inferences about policy changes can be drawn. Under normal conditions, the prescribed penalty for a particular offense will ordinarily remain stable over a period of time. Moreover, those occasions on which punishment policy is changed by a legislature will usually be associated with special conditions, and in particular with changing trends in the crime rate. More specifically, penalties for a particular crime will be more likely to decrease during periods when the rate of that particular crime is either stable or trending downward. On the other hand sharp upward shifts in the level of punishment prescribed for a particular crime will usually be associated with an increasing rate of crime.

Thus, when examining crime rates after a change in legislative policy has occurred, we must not assume that any changes in the crime rate are necessarily effects of the policy change. We must also be aware of the substantial possibility that some other factor or factors may have been the cause both of the change in punishment policy and the change in crime rate. In most cases, pressure for strong new countermeasures to crime comes when the crime rate increases. If this pattern forms the background for upward shifts in the level of punishment policy associated with particular crimes, one possibility should always be borne in mind: a crime rate which has increased to a high and unnatural level just before a countermeasure is introduced, will of and by itself regress to a more normal level whether or not a change of punishment policy occurs. This process is analogous to the regression of abnormal figures toward the mean in a statistical sample of a true population. But it can

24. Figures 1 and 2 are adapted from figures 3 and 4 in the U.S. President's Commission on Law Enforcement and Administration of Justice, Report, *The Challenge of Crime in a Free Society* (1967) at 22 and 23.

sometimes cause observers to make false assumptions about the relation between a drop in the crime rate after it has risen and the countermeasures which have been introduced.

One example is Connecticut's famous crackdown on speeding drivers in the mid-1950s. Just before the crackdown, Connecticut's rate of driving fatalities increased dramatically, compelling the governor of that state to introduce a strict new series of countermeasures. Soon after the introduction of the measures, Connecticut's rate of traffic fatalities decreased dramatically to a level much lower than that experienced during the period just before the crackdown but not substantially lower than normal levels for the state of Connecticut.[25]

Investigators later found that the death rate from traffic accidents in Connecticut just before the introduction of the countermeasures was abnormally high for the state. They also found some reduction in traffic fatalities in states adjoining Connecticut which had not instituted a speed crackdown and had not experienced the sharp increase which had led to Connecticut's unique policies.[26]

These two findings led to the conclusion that the Connecticut drop may well have been a decrease normally to be expected. "The fact that Governor Ribicoff was prompted to take action in late 1955 by the alarmingly high fatality rate for that period introduces the possibility of a regression effect from the observations immediately preceding his actions to the observations immediately following."[27] In other words, although the decrease might have resulted from the crackdown, it might have occurred simply because of the abnormally high level of traffic fatalities just before the change in policy.[28]

In New York City in 1966, the rate of taxicab robberies increased sharply. As a result of the sharp increase, the police department authorized off-duty police officers to take after-hour

25. Campbell and Ross, "The Connecticut Speed Crackdown" (1968) 3 *Law and Society Rev*. 33–53.

26. *Ibid*; see also Glass, "Analysis of Data on the Connecticut Speeding Crackdown as a Time-Series Quasi-Experiment" (1968) 3 *Law and Society Rev*. 55–76.

27. Glass, *supra* note 26, at 75.

28. Campbell and Ross, *supra* note 25, at 47: "This effect, it must be restated, could be due to the crackdown, or could be due to the regression effect."

jobs driving taxicabs, and just subsequent to the introduction of this new preventive measure the taxicab robbery rate fell sharply, although it remained higher than it had been prior to the sharp increase in 1966.[29]

It is unwise to assume that the introduction of countermeasures motivated by a sharp upward shift in a general crime rate is necessarily responsible for a subsequent decrease in the crime rate that does not move below normally experienced historical levels of crime. But it is even more unwise to draw positive conclusions from before-and-after statistics dealing with the treatment of special groups which have been selected from the population because of their increased propensity to commit or experience, during the period just prior to treatment, the crimes which led to that treatment.

For example, one Chicago study concentrated on schools whose students were responsible for a high number of false fire alarms. Fire department personnel were sent out to those schools and delivered various different appeals to the student populations to refrain from turning in false fire alarms. In most cases, the false alarm record attributable to the student population of the schools concerned decreased sharply after the presentation of the fire department program. At the same time, no school's record of false alarms dropped to the average for city schools in the Chicago area. On the basis of the data outlined here, it would be impossible to decide whether the fire department presentations were responsible for the subsequent decrease or not. For, clearly, the decrease might merely have represented regression toward the mean.[30]

Perhaps more typical of correctional intervention policies is a Detroit study made of the records of individuals sentenced to a "driver improvement school" (1) in the year before they were subject to such a sentence and (2) in the year just after

29. The countermeasure was introduced in mid-1967. Cab robberies for the period August through December for the years 1964–67 were as follows:

1964	1965	1966	1967
241	245	535	346

(Data derived from letter from Gordon F. Dale, Technical Services Bureau, New York Police Department, March 1968.)

30. "The Chicago False Fire Alarm Project: Interim Report" (1967) unpublished. Center for Studies in Criminal Justice, University of Chicago Law School.

they graduated from the driver improvement school. The comparison showed a dramatic decrease in the propensity of individuals who attended the school to be cited for traffic violations. In the year before the sentence, the average number of tickets for individuals subsequently treated by the driver improvement program was 3.5, whereas in the year after, the average number was 1.57—a decrease of more than 50 percent.[31]

The problem with both the fire alarm and the driver improvement examples is that, in each case, the particular units were chosen for treatment because they had displayed an extreme propensity for indulging in, or being apprehended for, the behavior which led to the treatment.

In Chicago, a school noted for the very highest propensity toward false fire alarm offenses might be expected to show a decrease in the number of false fire alarm offenses reported, whether or not any countermeasure were introduced, as in the Connecticut speed crackdown. And this possibility is the more pronounced because of the small size and specially selected nature of the units chosen for the Chicago study.

In the Detroit sample, the problem is, if anything, considerably worse. The drivers in the sample were chosen and sentenced solely because they had had abnormally high traffic violation records in the year before they were subjected to the driver improvement school. Not only were they a specially selected group of bad drivers in that year, but they may have been a group of very unlucky drivers. In the year after their attendance in such school, whether or not they became better drivers, it is reasonable to suppose that this group of students would at least be subjected to a normal rather than an abnormal risk of apprehension for such driving infractions as they might commit. It is reasonable to suppose that very different factors in terms of chance, and in terms of the normally expectable crime rate associated with this particular group, may have functioned to create a misleading impression that the countermeasure effected a change in the number of offenses committed by a select group of people.

31. "The Detroit Driver Improvement Program (1967) unpublished. Center for Studies in Criminal Justice, University of Chicago Law School.

For this reason we are inclined to be skeptical about what has recently been described as "a successful experiment in San Jose, California."[32] The experiment involved the referral by the traffic court of "chronic traffic violators" to "group therapy sessions." It is reported that "a sample of the driving records of . . . drivers attending group therapy sessions showed 64% had fewer convictions of moving traffic offenses after the therapy sessions than driving comparable periods before they completed the program."[33] Here, as in the case of the Detroit driver improvement school, we think it probable that no basis more unsuitable for evaluating the program could have been found than comparing the record of the group during the period that led to its selection with its record immediately after treatment.

On the other hand, there are instances in which an upward trend just before the introduction of a countermeasure is not followed by a normal regression toward the mean level of offenses experienced previously. For the crime rate may be rising for a reason which can serve as a basis for prediction that the crime rate will rise in the future.

In California, a study already referred to was made of an increase in the rate of assaults against police officers that was followed by the introduction of increased penalties for attacks on the police. This was in turn followed by a further increase in offenses against police officers. Because the same factors that may have been at work increasing the initial rate may still have been at work increasing the subsequent rate, it was incautious to conclude, as some observers did conclude, that the increased penalties had had no deterrent effect.[34]

Similar to the California experience with assaults against police officers, was the California experience with marijuana offenses. In the case of marijuana offenses, no statistics are available on the gross number of offenses committed. The figures deal only with the number of reported arrests. Because such crimes are without victims likely to report to the police, the number of arrests reported is likely to be vastly less than

32. Beresford, "Group Therapy for Chronic Violators" (1971) 7 *Trial* 42.
33. *Ibid.*
34. California Assembly Office of Research, *Crime and Penalties in California* (1968) 10–12.

the number of offenses committed. In any event, the California statistics show that the rate of marijuana arrests by the police, which had risen substantially before the increases in the legislative minimum and maximum penalties provided for possession of marijuana, continued to increase afterward.[35] Again, these statistics were regarded by some observers as proof that the increase in legislative penalties had had no effect upon the crime rate. But there are reasons to believe that the crime rate would have continued to rise in any event. And since it is difficult to estimate how much the rate would have continued to increase if there had been no change in punishment policy, a negative conclusion cannot legitimately be drawn from the evidence.

It has already been suggested that ordinarily penalties will not change drastically, particularly in an upward direction, unless other changes in society have produced a situation where special penal measures are felt to be warranted. In such circumstances, as we have said, the very social conditions that precipitate the change in punishment policy may also lead to further upward or downward movements in the crime rate. Beyond this possibility however, there is a further complication. The social forces causing the change in punishment policy may at the same time give rise to other developments which may have an influence on subsequent rates of criminality. Let us assume that a sharp rise in the burglary rate, or the development of special awareness of the harm done by burglary, produces an upward shift in the punishment level for that crime. It is not unlikely that the same conditions will also lead both to an increase in the police resources invested in the detection and apprehension of burglars, and to more attention to anti-burglary precautions on the part of individual citizens. These latter developments, rather than the upward penalty shift, may well be responsible for any subsequent fall in the burglary rate. It should be noted that these collateral changes would not be merely coincidental. Far from being exceptional, such multiple changes in response to the same social forces are the rule. It is therefore possible that significant changes in a crime rate will be falsely attributed to one of many changes in crime preven-

35. *Id.* at 12.

tion strategy, *and* that apparently discouraging crime statistics will mask what may be a genuine deterrent effect of a particular change.

An example of the first type of effect comes from Professor Chambliss's study of parking offenses at a midwestern university referred to in chapter 3.[36] Chambliss describes how the university responded to a rapid increase in prohibited parking on campus in the early fifties. The response involved both changing the severity of fines imposed on multiple parking offenders, and providing for the first time an efficient mechanism to enforce the regulations in relation to faculty members who could previously ignore parking summonses if they chose. Professor Chambliss's data show that after the change in university policy a significant decrease in prohibited parking occurred. The decrease, however, cannot be interpreted solely as a response to the increased penalties. It seems likely that it was largely due to the changes in enforcement.

In most cases the failure to consider changes other than those in penalties results in an overestimate rather than an underestimate of the relative impact of the change in penalty level. But failure to note other changes may also lead observers to conclude with unjustified confidence that a change in punishment level has had no preventive effect on the crime rate.

The danger of the preventive effects of penalty increases being masked is most extreme when the amount of effort expended by police influences the proportion of crime that is reported. A masking effect may be expected whenever the arrest rate bears little relation to the offense rate. This will be particularly marked in the case of "victimless" crimes such as drunkenness, sexual offenses involving consenting parties, and narcotics offenses.

Another difficulty arises where the only reliable information available is on the number of arrests rather than on the number of crimes reported for a particular area. This derives from the fact, already mentioned, that the social pressures leading to a change in punishment policy may also lead to a greater commitment of resources to the enforcement of that particular

36. Chambliss, "The Deterrent Influence of Punishment" (1966) 12 *Crime and Delinquency* 70–75.

criminal law. Intensified enforcement efforts may result in a greater ratio of arrests to offenses. But the greater number of arrests may create the illusion of a crime wave when, in fact, the crime rate may have diminished.

This point is relevant to the California experience with marijuana offenses.[37] Any conclusions one would like to draw about the effect of the increased marijuana penalties should be tempered by the recognition that the pressures leading to the penalty changes may have led also to a greater effort on the part of the police to discover such crimes.

A striking increase in the number of reported sex offenses occurred after an upward shift in the penalty for such offenses in Norway in 1927. "Comparing the five-year period before the change with the five-year period after the change, the average rose . . . 68 percent."[38] Professor Andenaes attributes this increase to the fact that "the discussion and agitation that went with the revision [in the penal code] and the stricter view that the new provisions gave expression to, doubtless caused many sex offenses that would not have been reported to be reported now—and perhaps the police now investigated such cases more energetically as well."[39]

In sum, studies of rates of crime before and after changes in penalty levels are hindered by a number of confounding possibilities. So we should always bear in mind that rates of crime may fluctuate independently of any change in crime prevention policy; that the conditions leading to changes in penalties or enforcement techniques may themselves independently influence the crime rate; and that the special social conditions leading to a change in penalty levels may produce other social responses which influence the crime rate.

It is our position that such possibly confounding phenomena, far from being rare, should be expected in most studies of an upward shift in the level of punishment for a particular crime. Yet such difficulties do not justify the total rejection of retrospective studies as a research method. As with comparative

---

37. California Assembly Office of Research, *supra* note 34, at 12.
38. Andenaes, "General Prevention—Illusion or Reality?" (1952) 43 *J. Crim. Law, Criminology, and Police Science* 191.
39. *Ibid.*

studies, a number of techniques can improve the reliability of before-and-after studies. Moreover, although these correctives are far from absolutely effective, they can in many cases render before-and-after studies as meaningful as any other research in a nonexperimental setting can hope to be.

B Controls for Retrospective Research: Long Range Trends

One natural way of testing whether a change in crime rate is attributable to a change in penal policy is to expand a short-run before-and-after study so as to cover a longer period. This expansion of perspective, while no panacea, will often expose incautious inferences. On the other hand it can, on occasion, lend credibility to the original inferences drawn from a short-run study. Both these possibilities are illustrated in a number of the studies mentioned earlier in this discussion.

To begin with the most extreme example, the reader will recall the dramatic "improvement" of drivers sentenced to the Detroit driver improvement school when their traffic records the year after graduation from the school were compared to their records the year before they entered it. Now, if we extend the period of comparison backward in time to the period from 24 to 12 months before sentence, we can test whether exceptional bad luck and other special factors may have played a role in the extremely high year-before traffic ticket averages used in the initial comparison. The results of such an extension are given in table 10. It has to be borne in mind that in the year immediately preceding attendance at the school the mean

TABLE 10
Records of Moving Violations of Persons
Attending Driver Improvement School

	No. of Drivers	Total No. of Violations	Mean No. of Violations
During the period from 24 to 12 months before attendance	280	440	1.57
During the year after completion of school	280	441	1.57

number of violations per individual was 3.50.[40] Going back one year, we find that the average number of moving violations in the period from 24 to 12 months before attendance at driver improvement school is precisely the same as the average number of moving citations in the period from 0 to 12 months after graduation from the driver improvement school. The striking similarity between the two averages cannot, however, be taken as a conclusive indication that no improvement was experienced by the members of this group. It is perfectly possible that without the treatment the records of the group might have worsened as time went on.

On the other hand, the data from the year immediately before driver improvement school are tainted by the fact that luck as well as other factors play a significant role in the number of moving violations recorded. So we are left with a comparison of only two periods of time and a group which experienced remarkably similar traffic offense rates in each period. We certainly cannot conclude from these results that the driver improvement program exerted a preventive influence on its subjects.

The Chicago false fire alarm study presented a different, and superior, method of determining whether the sharp drop in fire alarms in specially selected high false fire alarm schools could be attributed to the fire department's prevention program. In that study, a randomly selected control group of high false fire alarm schools was left untreated, while other randomly assigned problem schools were being treated. Records were kept of the false alarms attributed to these control schools before and after the other high risk schools were subjected to treatment. The results were that the number of alarms reported from all the high risk schools dropped significantly. But there was no significant difference between the drop experienced by schools subjected to the treatment programs and schools in the control group. Here it was apparent that the particular countermeasure was not the cause of the decrease in reported rate.[41]

40. "The Detroit Driver Improvement Program" (1967) unpublished. Center for Studies in Criminal Justice, University of Chicago Law School.
41. "The Chicago False Fire Alarm Project: Interim Report" (1967) unpublished. Center for Studies in Criminal Justice, University of Chicago Law School.

We have already referred, in chapter 4, to the British experience after the introduction of the Road Safety Act of 1967, which provided, effective October, 1967, for a new definition of drunk driving and more convenient methods of proof of intoxication of drivers once arrested. It was found that the number of serious and fatal nighttime accidents decreased 38 percent when the seven-month period following the introduction of the new law was compared with a similar seven-month period in the year prior to its introduction.[42] In that case, extending the comparison to a longer time span shows that, rather than being a regression to more normal historical rates, the decrease was both significant and unexpected in terms of Great Britain's long-range traffic accident experience. The "fatalities plus serious casualties" figures for the years 1961 through 1968 have been subjected to a time-series analysis which demonstrates that what the authors call "the Breathalyser crackdown" was "not a reaction to a peak crisis, but rather to a chronic condition."[43] It also shows that, though the initial reduction was not fully maintained but "leveled off," the crackdown "did save lives and prevent injuries" and "continues to have an important beneficial effect on British highways."[44]

Just as marked discontinuities following the introduction of a change in punishment policy, which are apparent in the light of long-term trends, can corroborate conclusions drawn from short-range comparisons, so the existence of *uninterrupted* long-term trends can throw doubt on those conclusions. A number of studies of trends in the homicide rate before and after either the introduction or the abolition of capital punishment for homicide have shown that, while both increases and decreases are experienced after a change in punishment policy, in the great majority of cases the short-term movements are quite consistent with the longer-term trends experienced in the same jurisdictions in the years before the change in punishment policy.[45]

42. *Ministry of Transport Press Notices*: no. 892 of 19 Dec. 1967; no. 78 of 8 Feb. 1968; and no. 157 of 1 March 1968.
43. Ross, Campbell, and Glass, "Determining the Social Effects of a Legal Reform" (1970) 13 *American Behavioral Scientist* 504.
44. *Id.* at 507.
45. See Sellin, *supra* note 8, at 34–50 for a summary of the evidence relating to the effect of the abolition of the death penalty on homicide

The results of such comparisons are not solely negative. The continuity in trend before and after the change in punishment policy is positive evidence that the changed rate of crime cannot properly be attributed to the penalty change. For the examination of a longer time span than can be covered by a short-term before-and-after study may show that apparent discontinuities, when viewed in perspective, either form part of a continuous long-range trend, or are a return to more normal levels of crime after a brief interruption.

The net result of introducing the longer time dimension in a before-and-after study is frequently to cast varying degrees of doubt on the proposition that the change in punishment policy resulted in the change in crime rate. Where the long-range comparison only shows that after a brief interruption there was a return to more historically normal crime rates, the evidence is not totally persuasive. We simply don't know whether regression or marginal deterrence, or both, have influenced the crime rate.

Even where the data show an uninterrupted long-range trend, this still cannot be taken as conclusive evidence of the lack of punishment policy effect. Trends are not necessarily immutable, and the apparent continuity may conceal what has in fact been a change in trend compensated for by the effects of the change in punishment policy. While dangers exist both in the continuity and discontinuity situation, the danger of false inference seems to be less severe when a trend has been continuous and uninterrupted. Nevertheless, the longer the time span encompassed, the greater is the possibility that changes due to factors other than punishment policy will assume prominence. Great cyclical changes in the crime rate will tend to obliterate smaller changes which may be due to punishment policy. The significance of this problem becomes apparent when it is recognized that even when changes in punishment policy do make a difference in crime rates, that difference may often be small when expressed in terms of a rate per 100,000. Yet relatively small changes in the rate of serious crimes are not necessarily unimportant and can be quite significant in terms of public policy.

---

death rates in both American states and foreign countries which either tried abolition for a period or permanently abolished the death penalty.

C Controls for Retrospective Research: Historical Context

If we can determine why a particular political unit chose a particular time in history to make changes in punishment policy, we may discover whether the social forces that led to this change might also have led to others. Information about the legislative history of changes in punishment policy, about the social forces operating just before change, and about trends in crime just before change, may all be relevant to such a determination.

A study of the conditions prevailing in California before the repeated escalations in penalties for possessing marijuana suggests that the use of marijuana was increasing at a substantial rate before the upward shift in punishment. This impression could be confirmed or refuted by an analysis of the marijuana arrest rates over the years just prior to the change in punishment policy. Newspapers, testimony before legislative committees, and other sources might reveal the degree to which law enforcement officials were recognizing, at the time of pending legislative change in punishment policy, that further or increased enforcement efforts might be necessary to implement public policy against marijuana consumption.

The results of such an inquiry might cast doubt on the inference that the penalty escalations had no effect on the crime rate.[46] For when the trend in rate of reported arrests or of offenses after a change in legislative policy is viewed in the light of contemporary social conditions and changes in enforcement strategy, trends in the crime rate that first appeared to have unequivocal significance may be rendered ambiguous. Alternatively, historical analysis may suggest that no third forces were at work to negate the effects of the change in punishment policy and that the ineffectiveness of such a change cannot be explained in any other way than by attributing little or no force to the change in policy itself.

It is not inevitable that the study of the conditions surrounding a change in punishment policy will produce plausible rival hypotheses to explain any change or lack of change in the crime rate. It may provide reasons for questioning the easy inference regarding policy effect that comes from a before-and-after com-

46. California Assembly Office of Research, *supra* note 34, at 10–12.

parison. It may, on the other hand, buttress the strength of an inference that a change of punishment policy and only such a change is the cause of a change in the crime rate. Whatever the impact of such historical study may be, the necessity for it is plain in any area where the possibility of confounding variables is so considerable.

D Controls for Retrospective Research: Independent Evidence

We have indicated that before-and-after studies that focus solely on the change in the quantity of crime may be misleading or may lead to equivocal conclusions. Yet, as with comparative studies, it is sometimes possible to find independent evidence which may enable us to supplement raw data on crime rates and thus make more meaningful comparisons. In particular it may be possible to find an independent but parallel measure of the impact of the law on behavior.

Perhaps the most illuminating example of the use of independent measures as indices supplementing a quantitative before-and-after comparison can be found in the evaluation of the Road Safety Act of 1967 and its impact on drunk driving in Great Britain. Because drunk driving does not necessarily have a victim and will not necessarily be reported, criminal statistics relating to the number of violations of the law known to the police provide an extremely defective measure of the actual number of violations. But because of the overwhelmingly high association of abnormal alcohol concentrations and serious and fatal traffic accidents, the measure of fluctuations in the rate of drunk driving which was employed was the trend in the number of serious highway traffic casualties in Great Britain during the period just before and just after the introduction of the new law.

Because serious highway traffic casualties are in many instances not the result of driving under the influence of alcohol, some measure of the extent to which alcohol involvement in traffic fatalities might have changed before and after the new law was considered necessary. Two independent measures of the contribution of alcohol to traffic fatalities were studied.

The first was a comparison between nighttime and daytime trends in accidents that resulted in serious or fatal injuries. Because nighttime accidents are far more closely related to abnormal blood alcohol levels, such an analysis could be expected to indicate whether or not the change in the drunk driving rate was responsible for the substantial decrease in the total rate of fatal and serious accidents that occurred after the introduction of the new legal standards and enforcement policies. As table 11 shows, nighttime fatal and serious accidents decreased far more substantially than daytime serious and fatal accidents.[47] The net result of this comparison is to make it appear highly probable that a change in the level of drunk driving was indeed responsible for the decrease in total accident experience.

TABLE 11
Percentage Decrease in Road Casualties in Great Britain:
October–December 1966 to October–December 1967

	October	November	December
Daytime (8 A.M. to 6 P.M.)	2	2	7
Nighttime (8 P.M. to 4 A.M.)	36	38	41

In evaluating the Road Safety Act of 1967, however, it was possible to go a step further, and to determine the extent to which abnormal blood alcohol concentrations themselves were related to accident fatalities before and after the introduction of the new standards. Figures were available on the blood alcohol concentrations of drivers killed before and after the implementation of the act. Post mortem examinations of drivers killed in road accidents revealed that the percentage of those killed with blood alcohol levels over 0.08 percent dropped from 28 percent in the year before the effective date of the Road Safety Act to 15 percent in the first year after the act came into force.[48] Table 12 offers compelling evidence of the relation between the decrease in serious accidents and the decrease in drunk driving. It further suggests that virtually all

47. *Supra* note 3.
48. Ministry of Transport Road Research Laboratory Report, by R. F. Newbay (in preparation), cited by Andenaes, "Deterrence and Specific Offenses" (1971) 38 *U. Chi. L. Rev.* 550 n. 41.

of the decrease was attributable to the diminution in drunk driving.[49]

TABLE 12
Blood Alcohol Figures of Drivers and Riders Killed in Road Accidents

	Numbers Killed		
Blood Alcohol Levels in milligrams per 100 milliliters	Dec. 1966 to Sept. 1967	Oct. 1967 to Sept. 1968	Percentage Change
00 to 09	578	536	−7
10 to 50	80	57	−28
51 to 80	48	19	−60
81 +	279	114	−59

It is difficult to conceive of a more effective demonstration of the impact of the law than the combination of the comparison of general traffic accident trends and the estimates of the reduction in deaths due to driving under the influence of alcohol, as done in tables 11 and 12.

Another type of parallel study is the analysis of the component parts of a crime rate, which may produce more useful information than comparisons of gross rates before and after a change in punishment policy. One remarkable if not wholly successful attempt to use this method was the analysis conducted by Gibson and Klein, of the British Home Office Research Unit, of the impact of the abolition of capital punishment on types of homicide as well as on the overall rate of homicide in Great Britain.[50]

There is some reason to believe that homicides involving mental abnormality are less responsive to the threat of criminal sanction than those committed by normal persons. One strategy, therefore, for performing an analysis of before-and-after rates of homicide in order to determine whether or not a change from capital to noncapital sanctions had any effect on the rate, would be to trend "normal" and "mentally abnormal" types of

---

49. Ministry of Transport data supplied in personal communication, October 1969, from J. Betts.
50. Gibson and Klein, *Murder from 1957 to 1968* (1969).

homicide into two categories—those homicides that resulted in the subsequent determination that they were committed by mentally abnormal individuals, and those homicides that did not. The results of such a breakdown of the data are shown in table 13.[51]

The Gibson and Klein data raise doubts about the apparent evenness of trend in the gross rate, with an upward swing in homicide before and after complete abolition of capital punishment. Moreover, they show an increase in the rate of "normal" homicide which might easily be attributed, although Gibson and Klein do not do so, to abandonment of the death penalty. The problem with drawing this inference, however, is twofold.

In the first place, it is difficult to understand how, independently of any change in policy that might influence the number of mental abnormality claims and the number of mental abnormality findings, the rate of abnormal murder could decrease precipitously over a period of one year. In the second place, the presence or absence of capital punishment may influence both the number of offenders who commit suicide after committing murder and those who are found mentally abnormal. At the same time more offenders may be found to be normal when the consequences of such a finding are less drastic than the death penalty. Table 14[52] suggests that people are more likely to want to be found mentally abnormal in a situation where capital punishment is the alternative to such a finding than they would be in a situation where the alternative is, at worst, a long term of imprisonment. Moreover, it is not improbable that the authorities would be more inclined to classify a homicide as normal when this classification would not have lethal consequences. These considerations raise a serious obstacle to drawing any inference from the Gibson and Klein data.

Our analysis of these data points up a general problem in the content analysis of before-and-after crime rates. A change in punishment policy, or the social forces that lie behind it, may well influence the extent to which individuals will fall in one or another category of crime, such as the categories of mentally abnormal homicide and mentally normal homicide. The

51. *Id.* at 3; data derived from table 2.
52. *Id.* at 8 and 27; data derived from tables 6 and 22.

TABLE 13
Abnormal and Normal Murder Rates, 1957–68

Year	Abnormal Homicide			Normal Murder	Total
	Abnormal Murder	Murder Reduced to Manslaughter by Reason of Diminished Responsibility	Total		
1957	78	22	100	57	157
1958	77	29	96	47	143
1959	78	21	99	57	156
1960	72	31	103	51	154
1961	66	30	94	54	148
1962	73	42	115	56	171
1963	63	56	119	59	178
1964	59	35	94	76	170
1965[a]	58	50	108	77	185
1966	34	65	99	88	187
1967	64	57	121	90	211
1968	52	57	109	96	205

[a]The Murder (Abolition of Death Penalty) Act of 1965 came into operation on 9 November 1965.

TABLE 14
Murder Suspects Found Insane and Executions 1957–68

Year	Suspects Found Insane	Executions
1957	21	3
1958	19	5
1959	27	4
1960	22	7
1961	20	4
1962	15	2
1963	12	2
1964	10	2
1965	8	0
1966	5	0
1967	9	0
1968	6	0

change, of and by itself, can produce changes in the nature
or content of the crime rate. These changes, which will be
independent of changes in the gross crime rate, may seem to
provide a measure of the effects of policy change but will in
fact be an unreliable index as to whether the change in punishment policy has achieved any significant measure of crime
prevention.

Yet such content analyses of crime rates can be a useful
supplement to purely quantitive crime rate analyses. An intelligent blending of the gross data on crime rates with whatever data exist on the nature of such crime rates before and
after changes in punishment policy may sometimes provide a
basis for discriminating between real and spurious changes in
crime rates following policy changes.

One final example of content analysis as a supplement to the
comparison of gross rates, while more trivial in substance than
the Gibson and Klein study, is worthy of mention. Professor
Chambliss, in a study we have previously cited, surveyed a
number of university professors affected by changes in both
the amount of fine threatened for repeated prohibited parking
and in the methods of enforcement. The enforcement changes
meant that faculty members who had successfully evaded fines
for parking violations in the past would not do so in the future.
Chambliss's findings were that, taken as a whole, the sample
evidenced a substantially smaller amount of prohibited parking

after the change than before.[53] But when the sample of responding faculty members was divided with respect to whether or not they had actually paid the fines before the change in policy, it was found that the overwhelming majority of the decreases in parking violation were attributable to individuals who had not previously paid. Thus, while either the escalation of fine or the change in enforcement policy might have been responsible for the change in the gross rate of reported prohibited parking, content analysis suggests that the change in enforcement policy rather than the change in fine level was the crucial factor.[54]

The problems encountered when one seeks to draw conclusions from a before-and-after analysis in a single jurisdiction are similar in one respect to those encountered in a comparative analysis of the crime rates that obtain in different jurisdictions. In both cases, independent evidence untainted by the particular flaws that may affect either type of study will always be a desirable adjunct.

There is a certain logical symmetry about the conclusion that a natural adjunct to the retrospective study is the comparative study and vice versa. If we doubt the validity of assuming continuity in California's marijuana crime rate, one natural strategy for testing the effect of escalations in California sanctions is to examine the sanction policies and resultant crime trends in other jurisdictions which are as close in nature to California as is possible. Such comparisons will, of course, be imperfect because there is no place quite like California. Nevertheless, this combination of comparative and retrospective methods, while by no means invulnerable, suggests an inversion of a familiar maxim: two wrongs, if carefully combined, may make a right.

SECTION 4 THE INDUCED RETROSPECTIVE STUDY

When the criminologist, having heard of a change in punishment policy, responds by attempting to study the rates of a particular crime before and after that change, he may have

---

53. Chambliss, "The Deterrent Influence of Punishment" (1966) 12 *Crime and Delinquency* 70–75.

54. For a more detailed analysis of the Chambliss study, see Zimring and Hawkins, "Deterrence and Marginal Groups" (1968) 5 *J. Research in Crime and Delinq.* 111–14.

arrived on the scene of change too late for an effective study to be carried out. It may not be possible to make a satisfactory study of the conditions that existed just before the change in law. If the police-recorded rate of an offense is unreliable, it will be too late to take a victim survey to determine the rate of a particular crime before a change in policy.

Moreover, it may be difficult to determine precisely what social forces led to the decision that a change in policy was needed. In addition, account must be taken of the possibilities already discussed: that the social forces that led to a change in policy may themselves have led to a change in crime rate, and that the social forces which led to the change in punishment policy may have led to other changes which themselves influenced the crime rate.

We mention these possibilities again now in order to contrast the traditional retrospective study of punishment policy changes with an alternative method—one we may call the planned or induced retrospective study. Insofar as it is possible for the researcher to choose areas in which he would like changes to take place and to persuade the relevant authorities to effect such changes, the task of studying the historical context surrounding change and the effects that factors other than penalty changes might have on a crime rate becomes much easier.

In addition, if the researcher has any choice in that matter of which jurisdictions make changes in punishment policy, he can avoid many of the problems that arise in the case of normal punishment changes. For example, he can select areas in which the crime rates have been stable or predictable. Having thus assumed some control over the conditions that determine whether or not changes in punishment policy are made, he will be protected from some of the confounding factors which commonly vitiate the conclusions of retrospective studies. Moreover, when combined with comparisons with areas previously chosen as similar to the area experiencing the change, the induced retrospective study may well provide the most reliable of all nonexperimental assessments of the effect of a particular change.

It differs from the classical model of the controlled experiment because there will be no large number of units to be assigned into test and control categories. The absence of such large numbers of control areas makes us depend far more heavily, for comparison, on the record of the selected jurisdiction just before the change in policy. But the induced retrospective study is similar to the controlled experiment in that the researcher has a large measure of control over what variables will be changed and what areas will experience the change. Although, for the lack of some marginal controls, the exercise will be far from perfect, it deserves high priority in any list of possible research methods into the deterrent effect of punishment.

In the United States, incidentally, both the Law Enforcement Assistance Administration and the Department of Transportation, National Highway Traffic Safety Administration will make grants for implementing innovatory crime prevention and control programs and for the evaluation of the effects of such programs.[55] The National Institute of Law Enforcement and Criminal Justice, which is the research and development arm of L.E.A.A., has a research center which is devoted to "programs in crime prevention and deterrence."[56] The availability of such funds makes possible induced retrospective experiments in such areas as the control of drunk driving, changes in methods of detection and police patrol, and variations in levels of prosecution. But the considerable expense and great responsibility inevitably associated with induced retrospective studies render it advisable that tests be restricted to well-established hypotheses and to changes in punishment policy that do not involve serious social costs. Within these limits, the induced retrospective study is one of the most promising possibilities for future research.

SECTION 5 THE FIELD EXPERIMENT

Dr. Max Grunhut, writing on the treatment of juvenile offenders some years ago, declared: "In the administration of justice no experiments are feasible."[57] But more recently it has

55. See (1) Law Enforcement Assistance Administration, *Guide for State Planning Agency Grants* (1968) and (2) U.S. Department of Transportation, National Highway Safety Bureau, *Alcohol Safety Action Projects, Guide for Applicants* (1970).

56. Law Enforcement Assistance Administration, *L.E.A.A. 1970* (1970) 47–51.

57. Grunhut, *Juvenile Offenders before the Court* (1956) 10.

been urged that "whenever a legal innovation is introduced it should be done if possible under circumstances which will permit thorough evaluation of its effects."[58] Professor Schwartz has argued the case for "field experimentation" as a means of improving our ability "to use law as an effective instrument of control."[59]

The field experiment is "designed to bring to natural situations some of the precision of the laboratory."[60] It is relatively little used in the social sciences, although where practicable it is an appropriate and valuable strategy of research. Unfortunately, in all but a few instances it will not be possible randomly to assign individuals into test and control groups and to vary as between the groups the conditions of threat and punishment that accompany the detection and conviction of an individual for law violation. It is difficult to conceive of an acceptable experiment in which, after random assignment, the severity of sanctions threatened for a violation of a particular criminal law was varied between the two groups. There are, on the other hand, a number of threat variables other than penalty which could be varied so as to carry out random assignment of different variables to different groups.

One example of a variable susceptible to such manipulation may be found in a field experiment conducted by Professor Schwartz and Sonya Orleans in the Chicago area on the effectiveness of different types of persuasive appeals on the taxpaying behavior of individual citizens.[61] Schwartz and Orleans took a sample of four hundred 1961 taxpayers and randomly assigned them to four groups: one group receiving a threat appeal, one receiving an appeal to conscientious motives for tax paying, one receiving a neutral message on taxpaying behavior, and one receiving nothing at all. The data on tax paying during the subsequent taxable year showed that the conscience- and threat-appeal groups both tended to pay more taxes than the groups subjected to the neutral appeal or no appeal. Be-

58. Zeisel, Kalven, and Buchholz, *Delay in the Court* (1959) 24.
59. Schwartz, "Field Experimentation in Sociological Research" (1961) 13 *J. Legal Ed.* 403–8.
60. Schwartz and Orleans, "On Legal Sanctions" (1967) 34 *U. Chi. L. Rev.* 285.
61. *Id.* at 274–300.

tween the appeal to the conscience and threat appeal, the former appears to have had a greater influence.[62]

The Schwartz and Orleans study illustrates an aspect of deterrence suitable for field experiment: the effect of variations in the communication of a threat. For when we vary the manner in which a threat is communicated rather than the terms of that threat, there are no major ethical objections to carrying out such experiments. Moreover, the cooperation and assistance of administrative agencies will not be too difficult to obtain.

A greater problem is encountered when variables such as law enforcement strategies affecting the probability of apprehension are subjected to field experimentation. In the first place, with the exception of specialized enforcement practices, such as the auditing of tax returns, it is normally difficult to alter the probability that an individual offender will be apprehended without general changes in apprehension rates.

It is possible, where a political unit is made up of a number of distinct and separate subunits, randomly to assign various levels or techniques of enforcement to test and control units and to conduct what will be in effect a unit field experiment. In order to make random assignment possible, however, the units subject to the new enforcement strategy will have to be fairly small. And this raises some problems. First, it may be difficult to ensure that variations in enforcement technique as between small units such as a police precinct will be clearly perceived by the intended audience. Second, the manipulation of enforcement strategies may merely persuade criminals to transfer their attentions elsewhere. In such circumstances any deterrence which is achieved may in fact be an "export" effect rather than a crime prevention effect.

At this point it is important to distinguish between the field experiment and some of the other methods we have discussed. First, there is the situation where a change in punishment policy or enforcement methods which occurs naturally in a high crime rate area is subjected to a retrospective study. In such circumstances, as we have indicated, there is always the danger of regression effects. To some extent the induced retrospective study will be protected against this danger. In the

62. *Id.* at 294–99.

field experiment, with random assignment into test and control units, the protection provided will be even more effective. Unfortunately, the use of the latter method is less often feasible.

We conclude, then, that in the limited number of situations within which the field experiment is possible and ethically unobjectionable, it is the preferred method of assessing the consequences of changes in legal threats. Again, as with the induced retrospective study, the costs in human terms impose stringent limits. But this should not be regarded as an absolute barrier to field experimentation. In conducting this type of research, we should proceed with caution, but we should proceed.

SECTION 6 SURVEY RESEARCH
A Introduction

It has been suggested that, as the effectiveness of deterrence must depend upon the public's response to the multiple threats and examples of punishment provided by the criminal law, survey research techniques should be employed in order to determine the real nature and extent of that response.[63] The Report of the President's Commission on Law Enforcement and Administration of Justice stated that "the survey technique has a great untapped potential as a method for providing additional information about the ... relative effectiveness of different programs to control crime."[64]

There is no doubt that reliable information about public knowledge of, and attitudes and responses to, elements of a threat and punishment system would be of value to the manipulation of deterrent processes in our criminal justice system. Given the limited opportunities available for experimental programs, and the difficulties associated with retrospective and comparative research, the direct method of investigating public response to punishment policy by questioning individuals seems initially attractive. We are of the opinion that survey research can make a contribution to the understanding of deterrent processes as long as it is conducted with care and its limitations are appreciated.

63. This suggestion can be found stated explicitly by Wootton in *Crime and the Criminal Law* (1963) at 98.
64. *Supra* note 24, at 22.

The tone of some of our remarks in this section might suggest that survey research can be of little utility for empirical investigation of deterrence. Yet finding out what people say about crime and punishment or what prisoners say about police or prisons is not necessarily an idle task. As Nigel Walker says in this connection, "This is a case where some information . . . is better than no information."[65] Usually, however, the proper role of survey research is either as a preliminary or supplement to other methods of investigation.

Survey research can be directed at a variety of goals, including knowledge of (1) the extent of public knowledge of the elements of a punishment policy, (2) the nature of public attitudes toward punishment policy, and (3) behavioral responses to particular criminal regulations. The opportunities and problems associated with survey research vary in relation to the goal of the research. The following subsections discuss the prospects for accurately obtaining these three distinct end products by survey methods.

B Survey Research and Public Knowledge

Survey research may be of some value as a means of obtaining information about public awareness of changes not only in penalties but also in techniques of enforcement and apprehension. Surveys conducted before and after such changes provide a means of assessing their effect in terms of public knowledge. They may also provide information about the effectiveness of publicity campaigns associated with such changes.

It is crucial to survey research of this kind that its findings relate directly to the operation of a penal system. We have already discussed some of the difficulties involved in the interpretation of research findings in this area.[66] It may be as well to enumerate here the principal obstacles to drawing straightforward categorical conclusions.

In the first place, even if it is found that public knowledge of the specific levels of a criminal penalty is extremely limited, this does not necessarily mean that the sanction for the crime is not achieving a deterrent effect among the population. As long as the public feels that unpleasant consequences are at-

---

65. Walker, *Sentencing in a Rational Society* (1969) 63.
66. See chap. 4, sec. 1, subsec. D *supra*.

tached to apprehension for forbidden behavior, a deterrent effect is possible. Public ignorance of the level of penalties may produce a pattern of responses from that public which includes both overestimates and underestimates. And as we have already noted some scholars have suggested that an uncertain sanction, the behavioral equivalent of an unknown one, may be a better deterrent than a specifically defined punishment.[67]

In the second place, general lack of knowledge regarding penalty levels does not mean that subgroups of the population associated with particular types of criminal behavior may not have considerable knowledge of the penalties for that behavior. This is of some importance because serious criminal activity is normally confined to a group of persons smaller than the total population. In any particular form of criminal activity such factors as the degree of socialization, lack of motivation, failure to recognize opportunities, and lack of skill or ability will preclude participation by a substantial proportion of the population.[68] It would therefore seem that the utility of severe threats designed to prevent specific serious crimes must be in large measure determined by the effect of such threats on this limited group of potential criminals.

In the third place, the finding that a substantial proportion of the population in a particular jurisdiction was ignorant of, or significantly underestimated, the maximum or average pen-

67. E.g.: (a) Morris, *The Habitual Criminal* (1951) 12: "Frequently it is the unpredictable quality of punishment that conditions its deterrent force." (b) Wilkins, "Criminology: An Operational Research Approach," in A. T. Welford (ed.), *Society: Problems and Methods of Study* (1962) at 325, "It might perhaps be argued that a measure of uncertainty is necessary to maximize the effect of deterrence to crime. In terms of the theory of strategy, this means that an element of randomness may be necessary to achieve the maximum social controls of deterrence." (c) Campbell, *Defense of the Middle East, Problems of American Policy* (1958) 177, cited in Halperin, *Deterrence and Local War* (1963) at 21. "The maximum deterrent effect, then, should come from creating in the minds of the Soviet leadership a mixture of uncertainty and certainty."

68. This is not to suggest that what the *Report* of the U.S. President's Commission (*supra* note 24, at 43) refers to as the "common belief that the general population consists of a large group of law-abiding people and a small body of criminals" is well founded. But although there is considerable evidence dealing with unreported crime, criminal case mortality, impunity rates, self-reported crime, and white-collar crime which suggests that the "hidden" offender group is very substantial, it in no way invalidates our assumption.

alty for a particular offense would not negative a marginal deterrent effect attributable to the particular penalty. This is because individual underestimates might vary in proportion to the actual severity of the sentence. Raising an armed robbery maximum sentence from twenty to forty years might give the public the impression that armed robbery is "more serious," and might thereby raise *the average notion* of the penalty's severity.

We should here briefly consider two competing theories concerning the communication and perception of legal commands to citizens. The "classical" theory of communications appears to assume an immediate, direct, and literal relationship between the provisions of legal commands and citizen perception.[69] Thus, on a Tuesday afternoon, the California legislature passes a law raising the minimum penalty for possession of marijuana from x to y. The law is due to go into effect the next day. According to the "classical" theory, overnight all citizens who might be affected in this state perceive: (a) that there has been a change, (b) the nature or direction of the change, i.e., that the new penalty is more severe than the old, and (c) the extent of the change, i.e., that the minimum punishment has been elevated from level x to level y.

The other theory of communication, here termed a "diffusion" theory, would stress the unreality of the classical model. The proponent of a diffusion theory would argue that individuals are probably informed about punishment policy and that this information probably has an influence on behavioral decisions among some populations. And he would concede that the attention paid by violators of a particular statute may be greater than that of the general population. But he would argue that the timing of the communication process and the nature of that process are not as the classicists have supposed.

First, he would assert that information about punishment policy "trickles down" to significant subgroups in society rather

69. However, Bentham in "On the Promulgation of Laws" 1 *Works* (1843) 157–63 is clearly aware that "the dissemination of the laws" is not so simple a matter. Nevertheless, the British Road Safety Act of 1967 appears to offer a perhaps unique example of the classical theory of communication in practice. For discussion of the operation of this legislation, see *supra* chap. 4, sec. 1, subsec. E (iv), and *infra* chap. 6, sec. 2, subsec. A.

than being immediately poured into public vessels of knowledge.[70] Second, he would maintain that the particulars of legislative punishment policy are not perceived as precisely as the classical model assumes. The perception of a particular group might vary in direct relation to a change in official punishment policy, but the variance might not be in terms of the literal penalties provided before and after the change. Third, the diffusion theory proponent would suggest that, since the process of communicating official punishment policy is more approximate and takes more time than has been sometimes supposed, an individual's perception of the penalty for a crime may change without that individual's actually being aware of a legislative change. The change in perception may take place months or years after legislative action. While an individual's previous impression was that the particular offense was not very severely punished, he now finds himself thinking that the punishment for the offense is rather more severe than he had previously supposed.

This brings us to the last of the limits on the reliability of inferences which can be drawn from survey research dealing with public knowledge of punishment policy. Even if there is a general lack of knowledge regarding penalties, and even if some high criminal risk subgroups are ignorant of the penalties for some offenses in relation to which they are at risk, it does not necessarily follow that lack of knowledge results in failure of deterrence.

In relation to certain offenses, such as income tax evasion, the population at large might be regarded as potentially criminal. But in relation to most offenses the potential offender

70. See Barmack and Payne, "The Lackland Accident Countermeasure Experiment" (1961) 40 *Highway Research Board Proceedings* 513–22, where a research program to develop and evaluate measures for the prevention of personal injury accidents among servicemen is reported. The authors report a three-month lag between the time the countermeasure (a program designed to undercut the favorable image many young adults have toward "tanking up and taking off" in a car) was first announced and the time it began to exert a detectable effect. They suggest that the lag between application and detectable effect may have been due to the fact "that the spread of information about the countermeasure is an *accretive process* which necessitates repeated announcements . . . and word-of-mouth communication until a substantial majority of the population becomes aware of the countermeasure" (our italics).

group will usually be only a limited proportion of the population. It will be confined to demographically definable subgroups in respect of, e.g., rape, prostitution, antitrust offenses, and vagrancy. It will be confined to otherwise definable subgroups in respect of, e.g., drug addiction, homosexuality, and armed robbery. Again persons with criminal records may be regarded as constituting a special subgroup in virtue of their distinctive character and experience.

It follows that, even if only 10 percent of the whole population knows the penalty for a particular offense, this 10 percent may belong to the potentially criminal population in regard to the offense—a fact which may be significant in relation to deterrence. The California findings which we have already discussed have relevance here.[71]

Table 15 illustrates the degree to which knowledge regarding penalties varies among different population groups.[72] It is notable that 65 percent of the college students were correct on the question about marijuana, with those confined to adult correctional institutions coming next. On the other hand, whereas 76 percent of the adult prisoners were correct regarding robbery with bodily injury, the general population scored only 20 percent. The general population, college students, and high school students, however, appear to have been better informed than adult prisoners regarding drunk driving penalties. With the exception of drunk driving and the possession of marijuana, it is clear that adult criminals have the greatest knowledge about penalties.

It is necessary here, however, to make a basic point: that the way in which a question is asked may have considerable influence on the nature of the response it elicits. In the California survey, respondents were asked to indicate—by checking a space on the questionnaire next to the answer "which best describes your knowledge"—"what the Legislature did last year in regard to the minimum penalty (the least a person could get) for the crime listed." For three of the offenses listed the legislature had increased the minimum penalty to fifteen

71. See Social Psychiatry Research Associates, *Public Knowledge of Criminal Penalties: A Research Report* (1968); also our discussion at chap. 4, sec. 1, subsec. D, *supra*.
72. *Id.* at 11. Table 15 is table 5 in the report.

TABLE 15
Percentage of Correct Answers on Recently Increased Penalties for Crimes by General Public, High- and Low-Delinquency Groups, and Institutional Populations

Knowledge of Increased Penalties	General Population	College	Low-Delinquency High School	High-Delinquency High School	Institutional Youth Auth.	Adult Corr.
Rape	16	17	30	27	24	43
Drunk driving	39	46	48	34	26	37
Robbery with bodily injury	20	20	23	33	30	76
Burglary with bodily injury	16	15	25	29	21	57
Possession of marijuana	36	65	38	16	25	47

years' imprisonment, but the minimum penalties for driving under the influence of alcohol and the possession of marijuana had *not* been increased. Although there was a tendency for respondents who did not know whether there had been a change in penalty to check the answer "No change in the minimum,"[73] the percentages of "no change" responses in regard to marijuana possession and drunk driving were too high to be explained on that basis alone.

In general it may be said that survey research regarding public knowledge is most usefully directed at samples of distinct subpopulations, whose responses to punishment policy can be assumed to be different from those of the general population, and whose involvement in particular types of criminal activity is extensive enough to make distinct subgroup response of some significance to criminal regulation.

Another type of survey which would be of some value would be one aimed at determining whether the public estimate of penalties for particular crimes is higher in jurisdictions with more severe sanctions for particular crimes than in jurisdictions with less severe sanctions for the same crimes. Survey research could be conducted in a number of jurisdictions, and the research exercise in each jurisdiction could include samples of both a general public and specific sub-publics. Such surveys could also be used to test experiments in the field of communications.

Some of the reservations we have mentioned in relation to public knowledge surveys are equally applicable to before-and-after surveys of public perception of policy changes. However, with before-and-after surveys we could assess not only the degree of public awareness of changes but also to what extent increases in severity are reflected in an "impression" that the penalty for a particular offense has been increased rather than in knowledge of the details of a penalty change.

At the same time, survey research aimed at knowledge of recent changes in the law is not an efficient tool for determining the potential of the diffusion process for distributing information (and thus susceptibility to marginal deterrence) among a

73. *Id.* at 11: "When answers were given, people were more likely to respond that the Legislature had not acted at all. Very few were able to give correct answers."

population. Since changes of punishment policy may, under the diffusion theory, not even be perceived as such by the individuals who ultimately gain access to the information, the recent-change strategy is not a complete one—it may miss the relevant communication process. If researchers waited long enough after a change, they could pick up whatever "trickle down" effects a change in punishment policy might produce.

We are dealing here with nonexperimental changes in punishment policy. Before a change of this kind takes place, other events must provide the motive force for change. The level of publicity regarding the behavior for which the penalty is changed may have varied independently of the penalty change itself. And the social forces which alter the official penalty policy may also have altered the public's notion of the gravity of the crime and affected the public's basic estimate of the appropriate punishment level for such a crime. Moreover, the longer the period between the penalty change and the implementation of the survey, the greater the possibility that factors other than the penalty change may have influenced the responses obtained.

Another complication is that legislatures can only change the minimum and maximum legislative prescriptions of penalties. The actual punishment policy of any jurisdiction is the range of sentences which courts impose for a particular crime. The possibilities of charge reductions, probation, selective or discriminatory prosecution, and station adjustments by the police will all affect the public's perception of what a punishment policy is. Thus, the data upon which public perception of penalties is based may well be not legislative but judicial behavior.[74] Responses to judicial changes are unrelated to the timing of legislative change, and difficult to pin to a time schedule.

74. Experience from the Scandinavian countries, incidentally, shows that an increase in the maximum penalty rarely has any appreciable effect on sentencing. See Andenaes, "Choice of Punishment," in Schmidt (ed.) 2 *Scandinavian Studies in Law* (1958) 67: "It is extremely difficult for the legislator to interfere, by means of directions to the courts, with established practice in penalty decisions. If such directions are not of an absolute binding nature—in that, for example, they fix a definite minimum punishment—general practice will continue more or less unaffected by the admonitions of the legislator."

An example of the difficulties involved in interpreting survey research data may be found in the study by Professor Claster, referred to earlier. Claster set out, among other things, to test the hypothesis that "delinquents perceive their chances of apprehension and conviction . . . to be less than non-delinquents perceive their own chances."[75] Finding that delinquents' perception of their likelihood of arrest if they committed hypothetical crimes was significantly lower than that of non-delinquents, Claster concludes that a "mechanism of perceptual distortion leads delinquents to perceive themselves invulnerable to arrest."[76] He is puzzled, however, because "there is not a corresponding significant difference in perceived immunity from conviction,"[77] which was also hypothesized.

Claster suggests, as a possible explanation, that "if a magical belief in immunity from arrest serves to neutralize fear of punishment a simultaneous belief in immunity from conviction is unnecessary."[78] "The perception of immuniy was shown among boys who were caught and incarcerated, many of them repeatedly, for delinquent offenses";[79] their greater belief in their ability to evade arrest than that of non-delinquents is held to "provide quantitative evidence for the 'magical immunity' mechanism posited in psychoanalytic ego psychology."[80]

But in view of what is known about impunity rates, even in relation to very serious offenses,[81] and the lack of reliable information about actual arrest to crime ratio for most offenses, the boys' estimates may well have been based quite simply on experience of a very large degree of immunity to arrest before they were actually caught. Their lack of belief in a similar immunity to conviction may have been based on the repeated experience that conviction almost automatically follows arrest.

75. Claster, "Comparison of Risk Perception between Delinquents and Non-Delinquents" (1967) 58 *J. Crim. Law, Criminology and Police Science* 80. See also, discussion of this study at chap. 4, B Differences among Men *supra*.

76. Claster, *supra* note 75, at 85.

77. *Ibid.*

78. *Ibid.*

79. *Ibid.*

80. *Id.* at 84.

81. See Radzinowicz on impunity rates in his preface to McClintock and Gibson, *Robbery in London* (1961) xi to xiii.

In short, so far from supporting the hypothesis that delinquents are subject to the "delusion of exceptionalistic exemption from the laws of cause and effect,"[82] these same data might be advanced as evidence that delinquents are unusually realistic in their attitudes.

Our general conclusion is that surveys of the population at large are inadequate for effective research into public knowledge. It is much more important to obtain estimates of levels of knowledge in those critical sections of the population presumably most susceptible to engagement in criminal behavior. Such research can show us which penalties are now most widely recognized, and this data in turn can suggest where a broad deterrent effect is most likely and how we can more efficiently disseminate information about penalties. What has been said about the use of penalty surveys applies also to surveys of other threat variables, such as the probability of apprehension and new enforcement methods as in the case of the British Road Safety Act of 1967. As long as such surveys are administered with care and modestly interpreted, they can be of value in assessing the extent of present knowledge and evaluating the effects of change.

Two surveys carried out among drivers for the British Ministry of Transport in connection with the ministry's publicity campaign on the subject of the 1967 Road Safety Act[83] provide an excellent example. The surveys, which were conducted just before and shortly after the campaign, were designed to assess the effect of the new drinking and driving law[84] and of the publicity campaign. It was found that knowledge of the law had significantly increased by the time the second survey was done, although there was little exact knowledge of penalties.[85]

Questions in the survey were framed to provide information about changes not only in knowledge but also in attitude and

82. Redl and Wineman, *The Aggressive Child* (1957) 163 cited in Claster *supra* note 75, at 81 n. 9.
83. Sheppard, *The 1967 Drink and Driving Campaign: A Survey among Drivers* (1968).
84. See *supra* note 69.
85. Sheppard, *supra* note 83, at 33–37.

behavior. It was found that "attitudes to drink and driving have hardly changed."[86] As to behavior, it is reported that "drivers are no less likely to drink or to drink away from home, but that they are less likely to drive themselves back afterwards."[87] In the following subsections, we discuss some of the problems which arise in connection with the design, administration, and interpretation of surveys dealing with attitudes and behavior.

C Survey Research and Attitudes
i Some Problems

A second task that survey research might undertake is the investigation of public attitudes to punishment policy. This is clearly of fundamental importance, for criminal laws are not usually regarded as divine fiats, nor is obedience to them automatic. It is true that men cannot act on information which they do not possess (hence our previous inquiry about public knowledge), but the nature of their response to that information is a function of more than merely cognitive or perceptual processes, being conditioned by those basic response tendencies we call attitudes.

For a number of reasons which will be made explicit in what follows, we are rather more skeptical about the value of survey research relating to attitudes than some other scholars in the field appear to be. It is not clear to us that the conventional attitude survey has any great potential as a means of obtaining information about deterrence.

Attitude measurement involves a number of technical problems, and we shall not here give an extended treatment of attitude definition and measurement, which may be found in general texts on research methodology in the social sciences.[88] Attitude surveys have long been used in the fields of market research and politics, and, although responses to questionnaires

86. *Id.* at 37.
87. *Id.* at 33.
88. Jahoda, Deutsch, and Cook, *Research Methods in Social Relations* (1951); Festinger and Katz (eds.) *Research Methods in the Behavioral Sciences* (1953). See also Thurstone and Chave, *The Measurement of Attitudes* (1929).

of this type are subject to both intentional and unconscious distortion, they have proved useful.

Nevertheless, it has to be recognized that attitudes "differ greatly in their amenability to observation and measurement."[89] There are certain "sensitive" subjects such as sexual behavior, religion, and race in regard to which attitudes are much less easily surveyed than where preferences for different types of consumer goods, or even party political programs, are concerned. There is little doubt that punishment is another such subject. As Margery Fry put it: "One has only to propose some change in our penal laws . . . to become aware at once that ages of traditional emotion, of obscure thinking, or desire for vengeance, of terror of 'bad men', of distrust of authority, or religious doctrine, of sadism and of love of power have woven around the subject a complex tangle of motives and beliefs."[90] The answers given to questionnaires in an area of this kind can hardly provide objective indices of attitude.

A number of difficulties attendant upon almost all attitude surveys assume particular significance in this context. The principal problem is that it is a matter of some difficulty to determine exactly what attitude studies actually measure. One of the most influential definitions of the term is G. W. Allport's: "An attitude is a mental and neural state of readiness organized through experience, exerting a distinctive or dynamic influence upon the individual's response to all objects and situations with which it is related."[91] But attitude surveys elicit merely verbal responses, from which it would be perilous to infer any "directive or dynamic influence" more powerful than was required to produce the verbal responses themselves.

And in ordinary usage, although the word *attitude* is commonly employed to refer to an individual's behavior or manner of acting as indicative or representative of his mood, feeling, or opinion, it is also used to refer to the feeling or mood itself, independent of any potential action apart from purely verbal expression. (Thus no contradiction would be involved in say-

89. Stephan and McCarthy, *Sampling Opinions: Analysis of Survey Procedure* (1958) 355.
90. Fry, *Arms of the Law* (1951) 21.
91. Allport, "Attitudes," in Murcheson (ed.), *Handbook of Social Psychology* (1935) 810.

ing, for example, "His attitude is sympathetic but he will do nothing to help.") This distinction between a sentiment and a tendency to act may be obscured when we talk of attitudes, but in interpreting survey results it is important to observe it.

Another difficulty has been noted by R. E. Vernon. He points out that most people, in answering questions relating to attitudes, "will naturally express their 'public' rather than their 'private' views, and their responses will not necessarily tell much about their actual behavior."[92] This is a serious complicating factor in an area where "public" and "private" views may frequently be conflicting. For there can be no doubt that considerations of prestige and concern about the individual respondent's public image play a significant part here. Individuals who are anxious to be identified with authority or the establishment—or with liberal or progressive causes—may respond in ways which reflect that anxiety but do not correspond to their real feelings or opinion.

There remains a further difficulty, to which we have already referred. It is not merely a matter of unwillingness to be candid. Dr. Mildred Parten, describing opinion and attitude surveys as attempts "to discover the number or percentage of the people who respond in a particular way to a single statement, phrase, or other attitude indicator,"[93] points out that "the surveyor cannot be sure that his counts would not have come out very differently had he worded the question a little differently or placed it in another context."[94] Even series of questions, unless they are carefully constructed to reflect the complexity of real life situations, are likely to elicit misleading responses. For if only selected aspects of a milieu are identified or reflected in a questionnaire, then it is only the reaction to those aspects which will be obtained.

This raises another problem: an individual's reactions or attitudes may not be deliberately adopted modes of regarding a particular subject. Unconscious personality factors may exercise a considerable influence. Punishment, after all, is some-

92. Vernon, "Measurement of Abilities, Attitudes, and Personality Traits," in Welford (ed.), *Society: Problems and Methods of Study* (1962) 71.
93. Parten, *Surveys, Polls and Samples* (1950) 193–94.
94. *Id.* at 194.

thing which most human beings will have experienced in some form, and very commonly that experience will have been a highly emotional one. As a result, people's attitudes in this area are frequently both ambivalent and labile.

We have to deal, then, not merely with deliberate disingenuousness (which is in itself a considerable problem) but also with inconsistency and deception which the respondent may not be aware of, and over which he exercises no conscious control. It is by no means uncommon for identification with and sympathy for the victims of crime to inspire feelings of indignation and aggression. Contrarily, identification with offenders may induce feelings of tolerance and compassion.

When, as is frequently the case, these contrary feelings coexist in the same individual, it is impossible to distinguish between different responses, both of which may be "valid." Even the repetition of a survey after an interval with the identical schedule, interviewers, and procedures, which is a common method of validation,[95] would serve little purpose here. For whether the second survey revealed considerable inconsistencies, as is not uncommon in surveys dealing with ideologies rather than factual information,[96] or whether consistency prevailed, it would be difficult to know what significance to attach to either.

It is not merely that the data are intrinsically difficult to interpret. The interpretation of responses is itself peculiarly liable to be conditioned by factors of the same kind which may have exercised a dominant influence on the responses themselves. For the drawing of inferences from material dealing with punishment is neither deduction from given premises to a necessary conclusion nor straightforward induction from purely factual material. The data available for interpretation are not only qualitative data but the kind of qualitative data which will rarely, if ever, be handled with objectivity. Here again, it is not conscious bias which is the principal problem (although it cannot be ruled out) but rather that both *what* is seen as significant and *how* it is seen as significant may be conditioned by motivational and emotional processes—uncon-

95. *Id.* at 496–98.
96. *Id.* at 497.

scious personality dynamics, of which the observer is not himself aware.

ii Some Examples

Two recent studies of the type recommended earlier—dealing with subgroups rather than the general population—illustrate the problems just discussed. Indeed, in both instances the subgroup involved was an imprisoned criminal group, which may be said to represent a sample of an unambiguously criminal population.

Surveys of such groups are valuable because they are so unambiguously a high criminal risk group; because their future behavior constitutes such a substantial proportion of what we define as the "crime problem"; and because they may give us some indication of what the experience of punishment adds to the information an individual has about penalty levels in society. It could be argued that, as they deal only with that part of a potentially criminal population which has not been deterred, they will provide unreliable indices of the deterrent potential of marginal increments in penalties. A number of other problems, too, relate to the interpretation of surveys of this nature.

The first study, which was carried out by the Bureau of Social Science Research, Inc., was designed to investigate "the deterrent value of crime prevention measures as perceived by criminal offenders."[97] Because our review of it is largely critical, it is only fair to begin by acknowledging that it is one of the few serious attempts to obtain information about responses to deterrents, which explains why we deal with it at some length. Moreover, although we imply that it exemplifies what we have earlier called "the Warden's Survey fallacy,"[98] this criticism is directed not at the nature of the survey but rather at the interpretation of the data. Last, the study has some claim to uniqueness in this field insofar as it focuses on the career rather than on a criminal act.

97. Goodman, Miller, and DeForrest, "A Study of the Deterrent Value of Crime Prevention Measures as Perceived by Criminal Offenders (1966). Unpublished paper submitted by the Bureau of Social Science Research, Inc., to the Institute for Defense Analyses.
98. See chap. 2, sec. 2, subsec. B *supra*.

The purpose of the study was "the development of data from which . . . certain inferences about behavioral deterrence might be made."[99] It was "initiated by the simple question how do convicted felons perceive and respond to deterrents?" for "obviously, 'deterrents' do not deter unless they are at least perceived as such by prospective offenders."[100] The study was based on interviews with a sample of 124 inmates drawn from the population of a reformatory for men. Those interviewed were "men (1) who had been convicted of at least two serious property offenses (as adults); (2) whose crimes had been principally offenses against property; and (3) who were not scheduled for release until at least one month after the interview was scheduled for completion."[101] The decision to restrict the sample to property offenders was based on the assumption that such offenders "are much more likely to be deliberative in the commission of crimes, less likely than those who commit crimes against the person to be impulsive. Therefore, to ask them questions about deterrents would make more sense."[102]

The inmates were asked series of questions designed to test their "responsiveness" or "amenability" to both "police deterrence" and "prison deterrence." The responses to the questions were then classified and analyzed, and inferences were drawn regarding the "deterredness" of the offenders and the "effectiveness of certain police strategies and prison policies as deterrents of crime." It is not necessary for our purposes to reproduce or to examine in detail here all the response data presented, for we are concerned merely with certain patterns which emerge in the responses and their interpretation.

The authors of the study were clearly aware of some of the difficulties we have touched on. Commenting on the question put to the inmates, "What percent of the guys who get out of here will go straight? What's your guess?" they say: "It may be assumed that the answers *to this question* are not entirely dispassionately neutral, but that to some degree they reflect the respondent's personal attitudes"[103] (our italics). Unfortu-

99. Goodman, Miller, and DeForrest *supra* note 97, at 4.
100. *Id*. at 3.
101. *Id*. at 4–5.
102. *Id*. at 4 n. 2.
103. *Id*. at 46.

nately, what is here suggested as a possibility in relation to a particular question is something which has to be borne in mind throughout the study. In view of both the respondent's situation and the nature of the subject matter it would be extremely sanguine to expect dispassionate neutrality at any point.

For example, in the case of "police deterrents" the authors say:

It is not insignificant, perhaps, that the inmates rated, 'more respectful treatment from police' higher than 'greater numbers of uniformed patrolmen,' a finding which suggests that the prisoners may believe that the police provoke a certain amount of crime by virtue of the manner in which they treat suspects and ex-convicts.[104]

But this finding might equally—and somewhat more plausibly —be taken to suggest merely that prisoners took the question-naire as an opportunity to express an understandable feeling that they would *prefer* "more respectful treatment from police" than they had experienced in the past. The fact that they were *supposed* to be rating the items in terms of their *deterrent* efficacy does not mean that they actually did that. It would be interesting to know on what grounds they could think police politeness a more effective deterrent than greater numbers of uniformed patrolmen.

In regard to parole the authors conclude:

Responses to the item on the stringency of parole, together with certain qualitative data, indicate that many of the inmates hold the over-zealous enforcement of parole rules and harassment by parole officers responsible in some measure for recidivism.[105]

But might not these responses and the "qualitative data" (which admittedly we cannot assess, as they are not made available to us) be taken to indicate no more than the fact that many inmates find parole rules and their enforcement extremely irksome.

On the deterrent value of imprisonment and prison discipli-nary measures, take the following passage:

104. *Id*. at 38.
105. *Id*. at 39.

More interesting, however, is the fact that nearly all of these men, in answer to the question on the number of offenders who would go straight if 'prisons made life a bit rougher for inmates,' said that this would make no difference.[106]

It would surely be very surprising if prisoners were to give a positive answer to this question and, in effect, invite authority to make life more unpleasant for them. The authors seem unaware that responses to their questions are likely often to reflect the subjects' calculations as to the possible consequences of their answers.

What the authors refer to as "a highly consistent and reliable set of data"[107] can hardly be accepted at face value in this way. The following passage is illustrative of the dangers involved:

Thus, few inmates regard imprisonment as a deterrent (in career terms) and, more or less independently of this fact, few believe that other inmates are deterred by it. This raises two questions: (1) Why does imprisonment fail to deter (more than it does)? (2) If prison (along with police action) fails, by and large, to deter, what, if anything, has crime-deterrent value?[108]

Here what may have been expressions of attitude or opinion are assumed to be veridical. For if this were not the case, the two questions which are then directly raised would not necessarily follow.

A final example illustrates the way in which an uncritical assumption regarding the candor and reliability of responses can lead to conclusions which are of questionable validity. At one point the authors say that the responses they received provided

clear evidence that the inmates overwhelmingly subscribe to the rehabilitative goals of the correctional system rather than to the doctrine that punishment deters crime.[109]

They also noted an

almost universally voiced resentment over what they felt were departures from, or failures to realize equitably and adequately, the goals of these programs,[110]

106. *Id*. at 48.
107. *Id*. at 56.
108. *Id*. at 47.
109. *Id*. at 39.
110. *Id*. at 50.

and considerable dissatisfaction with

the alleged rigidity and parsimoniousness of the parole board.[111]

They go on to say:

Were it not for the implicit, underlying endorsement of rehabilitative goals, these would not have been the preeminent kinds of complaints. It is apparent, then, that most of these men are markedly oriented to conventional middle-class values . . . even to the acceptance of official correctional system doctrines. Crime, for most of them, does not appear to be either a "profession" or a way of life. Very few seem basically to oppose themselves to society or to its normative system. The data suggest that many are no more than amateur criminal "moonlighters," despite the fact that they may have long records of arrest, conviction and commitment. Inferentially, they commit criminal offenses to a considerable extent for reasons of economic need—much of which is attributed to the fact that their chances on the job market are impaired by the stigma of "ex-con" status. . . .[112]

The use of the term "inferentially" is interesting. Although what "the data suggest" must to some extent be a matter of individual interpretation, at least two possibilities seem here to have been overlooked. First, let us assume that the inmates' overwhelming subscription to the "rehabilitative goals of the correctional system rather than to the doctrine that punishment deters crime" can be accepted as a genuine commitment. If it can, it must surely raise some doubts whether inmates' expressions of attitude and opinion regarding the efficacy of various deterrent measures can be viewed as completely candid and reliable. For their rejection of "the doctrine that punishment deters crime" might to some extent have determined their responses to questions.

Second, let us assume that the inmates' "acceptance of official correctional system doctrines" was entirely disingenuous and reflected no more than a preference for the relative amenity of avowedly rehabilitative systems as compared with the possibly oppressive rigor of purely deterrent ones; and, moreover, that this preference is reflected in their responses throughout the survey report. That this is a real possibility is confirmed

111. *Ibid.*
112. *Id.* at 50–52.

by a Norwegian prison study, Thomas Mathiesen's *The Defences of the Weak*.[113]

Mathiesen concluded that, while prisoners frequently "appear to be in agreement with staff members on norms and values, arguing that staff members deviate from established principles,"[114] their criticisms may well reflect no more than the "paramount interest of the inmate in his own situation only, couched in terms giving a less 'egoistic' appearance."[115] Mathieson found that inmates justify their censoriousness by reference to the value system which best serves their "individual interests within the institution."[116] Thus in a "treatment-oriented institution" they complain that principles of justice and equality are violated; in a "regular maximum-security prison" they insist on "the uniqueness of the individual inmate's situation."[117]

So, in the Bureau of Social Science Research study, what the authors refer to as an "implicit underlying endorsement of rehabilitative goals" may not have been implicit or underlying at all. Indeed, their reference to this "endorsement" immediately follows three complaints about "the alleged rigidity and parsimoniousness of the parole board." But complaints of the kind cited—e.g., "chances of making parole are almost nonexistent"—are almost universal among prisoners, and may very well reflect merely a desire to get out of prison as soon as possible and constitute an implicit, underlying endorsement of nothing more than that very natural ambition.

In sum, it may be said that the authors' conclusions about the character of the offenders ("fairly ordinary citizens in most respects"),[118] about the effectiveness of deterrents ("except under certain highly specific conditions, deterrence does not work for these kinds of offenders"),[119] and about "the solutions" (mechanisms designed to afford greater economic advantage, greater self-respect and dissolution of the stigma of the police and prison record")[120] are not warranted by the

113. Mathiesen, *The Defences of the Weak* (1965).
114. *Id.* at 181.
115. *Id.* at 182.
116. *Ibid.*
117. *Id.* at 150–93.
118. Goodman, Miller, and DeForrest, *supra* note 97, at 56.
119. *Ibid.*
120. *Id.* at 57.

evidence cited. This is not to say that there may not be independent grounds for regarding them as valid. In regard to deterrence specifically, we find no warrant for drawing any inferences from the data presented.

Another study which illustrates the difficulties involved in interpreting an attitude survey of an imprisoned criminal group is Professor Rettig's "Ethical Risk Sensitivity in Male Prisoners,"[121] to which we have already referred briefly. This study seeks to compare "the ethical decision-making process"[122] of a sample of young male prisoners at a federal reformatory in Ohio with that of a sample of students at a nearby state university of similar age, sex, and socioeconomic status. The method used was to ask both groups to make a series of predictions on the likelihood, in varying circumstances, that a hypothetical bank teller would embezzle bank funds. The situations were varied systematically such that the embezzlement would bring great or little gain to the teller, the teller would or would not be caught, and the teller would or would not be censured. The teller intended either to steal or to borrow the money.

One striking result that emerged from the study was that the overall mean prediction score of the prisoners fell considerably below that of the students. "The prisoners state in general that the hypothetical bank employee is less likely to take the money in any circumstances."[123] It is not surprising therefore when Professor Rettig infers that "the prisoners, in comparison with the students, are highly defensive and cautious in their questionnaire behavior."[124] The assumption of a "generalized defensive 'response set' on the part of the prisoners"[125] seems reasonable.

It *is* a little surprising, however, that Professor Rettig then goes on, on the basis of "the comparison of the prediction score of prisoners with that of students," to observe, for example, that "in comparison with students, prisoners are relatively insensitive or inattentive to the expectancy and the

121. Rettig, "Ethical Risk Sensitivity in Male Prisoners" (1964) 4 *Brit. J. Crim.* 582–90.
122. *Id.* at 583.
123. *Id.* at 586.
124. *Ibid.*
125. *Ibid.*

magnitude of gain," and that these "considerations" appear to play a lesser role in the ethical decision-making process of prisoners than of students.[126]

It would surely not be too fanciful to suggest that the apparent indifference to gain on the part of a group of convicted property offenders (including forgers, thieves, and bank robbers)[127] might be due less to any "ethical decison-making process" than to a desire to project a socially acceptable image. Similarly, in view of the fact that "nearly all of the convicts under study were recidivists,"[128] the finding that "the prisoners are more sensitive to the severity of censure than to the other components of the decision-making process measured in this study"[129] might be regarded somewhat skeptically. Undue sensitivity to censure is unlikely to be so salient a feature of the motivational process of this category of prisoner.

iii Conclusions

Neither in relation to the two studies mentioned here, nor in relation to attitude research generally, is it suggested that no positive results whatever could have been achieved or can be anticipated. Both in the studies of prisoners and in the study of youths, the particular interpretations offered by the authors seem to have been not so much *drawn from* the data as *imposed on* them. The difficulties we have discussed in this section may be summed up as follows.

Attitude surveys elicit verbal responses which may be regarded as indices of attitude in the sense of sentiments or feelings. Factors tending to render the responses unreliable as indices of sentiment are (a) the fact that questionnaires are inevitably selective and may thus condition the nature of the responses, (b) lack of candor on the part of respondents, and (c) the influence of competing emotional or psychological components which may not be conscious.

Nevertheless, carefully constructed questionnaires designed to present situations in their full complexity, coupled with conservative principles of interpretation rigorously applied, could render such surveys useful for sentiment sounding. We

126. *Id.* at 587.
127. *Id.* at 585.
128. *Id.* at 590.
129. *Id.* at 587.

should bear in mind that some degree of discrepancy or error of measurement between the response that we use as an index and the sentiment that we infer from it is probably inevitable.[130]

When we are considering whether respondents are likely to act in accordance with the sentiments they express, we have to recognize, as Thurstone and Chave point out, that "the measurements of attitudes expressed by a man's opinions does not necessarily mean the prediction of what he will do."[131] People's conduct is inconsistent with their professed sentiments on so large a scale and for so great a variety of reasons that survey techniques cannot be regarded as very precise instruments for predicting overt conduct.

It is possible, however, that attitude surveys supplemented by intensive and aggressive interviewing closer to the pattern of psychotherapy might enable us to reconstruct patterns of relation between sentiment and action set. An example, although not a model, of what we have in mind may be found in the study carried out by Dr. Donald Newman for the Task Force on Firearms of the U.S. National Commission on the Causes and Prevention of Violence.[132] Another possible method may be found in Professor Hans Toch's use of the "peer interview" in his *Violent Men*.[133] Studies of this nature are not without their own problems and would be unlikely to produce the kind of hard data upon which changes in sanction or enforcement policy could be based without reference to other evidence. But taken in conjunction with other evidence, the information de-

130. Thurstone and Chave, *supra* note 88, at 8 say: "But this discrepancy between the index and 'truth' is universal."

131. *Id.* at 9. In this connection the findings of a national survey carried out in 1966 by the National Opinion Research Center of the University of Chicago for the National Association of Broadcasters are suggestive. The study revealed that 67 percent of a cross section of the population felt that TV commercials cause too many interruptions; 63 percent that they are too frequent; and 58 percent that they are irritating (report in *Parade Magazine,* 7 January 1968). In the circumstances, however, it would be unwise to assume that the commercials thus stigmatized necessarily elicit a negative response in terms of conduct on the part of those who express critical views. Indeed, it may be true that a commercial that is "irritating" can be extremely effective precisely because it is irritating and thus memorable.

132. Newman, "Firearms and Violent Crime: Conversations with Protagonists," Appendix E in Newton and Zimring, *Firearms and Violence in American Life* (1969) 183–94.

133. Toch, *Violent Men* (1969).

rived from such studies might prove an aid to more rational policy making.

D Survey Research and Behavioral Response

It might seem obvious that a straightforward way of finding out how people respond in action to variations in punishment policy would be to ask them questions about behaviors threatened in various jurisdictions. Although relatively little work has been done in this area, survey techniques have in fact been used to obtain information about criminal behavior from cross sections of the population.

Two types of study have been made. In the first, surveys of victim experience or victimization, individuals were asked whether they (or any member of their household) had been a victim of crime during a specified period. In the second, surveys of "self-reported" crime, individuals were asked whether and to what extent they themselves had engaged in conduct for which they might have been sentenced if they had been apprehended.

i Victim Studies

The first national survey ever made of crime victimization was that initiated by the President's Commission on Law Enforcement and Administration of Justice and is described in the commission's report.[134] Although we have already cited the commission's recommendation of the survey technique as a method for providing information about "the relative effectiveness of different programs to control crime,"[135] it is a method which is subject to severe limitations.

Thus the data obtained from the survey (carried out for the commission by the University of Chicago's National Opinion Research Center, the University of Michigan's Survey Research Center, and the Bureau of Social Science Research of Washington, D.C.) are used, among other things, to demonstrate that the crime rates published in the FBI's Uniform Crime Reports greatly understate the actual amount of crime in the United States today. But in attemping to estimate responses to

134. *Supra* note 24, at 20–22 and 38–42.
135. *Id.* at 22.

punishment policy, we are concerned with much more than crime rates.

This is not to say that asking individuals whether or not they had been victims of criminal activity might not serve a number of useful functions. For, as the President's Commission report points out, one of the most neglected subjects in the study of crime is the victim. And more knowledge about "the part the victim can play in the criminal act and the part he could have played in preventing it"[136] might well lead to more effective efforts to control and prevent crime. But most victims probably could not estimate the extent to which variations in punishment policy might have played a role in the decision to engage in the criminal activity they have suffered.

Thus, it seems that the important function which victim reports might serve in deterrence research would be to eliminate one of the possibly confounding variables involved in comparative or retrospective studies using crime rates, that is, the danger that different proportions of crimes committed might be reported by the police in different periods or areas being compared. Still, in eliminating this possibly confounding factor, the victim survey might import to the interpretation of data a number of additional problems. We shall not here enter into a discussion of the survey method with respect to victimization. An excellent summary of the limitations of this kind of enquiry may be found in Hood and Sparks's recent treatment of this subject.[137]

ii Self-Report Studies

Asking individuals to report criminal activity that they themselves have committed does hold out the possibility of revealing whether, and to what extent, provisions of a punishment policy have influenced their behavior. Such studies would necessarily have to be bifocal, for individuals must be asked questions about their conduct and must also be asked to give opinions as to factors affecting their conduct. Most of the studies which have been made in this field to date have been concerned only with the first aspect. Two of the most frequently cited are

136. *Supra* note 24, at 38.
137. Hood and Sparks, *Key Issues in Criminology* (1970) 23–36.

Austin L. Porterfield's "Delinquency and Its Outcome in Court and College"[138] and James S. Wallerstein and Clement J. Wyle's "Our Law-Abiding Law-Breakers."[139] Critical examination reveals that the results of such studies must be viewed with considerable caution.

In the first place there is the problem of definition. Porterfield notes that in his study, which dealt with college students, "space limits in the questionnaire confidentially presented to the students precluded adequate definition of all the offenses about which inquiry was made."[140] But the fundamental problem is that, even assuming adequate definitions were presented in questionnaires, behavior perceived subsequently by individuals as conforming to those definitions might well not have conformed with prosecutional definitions.

In any event, much of the behavior would probably not be of the kind regarded by society as part of "the crime problem." That this is so can be seen clearly from the details of offenses given in the Wallerstein and Wyle study, which dealt with criminal behavior by adults.[141] "Many of the offenses were no doubt committed against friends and relatives. . . . What is technically an offense and therefore within the scope of this study may actually be a relatively harmless act."[142]

Martin Gold, in a study of five hundred high school students in Michigan, interviewed respondents in detail about their reported acts. He found that "half the acts of property destruction, one fourth of the confidence games, and one fifth of the personal assaults to which our sample initially admitted could not conceivably be called chargeable offenses."[143]

A second problem is that of misestimation of frequency, in the form both of overreporting and of underreporting, due to factors other than definition such as exaggeration and concealment. In the part of their study dealing with "what crimes were

138. Porterfield, "Delinquency and Its Outcome in Court and College" (1943) 49 *Am. J. Soc.* 199–208. See also A. L. Porterfield, *Youth in Trouble* (1946) 36–51.

139. Wallerstein and Wyle, "Our Law-Abiding Law-Breakers" (1947) 25 *Probation* 197–218.

140. Porterfield, *supra* note 138, at 200.

141. Wallerstein and Wyle, *supra* note 139, at 109–111.

142. *Id.* at 112.

143. Gold, "Undetected Delinquent Behaviour" (1966) 3 *J. Research in Crime and Delinq.* 30.

committed,"[144] Wallerstein and Wyle remark, "The high rate for assault may be explained by the inclusion of such episodes as fist fights. . . . Probably most males don't mind admitting this type of offense."[145] From both male college students and adult males, some exaggeration in regard to such offenses as assault, auto misdemeanors, and certain sexual offenses may be expected as part of an attempt to project a "masculine" image. Some of the comments appearing on the Wallerstein and Wyle questionnaires (e.g., "Thrashed a lot of men in my time but they all jolly well deserved it," and "Too much trouble, I've done them all")[146] seem to bear out this suggestion. Some supporting evidence may be found in a study by Clarke and Tifft, who used follow-up interviews and polygraph tests to check the self-report responses of male university students. They found that overreporting was most marked in respect of sexual offenses and offenses involving violence."[147]

As to underreporting, a survey designed to elicit self-report information relating to what must, in many cases, be extremely sensitive areas of behavior cannot expect to be met with absolute candor on the part of all subjects. Many personal comments cited by Wallerstein and Wyle are attempts at self-justification by individuals who clearly feel the need to offer some excuse for their behavior.[148] It is not insignificant that these excuses were offered in questionnaires which "were returned anonymously to ensure frankness."[149]

At a more intense level, that sort of feeling may frequently lead to significant omissions. Martin Gold, checking the validity of his respondents' answers, found not only that there was deliberate concealment of offenses but also that this concealment generally pertained to the more serious offenses.[150]

If, then, more trivial offenses are likely to be overreported, whereas more serious offenses, "real crimes," are likely to be underreported, the distortion produced by the former will be reinforced by the latter.

144. Wallerstein and Wyle, *supra* note 139, at 109.
145. *Id.* at 110.
146. *Id.* at 111.
147. Clark and Tifft, "Polygraph and Interview Validation of Self-Reported Deviant Behavior" (1966) 31 *Am. Soc. Rev.* 516–23.
148. Wallerstein and Wyle, *supra* note 139, at 110–11.
149. *Id.* at 108.
150. Gold, *supra* note 143, at 31–34.

A number of other self-report studies have been published.[151] One of them is unusual in that it includes a lengthy discussion of some of the major difficulties in the use and interpretation of self-report data. "A Study of Self-Reported Crime," by Nils Christie, Johannes Andenaes, and Sigurd Skirbekk[152] deals with two urban and two rural districts in Norway, the subjects being males assembled for premilitary classification. The authors caution against "exaggerated expectations concerning the usefulness of the method" and "the pretension that we here have an instrument which can give the final answer to fundamental questions."[153] In addition to the question of the *willingness* of subjects to give honest answers, Christie *et al.* raise the problem of "the informants' *ability* to give honest answers."[154] They claim, "We must expect to get more information—and more precise information—from the better educated informants" because they "are more trained in that type of work, they read and write faster, become less exhausted, and have probably more time to think."[155] At the same time, they suggest that "informants with an unusually rich and varied criminal background will probably under-report" because "they will have so much to report that it is difficult to remember exact details."[156]

151. Among the best of these are: Murphy, Shirley, and Witmer, "The Incidence of Hidden Delinquency" (1946) 16 *Am. J. Orthopsych.* 687–96; Short and Nye, "Scaling Delinquent Behavior" (1957) 22 *Am. Soc. Rev.* 326–31, and "Extent of Unrecorded Juvenile Delinquency" (1958) 49 *J. Crim. Law, Criminology, and Police Science* 296–302; Reiss and Rhodes, "The Distribution of Juvenile Delinquency in the Social Class Structure" (1961) 26 *Am. Soc. Rev.* 720–32; Dentler and Monroe, "Social Correlates of Early Adolescent Theft" (1961) 26 *Am. Soc. Rev.* 733–43; Erickson and Empey, "Court Records, Undetected Delinquency and Decision Making" (1963) 54 *J. Crim. Law, Criminology, and Police Science* 456–69; Empey and Erickson, "Hidden Delinquency and Social Status" (1966) 44 *Social Forces* 546–54; Vaz, "Self-Reported Juvenile Delinquency and Socio-Economic Status" (1966) 8 *Can. J. Corrections* 20–27; Voss, "Socio-Economic Status and Reported Delinquent Behavior" (1966) 13 *Social Problems* 314–24; Akers, "Socio-Economic Status and Delinquent Behavior" (1964) 1 *J. Research in Crime and Delinq.* 38–46; Christie, Andenaes, and Skirbekk, "A Study of Self-Reported Crime," in Christiansen (ed.), *Scandinavian Studies in Criminology* (1965) 86–116; Elmhorn, "Study in Self-Reported Delinquency among Schoolchildren in Stockholm," *ibid.*, 117–46.

152. Christie, Andenaes and Skirbekk *supra* note 151.

153. *Id.* at 94.

154. *Id.* at 93–94.

155. *Id.* at 94.

156. *Ibid.*

Another study in which "the reliability problem" is discussed briefly is Kerstin Elmhorn's "Study in Self-Reported Delinquency among Schoolchildren in Stockholm."[157] She points out that "the least gifted children found the questions more difficult to undersand than did the other children"[158] and gives details of the extent to which, in her study, "the interpreted significance" of questions diverged from "the intended significance."[159] "Another complication," mentioned by D. J. West in reviewing some of the studies cited here, is whether in addition to "the greater verbal fluency and readier adaptability to interviews and tests displayed by middle-class children . . . lower-class children may [also] be less ready to confide."[160] This of course is a problem not confined to studies dealing with schoolchildren.

The second kind of self-report study, dealing with motivation, is essentially an attitude or opinion study. This is because the only information that can realistically be expected here is an individual's public or private opinion of what factors motivated his conduct. It could be argued that such a strategy is the most dangerous of all because it combines the hazards of self-report information sampling with the hazards of attitude sampling. An example of this type of study is in Willcock and Stokes's *Deterrents and Incentives to Crime among Youths Aged 15–21 Years* to which we referred in our discussion of types of threatened consequences.[161] We have already cited the finding that 68 percent of those questioned rated the possibility of unofficial disapproval the most important of eight possible deterrents including such items as the possible penalty and the possibility of loss of employment. Unfortunately, as we pointed out earlier, because the nature of the offense involved was not specified, and this would be likely to affect the ranking of the deterrents, the finding cannot be accepted without reservation.

At another point, however, informants were asked about their "introspective beliefs about the things which might deter them from committing each of nine offences." the results of this in-

157. Elmhorn *supra* note 151, at 123–25.
158. *Id.* at 123.
159. *Id.* at 123–24.
160. West, *The Young Offender* (1967) 60.
161. Willcock and Stokes, *Deterrents and Incentives to Crime among Youths Aged 15–21 Years* (1968). See also discussion at chap. 4, sec. 1, subsecs. E and F, *supra*.

quiry are shown in Table 16.[162] There are considerable variations in the ranking of the different deterrents in relation to
the nature of the offenses; and it is likely that the variations
would have been greater had some more serious offenses been
included. This result also illustrates the general point that the
responses obtained will be largely dependent on the way the
questions are asked, and that in many cases it may be necessary
to use more than one questionnaire in order to obtain reliable
results. An interesting finding is that the punishment and the
disadvantages of being caught are rated as greater deterrents
in respect of the more serious offenses where they are likely
to be more severe.

Nigel Walker, commenting on the results of this survey, remarks that "what these 808 young males said about the considerations which would or would not deter them from offences
cannot be accepted without reservations," because "what someone says in response to a questionnaire or interviewer may not
be a reliable indication of the way in which he will think and
act when faced with a real situation of the kind which he is
talking about."[163] But perhaps an aggressive, interpretive tie-in
of self-reporting and attitude strategies together with the use
of the sort of checks on validity employed by Gold[164] and by
Clark and Tifft[165] would create a situation in which we are
controlling for a few of the inherent hazards of attitude surveys alone. It seems likely that, for such an approach to achieve
any positive results, the survey would have to take the form of
(or at least be supplemented by) interviews which were in
depth and of a quasi-psychotherapeutic nature. Clearly the sort
of mass sample commonly used in survey research would not
be feasible here.

It might also be worthwhile to use self-report data to determine responses to particular control measures by those who
have been personally subjected to them, that is, in the assessment of the effects of punishment on those actually punished.
For in the case of a particular penal measure, if we were to
compare a group who had been exposed to treatment with a

162. Willcock and Stokes, *supra* note 161, at 75, table 43.
163. Walker, *supra* note 65, at 63.
164. Gold, *supra* note 143.
165. Clark and Tifft, *supra* note 147.

group not exposed, or with a group exposed to different types of treatment, it would be possible to attribute differences in reported behavior to the penal experience—assuming there were no other reasons why the response patterns should be different —and we could make this attribution without trusting respondents' opinions of their motives for conduct.

SECTION 7 PROBLEMS OF MEASUREMENT
A The Crime Rate and Crime Control Research

The number of people deterred from a particular criminal act cannot be measured directly. In theory it might be possible to devise a survey in which potential criminals who would have become actual criminals would confess that this was their intention and candidly admit that only penalty threats restrained them. In practice, however, such a survey is incapable of being executed. It is usually assumed that we can make valid inferences about the number of people restrained from committing criminal acts by studying trends in the number of individuals convicted or in the number of crimes reported.

Using the crime rate reported or known to the authorities as a dependent variable in studies of the effectiveness of crime control policy involves a number of risks. In the first place, the number of crimes known to authorities in almost all situations is only a fraction of the number of crimes committed, although that fraction varies from crime to crime.[166] This would not constitute a significant problem if it were true—as Adolph Quetelet, the father of criminal statistics, believed it to be—that the relation between reported and unreported crime was constant.[167] But although the validity of calculations of changes in crime rates depends upon such an assumption, there is considerable evidence that the relation is highly variable.[168] Changes in policy, or the social forces that lie behind them, can and do result in changes in the proportion of reported crimes. And the pro-

166. See U.S. President's Commission on Law Enforcement and Administration of Justice Task Force Report, *Crime and Its Impact— An Assessment* (1967), "The Extent of Unreported Crime" 17–19. See also Sellin and Wolfgang, *The Measurement of Delinquency* (1964).

167. Quetelet, 1 *Essai de physique sociale* (1835) 7 and 9, cited in Van Bemmelen "The Constancy of Crime" (1952) 2 *Brit. J. Delinq.* 213.

168. U.S. President's Commission, *supra* note 166, at 17–25.

TABLE 16
Answers to Question, "What sort of things hold you back, or worry you about doing it?"

Things which informants believed would hold them back, or worry them about doing it	Breaking into a lock-up shop	Picking up a wallet	Breaking into a private house	Taking unknown person's car	Stealing from a large store	Throwing stone at a street lamp	Stealing from a coat	Starting punch-up in dance hall	Stealing from small shop
	%	%	%	%	%	%	%	%	%
1. *Personal restraints* (excluding physical inability) including reasons of conscience; consideration for the injured party, and the situation is not (sufficiently) a temptation	42.7	60.9	43.8	38.7	33.9	51.0	65.0	34.4	45.9
2. *Inability to execute deed itself* (excluding "being caught") e.g. "can't drive a car"; "afraid might get hurt/smash car/injure innocent people"; "can't fight"; "might lose fight"; "wouldn't be able to get in"; "would miss street light anyway"	1.5	0.0	2.6	15.6	0.4	1.9	0.6	26.9	0.0
3. *Effect on parents/opinion of others / on own future*	9.9	3.4	6.1	3.5	7.4	3.7	5.9	7.7	5.3
4. *Difficulty of concealment of offence —easily caught*	7.7	11.9	7.7	6.3	21.4	8.3	5.5	2.1	8.6
5. *The punishment/sentence*	5.3	1.3	4.7	8.4	4.1	2.1	1.4	4.2	4.5

6. *Miscellaneous and unspecified disadvantages of being caught not covered above—e.g. "being caught (unspecified further)", "scared of being caught for something so petty"*	24.7	8.9	27.4	19.6	24.9	11.5	12.9	9.3	26.1
7. *Nothing would deter* (including "have done it, undeterred")	1.6	9.3	1.2	2.1	1.9	13.2	1.6	5.3	3.2
8. *Vague answers*	1.8	0.8	1.5	1.0	0.6	1.9	0.7	4.7	0.7
9. *Don't know*	0.5	0.7	0.4	0.6	0.7	0.7	0.7	1.0	0.9
10. *No information*	4.3	2.8	4.7	4.2	4.8	5.7	5.6	4.5	4.8
Base	808	808	808	808	808	808	808	808	808

portion of reported crimes can vary markedly as between areas. Even the experimental introduction of particular penal measures can itself influence not only the actual amount of crime but also the proportion of crimes that are called to the attention of authorities.

B The Arrest Rate and Probability of Apprehension

Insofar as it is true that "certainty of detection would be the best deterrent,"[169] it is clearly important to investigate the effect on the crime rate of variations in probability of apprehension. Some measure of the probability of being apprehended for a particular crime is required.

The measure most commonly used is a percentage derived by dividing the number of crimes recorded by the police by the number of arrests made by the police. The resultant figure is sometimes referred to as the "clearance rate." But "the fact that a crime is recorded as 'cleared up,'" McClintock and Gibson point out, "does not necessarily mean that someone has been convicted; it mearly means that someone has been arrested."[170] For this reason, we prefer to talk of the arrest rate. To what extent does this measure provide adequate support for inferences about the degree of influence that variations in the probability of apprehension will have on rates of crime?

A reliable index of probability of apprehension would be valuable in both retrospective and comparative studies. In a retrospective study, if the percentage of recorded offenses resulting in arrests increased, the inference would be that the probability of being arrested for a particular offense had increased over time. In a comparative study, if area *A's* percentage of recorded crimes resulting in arrests were greater than that of area *B*, then it could be assumed that area *A* must be detecting a greater proportion of its crime than area *B*.

Unfortunately both the numerator and the denominator of the fraction used to arrive at this index of probability of apprehension are derived from police records. The number of *individuals arrested* for a particular crime is, in a very important sense, a police-created statistic. So also is the number of *offenses recorded*.

169. McClintock and Gibson, *supra* note 81, at 30.
170. *Id*. at 39.

It is clear that the police are largely responsible for the number of arrests made. In fact, the President's Commission Task Force on the Police found that "almost unlimited discretion is given to the police officer to arrest persons."[171] At the same time, it is likely that the number of individuals arrested for a particular crime will reflect police policy if that policy is such as to encourage variations in either an upward or downward direction in the number of individuals arrested for a particular crime. Thus, if a police drive against burglary is in progress, it is probable that merely by the reallocation of enforcement resources the number of arrests for burglary will be increased.

But the police normally not only have the power to decide when to arrest but also have the power to choose which of a number of crimes an individual will be listed as arrested for in a particular situation. If a drive against burglary is in progress, this may well influence the decision whether an individual is charged with burglary, simple larceny, or criminal damage to property in a situation consistent with the commission of any of these three offenses.

Some years ago the British Home Office Statistical Advisor, commenting on an apparent increase in serious crimes of violence, wrote: "In 1952 the number of convictions of indictable woundings and assaults exceeded by one thousand the number for 1948, while the number of convictions of non-indictable assaults was less by two thousand: the explanation may be that the tendency to commit serious offences of violence is increasing while disorder in general is declining but it is alternatively —or additionally—possible that the publicity about offences of violence may have caused the police, consciously or unconsciously, to view these offenses more seriously and carry out a general upgrading of the legal classification attached to a particular set of facts."[172]

It is evident that the relation between police policy about the allocation of enforcement resources, and the way in which police discretion is exercised, is an extremely complex one. Moreover, these considerations lead to the conclusion that the number of arrests made is an unreliable index of real enforcement

171. U.S. President's Commission on Law Enforcement and Administration of Justice Task Force Report, *The Police* (1967) 188.
172. Lodge, Appendix to Longford, *Causes of Crime* (1958) 186.

conditions. If law enforcement agencies only controlled the number of *arrests made* for a particular offense, and did not also control the number of *offenses recorded,* our skepticism might be less necessary. Indeed, the reservations we have expressed about arrest rates are compounded when it is realized that the police have an even greater control over the number of offenses recorded. For the denominator of the most commonly used index of the probability of apprehension is not the number of offenses that take place—it cannot be that—but rather the number of such offenses that the police record.

A number of intermediate steps stand between the occurrence of an offense and the recording of such an offense by the police. Of major significance is the fact that many victims may not wish to report the fact of their victimization to a police agency. We have already pointed out that the survey technique as applied to criminal victimization involves a number of methodological problems. Nevertheless, the findings of the first national survey of crime victimization which was carried out by the National Opinion Research Center of the University of Chicago for the President's Crime Commission indicate a substantial disparity between reported and unreported crime. The amount of personal injury crime reported to N.O.R.C. was almost twice the *Uniform Crime Reports* rate and the amount of property crime more than twice as much as the *Uniform Crime Reports* rate for individuals. "Forcible rapes were more than 3½ times the reported rate, burglaries three times, aggravated assaults and larcenies of $50 and over more than double, and robbery 50 percent greater than the reported rate."[173]

The gap between actual offenses and offenses reported *to* the police constitutes a serious problem in comparative crime control studies. For it is apt to change over time, and existing data illustrate very clearly that it is not constant when different areas are being compared. Those regions of the United States where violent crime is most common, for example, are precisely those areas where actual offenses of this nature are least likely to become reported offenses.

But if the failure of victims to report to the police is one important source of error, the possibility that police will not

173. U.S. President's Commission, *supra* note 166, at 17.

choose to record all those apparent offenses reported to them is another. Honest doubts held by the police about the probability that a reported crime is an actual crime may influence their decision. Moreover, the police investment in crime prevention creates a situation in which every crime recorded is in a sense an admission against interest. In such circumstances, it is not surprising that some police do not record all reported crimes.

When the police are seen as controlling both the number of arrests and the purported number of offenses known, a number of possibilities of distortion become evident. The first of these and the simplest, is that the police may seek to make as high as possible the number of *arrests* for a particular offense, especially when a special crime prevention program has been adopted with respect to that particular offense, while seeking to depress as much as is possible the number of recorded *offenses*. In this case, the "probability of apprehension" will be greatly exaggerated. A second possibility is that both the number of arrests recorded and the number of offenses recorded will increase dramatically when the police, for budgetary or other reasons, seek to accentuate a particular crime problem as being worthy of attention. Yet a third possibility is that the police, unwilling or unable to fully control the number of individuals arrested for a particular crime, will seek to minimize the number of offenses in order to create an illusion of effective law enforcement without affecting arrest statistics.

Lest these possibilities be viewed as merely theoretical, we reproduce in table 17 the recorded figures for the number of offenses known to the police in relation to certain FBI index offenses for the city of New York before and after a change of police administration in 1965.[174]

The figures suggest either that the new police administration was unduly criminogenic, or that something less than the whole truth, or even the whole truth known to the police, had been recorded in the city of New York prior to the change in administration. Is every city like New York? How many are? We do not know, but it is clear that police records of crime

174. The source of the figures is *Uniform Crime Reports* (1964) 171, (1965) 176, (1966) 170.

TABLE 17
Offenses Recorded before and after Change of Police Administration, New York, 1965

	1964	1965	1966	Percentage Change between 1965 and 1966
Murder and nonnegligent manslaughter	636	631	653	+3
Robbery	7,988	8,904	23,539	+164
Burglary— breaking or entering	45,693	51,072	120,903	+137
Larceny—theft $50 and over	70,348	74,983	108,132	+44

cannot be accepted as a satisfactory index of the actual amount of crime. And if the recorded rate of crimes known to the police is itself suspect, then the compound statistic of recorded arrests over recorded crimes, must be doubly suspect.

A discouraging aspect of this situation is that we are unable to suggest a better measure of "probability of apprehension" than that discussed here. It is possible, however, to suggest some correctives to the uncritical acceptance of police statistics as an index of variation. In the first place, not all police statistics are equally unreliable. In some cases, notably homicide and bank robbery, police records are likely to be more veridical than in others. This provides some measure of control by enabling us to compare as between areas, or over time, trends in these offenses with trends in other crimes, to determine whether or not a change in police practice or a change in the actual incidence of crime is responsible for statistical variations.

With respect to certain other crimes such as aggravated assault, it is possible to compare trends in recorded homicides and recorded aggravated assaults, or, as in the British example cited above, between serious and less serious assaults. The ratios between these offenses can sometimes provide a fairly accurate index of whether the number of violent attacks is increasing or decreasing, or whether police and public sensitivity to violent attacks is increasing or decreasing. In comparative studies, however, the problems are more complicated.

In property crimes, it is more likely that a crime as serious as armed robbery at a place of business will be reported to the police and recorded by the police than more minor crimes such as larceny. This differential likelihood gives us a base line in robbery statistics for assessing the relative influence of actual trends in crime and variations in police recording practices on the rate of crimes recorded. Thus we might have some measure for the independent assessment of police reporting practices. But since robbery and other crimes against property may very well be subject to different trends, and the New York robbery figures suggest that general robbery statistics are not trustworthy in all cases, the test is far from conclusive.

Another test is the study of the particular historical conditions that may or may not provide a motive for changes in police reporting practices. This may be supplemented by a study in some detail of the mechanics of police reporting practices. Such studies may provide plausible rival hypotheses to real change in explaining variations in recorded crime rates.

A possible corrective lies in the use of prison admission or correctional statistics. These, while not being an accurate independent index of fluctuations in enforcement policy, can provide some check against wide variations in reported arrest rates, although not in respect of "offenses known to the police." In cases such as homicide, however, the punishment rate may tell us more about the mores and rules of criminal procedure than about probabilities of apprehension.

Finally, where victimization studies are available with respect to particular crimes in the different areas being compared, or in the same area before and after a change both in punishment policy and recorded crime, such studies can provide a natural control. Even in cases where victimization studies before and after changes in the crime rate are not available, studies which focus on victimization after a change in punishment policy and also attempt to determine whether there has been a change in historical victimization rates can provide some indication whether police statistics accurately reflect real trends in the incidence of crime.

C The Average Sentence and Severity of Punishment

Less formidable, but nevertheless serious, problems arise
when we consider a common method of defining severity of
penalty as an intermediate step in the analysis of whether variations in the severity of punishment, over time or between areas,
influence the incidence of crime. Thus, the measure of severity
selected by Professors Gibbs, [175] Tittle [176] and Erlich[177] in separate analyses of whether variations in severity of punishment
affect the crime rate, was the average length of prison sentence
served by individuals convicted of particular offenses, in various different jurisdictions.

Some of the problems that arise when this measure is used,
are immediately apparent in figure 3, which represents dia-
grammatically some of the decisional and classificatory steps
that exist between the occurrence of an act of crime and a
prison sentence for a particular offender.

One immediate and valid inference from figure 3 is that the
proportion of actual offenses that result in prison sentences is
likely to be an extremely small fraction. It is in fact commonly
estimated as being 1 percent of the total number of actual
crimes committed, although it varies from crime to crime. It is
important also to realize that the percentage of crimes resulting in a prison sentence is likely to vary over time and between
areas, as conditions that affect classification along the road from
actual crime to prison sentence themselves vary.[178]

It is evident too, that such enforcement-related variables as
the number of crimes reported to police and recorded by police
and the number of detected and arrested may vary drastically
both over time and between areas. The same applies to the
proportion of prosecutions on lesser charges, the proportion of
individuals convicted, and the proportion of convicted individuals sentenced to prison. To the extent that they do vary,

175. Gibbs, "Crime, Punishment, and Deterrence" (1968) 48 *Southwestern Soc. Sci. Quarterly* 515–30.
176. Tittle, "Crime Rates and Legal Sanction" (1969) 16 *Social
Problems* 409–23.
177. Ehrlich, "Participation in Illegitimate Activities: An Economic
Analysis" (1970) unpublished.
178. For details of wide variations in incarceration rates, see Wilkins,
"Crime Prevention and Costs in National Planning: A Discussion of
Concepts and Issues" (1967), 25 *Internat. Rev. Crim. Policy* 23–24.

FIGURE 3

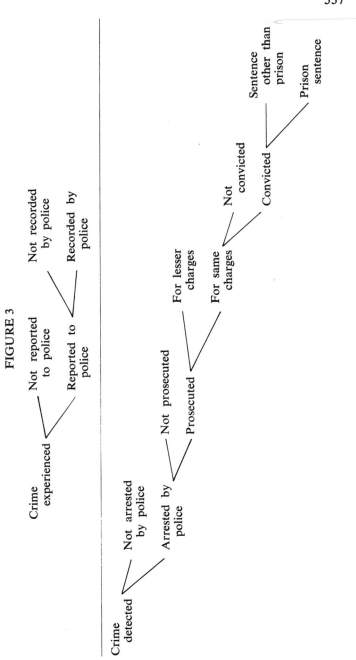

comparative studies or retrospective studies of "severity" may interpret a difference in the length of sentence served by essentially different groups of offenders in two areas, or in one area over time, as a difference in sentence severity for the same types of offenders.

For instance, if the proportion of convicted individuals sentenced to prison is much greater in area *A* than in area *B*, it is quite possible that the average length of sentence served in area *B* will be greater than that served in area *A*. Yet the same type of offender in each situation may be receiving the same type of sentence. In fact, the average sentence may be more lenient in the apparently stricter jurisdiction. This is a possibility and not a probability, but it is a possibility that cannot be ignored in evaluating the reliability of an index of severity of punishment which is based on the length of sentence served by offenders.

Our discussion of crime rates, indices of probability of apprehension, and a commonly used index of severity of punishment has not been exhaustive. Deterrence research utilizes a great variety of indices. We have illustrated some of the problems that arise in the use of some of the more important index variables. But we do not claim to have completely covered all the problems associated even with those index variables which we have considered.[179] The basic principle is that as a general rule we have to be content with what John Stuart Mill called "narrow conclusions."[180] Indeed, the problems discussed here may be seen as further evidence in support of the conservatism we have recommended in regard to drawing inferences from comparative and retrospective studies.

179. In this connection, see discussion of comparative studies of sentence severity, sec. 2 *supra*.

180. Mill, *Auguste Comte and Positivism* (1865) 82: "As often as a study is cultivated by narrow minds, they will draw from it narrow conclusions."

6 An Agenda For Research In Deterrence

The force of the relatively few available studies on the deterrent effectiveness of particular crime control policies is tempered by two factors: (1) most methods for assessing the influence of crime control policies are imperfect; and (2), insofar as reliable findings *are* available, such findings are likely to be specific to a particular crime and a particular audience of potential offenders.

Since only a small fraction of 1 percent of the total national expenditure for crime control has, in the past, been devoted to research[1] it is not altogether surprising that knowledge is deficient. Moreover, although more funds for research in crime control are currently being made available[2] the amount allotted to research in deterrence will inevitably, and rightly, be limited. In view of the scarcity of research resources and the recalcitrance to research of many of the problems encountered in this area, some attempt at a scheme of priorities for future research is necessary.

1. U.S. President's Commission on Law Enforcement and Administration of Justice, Report, *The Challenge of Crime in a Free Society* (1967) 273.

2. See: Law Enforcement Assistance Administration, *Guide for State Planning Agency Grants* (1968), and *L.E.A.A. 1970* (1970).

We do not, however, offer a hierarchical list of research priorities in ascending or descending order of importance. Rather, having discussed research from the point of view of methodology, we now move to consider it in a programmatic perspective. We shall first propose some criteria which should govern the selection of problems in deterrence for intensive study, and shall then indicate some specific areas which conform to those criteria.

SECTION 1 SOME CRITERIA FOR DETERMINING RESEARCH PRIORITIES

As a preliminary, we must say something about the kind of academic retrospective and comparative studies which we have considered in our general discussion of research strategy. Our view is that, since such studies are not expensive and may sometimes produce useful results, they should be pursued. The probability is that they will generate further hypotheses rather than produce solutions to practical problems. But the disinterested pursuit of truth without reference to its practical application is no harder to justify in this field than in any other, as long as it does not involve great costs. And, quite certainly, the generation of useful hypotheses is important, given the lack of satisfactory theory at the present time.

The emphasis in what follows, however, is on the use of research methods and techniques which require changes in the operation of the criminal justice system. Their use involves costs not only in terms of human and financial resources but also, it may be, in the form of human suffering on the part both of victims and offenders. Moreover, we are specifically concerned with the policy significance and the practical implications of that research. These considerations inevitably determine the nature of the criteria which follow. It may be added that we see these criteria as applicable to research not only in deterrence but in the whole field of crime control.

The first criterion is the social importance of the problem proposed for study. By social importance in this context we mean specifically the social costs involved in the incidence of a particular crime or punishment. To give a concrete example, homicide is clearly of greater social significance than illegal parking. An annual rate of fifteen thousand homicides in the

United States[3] is of greater significance as a social problem than an annual rate of two hundred or even eight hundred million acts of illegal parking. The determination of the degree of social importance or significance of an issue has to be made in terms of the generally accepted value system of society. It will not, of course, always be on the level of self-evidence displayed in our example. Indeed, it is unlikely that the application of this criterion alone will often be completely dispositive. For it is probable that many problems of undoubted social significance will prove relatively insusceptible to solutions based on variations in penal policy. It is likely also that many of them may prove not to be possible subjects for research projects.

A second criterion is the social significance, not of the particular crime problem to be investigated or subjected to experiment, but of the hypothesis about the effect of deterrent variations to be tested. The essence of this criterion is the extent to which establishing the truth of hypotheses may lead to a significant saving of social resources, either by reducing the rate of crime or by reducing the waste of resources used in the ineffective pursuit of marginal increments in deterrence. Among the many areas where present rates of crime constitute a significant social problem, we would choose for study those where present knowledge suggests that changes in penal policy may lead to important changes in the crime rate. Alternatively, we might select for investigation those where, despite a heavy investment in punishment based on deterrent expectations, there is some reason to believe that variations in the level of punishment have little in the way of marginal deterrent results.

A third criterion is the amenability of the issue to reliable assessment. Research opportunities are distributed unevenly over the range of deterrence issues. Other things being equal, it is easier to manipulate conditions of punishment for those crimes not subject to substantial social stigma or massive punishment than for those traditionally subject to serious condemnation.

As to experimentation, not simply with the *extent* of consequences threatened for a particular offense, but, more basically, with the *type* of consequences threatened for criminal behavior,

3. *Uniform Crime Reports—1969* (1970) 6: "In 1969, there was an estimated 14,590 murders committed in the United States."

less seriously punished crimes seem by far the most likely subjects.

In the light of the criterion of amenability, radical experiments in the treatment or threatening of criminal behavior will tend to be confined to categories of behavior which are not considered too serious. Investigations of the deterrent effectiveness of punishment threats on serious crimes will be confined, in the main, to relatively modest upward and downward shifts in penalty level. Experiments in enforcement, however, need not be confined to minor offenses, when they involve sharp increases in enforcement levels.

It is of course impossible to determine with any precision just which deterrence issues will be most amenable to research. That would require a prediction of the changes which political and social pressures in the coming decade will produce. To some extent, the criminological researcher must be an enlightened opportunist, ready to study changes in punishment level or enforcement policy where they occur, measuring effects as precisely as is possible under the circumstances.

A final criterion for research priority is the significance of a particular issue for deterrence theory as a whole. Because of the incompleteness of present knowledge, and the specificity to be anticipated in the results of much deterrence research, the application of this criterion is also a matter on which no very specific guidance can be provided in advance. It is possible, however, to give an example of the kind of issue to which this criterion could be applied. There is no reason why research into the deterrent consequences of changes in crime control policy should be concentrated entirely on modest changes in the penalty, or the intensification of enforcement procedures, associated with major crimes. It would seem desirable to fill out the picture by investigating the effect of more drastic changes associated with crimes of lesser seriousness which are committed by broader cross-sections of the population and which occur far more frequently than serious offenses. As the extent of knowledge increases, other ways in which particular studies may contribute to the general understanding of the deterrent effect will no doubt become apparent.

For reasons indicated in the text above, our criteria cannot be applied simply to the real world so as to produce syllogistically a list of research priorities for the decade ahead. Nevertheless, having outlined the sort of criteria which should be employed, in the section which follows we shall discuss a number of areas which seem to us both to conform with those criteria and to be promising areas for research, namely:

A. Social control of the drunk driver
B. Intensive enforcement and urban street crime
C. Countermeasures to folk crimes
D. Traffic offenses: threat and punishment
E. Variations in the sanctions for serious crimes
F. The establishment and repeal of criminal prohibitions on behavior

SECTION 2 SOME AREAS FOR RESEARCH AND EXPERIMENT

A Social Control of the Drunk Driver

In 1970, road accidents killed 55,300 Americans. A conservative extrapolation of research findings on the relation between alcohol and traffic accident fatalities would indicate that between one-third and one-half of those fatalities were attributable to excessive drinking.[4] One way to put this fatality statistic in perspective is to compare it with the combined total of homicides (other than reckless homicides) and suicides in the United States. The total of traffic fatalities attributable to alcohol is about two-thirds of the combined total of homicides and suicides.[5]

It is clear that the control of the drinking driver merits priority consideration because of its importance as a social problem. It is equally clear that this problem merits priority because changes in levels of enforcement and detection techniques appear to exert a substantial influence on levels of drunk driv-

4. U.S. Department of Transportation, *1968 Alcohol and Highway Safety Report* (1968) 14.
5. U.S. Bureau of the Census, *Statistical Abstract of the United States* (1969) 58; the figures given for 1967 are as follows:

Cause of Death	Deaths	Deaths per 100,000 Population
Motor vehicle accidents	52,924	26.7
Suicide	21,325	10.8
Homicide	13,425	6.8

ing, and on the accident and fatality costs associated with driving under the influence of alcohol.

The case for considering drunk driving as a prime subject for assessment of the effectiveness of legal threats comes from a variety of sources. Experience in Scandinavian countries that have established and maintained energetic enforcement levels in drunk driving control suggests that the role of alcohol in accident fatalities can be diminished substantially, even in countries where drinking, often heavy drinking, is widespread. In Norway, for example, Andenaes cited figures which show less than 2 percent of highway accidents as due to alcohol, and only 3½ percent of drivers in fatal accidents as being under the influence of alcohol.[6]

More direct and more dramatic evidence of the effectiveness of changes in drunk driving regulation is furnished by the British Road Safety Act of 1967—already discussed in connection with retrospective research.[7] The law defined the level of blood alcohol concentration that led to conviction for drunk driving at .08 (a lower level than the previous maximum), and provided that the police be equipped with portable breathalyzer kits for detecting the presence of the relevant blood alcohol concentrations in drivers. Preceded by intensive publicity, the act reduced nighttime fatal and serious-injury accidents by 38 percent in the first three months after it came into effect, as compared with the same months in the previous year. That this change was due to the change in the law was, as we have shown, corroborated by evidence that the degree of intoxication noted among those drivers who were fatally injured in Great Britain was substantially lower in the period just after the introduction of the new law than in the period just before. Evidence to date shows that, while the short-term trends were somewhat moderated in subsequent years, a fair proportion of the reductions in serious and fatal accidents has been maintained.[8]

---

6. Andenaes, "The General Preventive Effects of Punishment" (1966) 114 *U. Pa. L. Rev.* 969. See also Klette, "On the Functioning of the Swedish Legislation Concerning Drunken Driving" (1966) unpublished.

7. See chap. 5, sec. 3, subsec. D, *supra*.

8. Ministry of Transport, *The Road Safety Act of 1967 and its Effect on Road Accidents in the United Kingdom* (undated), cited by Andenaes in "Deterrence and Specific Offenses" (1971) 38 *U. Chi. L. Rev.*

The relation between the level of drunk driving and the level of highway fatalities, and more particularly between drunk driving and serious and fatal *nighttime* accidents, provides a fairly reliable base for assessing whether substantial fluctuations in the rate of drunk driving have in fact occurred. The possibility of introducing blood tests as a standard procedure in all traffic fatality cases provides a second independent measure of the relative importance of drunk driving to the total accident fatality experience.

The promise drunk driving research holds for deterrence theory generally is also substantial. For drunk driving is a crime which has not traditionally commanded much public attention or police enforcement priority. Furthermore, it is an area where a broad sector of the population can be considered potential offenders. This provides an interesting contrast to other areas of crime control policy where potential offenders, according to the available evidence, constitute a relatively small segment of the population.

The problem of the drinking driver in the United States scores close to the top on all four of our criteria for according research priority. If drunk driving control is worthy of study in any circumstances, it is particularly suitable for induced retrospective study. If it proves possible to select typical metropolitan jurisdictions in the United States for study, and to create substantial changes in the conditions of enforcement that relate to drunk driving, the opportunities for serious research come as close to optimal as a criminologist is likely to encounter in a real world setting.

It should be added, however, that experiments in control should not be confined to replication of the British approach. There are great possibilities for experiment and variation. It is more important to achieve control than to verify or disprove hypotheses in deterrence theory. Many variables might be tested, including the use of random checks, increased police highway patrols, and variations in penalties.

It would be interesting to test the hypothesis, mentioned by Andenaes in connection with the British experience, that the publicity campaign rather than the law itself caused the de-

550 n. 40. See also Department of the Environment, Scottish Development Department and Welsh Office, *Road Accidents 1969* (1971).

crease.[9] Andenaes rejects this theory on the ground that, while "there had been long-standing public discussion of the problem of drunken driving, and the publicity campaign began two weeks before the law took effect," the reduction in highway accidents did not take place until after the act took effect. "It seems clear," he says, "that the dramatic reduction in highway accidents is directly attributable to the legislation."[10] However, since the publicity stressed that the act was to come into effect on 9 October 1967, the dramatic reduction in the latter part of October might conceivably have followed even if no attempt at enforcement had been made. Therefore, independent testing of the two variables—publicity and actual enforcement—would be a worthwhile experiment. Above all, our approach should be pragmatic and directed at securing maximum control at minimum cost rather than the construction or validation of general theories.

B Intensive Enforcement and Urban Street Crime

Among the crimes which are regarded as most serious in the United States are those that occur in streets and other public places between victims and offenders previously unacquainted. The category "street crime" is customarily restricted to crimes of personal contact, such as aggravated assault, and a variety of forms of crime including muggings, purse snatchings, and armed street robberies. Nationally, about one-half of all robberies are street robberies.[11] The financial losses involved are rarely great, but the shock and injury suffered by victims of street crime represent a substantial harm.

The existence of, and recent increases in, such forms of criminality have created an atmosphere in which many Americans feel it is unsafe to walk the streets of their neighborhoods after dark.[12] The use of "crime in the streets" as a political slogan may be seen as evidence of public concern.

As in the case of drunk driving, there are indications that

9. Andenaes, *supra* note 8, at 549.
10. *Ibid.*
11. U.S. President's Commission, *supra* note 1, at 18.
12. *Id.* at 50–51: "One-third of Americans feel unsafe about walking alone at night in their own neighborhoods. . . . In the high crime districts surveyed in Boston and Chicago . . . forty-three percent reported they stayed off the streets at night altogether."

street crime can be significantly reduced through variations in the conditions of the legal threats associated with it. There is, however, no evidence to suggest that any substantial marginal deterrence can be gained by increasing the maximum sentences that can be imposed for such crimes. Statutes already provide for sentences which are among the highest available in American courts.

Moreover, although there are wide variations in the sentences actually imposed, any significant increase in the severity of sanctions now on the statute books might blur what distinction exists between the penalties for common street crimes of violence and the penalties for street crimes resulting in injury or death. To the extent that variations in the severity of penalty can be expected to channel or influence behavior, there may be an advantage in preserving a further distinction between nonfatal and fatal injuries to victims, in the hope of minimizing the number of killings. With this in mind, the legislatures might find it more expedient to create mandatory minimum sentences than to escalate maximum sentences.

But if there is reason to be cautious about assuming that increasing the already substantial punishment for aggravated assault and most forms of robbery would have a measurable effect on the crime rate, the same cannot be said for measures which aim at increasing the probability that violent street crimes will be detected or prevented. According to FBI reports, approximately one out of four robberies (and most probably a much smaller proportion of all street robberies) are cleared by the arrest of an offender.[13] For reasons given earlier, the correct figure would probably be very much smaller.[14] Thus, the objective risk of apprehension for the commission of violent street crimes is generally less than for other crimes of violence,[15] although still probably greater than for many non-contact property offenses.[16]

13. *Supra* note 3 at 16: "In 1969, law enforcement agencies were successful in solving 27 percent of these crimes."

14. See chap. 5, sec. 7, *supra*.

15. *Uniform Crime Reports, supra* note 3, at 30 gives the following percentages for "Crimes Cleared by Arrest" in respect of other violent offenses against the person in 1969: murder 86 percent, negligent manslaughter 84 percent, forcible rape 56 percent, aggravated assault 65 percent.

16. *Ibid.* In respect of other offenses against property the percentages given are: burglary 19 percent, larceny 18 percent, auto theft 18 percent.

Available information suggests that changes in the allocation of police enforcement resources can substantially increase the probability that street criminals will be apprehended, and by doing so, significantly reduce the number of street crimes experienced in a particular area. In an age of unprecedented technical innovation, it is somewhat ironic that the most successful *known* strategy for increasing the probability of apprehension for street crimes is simply more intensive police patrol.

Certainly, experience to date with this method is at least hopeful. Some evidence may be found in an experiment known as Operation 25, which took place between 1 September and 31 December 1954 in a part of New York City that is one of the densest urban areas in the United States.[17] Operation 25 gave some indication that an increase in police enforcement that increases the likelihood of apprehension for street crimes will also reduce the rate of such crimes. This is not to say that there is necessarily a direct cause-and-effect relation between increasing probability of apprehension and a reduction in the amount of street crime. In the first place, when the number of police patrolling an individual area is greatly increased, this leads not only to an increased objective probability of apprehension, but also to recognition on the part of potential offenders of increased police presence in the area. Independent of the actual increase in chances of apprehension, the increased police presence may persuade potential criminals either to foreswear criminal intentions, or to transfer their attention to areas less saturated with law enforcement personnel. Thus, increases in the degree of police patrol may influence the rate of street crime by altering potential offenders' perceptions of enforcement chances, independent of an objective shift in probability of apprehension.

There are also other problems to be considered. In the case of Operation 25, the New York City Police Department selected the 25th Precinct—a small police district noted for its high crime rate—and quadrupled the number of foot patrol officers assigned to that district during the experimental period. When crime statistics for the period of Operation 25 were compared with those for the same period in the previous year, they re-

17. City of New York Police Department, *Operation 25* (1955).

vealed notable decreases in all major crimes where the victim was likely to report them. Yet the basis on which the experimental area was chosen, and the extremely small size of the area subjected to increased patrol, inevitably raise doubts about the extent to which one can draw valid inferences about the effects of intensive police patrol on crime rates in other situations.

The fact that the area selected for study had experienced exceptionally high rates of violent crime during the period just before the program was introduced might suggest that the reduction in violent crime was attributable to regression rather than to the change in police program. However, since the rates of all crimes did not decrease as significantly as the rates of street crimes, and since the high crime rate characteristic of the area was persistent over time and not a recent development, such a theory is less tenable than it might be in other situations.

The small size of the test area, however, raises more serious doubts. Increasing police patrols by a significant degree may persuade potential criminals to transfer their criminal activities elsewhere without causing them to desist from crime altogether. If the amount of police resources necessary to cause crime to be exported is significantly less than what would be necessary to reduce the number of actual offenses attributable to the same groups of criminals or potential criminals, an experiment within a very small geographical area may well produce apparent crime reduction. But these results might be belied in part if larger-scaled evaluations were made. Unfortunately, the report on Operation 25 does not provide the data for assessing whether or not the "exportation" of crime took place, or how significant the export may have been as opposed to the wholly deterrent effects of the operation.

A somewhat more careful analysis of a similar but more recent experiment in intensified enforcement in New York has been carried out by Professor Press. Again there was a significant decrease in the amount of street crime, but the possibility of an export effect is not precluded in that case either.[18]

18. Press, *Some Effects of an Increase in Police Manpower in the 20th Precinct of New York City* (1971) 1–18. In this study, crime rates in precincts adjacent to the 20th were analyzed to determine what were called "displacement effects." A "strong suggestion" of displacement is

The difficulties involved in interpreting the results of such experiments when conducted within extremely small areas suggest an alternative method of research. What might be attempted is a variety of the induced retrospective experiment, discussed earlier, addressed to significantly increasing the amount of police enforcement resources devoted to the prevention of street crime in a middle-sized to large urban area on a citywide basis. In such an experiment, careful selection of the city to be studied, together with collection of relevant crime data *before* the introduction of the change, could ensure reasonable conditions for assessing the true impact of the change in police patrolling practices. Taking a large urban unit, rather than a small section of a larger city, would reduce the chances of "export" effects. It should be added that any serious study will necessarily involve laying down a base line —independent of the police—for measuring the effects of the change.

It might be objected that introducing such changes in police patrol patterns on a large scale for purposes of retrospective evaluation would be very much more expensive than making similar changes within a smaller area. It could also be argued that careful study of crime patterns in adjacent areas might go a long way toward correcting the deficiencies of the small area study. To some extent this objection is well taken. However, it is also true that the best type of change in police patrol practices to evaluate is that which represents a practical alternative to present police practices over large areas. It may be of theoretical interest to discover that, if we quadruuple the number of police in a particular small area, we can reduce the crime rate. But if this is not a feasible countermeasure to crime, the finding will lack practical value. On the other hand, if a substantial but achievable increase in police patrol size can be shown to reduce street crime by a significant amount, it may provide a model for the reform of police procedures in cities with similar problems throughout the country. So the

---

reported in one neighboring precinct where major crime types increased, bnt generally by an amount less than the decrease observed in the 20th Precinct. Other problems include the possibility of a Hawthorne effect, where the police may have kept better or worse records, knowing that the experiment was being carried out; and the inherent problems of after-the-fact analyses such as lack of randomization.

apparent disadvantage of cost is outweighed by the fact that such experiments have a general practical significance only if the methods employed can be widely replicated. In addition, the selection of a large rather than a small area adds reliability to the inferences we may seek to draw from a study of intensive enforcement practices.

It is necessary to add two further points. One relates to the assessment of the effects of such intensive enforcement methods; the other to the question of the comparative costs of such methods. With regard to the first, if the probability that a particular type of offender will be apprehended is greatly increased, then the increased apprehension rate may achieve a substantial *preventive* effect which is quite independent of the *deterrent* effect of the escalation in enforcement. This is likely to be especially marked in relation to offenses like mugging, burglary, and automobile theft where one offender may, if he is at liberty, commit a number of similar offenses.[19] Nevertheless—and this brings us to the second point—it is crime prevention rather than deterrence which is the ultimate object of crime control measures. It follows that experiments in this field should not be confined to seeking to achieve simple deterrent effects. In regard to urban street crime there are a variety of stratagems including better street lighting, effective gun control, citizen police alarm devices, and cashless busses which may have a preventive effect and should also be tested. The objective should be the least-cost method of securing a reduction in crime. Experiments with more intensive police patrol may then help us to find out where investment in deterrence ranks as a preventive of street crime.

For political reasons the control of street crime may be seen as an attractive object of investment, as witness the Law Enforcement Assistance Administration's 1972 high-impact, eight-city, anticrime program directed at "street crimes and burglaries."[20] Nevertheless, there are dangers associated with

19. U.S. President's Commission on Law Enforcement and Administration of Justice Task Force Report, *Science and Technology* (1967) 63: A rearrest-crime-switch matrix prepared for the commission by the Institute for Defense Analyses shows that the probability of an arrested offender's having his next arrest for the same type of crime is higher with respect to robbery, burglary, and automobile theft than to any other index offenses.

20. See "U.S. to Aid 8 Cities in Fight on Crime" in *New York Times* 14 Jan. 1972.

programs which possess this kind of popular appeal. The political importance of achieving success may stimulate pressure against rigorous evaluation and hurry programs into operation before reliable base-line data have been acquired. It is to be hoped that these dangers will be recognized and avoided.

C Countermeasures to Folk Crimes

The general category of folk crime refers to "types of violation [which] are widespread and socially costly" but, although "criminal according to socio-legal criteria," are not generally "stigmatized as criminal" to the degree that other types of crime are.[21] Folk crime has been held to include "traffic law violations, white-collar crime, chiseling, black market dealings."[22] It is used here in a wider sense, to include also such offenses as shoplifting, tax evasion, petty thefts by employees, and other types of pilfering.

Such offenses are recognized as widespread without promoting either extensive fear or extravagant public condemnation. Our categorization of them as folk crimes is not meant to suggest that prevailing opinion considers such behaviors correct or even justifiable. Rather, the label is employed to indicate that they are very often condoned; and there is little tendency on the part of the general public to feel markedly guilty about committing such offenses if undetected, or to subject individuals apprehended for them to extreme stigmatization.

Another feature which is characteristic of folk crime is "the generally higher social status of the violators. . . . they tend to be from higher social classes than the typical stigmatized criminal."[23] Thus, Laurence Ross has shown that "traffic law violators have a higher social status than violators of other criminal laws" and that in this way they resemble Sutherland's description of "white-collar criminals."[24] Tax evasion, employee crime, and other types of white-collar offenses are not restricted to the higher social strata, but the opportunities and incentives

21. For discussion of the definition of the expression folk crime, see Laurence Ross, "Traffic Law Violation: A Folk Crime" (1960–61) 8 *Social Problems* 236–37.
22. *Id.* at 237.
23. *Ibid.*
24. *Id.* at 232–35: See also Sutherland, *White Collar Crime* (1959).

for committing such crimes are concentrated in the middle and upper strata of society. The more taxes one owes, the greater the rewards for tax cheating. The greater one's degree of responsibility and trust, the greater the opportunities for particular types of employee crime.

With respect to shoplifting, it is not necessarily true that the middle and upper economic levels of society commit a greater number of such offenses per capita than members of the lower social strata. But the fact that middle and upper income groups are prone at all to commit such offenses is in contrast to the clear relation noted between low social status and high rates of criminality with respect to other offenses. A study carried out in Chicago found that "most shoplifters are 'respectable' people" and that "the data on shoplifting" show "a strong middle-class component."[25]

Consideration of the type of offense categorized as folk crime suggests that there may be some class bias operating in the United States in the classification of crimes as either reprehensible or tolerable. For it would not be inaccurate to characterize these offenses as in large part middle-class crime. Yet although they constitute "the most frequent and costly kinds of antisocial behavior,"[26] they are frequently "not stigmatized by the public as criminal" and in many cases "not considered in public opinion to be 'real' criminality."[27]

It is difficult to assess the social cost of folk crime in America. By one measure—the amount of social discontent provoked by this type of offense—the social costs are by definition low, because the social toleration of such offenses is high. On the other hand, to the extent that objective estimates of economic loss or the dimensions of property transfers are regarded as measures of social cost, property folk crime represents a very substantial social loss. It is probable, for example, that shoplifting and employee theft result in a greater property loss to retail businesses in the United States than all other forms of property crime produce in all victim classes.[28]

25. Cameron, *The Booster and the Snitch* (1964) 100 and 173.
26. Laurence Ross, *supra* note 21, at 240.
27. *Id.* at 232.
28. U.S. President's Commission on Law Enforcement and Administration of Justice Task Force Report, *Crime and Its Impact—An Assessment* (1967) 48.

But we shall not here enter into discussion of the apparent contradiction between the objective and subjective costs of folk crime in the United States. It may well be that society does not wish to punish or even to apprehend, to a greater extent than is already done, those who commit these offenses. Nor are we inclined to urge the prevention of all crimes at all costs. Nor shall we argue that an individual act of petty larceny should be viewed as heinous because of the aggregate cost of millions of such offenses.

Our placement of crime control measures in this area on a list of possible subjects for deterrent research does not rest primarily on the social costs, except in the case of drunk driving. It rests on the belief that the rate of folk crime is peculiarly susceptible to variations in the conditions of legal threats. Small-scale folk property crimes involve small amounts of gain for individuals who in many cases are not desperately in need of money. Moreover, the characterization of acts as folk crimes indicates that there are few social barriers apart from the legal threat that stand between potential offenders' temptations to commit such crimes and their willingness to do so.

Available research data support this assumption. The Chicago study of shoplifting referred to suggests that the apprehension of nonprofessional criminals for shoplifting is an almost totally effective mechanism for reducing subsequent shoplifting among those apprehended[29] and, moreover, that most shoplifters are nonprofessionals.[30] By extension, any method of significantly increasing apprehension chances will reduce the crime rate through this preventive effect, even if it has no effect as a general deterrent. Yet there is no reason to suppose that a substantial and visible increase in credibility in the legal threat against shoplifting would not also function as an effective general deterrent. Also, since the high rate of such offenses depends in large measure on the absence of social stigma, this area would be an interesting subject for experiments in trying to enhance the "moralizing" quality of criminal law.

29. Cameron, *supra* note 25, at 151: "Among pilferers who are apprehended and interrogated by the store police but set free without formal charge, there is *very little or no recidivism*" (author's italics).
30. *Id.* at chaps. 4 and 5, pp. 70–120.

If the data on shoplifting suggests that change in the probability of apprehension can have significant effects on the behavior of potential folk criminals, Marshall Clinard's study of black market behavior among businessmen suggests that changes from nonpenal to penal sanctions may have a significant effect on the perceptions of businessmen about both the wrongness and the risks involved in black market behavior.[31] Clinard also cites an unpublished survey by the Enforcement Department of the Office of Price Administration which indicates that "where sentences were generally adequate, observance of regulations was best, and that a converse situation existed where sentences were inadequate."[32]

As between changes in the severity of sanctions threatened and changes in the enforcement levels and techniques associated with folk crimes, we favor the latter for a variety of practical and ethical reasons. The practical reasons are that the research, to date, suggests that variations in the credibility of threats aimed at this type of crime have a more substantial effect on behavior than variations in the amount of punishment threatened. We would add, on the basis of Clinard's study, one caveat to this. There may be situations in which the change from minor to more serious penalties will create a change in the perceptions of offenders about the seriousness of the offense; and this may be necessary to achieve significant deterrent effects in some areas of folk crime. But it is in relation to folk crime that attempts to escalate sanctions are most likely to result in selective prosecution and inequitable punishment policies. It is only where there is an urgent necessity, and even then caution must be exercised, that recourse should be had to substantial penalty increases.

The necessity for escalations in penalty can easily be overemphasized. The Chicago shoplifting study demonstrates that apprehension and the following unpleasantness of interrogation and confrontation are the only sanctions employed against the majority of amateur shoplifters, yet they prove effective to those apprehended.[33] In the light of the finding that minor

31. Clinard, *The Black Market: A Study of White Collar Crime* (1952) 243–45.
32. *Id.* at 244–45.
33. Cameron, *supra* note 25, at 151.

sanctions can sometimes achieve significant preventive effects, we believe it is always preferable to test changes in enforcement conditions before deciding to employ the more drastic measure of gross escalations in penalty.

D Traffic Offenses: Threat and Punishment

We have already included the general range of traffic offenses in the category of folk crime, but for a variety of reasons they merit separate treatment. The United States is uniquely a nation on wheels. More people drive than vote. If the social impact of motor vehicles is great, so too is the cost of motor vehicle traffic. Laurence Ross pointed out ten years ago that "violations of the traffic laws are the most common form of reported crime in the United States, and the accidents associated with these violations are perhaps the most costly of our social problems."[34] Moreover, as Barbara Wootton has said of the British scene, "In half a century the invention of the internal combustion engine has completely revolutionized the business of our criminal courts."[35]

In 1970, some 55,300 persons were killed in highway traffic in the United States. As previously noted, close to one-half of those fatalities were associated with the consumption of alcohol. Indeed, "alcohol has been found to be the largest single factor leading to fatal crashes."[36] But, in addition, there is abundant evidence that a variety of traffic offenses are associated with the majority of traffic accidents. The National Safety Council reported that over 80 percent of all serious and fatal accidents in 1968 involved traffic violations.[37] We cannot, however, infer from the fact that traffic offenses are associated with serious and fatal accidents the conclusion, so easy to reach in the case of drunk driving, that the social cost of traffic offenses in the United States is disproportionately high. Except for the drinking driver, we have no reliable way of estimating what proportion of all drivers are constantly committing some

34. Laurence Ross, *supra* note 21, at 231.
35. Wootton, *Social Science and Social Pathology* (1959) 25–26.
36. U.S. Department of Transportation, *supra* note 4, at 11.
37. U.S. National Safety Council, *Accident Facts 1968* (1969) 48: Violations of a traffic law are reported in 90.6 percent of all accidents, in 80.3 percent of all fatal accidents, and in 87.7 percent of all accidents involving injury.

types of traffic offense. So we have no basis for assessing the relation that exists between traffic offenses and accidents.

Yet, apart from any possible relation between traffic offenses other than drunk driving and the social costs related to serious accidents, the criminal law regulation of traffic behavior is of substantial importance. To begin with, the great majority of adults in the United States are drivers and thus form one of the largest groups of potential criminals with respect to any crime presently defined. The number of actual offenders, as well as the number of potential offenders, is much larger in the traffic area than in any other area of the criminal law.

Moreover, most traffic offenses are not considered to be serious criminal offenses. Some twenty years ago Margery Fry observed that "many people who would cut an acquaintance found guilty of stealing £5 will still shake the hoof of a road hog."[38] She also noted that "quite respectable people seem to be a little proud of having been fined for dangerous driving."[39] This attitude, which is reflected in the low scales of penalties for such offenses, has proved conducive both to experiments in the degree of punishment meted out to traffic offenders, and to experimental changes in the types of punishment given to traffic offenders.

Miss Fry favored experimenting with penalties in this area and suggested, for example, that " 'Caution: I have been convicted of dangerous driving' affixed to the rear of an offender's car for a year or two would have a real effect in educating public opinion as well as in hindering a repetition of the offense."[40] We include the treatment of traffic offenders as a promising area for research largely because this area more than all others provides a wide-ranging freedom to experiment. Unfortunately, although this freedom has been exploited to some extent, almost no methods of treating traffic offenders have been subjected to a systematic assessment, and no studies of general deterrence have been attempted.

One controlled experiment that has come to our attention produced somewhat surprising results.[41] In that study, conven-

38. Fry, *Arms of the Law* (1951) 19–20.
39. *Id.* at 122.
40. *Id.* at 123.
41. Mecham, "Proceed with Caution: Which Penalties Slow Down the Juvenile Traffic Violator"? (1968) 14 *Crime and Delinq.* 142–50.

tional traffic treatments for juvenile violators, such as attendance at traffic school, being restrained from driving, and fines, were compared with the writing of an essay on traffic safety in a random-assignment controlled experiment. Those individuals subjected to the essay assignment did significantly better than the other groups as a whole and apparently better than any of the other treated groups.[42]

A second study tested the effects of fines, driver school, probation, and the combination of fines and driver education on four randomly assigned groups of convicted offenders. Both driver education and probation outperformed fines during the first year of treatment, with driver school continuing to work well in the second year after treatment while probation effects diminished. However, the combination of education *and* probation had no better record than fines and far less effectiveness than either probation or driver school alone![43]

Assessments of other methods, such as warning letters to errant drivers and variations on the theme of driver education,[44] underscore a basic conclusion that we are far from an acceptable theoretical framework to explain the great variety of results. Surprising results should not in themselves lead to premature endorsement of unusual traffic offender sanctions. On the other hand, the tolerance toward experimentation that exists within the area of traffic offender treatment, together with the paucity of evidence that our present traffic offender sanctions are working at all, let alone working better than any possible alternatives, make this an eminently suitable area for a series of controlled random-assignment experiments.

Such experiments appear relatively low on our list of areas for investigation because of the uncertain nature of the social cost of this type of offense, and the apparently low degree of public anxiety regarding the traffic offender. Given the present confusion in traffic offender punishment policy, however, experimentation in the *types* as well as *severity* of traffic offender

42. *Ibid.*
43. Owens, "Report on a Three Year Controlled Study of the Effectiveness of the Anaheim–Fullerton Municipal Court Drivers Improvement School" (1967) 7 *Municipal Court Rev.* 7–14.
44. See e.g., Coppin, Marsh, and Peck, *A Re-evaluation of Group Driver Improvement Meetings* (1965).

sanctions, and in enforcement conditions, could have nothing but salutary effects.

In the area of general deterrence of traffic offenses we are in favor of experiments in both publicity and enforcement, with one major reservation. The only reliable ways to assess changes in the rate of traffic offenses are through survey research about behavior and through accident statistics. In surveys, respondents have to remember and define offenses, and both memory and definition present problems in this context.[45] And accident statistics, so useful in drunk driving assessment, are problematic because the relation between accidents and offenses other than speeding is unconfirmed. If changes in enforcement do not produce changes in accident rates, is this evidence of the effectiveness of the enforcement strategy or of the irrelevancy of the measure? Sharp changes in accident rates are less ambiguous. But will there be any? We recommend campaigns focused on those offenses most likely to relate to accidents, with careful evaluations of their results. This approach serves both social policy and the needs of research methodology.

E Variations in the Sanctions for Serious Crime

Whether judged by the provisions of penal codes or the average time served by prisoners in states and federal penal institutions, the United States follows an unusually severe punishment policy with respect to offenders apprehended and convicted of homicide, rape, robbery, burglary, narcotics offenses, serious larceny, and other major crimes. It is, of course, true that many offenders are not involved in these statistics because they do not receive prison sentences or are convicted of lesser offences. But this does not establish that penal policy in practice is lenient so much as that it is both lenient (on occasions) and quite severe (on other occasions). Deterrence seems to be a principal, but not exclusive, motive for this relatively severe sanction policy. Yet the marginal deterrent impact of modest upward or downward changes in severe penalties for major offenses is far from established.

The evidence available, and that evidence is slight, suggests that fluctuations this far up the scale of available penal sanc-

45. See Hood and Sparks, *Key Issues in Criminology* (1970) 64–70.

tions have little or no effect on the rate of serious crimes. Yet, although the base penalties are already high, the escalation of sanctions is often recommended for serious offenses as a general deterrent measure. In the circumstances, it seems to us that an appropriate way of testing the effectiveness of severe penal sentences for serious crimes is to experiment with modest downward shifts in the average penalty imposed for a number of the most serious offenses under present American criminal law. It may seem incongruous to include in a work on deterrence a recommendation for the reduction of penalties, involving the risk of diminution in deterrent effect. But on the theoretical level this proposition could be defended on the ground of logical symmetry. And on the practical level, in spite of contrary theory, the risk involved would be extremely small, from the standpoints of both general deterrence and individual prevention.

One or a number of jurisdictions could arrange for an experimental downward shift in the average sentence imposed on all those convicted for a series of offenses. The change in punishment policy could be evaluated by comparisons of crime rates and of recidivism rates before and after the change. A danger inherent in such a comparison is that something other than the severity of punishment might change over the period of time covered in the comparison. Moreover, that "something" might include conditions which would produce a class of offenders different from those active prior to the period studied. Such a downward test should be subjected to rigorous before-and-after analysis. And if such controls as full information about the prior criminal records, age, and other characteristics of those sentenced both before and after the change in punishment policy were included, the dangers that come from lack of random assignment at a particular point in time could be minimized.

A second and more reliable method for assessing the efficacy of shorter rather than longer sentences, in relation to those punished, is the random assignment experiment. In such an experiment, every second offender convicted would receive a lower penalty than that normally imposed for his offense. The random assignment model is of limited utility, because it could only test the effect of the threat and punishment and subsequent threat of further punishment for further crime on those individuals actually punished. If random assignment were used, the actual punishment threat for potential criminals would be an uncertain combination of the more and less severe penalty, and, while this would represent a downward shift, it would not constitute an entirely satisfactory example for testing general deterrent efficacy.

The mechanism of random assignment gives rise to the further objection that it involves inequitable discrimination. If one group essentially indistinguishable from a second is to be treated more leniently, members of the second group can object that justice is being abrogated in the interests of science or social welfare.

It has been argued that downward tests of the effect of sanctions by random assignment methods involve no injustice, since, though some offenders will be treated better under experimental conditions, the rest will be treated no worse than usual.[46] It could be added that, since everybody has an equal chance of being awarded the smaller punishment, there is no real inequity involved in random assignment. These arguments would be more cogent if no alternative methods of testing were available, that is, if in the absence of random assignment experiments no experimental downward testing in penalties at all could be conducted.

Insofar as that is not the case, the questionable moral propriety of at-random experimentation must be recognized; for it would mean that a substantial number of offenders would be deprived of advantages which would accrue to them if the downward shift method were employed. Moreover, as to the question of equity, while offenders may *momentarily* stand on an equal footing before assignment to one or another punishment group, the whole essence of the random assignment method is that *similar* groups should be treated *differently*.

Because a conflict between antithetical principles and interest is involved, the debate as to the morality of random assignment experimentation in the field of punishment is not finally resolv-

46. See Morris, "Impediments to Penal Reform" (1966) 33 *U. Chi. L. Rev.* 645–56, for discussion of the principle of "less severity" as a safeguard against the abuse of human rights in evaluative research of this nature.

able. But we would make two points in regard to the ethical issues. First, when severe sanctions are the subject of inquiry, the experimental evaluation of downward rather than upward shifts is clearly less morally objectionable. Second, when random assignment rather than total downward shift models of experimentation are being considered, the extra suffering involved in the use of the former method should be counted as a major cost.

There is at least one method of experimentation open to us in this field which avoids the objections we have been discussing. This is "the indirect experiment,"[47] a compromise design which exploits the actual chance distribution involved in judicial discretion as a means of meeting the random requirements of controlled experiments. A number of experiments have already been successfully conducted within the field of law by this indirect method.[48]

We should here say something about the magnitude of the downward shifts that we have in mind. Such experiments would *not* involve the immediate release to the streets of great numbers of dangerous criminals. Rather, the downward shift experiment would begin by lowering the term of penal servitude prescribed for selected serious offenses from one term of years in prison to a smaller term of years in prison.

Beyond such preliminary experiments, there lies the possibility of experimentation with measures of social security less extreme than the physical restraints of the modern prison and with methods of punishment that focus on keeping the offender in the community rather than removing him from it. But we are not here concerned to endorse any particular items among these possibilities. Our proposal is merely that we should attempt to discover whether the expensive and lengthy terms of penal confinement now imposed in most of our jurisdictions for many crimes are any more effective than less expensive and less brutal alternatives might be.

Within the area of serious crimes, our view is that the most suitable subjects for experimental variation in penalty level are

47. Zeisel, "The Indirect Experiment" (1968) 2 *Law and Society Rev.* 504–8.
48. *Id.* at 505–8.

the illegal possession of narcotics and a range of nonviolent property offenses. Such a selection may be justified on the ground that in these areas there is a notable disproportion between the social dangerousness of the offenses and the present penalty levels. These offenses should not, however, be the exclusive focus of downward shift experiments in the coming years. There are, in the federal system and in the states, many other offenses that could be regarded as proper objects for such experimentation.

F The Establishment and Repeal of Criminal Prohibition on Behavior

One common characteristic of the five topics dealt with above is that they relate to marginal rather than absolute deterrence. In each case, it is the variation in conditions surrounding a threat rather than the presence or absence of that threat which forms the basis of the proposed study. None of the studies deals with differences between behavioral patterns when a threat is present and those obtaining when it is removed. Yet such differences are both of practical significance in a limited number of situations, and of undoubted theoretical importance to those interested in the deterrent effect of legal threats.

We do not suggest that interest in the nature of absolute deterrent processes is sufficient justification for either defining as criminal certain behaviors previously not criminal, or abolishing criminal sanctions for behaviors previously treated as criminal. Therefore, we do not advocate in this section, as we have in previous sections, changes to be made in the criminal justice system in the interest of research. Nor is it our intention to argue the case for redefining the limits of the criminal law or to suggest likely subjects for inclusion or exclusion. However, as changing social conditions generate pressures to establish or abolish categories of criminal offense, such occasions present an opportunity to study the effects of criminalization and decriminalization.

In this connection one study, to which we have already referred,[49] sought to determine by means of a survey the effects on attitudes of the passage of the British Suicide Act of 1961,

49. See chap. 4, sec. 1, subsec. D, *supra*.

which provided that attempted suicide should no longer be a criminal offense.[50] The authors of the study acknowledge that "there are obvious limitations ... to this sort of evidence" and point out that their particular survey related "only to attempts at suicide, which is not an act that most people seriously consider the possibility of committing themselves."[51]

They go on to say that "since no other crime (excluding offences under emergency legislation and analogous measures) has been removed from the statute book in the last hundred years, the prospect of a similar opportunity to test ... by a field survey about other types of conduct is remote."[52] Nevertheless, the passage since then, in Britain, of both the Abortion Act 1967, which permits abortion in a wide range of circumstances, and the Sexual Offences Act 1967, which decriminalized homosexual acts in private between consenting males over the age of 21, indicates that the law is not quite immutable. If opportunities for research in this area cannot be made to occur, they can be seized when they do occur.

It is perfectly true, as Walker and Argyle say, that surveys designed to measure the effect of changes in the law on attitudes are subject to limitations, many of which we have already discussed in some detail.[53] The question arises whether decriminalization may lead people to approve of, or at least no longer condemn, the behavior which is no longer prohibited by law. The difficulty is that of distinguishing between public approval that may have been a factor in causing or facilitating the legislative change, and approval that is a consequence of it. In regard to both criminalization and decriminalization, this constitutes a problem for survey research. Decriminalization may involve an obsolete law (the British Suicide Act 1961 might be said to have done this) or alternatively, as in the case of the Sexual Offences Act of 1967, it may represent a change in advance of public opinion regarding the moral significance of certain deviant behavior. Similarly, the creation of new categories of criminal behavior may be due to public pressure

50. Walker and Argyle, "Does the Law Affect Moral Judgments?" (1964) 4 *Brit. J. Crim.* 570–81; see also Walker, "Morality and the Criminal Law" (1964) 11 *Howard Journal* 209–19.

51. *Id.* at 572.

52. *Id.* at 572–73.

53. See chap. 5, sec. 6, subsec. C, *supra.*

and may confirm a widely held social judgment, or it may be a response to technological or social developments of which the general public are little aware. But it will not always be possible to decide with certainty into which category a particular legislative change falls.

It will sometimes be possible to measure the effects of legal change on the dimension of conduct rather than attitude. This was the case with the British Road Safety Act of 1967, which introduced a new offense in addition to the existing provisions relating to drunk driving: driving with an undue proportion of alcohol in the blood. Similarly, in the legalization of abortion, decriminalization may provide both qualitative and quantitative data. Birth rate trends can give some measure of the impact of legalization as well as provide information as to what the situation was prior to the change. Professor Andenaes cites birth rates in Eastern European countries as evidence that "the legalization of abortion has had a depressant effect on the birth rate."[54] But it is necessary to be cautious when drawing inferences about the effects of legal change in this area from birth rates alone. It is always possible that the social factors which lead to changes in the law also exert an influence on birth rates independently of the legislation. Thus, Andenaes gives as his "most striking example" the case of Romania, where the legalization of abortion in 1957 was followed by a decline in the birth rate and the prohibition of abortion in 1966 was followed by a sharp increase. "The effects of the new law [i.e., prohibition] were dramatic" Andenaes says.[55] But in view of the fact that the reversal of abortion policy was accompanied by both an increase in family allowances and the cessation of official importation of contraceptives, it is conceivable that the effects noted were to a large extent due to these changes rather than the abortion legislation.

Another area in which at least partial decriminalization is a political possibility concerns the drug marijuana, the acquisition and/or possession of which is currently punishable by law in the United States. It is notable that the President's Crime Commission remarked on the existence of "the greatest discrepancy

54. Andenaes, "Deterrence and Specific Offenses" (1971) 38 *U. Chi. L. Rev.* 544.
55. *Id.* at 544.

. . . between present versus reasonable legislation" in relation to marijuana.[56] We suspect that decriminalization might have spectacular consequences in this area. No matter how widespread marijuana use is now, it is possible that demand would prove to be quite elastic. The moral barriers to its use in this country, as distinct from the legal prohibition, do not appear to be very strong. It might well be that decriminalization would result in a level of demand much higher than would have existed without prohibition. Here, however, it would be necessary to rely almost wholly on survey research to obtain information about the effects of change in the law. Hard data like the statistics relating to traffic fatalities and blood alcohol levels or birth rates would not be available. Moreover, the epidemiological data available about current usage are so confused and conflicting[57] that we would have no base line for measuring change. A major problem is that legalization might very well affect willingness to respond candidly to surveys and thus render the data from before-and-after studies incomparable.

None of the foregoing remarks is intended to suggest that research in this area is not possible. what we have said is that the effects of some changes in the law are more readily susceptible to accurate measurement than others. But we should try to anticipate changes in the law and to lay a behavioral base line where possible. The vastness of the area of ignorance is due, at least in part, not to the intractability of the terrain but to the fact that in the past little effort has been made to explore it. If we found out anything, what we found out would provide a useful counterpoise to what we think we know already.

To the extent that opportunities occur, they should be taken. We are not in a position to present a comprehensive forecast of what offenses may be abolished or what offenses might be created in coming years. In general, offenses connected with matters which may be considered of marginal social consequence such as the regulations governing the use of the most innocuous prohibited drug substances, building codes, traffic ordinances, certain commercial regulations, and so on, would

56. U.S. President's Commission on Law Enforcement and Administration of Justice Task Force Report, *Narcotics and Drug Abuse* (1967) 26.
57. *Id.* at 24.

seem to be the most likely subjects for decriminalization in the near future. On the other hand, the category of behavior which might be called "crime against the environment" seems most likely to give rise to a new class of criminal offenses in coming years.

In that scientific interest alone provides insufficient justification for such radical changes, the student of deterrent effects had to rely on the normal processes of social and political change to provide opportunities to evaluate nonexperimentally the consequences of such changes in regulation. For this reason, retrospective and comparative studies will probably remain the most important means of obtaining information about the effects of the criminalization or decriminalization of behavior. Despite all the defects we have ascribed to retrospective and comparative studies, we suggest that such changes, when they occur, be carefully studied by these techniques.

INDEX

abortion, legalization in Britain, 364–65

Acton, H. B., 33, 34

aggressor, identification with, 153–54

alcohol, and risk taking, 105; and traffic fatalities, 285–86, 343–45. *See also* drunk driving

Alexander, F., and Staub, H., 87, 88, 97, 108, 109, 110, 111

Allport, G. W., 118, 308

Andenaes, Johannes, xiii, 10, 36, 44, 47–50, 62–63, 66, 68, 75, 80, 83–87, 128, 133, 135–36, 138, 162, 166, 173, 190–91, 194, 208, 224, 228, 229, 234–35, 279, 344–46, 365

antiwar movement, 220

apprehension: consequences of, and moral judgments, 231; and conviction, 245; and detention process, 174

apprehension, probability of, 161–62, 172, 333–34; apparent, 168; and arrest rate, 330–35; as deterrent, 157; index of, 330, 332; and pessimism, 102; and threat credibility, 164; variations in, 260

apprehension, risk of, 160–61; attitude toward, 230; communication of, 150; and crime rate, 170–71; objective judgment of, 163; and penalty severity, 196; personal experience of, 165; and police presence, 168–69; subjective judgment of, 102–3, 162–63, 165, 167, 196, 213, 226, 305–6; and threat sensitivity, 229

Armstrong, K.G., 33

arrest rate, and probability of apprehension, 330–35

assault on police, penalty for, 197

attitude: toward appropriate penalty, 246; defined, 118–